MAX-PLANCK-GESELLSCHAFT

Universität Augsburg University

TECHNISCHE UNIVERSITÄT MÜNCHEN

THE GEORGE WASHINGTON UNIVERSITY

WASHINGTON, DC

MIPLC Studies

Edited by

Volume 26

Nishantha Sampath Punchi Hewage

Promoting a Second-Tier Protection Regime for Innovation of Small and Medium-Sized Enterprises in South Asia

The Case of Sri Lanka

Nomos

MIPLC Munich Intellectual Property Law Center
Augsburg
München
Washington DC

Die Deutsche Nationalbibliothek lists this publication in the Deutsche Nationalbibliografie; detailed bibliographic data is available in the Internet at http://dnb.d-nb.de

a.t.: München, Ludwig-Maximilians-Univ., Diss., 2014

ISBN 978-3-8487-1885-6 (Print)
978-3-8452-5950-5 (ePDF)

British Library Cataloguing-in-Publication Data
A catalogue record for this book is available from the British Library.

ISBN 978-3-8487-1885-6 (Print)
978-3-8452-5950-5 (ePDF)

Library of Congress Cataloging-in-Publication Data
Punchi Hewage, Nishantha Sampath
Promoting a Second-Tier Protection Regime for Innovation of Small and Medium-Sized Enterprises in South Asia: The Case of Sri Lanka
Nishantha Sampath Punchi Hewage
331 p.
Includes bibliographic references.

ISBN 978-3-8487-1885-6 (Print)
978-3-8452-5950-5 (ePDF)

1. Edition 2015

Acknowledgements

This book is published on the basis of the doctoral thesis which was submitted to the Ludwig-Maximilians-Universität (Munich) in the winter semester 2013/2014. I am very grateful to all those who rendered me invaluable support in embarking on this daunting task. First and foremost, I owe a great debt of gratitude to my supervisor, Professor Dr. Josef Drexl, the Managing Director of the Max Planck Institute for Innovation and Competition and the Chair of the Managing Board of the Munich Intellectual Property Law Center (MIPLC), for his guidance, inspiring thoughts and encouragement, which has enabled me to undertake and complete this challenging task. I also express my heartfelt gratitude to Professor Dr. Annete Kur for her insightful comments on this dissertation.

Another debt of gratitude is owed to Professor Dr. Nari Lee of the Hanken School of Economics, University of Hanken, Finland, who was my Institute Advisor during this research. Her helpful comments and valuable suggestions enlightened me throughout this work. I would also like to sincerely thank Mr. Seth Ericsson, former Academic Director of MIPLC, who motivated me to undertake doctoral studies at MIPLC and who lent his helping hand whenever I needed assistance. I wish to express my gratitude to all those who helped me from Sri Lanka at various stages of my studies in Munich. I would like to especially thank Professor Kshanika Hirimburegama, Chairperson, the University Grants Commission of Sri Lanka, Professor Sharya Scharenguivel, Mr. N. Selvakkumaran, former Dean of the Faculty of Law, and other staff members of the Faculty of Law, University of Colombo, for all of the encouragement and support given to me during my doctoral studies in Munich.

The premises of MIPLC and the library of the Max Planck Institute provided me with the most conducive working atmosphere for this kind of research. Therefore, I wish to accord my deepest appreciation to all the staff of MIPLC and the Max Planck library for all the kind assistance extended to me at different stages of this thesis. Finally, I would like to thank my parents and brothers in Sri Lanka, Sundeep, Vatsala, Jayaram and Mark-Oliver from Munich, who encouraged and guided me in every aspect of my life. Most importantly, without the generous financial support of the Max Planck Institute for Innovation and Competition this research would not have been possible. Last but not least, the Graduate Center of Ludwig-Maximilians-Universität (Munich) deserves a special mention for the Completion Grant that enabled me to put the final touches to this thesis.

Table of Contents

List of Figures

List of Tables

Abbreviations

ACIP	Advisory Council of Intellectual Property
AIPPI	International Association for the Protection of Intellectual Property
ARIPO	African Regional Industrial Property Organization
ASIAN	Association of Southeast Asian Nations
CBD	Convention on Biodiversity
CGPDTM	Controller General of Patents, Designs and Trademarks
DPMA	Deutsches Patent- und Markenamt (German Patent and Trademark Office)
EPC	European Patent Convention
EPO	European Patent Office
EU	European Union
FDI	Foreign Direct Investment
FICCI	Federation of India Chambers of Commerce and Industry
FTC	Foreign Technology Collaboration
GATT	General Agreement on Trade and Tariffs
GDP	Gross Domestic Production
GERD	Gross Expenditure on Research and Development
GNE	Gross National Expenditures
ICT	Information and Communication Technologies
IIC	International Review of Industrial Property & Copyright Law
IIP	Institute of Intellectual Property (Japan)
IP	Intellectual Property
IPAC	Industrial Property Advisory Council
IPC	International Patent Classification
IPO	The Intellectual Property Organization of Pakistan
IPR	Intellectual Property Rights
IPRIA	Intellectual Property Research Institute of Australia
ISA	International Search Authorities
ISIC	International Standard Industrial Classification
ISR	International Search Report

JIPA	Japan Intellectual Property Association
JPO	Japan Patent Office
KIPI	Kenya Intellectual Property Institute
KIPO	Korean Intellectual Property Office
MNCs	Multinational Corporations
MyIPO	Intellectual Property Cooperation of Malaysia
NGO	Non Governmental Organization
NIPO	National Intellectual Property Office of Sri Lanka
NLR	New Law Reports (Sri Lanka)
NSF	National Science Foundation
OAPI	African Intellectual Property Organisation
OECD	Organisation for Economic Co-operation and Development
PCT	Patent Cooperation Treaty
SIPO	State Intellectual Property Office of People's Republic of China
SMEs	Small and Medium Sized Enterprises
SMMEs	Small, Medium and Micro Enterprises
Sri LR	Sri Lanka Law Reports
STP	Second-Tier Protection
TK	Traditional Knowledge
TKDL	Traditional Knowledge Digital Library
TRIPS	Trade Related Aspects of Intellectual Property Rights
UNIDO	United Nations Industrial Development Organization
UM	Utility Models
UI	Utility Innovations
US	United Sates
WIPO	World Intellectual Property Organization
WTO	World Trade Organization

1. Introduction and Background

1.1. Research Statement

> *'Innovators are those who see what everyone sees, but think of what no one else thinks. Innovators refuse status quo, they convert inspirations into solutions and ideas into products'.*
> *RA Mashelkar*[1]

The second decade of the twenty first century is witnessing the rise of global innovation competition. Undoubtedly, this century will be the century of knowledge and indeed the century of mind.[2] In a knowledge-based economy,[3] intellectual property (hereinafter 'IP') is considered as a tool for technological and economic development. The protection of IP is one of the building blocks of national innovation policies in many countries.[4] Innovation is not necessarily lacking in developing countries; however, harnessing innovation to generate wealth is a huge challenge for many of them[5] and this task is particularly daunting for most parts of developing economies in the South Asian region where a large part of innovation tends to be based on improvements or derived from traditional knowledge

---

1 RA Mashelkar, 'A Journey from Mind to Market Place' The Financial Express (India, 9 April 2012), available at: <http://www.financialexpress.com/news/a-journey-from-mind-to-marketplace/934242/> (accessed 30 April 2012).

2 RA Mashelkar, 'Intellectual Property Rights and The Third World' (2001) 81/8 Current Science 955, 955, available at: <http://www.iisc.ernet.in/currsci/oct252001/955.pdf> (accessed 20 April 2012).

3 "The phrase 'knowledge-based economy' describes the new economic environment in which the generation and management of knowledge play a predominant part in wealth creation, as compared with the traditional factors of production, namely land, labor and capital". WIPO, 'Intellectual Property (IP) Rights and Innovation in Small and Medium-sized Enterprises' (2004) WIPO Working Paper August 10/2004, 2 available at: <http://www.wipo.int/export/sites/www/sme/en/documents/pdf/iprs_innovation.pdf> (accessed 10 June 2011).

4 R Landry and others, 'Managing the Protection of Inventions and Technological Innovations in Canadian Manufacturing SMEs' (2009) 3/1 International Journal of Intellectual Property Management 57, 58.

5 See generally, U Suthersanen, G Dutfield and KB Chow (eds), *Innovation Without Patents: Harnessing the Creative Spirit in a Diverse World* (Edward Elgar 2007) 5-6.

and often subpatentable. As scholars have pointed out, a vast majority of scientific and cultural creations, if not all, are built on pre-existing creations and discoveries and do not represent giant leaps beyond what we already know.[6] Such innovations can be incremental in nature[7] and they are based on multiple small steps or increments.[8] Not surprisingly, they may not be able to satisfy the 'flash of genius test' in order to qualify for conventional patent protection. Thus, there is a great need to harness innovative potential, especially in developing countries such as Sri Lanka.

Inventions involving small inventive steps and short commercial lifecycles, gain growing importance each day. These innovations are routine and primarily devoted to product improvements or enhanced user-friendliness or searches for new use for those products.[9] More importantly, a large part of such innovations emanate from small and medium-sized enterprises (hereinafter 'SMEs'), which have been recognized as the principal engine of economic growth and technological progress in many countries.[10] Such incremental innovations are usually not protected, or not adequately protected because of the minor nature of the inventive activity involved in their creation. In other words, such innovations are the most vulnerable to unfair copying and misappropriation. In the absence of protection, incentives for investments for SMEs may dissipate. Obviously, there is a need to provide more incentive for such innovations with exclusive rights to commercialize, even though one can conversely argue that what does not qualify for patent protection should not be protected at all.

---

6 Ibid 7.

7 U Suthersanen, 'Incremental Inventions in Europe: A Legal and Economic Appraisal of Second Tier Patents' (2001) July, Journal of Business Law 319, 320.

8 U Suthersanen, G Dutfield and KB Chow (eds), Innovation Without Patents: Harnessing the Creative Spirit in a Diverse World (Edward Elgar 2007) 7.

9 Ibid.

10 The Government of India, *Annual Report of Ministry of Micro, Small and Medium Enterprises 2011-12* (New Delhi) 161 available at: <www.msme.gov.in> (accessed 31 July 2012). M Al-Mahrouq, 'Success Factors of Small and Medium-Sized Enterprises (SMEs): The Case of Jordan' (2010) 10/1 Anadolu University Journal of Social Sciences 1. See also, T Tambunan, 'Micro, Small and Medium Enterprises and Economic Growth (2006) University of Trisakti – Center for Industry and SME Studies Faculty of Economics Working Paper Series No. 14/2006 at 4-7, available at: <http://103.28.161.15/pusatstudi_industri/PUSAT%20STUDY%20TULUS%20TAMBUNAN/Pusat%20Studi/Working%20Paper/WP14.pdf> (accessed 12 January 2012).

In the eyes of conventional patent law, such creeping and incremental innovations are left unprotected being unable to meet stricter novelty and inventive step requirements though they are no less worthy and useful to society.[11] It is, therefore, possible to argue that there is a lack of incentives resulting from the said protection gap for this type of innovations in the existing IP paradigms.[12] While no protection may mean more access in developing countries, but no protection would also lead to dissipation of marketable value in innovation. As a corollary, this may reduce the incentives for investment for local innovation in improvement, in contrast to foreign ownership of major patentable inventions. A specifically designed second-tier protection (hereinafter 'STP') regime such as of a utility model (hereinafter 'UM') or petty patent system may be explored as one possible solution to this conundrum. Most remarkably, an STP regime can co-exist with other IP rights which can either be used as an important supplement or even a complement to an existing patent system. By its very nature, an STP system has been a national response to different national circumstances.[13] According to WIPO's World Intellectual Property Indicators 2011, there are currently around sixty countries[14] as well as three regional organizations[15] that provide for such a system of IP protection in one way or another.

---

11 See similar line of argumentation in Department of Industrial Policy and Promotion, Discussion Paper on Utility Models (23 May 2011) para 7, available at: <http://dipp.gov.in/English/Discuss_paper/Utility_Models_13May2011.pdf> (accessed 30 December 2011).

12 U Suthersanen, G Dutfield and KB Chow (eds), *Innovation Without Patents: Harnessing the Creative Spirit in a Diverse World* (Edward Elgar 2007) 5. See also, J Lahore, 'Designs and petty Patents: A Broader Reform Issue' (1996) 7 Australian Intellectual Property Journal 7, 8.

13 Bird and Bird, 'Why have Utility Models?, Legal Commentary: EU Green Paper' (1995) July/August, Managing Intellectual Property 3, 3-4.

14 WIPO, *World Intellectual Property Indicators*, 2011 edition 34, available at: <http://www.wipo.int/ipstats/en/wipi/index.html> (accessed 15 March 2012).

15 The three regional organisations which provide for a system of utility model protection are the Andean Community (comprising Bolivia, Colombia, Ecuador and Peru, OAPI (the African Intellectual Property Organisation) and ARIPO (the African Regional Industrial Property Organisation).

UMs are a form of patent-like protection given to minor and incremental innovations against unfair copying and imitation.[16] There is a plethora of terms used to describe "UMs".[17] The umbrella term "utility model" is used in many parts of the world, even though there is no global consensus on the term. A UM regime has also been given various names in different countries; such as petty patents, utility certificates, simple patents, short term patents, second-class patents, secondary patents, utility solutions, utility innovations, minor inventions, and innovation patents.[18] Nevertheless, policy makers, legislatures and lawyers anchor their definition to a secondary form of protection offering a cheaper, simpler and an easier, no-examination protection regime for minor and incremental innovations, usually characterized by less stringent patentability requirements (such as the degree of novelty and inventiveness required) which is often less than that needed for patent protection.[19]

In stark contrast to the South Asian legal landscape, many East Asian and South East Asian countries such as Japan, China, South Korea, Philippine, Malaysia and Thailand have adopted an STP regime in order to reward, incentivise and protect subpatentable innovations that have achieved remarkable progress in their innovative activities, particularly for local innovations. The evidence from recent scholarly investigations suggests that there is a reasonable nexus between such an STP system and the technological progress of a country. It means that there might have been a significant and positive impact on the country's innovation climate.[20] Per-

---

16 U Suthersanen, 'Utility Models and Innovation in Developing Countries' (2006) ICTSD Issue Paper No.13, vii, available at: <http://unctad.org/en/docs/iteipc20066_en.pdf> (accessed 15 March 2012).

17 See generally, U Suthersanen, G Dutfield and KB Chow (eds), *Innovation Without Patents: Harnessing the Creative Spirit in a Diverse World* (Edward Elgar 2007) 5.

18 See LH Gee, 'Second Tier Protection for Minor Inventions in Asia: An Appraisal of the Similarities and Differences' (3rd ASLI Conference Shanghai (China), 25-26 May 2006) 1-2.

19 U Suthersanen, 'Utility Models and Innovation in Developing Countries' (2006) ICTSD Issue Paper No.13, vii, available at: <http://unctad.org/en/docs/iteipc20066_en.pdf> (accessed 15 March 2012).

20 YK Kim and others, 'Appropriate Intellectual Property Protection and Economic Growth in Countries at Different levels of Development' (2012) 1/4 Research Policy 358, available at: <http://www.sciencedirect.com/science/article/pii/S0048733311001715> (accessed 2 June 2012). See also, N Kumar, 'Technology and Economic development: Experiences of Asian Countries' (2002) Commission of Intel-

haps even more importantly, some commentators in a most recent study who focused on East Asian countries have strongly argued that different types of IP rights may be more appropriate for countries at different stages of economic development, rather than different levels of strength of IP rights.[21]

In view of the above, this research investigates whether from a legal policy perspective it is desirable for Sri Lanka to foresee a specifically designed STP regime such as a UM or a petty patent system, in addition to the existing patent regime. It also examines whether such a system may be able to offer a solution to the problem of lack of incentives for incremental innovation and to the perceived protection gap without introducing undue costs. Thus, the underlying thesis of this study is that an STP regime, which is based on the legislative examples of other jurisdictions, would provide an efficient and locally accessible incentive system for innovation of SMEs in developing economies such as in Sri Lanka if it is properly tailored to suit the innovation landscape of the country with a mechanism to address the potential abuses.

1.1.1. Objectives

The primary aim of this research is to analyse, taking into account the specific characteristics of innovation landscape of the country, the adequacy of the existing IP paradigm to accommodate minor and incremental innovations and to establish whether Sri Lanka needs an STP regime to promote such innovations in the country. The study also investigates whether an STP system would be more suitable for SMEs as an important supplement to the existing IPRs. This research also aims to find out whether and

---

lectual Property Rights- Study Paper 1b, 4-5, available at: <http://www.twnside.org.sg/title2/FTAs/Intellectual_Property/IP_and_Development/IPR_TechnologyandEconomicDevelopment-Nagesh_Kumar.pdf> (accessed 10 January 2011). See generally, KE Maskus and C McDaniel, 'Impacts of the Japanese Patent System on Productivity Growth' (1999) 11/4 Japan and the World Economy 557, available at: <http://www.sciencedirect.com/science/article/pii/S0922142599000122> (accessed 10 January 2011).

21 YK Kim and others, 'Appropriate Intellectual Property Protection and Economic Growth in Countries at Different levels of Development' (2012) 1/4 Research Policy 358, available at: <http://www.sciencedirect.com/science/article/pii/S0048733311001715> (accessed 2 June 2012).

to what extent such a protection helps unleash the innovative potentials of grassroots innovators, especially the traditional knowledge (hereinafter 'TK') based or inspired innovations. Furthermore, it examines and recommends whether such regimes are warranted for other selected South Asian countries in order to further enhance economic and technological progress.

1.1.2. Research Problem

Even though the emerging markets in the East and the South East Asian region appear to have been continuously and effectively benefited from an STP designed to protect minor and incremental innovations,[22] Sri Lanka and other leading South Asian countries have been a notable exception to such regimes, arguably, in spite of the growing importance of creeping and incremental innovations in the technological progress of a developing country. It is of course difficult, if not impossible, to imagine the reason why there is no protection for innovations falling below the threshold required by patent law in view of the fact that a large part of innovations in the region tends to be based on improvements or derived from traditional knowledge and are often subpatentable. It is often claimed that minor and incremental innovations in developing countries are mostly created by individual innovators and SMEs.

1.1.3. Hypothesis and Research Questions

There is a general perception that, in the innovation landscape of South Asia, there is a protection gap in the existing patent laws and IP policies.[23] Apparently, the South Asian region has time and again failed to address

22 Ibid.

23 See generally, AK Gupta, 'Rewarding Traditional Knowledge and Contemporary Grassroots Creativity: The Role of Intellectual Property Protection' (Centre of International Development, Harvard University 2000), available at: <http://www.hks.harvard.edu/sustsci/ists/TWAS_0202/gupta_0500.pdf> (accessed 15 May 2012). See also, N Kumar, 'Technology and Economic development: Experiences of Asian Countries' (2002) Commission of Intellectual Property Rights- Study Paper 1b, 4-5, available at: <http://www.twnside.org.sg/title2/FTAs/Intellectual_Property/IP_and_Development/IPR_TechnologyandEconomicDevelopment-Nagesh_Kumar.pdf> (accessed 10 January 2011).

the issue of improvement innovations and falls short in providing them with an adequate protection mechanism.[24] Many innovations in developing countries such as in Sri Lanka, Pakistan, and of course with some exception in India, do not reach the high level of threshold that is required to secure protection under patent law. The high requirements for patent protection in these countries correspond to the international standards as required by Multinational Agreements. Thus, existing patent and other IP regimes do not adequately protect and incentivise incremental and minor innovations in Sri Lanka and in other South Asian countries and an introduction of an STP regime designed to protect such innovations would have a positive impact on innovations. Moreover, individual innovators and SMEs are more likely to benefit from such a regime.

The following research questions guide the study. First and foremost: what is the applicability of the existing patent system as an appropriate mechanism for the protection of minor and incremental innovations? Should such innovations be left unprotected? Secondly, is there any better way than patent to encourage such innovations? Can the design law successfully fill in the protection gap created by patent law? Would the existing Unfair Competition Law regime as a fallback protection provide an adequate protection for such innovations? Thirdly, is there a need to seek an alternative means of protection found in STP regimes or utility models and what are the lessons that can be learnt from other developed and developing countries? Then, is there a need for Sri Lanka to introduce an STP regime which will provide for minor and incremental innovations which fail to reach the requisite level of inventiveness under the existing patent system?[25] If there is such a need, which has not previously been fulfilled by the use of other forms of protection, can this newly created right be able to fill the protection gap? Is it possible to provide a distinctive rationale for justifying the adoption of such a second-tier protection regime?[26] What would be the implications of adopting such a regime? Would it be more appropriate in application for minor and incremental innovations which are mostly created by small and medium sized firms?

---

24 MD Nair, 'A Case for Grant of 'Petty Patents' *The Hindu* (New Delhi, 10 May 2001), available at: <http://hindu.com/2001/05/10/stories/0610000h.htm> (accessed 15 January 2010).

25 M Llewelyn, Utility Models/Second Tier Protection: A Report on the Proposals of the European Commission (1996) The Intellectual Property Institute 4.

26 Ibid.

Can large enterprises also benefit from this system? Would such a regime be more suited than any other type of IP for protecting TK-inspired innovations? Next, have other countries in the South Asian region felt the need for this form of protection and can they find valid reasons for supporting and adopting such a right? Why is it necessary to have such a drastic departure from the traditional patent threshold for these countries? Should such policy changes be applicable across the South Asian region or should it be addressed at a national level rather than regional level? Finally, what policy options can be recommended for consideration by policymakers in the South Asian countries?

1.1.4. Research Methodology

This research takes the form of a Hypothesis-Testing (Experimentation) Research. It was carried out primarily as a library-based research. In so doing, primary and secondary sources are used extensively. The primary sources consist of relevant Legislative Instruments and Case Law, while secondary sources include various documents such as Text Books, Research Articles, Journals and Annual Reports, and Statistical Data relating to the topic. Field research methodology was also used to ascertain evidence, in particular, from Sri Lanka. Visits and personal interviews of various organizations such as the Judiciary, IP offices, Law firms/IP attorneys, Companies/Industries and other business entities were conducted. Moreover, legal research and analysis concerning international legal framework and comparative legal analysis of STP regimes in selected jurisdictions have been carried out with support of the empirical research and analysis. Last but not least, interpretation methodology was also employed in order to enrich the arguments in the thesis.

1.1.5. How does this Research contribute to the Legal Science?

Limited academic attention has been paid to examine the issue of sub-patentable innovations, which remains by and large an unexplored territory of IP law landscape in the South Asian region. Not surprisingly, there is an acute dearth of relevant and helpful scholarly investigations on the protection of incremental and minor innovations which is almost non-existent in Sri Lanka. This research aims at an in-depth understanding of the usefulness and appropriateness of an STP regime in relation to Sri Lanka. To that extent, this doctoral thesis attempts to fill this gap by contributing towards designing a new legal framework for Sri Lanka which may be used as a model across South Asian countries. It will therefore contribute to advance the legal science in the South Asian region.

1.1.6. Limitations

The obvious challenge we face in this research is that there is no experience of a domestic second-tier protection system either in Sri Lanka or any other country in the region. Due to time and space constraints, this study was mainly confined to the Sri Lankan legal landscape. Nevertheless, it has an insight into the recent initiatives undertaken by two leading jurisdictions in the South Asian region, namely, India and Pakistan, to explore the possibility of adopting a UM regime. Nevertheless, perspectives of the other countries in the region were taken into consideration when common policy options are discussed depending on available resources, time and space for this study. Two jurisdictions each from the developed and emerging market countries, along with another developing country are selected for the purposes of comparative analysis.

1.2. Preliminary Thoughts and Definitions

1.2.1. Invention and Innovation

Ideas change the world, innovations shape our lives and improve our quality of life.[27] Innovation is not a new phenomenon. Arguably, it is as old as mankind itself.[28] There seems to be something inherently 'human' about the tendency to think about new and better ways of doing things and try them out in practice. An important distinction is normally made between invention and innovation.[29] Although the term 'innovation' is broadly

---

27 M Elmslie and S Portman, *Intellectual Property: The Lifeblood of Your Company* (Chandos Publishing Oxford 2006) 1.

28 J Fagerberg, DC Mowery and RR Nelson (eds), *The Oxford Handbook on Innovation* (Oxford University Press 2005) 1-4.

29 Ibid.

used, it is still without consistent definition across relevant disciplines. From a general perspective, innovation refers to the creation of better or more effective products, processes or technologies that are accepted by markets and societies.[30] As interpreted from a linguistic point of view, the term 'innovation' stems from the Latin word *innovare*, meaning to renew, alter, to make new or to introduce as new or change.[31] On the other hand, the term invention stems from Latin *invenire* which emphasizes 'original' rather than renewal or alteration.[32] Even though both terms involve an element of 'newness', there is a distinction between the originality of invention and the renewal of innovation.[33] Whereas the word 'innovation' is not a legal term, invention is legally defined. Therefore, the word invention is more associated with patent law terminology.

The economic literature on innovation has greatly been influenced by the theories of Joseph Schumpeter.[34] He argued that economic development is driven by innovation through a dynamic process in which new technologies replace the old; a process he labeled 'creative destruction'. In Schumpeter's view, 'radical' innovations create major disruptive changes, whereas 'incremental' innovations continuously advance the process of change. Schumpeter proposed a list of five types of innovations; (i) introduction of new products; (ii) introduction of new methods of production; (iii) opening of new markets; (iv) development of new sources of supply for raw materials or other inputs; (v) creation of new market structures in an industry.[35] Furthermore, Michael Porter has also attempted to define innovation from an economic perspective. According to him innovation is defined as "a new way of doing things (termed invention by some authors) that is commercialized".[36] Although there is no uniquely accepted definition, innovation is often defined as the conversion of knowledge into new

30 P Frankelius, 'Questioning Two Myths in Innovation Literature' (2009) 20/1 The Journal of High Technology Management Research, 40, 41.

31 Y Lee and M Langley, 'Invention and Innovation' (2004) August, The CIPA Journal 464.

32 Ibid.

33 Ibid.

34 OECD/Eurostat, *OSLO MANUAL: Guidelines for Using and Interpreting Innovation Data* (3rd edn, The Measurement of Scientific and Technological Activities, OECD Publishing 2005) 29.

35 J Schumpeter, *The Theory of Economic Development* (Harvard University Press 1934) 66.

36 ME Porter, *The Competitive Advantage of Nations* (Free Press 1990) 780.

commercialized technologies, products and processes, and how these are brought to the market.[37] According to OECD's Oslo Manual (2005), there are four types of innovations: product innovation, process innovation, organizational innovation and marketing innovation. For this analysis, product and process innovations warrant discussion. A product innovation is the introduction of a good or service that is new or significantly improved with respect to its characteristics or intended uses.[38] This includes significant improvements in technical specifications, components and materials, incorporated software, user friendliness or other functional characteristics. For example, replacing inputs with materials with improved characteristics (environmentally friendly plastics) or products with significantly reduced energy consumption (energy efficient stoves) and food products with new functional characteristics (margarine that reduces blood cholesterol levels).[39] A process innovation, on the other hand, is the implementation of a new or significantly improved production or delivery method. This includes significant changes in techniques and equipment, installation of new or improved manufacturing technology, such as automation equipment.[40]

Another aspect of innovation that merits discussion is the difference between radical and incremental innovations. Of course, radical innovations are technological breakthroughs that push the boundaries of global technology frontiers, for instance, the invention of the electric light. This kind of innovation can be considered an 'out-of-the-blue' solution to the problems existing in the field of technology which can create a far-reaching impact on our lives. Incremental innovations, on the other hand, take place in industries which continuously innovate to create products, which displace their own products with the fear that otherwise their competitors will do it for them.[41] In comparison, an incremental innovation is more concerned with improvements on an existing product or service, whereas a

---

37 WIPO, World Intellectual Property Report: The Changing Face of Innovation (2011) WIPO 23.

38 OECD/Eurostat, *OSLO MANUAL: Guidelines for Using and Interpreting Innovation Data* (3rd edn, The Measurement of Scientific and Technological Activities, OECD Publishing 2005) 151.

39 Ibid.

40 Ibid.

41 RA Mashelkar, 'An Eminent Scientist's new Road-map for India' (GoodNewsIndia, November 2000), available at: <http://www.goodnewsindia.com/Pages/content/inspirational/mashelkar.html> (accessed 30 January 2011).

radical innovation is an entirely new product, service or process. Besides, the development and life of an incremental innovation is much more ‘predictable’ than that of a radical innovation, and it will potentially generate less return and less benefits.[42]

At a very basic level, innovation is all about the practical application of creative ideas to the point it generates value to an organisation.[43] Innovation is key to the production as well as the processing of knowledge. A nation's ability to convert knowledge into wealth and social good through the process of innovation will determine its future.[44] Of course, the ultimate cause of all innovation is human creativity. But innovation does not occur in a vacuum; it requires a workable structure of incentives and institutions.[45] Furthermore, normally when we consider innovation, we refer to only formal systems of innovation; namely that is done in universities, industrial R&D laboratories, etc. Often not recognised is the technology innovation that takes place in an informal system of innovation, be it by artisans, farmers, tribes or other grassroots innovators. Such innovations are also taken into consideration as ‘innovations’ for purposes of this research.[46]

For the sake of clarity, it is worth drawing a clear distinction between the terms ‘invention’ and ‘innovation’. According to the general understanding, "‘invention’ is a specific patent law concept and ‘innovation’ is a broader economic term, encompassing incremental improvements".[47] Obviously, the ‘one-size-fits-all’ conventional patent system leaves an un-

---

42 UN-ESCAP, Managing Innovation in a Knowledge Economy: A Guidebook for SMEs in Asia and the Pacific (ESCAP 2010) 3.

43 A Dharmasiri, ‘The Triple ‘I’ for Transformation’, *Daily FT* (Colombo 20 June 2011), available at: <http://www.ft.lk/2011/06/20/the-triple-%E2%80%98i%E2%80%99s-for-transformation/> (accessed 2 August 2011).

44 RA Mashelkar, ‘Intellectual Property Rights and the Third World’ (2001) October – 18/8 Current Science 955, 955 available at: <http://www.sristi.org/material/1.2intellectual%20property%20and%20the%20third%20world.pdf> (accessed 30 January 2011).

45 Business and Industry Advisory Committee (BIAC) to OECD, Discussion Paper on ‘Creativity, Innovation and Economic Growth in the 21st Century: An Affirmative Case for Intellectual property Rights (BIAC Paris, December 2003) 3.

46 RA Mashelkar, ‘Intellectual Property Rights and the Third World’ (2001) 18/8 Current Science 955, 956.

47 KF Jorda, Utility Models: The Penacea for our Broken Patent System – Newsletter (Germeshausen Center 2007) 4, available at: <http://www.ipo.org/wp-content/uploads/2013/03/utilitymodels.pdf> (accessed 30 March 2013).

protected class of inventions of a lesser scope, which could not fulfil higher patentability criteria. Such inventions can well be described as 'innovations'. For purposes of this study, I shall therefore use the word 'innovation' to mean minor and incremental technical advances which represent improvements over prior art but with a lower level of inventiveness.

1.2.2. Second-Tier Protection

Even though second-tier protection has been considered a backwater of intellectual property, worldwide interest in such regimes appears to be substantial.[48] More than sixty countries currently offer second-tier patent protection, including key patenting jurisdictions such as Germany, Japan and China.[49] Generally, a second-tier protection (STP) system compliments a patent system to offer a more accessible form of protection for a shorter term, usually characterized by less stringent patentability requirements.[50] Given its origin in the late nineteenth century and the time-tested continuous existence, one can argue that the STP is neither new nor radical.[51] Such a system combines traditional IP protection with a 'lower tier' of previously largely unprotected or loosely protected subject-matter. In other words, a protection system consists of a top tier with a standard form of patent and a lower tier protection with a utility model or petty patent system.[52] In essence, this type of two-layered protection system is used in many regions of the world to provide an additional strategy in which access to the patent system can be enhanced by the expansion (or, in some cases, the creation) of an entirely separate regime of rights.[53]

---

48 MD Janis, 'Second Tier Patent Protection' (1999) 40/1 Harvard Law Journal 151, 152.

49 Ibid.

50 PA Cummings, 'From Germany to Australia: Opportunities for a Second Tier Patent System in the United States' (2010) 18/2 Michigan State Journal of International Law 300.

51 M Crinson, 'Is Some Novel Protection of Invention Needed in Canada' (1998) 12 Intellectual Property Journal 26.

52 A Kur, 'Two Tiered Protection-Designs and Databases as Legislative-Models?' in A Ohly (ed), *Common Principles of European Intellectual Property Law* (Mohr Siebeck, 2012) 99.

53 MD Janis, 'Second Tier Patent Protection' (1999) 40/1 Harvard Law Journal 151, 151.

Perhaps more encouragingly, the experience of different countries, especially those who have lived with STP regimes lend credibility for other countries to experiment with this supplementary protection system to provide a relatively quick, inexpensive, easy to obtain and simple protection mechanism for minor technical advances. Moreover, it is a lesser form of protection for low-level innovations which otherwise fall through the protection net of patent law. The most important advantage of this system is that it can be tailored to suit specific needs and circumstances of each country. While some regimes follow the classic utility model, others can be considered as modern second-tier regimes such as the innovation patent system in Australia that vary from the classic utility model, as exemplified by the original German *Gebrauchsmuster* regime. "Modern second-tier patent regimes are not easily represented by a singular example [single model]".[54] Most notably, neither Sri Lanka nor any other South Asian jurisdiction currently provides any form of STP for subpatentable innovations. Arguably, it may be high time for these countries to experiment with a two-track protection system with one dedicated to conventional patents and the other specifically attuned to incentivise small incremental innovations of SMEs.

For purposes of this study, the term 'second-tier protection regime' is used as a generic label encompassing utility models, petty patents, and other modern regimes such as innovation patents (Australia) or utility innovation (Malaysia) that are comparable to a utility model regime in most respects. For practical purposes, the terms second-tier protection, utility models and petty patents are treated as synonymous in this study. As a general matter, a 'second-tier protection' (STP), refers to a system that provides short-term protection for minor or incremental innovations with varying novelty standards (global, relative or local novelty depending on the jurisdiction) and with a lower level of inventiveness or without any requirement of showing an inventive step, and for which rights are granted without a substantive examination but after merely a check of formalities.

---

54 K Osenga, 'Entrance Ramps, Tolls, and Express Lanes-Proposals for Decreasing Traffic Congestion in the Patent Office' (2005) 33 Florida State University Law Review 119, 151.

1.2.3. A Developing Country

When it comes to dealing with the classification of countries based on their economic and social achievement, there is a plethora of indicators that have been adopted by different international organisations. As a result, currently, different standards determine whether a country is regarded as 'developing'. The United Nations agencies, the World Bank, the International Monetary Fund (IMF) use relatively different yardsticks in making this determination.[55] According to commentators, there is no generally accepted criterion (either grounded in theory or based on an objective benchmark) for classifying countries according to their level of development. "Classical economists were mostly preoccupied with what is now termed economic development in the sense of sustained increases in per capita real income, and neoclassical economists paid scant attention to the issue altogether".[56] Against this backdrop, the Preamble of the TRIPS Agreement particularly addresses least-developed countries. They comprise some 50 countries as defined by United Nations Economic and Social Council (ECOSOC) Development Committee on the basis of low income per capita under USD 750 to USD 900, weak human assets, measured by a composite Human Assets Index and Economic Vulnerability Index.[57] Most recently, in its country classification, the World Economic Outlook Report 2012 of the IMF has divided the world into three major groups: advanced economies (examples, Germany, Japan) and emerging (examples, Korea, China) and developing economies (examples, India, Thailand).[58]

Moreover, for analytical purposes, the World Bank classifies economies in the world into four groups namely low-income (USD 1,005 or less) lower middle-income (USD 1,006 to USD 3,975) upper middle-income

55 S Ragavan, 'Can't We All Get Along? The Case for a Workable Patent Model' (2003) 35 Arizona State Law Journal 117, 124.

56 L Nielsen, 'Classifications of Countries Based on Their Level of Development: How it is Done and How it could be Done' (2011) IMF Working Paper No. 11/31, 3-5.

57 T Cottier and P Véron, Concise International and European IP Law: TRIPS, Paris Convention, European Enforcement and Transfer of Technology (Kluwer Law 2008) 9.

58 IMF, *World Economic Outlook Report* (Washington, April 2012) 177-178, available at: <http://www.imf.org/external/pubs/ft/weo/2012/01/pdf/statapp.pdf> (accessed 10 June 2012).

(USD 3,976 to USD 12,275) and high-income (USD 12,276 or more), based on their gross national income (GNI) per capita.[59] Importantly, under this classification, low and middle income economies are commonly referred to as 'developing economies'.[60] Most strikingly, based on the above benchmarking, all eight countries in the South Asian region can be categorized as 'developing nations'. A closer look at World Bank statistics further reveals that only one country (Maldives) in the region belongs to upper-middle-income economies, while India, Sri Lanka, Pakistan and Bhutan belong to Lower-Middle-Income economies; and all the other countries, namely, Afghanistan, Bangladesh and Nepal are in the group of low-income economies. In essence, no country in the South Asian region has achieved the status of a 'developed economy' although India has in recent years become an emerging economic powerhouse in the global economic arena with a high GDP growth. For purposes of his paper, I shall utilize the same World Bank classification of a 'developing country' which is more acceptable than the other indicators as it has been relied on by IP specialized agencies such as the WIPO.[61]

1.2.4. SMEs

Small and medium-sized enterprises, better known as SMEs, are a very heterogeneous group of enterprises engaged in business activities across a large spectrum of sectors such as agriculture, manufacturing, construction, trade and services.[62] The SME sector is well recognised for its contribution to employment, innovation and economic dynamism and is consid-

---

59 World Bank, *World Development Indicators* (World Bank, 2012), available at: <http://data.worldbank.org/sites/default/files/wdi-2012-ebook.pdf> (accessed 30 June 2012). See also, World Bank, *Changes in Country Classification* (World Bank, 2011), available at: <http://data.worldbank.org/news/2010-GNI-income-classifications> (accessed 30 June 2012).

60 World Bank, *Changes in Country Classification* (2011) <http://data.worldbank.org /news/2010-GNI-income-classifications> (accessed 30 June 2012).

61 WIPO, World Intellectual Property Report: The Changing Face of Innovation (2011) WIPO 5.

62 AL Somaratne, 'Access to Finance by SMEs in Sri Lanka' *The Island* (Colombo, 13 August 2012), available at: <http://www.island.lk/index.php?page_cat=article-details&page=article-details&code_title=59129> (accessed 14 August 2012).

ered as an engine of growth and an essential part of a healthy economy.[63] SMEs are considered to be the backbone of a country and the 'real economy' in terms of economic contribution. This sector plays a very important role in both developed and developing countries.[64] Undoubtedly, the South Asian region is no exception to this reality. Generally speaking, SMEs represent 90 percent of all business operations in many of South Asian Countries. In Sri Lanka, SMEs account for more than 75 percent of the total number of enterprises, provide 45 percent of the employment and contribute to 52 percent of the Gross Domestic Production (GDP).[65]

There is no internationally accepted definition of SMEs. The definition of SMEs varies from country to country due to the diverse nature of economies and also due to the difference in the level of economic development of those economies.[66] Many countries and multilateral development agencies have their own definitions. The definition of SMEs is generally based on one of three criteria namely the annual turnover of the enterprise, number of workers employed or value of assets (investment).[67] For instance, the European definition is based mainly on the number of people employed; accordingly a business that employs fewer than 250 persons is classified as medium-sized, while a business that employs fewer than 50 persons is classified as small, and a business with fewer than 10 employees is considered a micro-sized enterprise.[68] Similarly, "the UK

---

63 SI Wickremasinghe, 'The Status of SMEs in Sri Lanka and Promotion of Their Innovation Output Through Networking of S&T Institutions' (2011) July-August, Tech Monitor 11, 11, available at: <http://www.techmonitor.net/tm/images/1/1d/11jul_aug_sf1.pdf> (accessed 30 June 2012).

64 AS Gamage, 'Small and Medium Enterprise Development in Sri Lanka: A Review.' Meijo University, Faculty of Business Management, Nagoya, Japan. 133-134, 149, available at: <http://202.11.2.113/SEBM/ronso/no3_4/aruna.pdf> or <http://wwwbiz.meijo-u.ac.jp/SEBM/ronso/no3_4/aruna.pdf (2003)> (accessed 25 January 2012).

65 Ministry of Traditional Industries and Small Enterprise Development & Department of Development Finance of the Ministry of Finance and Planning, *National Policy Framework for Small Medium Enterprise (SME) Development* (Draft SME Policy Framework 2014) 1.

66 AL Somaratne, 'Access to Finance by SMEs in Sri Lanka' *The Island* (Colombo, 13 August 2012), available at: <http://www.island.lk/index.php?page_cat=article-details&page=article-details&code_title=59129> (accessed 14 August 2012).

67 Ibid.

68 European Commission, 'Commission Recommendation concerning the definition of micro, small and medium-sized enterprises' 2003/361/EC of 6 March 2003. Article 2 of the Recommendation states that the category of micro, small and medi-

definition is based on turnover and the US definition is based both on number of employees as well as turnover".[69] Furthermore, "in China the categorization is between the sectors based on number of employees and turnover".[70] The Indian definition is based only on the basis of investment in plant and machinery.[71] In Sri Lanka, there is no clear definition for SMEs and different government institutions use different criteria.[72] The Task Force that prepared the White Paper of the government in 2002 had agreed upon the concept of (a) small scale enterprises, as those with asset values not exceeding Sri Lankan Rupees (SLRs) 20 million and (b) medium-scale enterprises, as those with asset values not exceeding SLRs. 50 million, excluding land and buildings.[73] The Department of Small and Medium Industries defines SMEs as those with a capital investment of less than SLRs. 5 million, and that employ less than 50 persons.[74] However, as per the practice adopted by the Department of Census and Statistics in compiling data relating to the industrial sector, the small-sized establishments are those enterprises that employ between 5 and 29 people, medium 30 and 149 people and large 150 or more.[75] Furthermore, according to the SME Policy Framework (Draft) of 2014, the category of small and medium sized enterprises is made up of enterprises which employ less than 300 employees and which have an annual turnover not exceeding

---

um-sized enterprises (SMEs) is made up of enterprises which employ fewer than 250 persons and which have an annual turnover not exceeding 50 million Euro, and/or an annual balance sheet total not exceeding 43 million Euro.

69 KD Raju, 'Small and Medium Enterprises (SMEs): Past, Present and Future in India' (2008) PHDCCI Working Paper 1-16, available at: <http://papers.ssrn.com/sol3/papers.cfm?abstract_id=1080505> (accessed 3 March 2013).

70 Ibid.

71 Ibid.

72 AS Gamage, 'Small and Medium Enterprise Development in Sri Lanka: A Review.' Meijo University, Faculty of Business Management, Nagoya, Japan. 134, available at: <http://202.11.2.113/SEBM/ronso/no3_4/aruna.pdf> or <http://wwwbiz.meijo-u.ac.jp/SEBM/ronso/no3_4/aruna.pdf (2003)> (accessed 25 January 2012).

73 SI Wickremasinghe, 'The Status of SMEs in Sri Lanka and Promotion of Their Innovation Output Through Networking of S&T Institutions' (2011) July-August, Tech Monitor 11, 12-13, available at: <http://www.techmonitor.net/tm/images/1/1d/11jul_aug_sf1.pdf> (accessed 30 June 2012).

74 Ibid.

75 Ibid.

SLRs. 900 million.[76] For want of a working definition, arguably, the number of employees and annual turnover seem more reasonable and appropriate.

Indeed, SMEs play a strategic role in relation to innovation and rapid response to market requirements.[77] Unfortunately, however, SMEs in developing countries face several challenges such as lack of access to finance, low R&D investment, technological backwardness, low production efficiency and quality of products due to lack of innovation etc.[78] Most notably, despite the growing importance, SMEs remain in technological backwaters for decades resulting in untapped and under-maximised potential. When it comes to IP, according to a recent survey conducted by the UK government, SMEs and micro-enterprises, which form the cradle of IP, are unaware of the IP system.[79] Moreover, a recent study of WIPO has revealed that, in many sectors, innovation by SMEs mainly consists in minor adaptations to existing products, innovation in designs, mode of service delivery or management and marketing practices.[80] Perhaps even

---

76 Ministry of Traditional Industries and Small Enterprise Development & Department of Development Finance of the Ministry of Finance and Planning, *National Policy Framework for Small Medium Enterprise (SME) Development* (Draft SME Policy Framework 2014) 3. Under this Policy Framework, the category of Micro Enterprises is made up of enterprises which employ 1-10 employees and which have an annual turnover SLRs. 1-15 million. Similarly, Small Enterprises are those employ 11-50 employees and which have an annual turnover SLRs. 16-250 million. The category of Medium Enterprises is made up of enterprises which employ 51-300 employees and which have an annual turnover not exceeding SLRs. 900 million.

77 European Commission, 'The amended proposal for a Directive approximating the legal arrangements for the protection of inventions by utility model' COM (1999)309 final, recital 5.

78 See also, SI Wickremasinghe, 'The Status of SMEs in Sri Lanka and Promotion of Their Innovation Output Through Networking of S&T Institutions' (2011) July-August, Tech Monitor 11, 11, available at: <http://www.techmonitor.net/tm/images/1/1d/11jul_aug_sf1.pdf> (accessed 30 June 2012).

79 R Pitkethly, 'The UK Intellectual Property Awareness Survey-(2006)' Intellectual Property Office of the UK, 9, available at: <http://www.ipo.gov.uk/ipsurvey.pdf> (accessed 20 June 2012).

80 WIPO, 'Intellectual Property (IP) Rights and Innovation in Small and Medium-sized Enterprises' (2004) WIPO Working Paper August 10/2004, 5-6, available at: <http://www.wipo.int/export/sites/www/sme/en/documents/pdf/iprs_innovation.pdf> (accessed 10 June 2011).

more importantly, the cost of IP protection erects access barriers for SMEs hindering efficiency and minimum utilization.

For purposes of this research, given that there is no generally accepted international or national definition for SME, the basis on which SMEs are defined depends on the stage of economic development of the country and the broad policy purposes for which the definition is used.[81] In this study, the term 'SME' is used in the sense that prevails in the given jurisdiction as the basis for this analysis. Such an open approach is required to avoid unnecessary confusion.

1.3. Sri Lankan Innovation Landscape

Sri Lanka, formerly known as Ceylon, is an island nation lying off the Southern tip of India. Because of its geographical location it was also known as the 'Pearl of the Indian Ocean'. Sri Lanka is a tropical island home to just over 20 million people.[82] It is a nation with a rich cultural heritage and a written history of over 2,500 years.[83] Sri Lanka was partly ruled by Portuguese and Dutch since 1505 and 1656 respectively. The coastal area of the island fell into the hands of British in 1796. Sri Lanka gained independence from the Great Britain in 1948. It is currently a member of the Commonwealth of Nations as well as the South Asian Association for Regional Cooperation (hereinafter 'SAARC'). Since independence Sri Lanka has achieved considerable progress in the socio-economic field in spite of a three-decades-long civil war which ended in 2009. Interestingly, this tiny island nation has pioneered South Asia's economic liberalization in 1977. In hindsight though, the country has not been able to reach its full potential in terms of economic development.

---

81 SI Wickremasinghe, 'The Status of SMEs in Sri Lanka and Promotion of Their Innovation Output Through Networking of S&T Institutions' (2011) July-August, Tech Monitor 11, 12, available at: <http://www.techmonitor.net/tm/images/1/1d/11jul_aug_sf1.pdf> (accessed 30 June 2012).

82 According to the latest statistics issued in March 2012 by Department of Census and Statistics of Sri Lanka, the country has recorded a total population of 20,277,597.

83 Fox News, 'Sri Lanka, Rising Star of Asian Economy' *The Island* (Colombo, 26 February 2011), available at: <http://pdfs.island.lk/2011/02/26/p2.pdf> (accessed 20 January 2012).

Sri Lanka's legal system has been influenced by several European legal traditions during its development. Nowadays, Sri Lanka's legal system is a rich mix of native laws and two European legal traditions, Roman-Dutch Law and English Law.[84] British laws were introduced to the country through legislation and judicial decisions. One area of the law which was greatly influenced by English law was the commercial law of the country and which is the reason why it has largely inherited IP laws from the UK. With the advent of new technologies and globalization, Sri Lanka has tried to keep up with development and adopted its IP regime to suit the new innovation climate. It has modernized its IP regime in line with TRIPS obligation with the introduction of the new IP Act which came into force in 2003.

On the demographic landscape, as in most parts of the South Asia, Sri Lanka too, has a majority portion of its population living in rural areas which is estimated to be nearly 80 percent of the country's total population.[85] Most industries are located in rural areas the rural economy heavily depends on agriculture and small industries. The technological progress that the country has so far achieved is not at all satisfactory in view of most recent figures and indicators. As a fact, Sri Lanka has fallen far behind in terms of technology and innovation compared with its neighbors, as well as East Asian countries. As pointed out by many, the innovation performance of the country is far from satisfactory. From a policy perspective, many factors influence the innovation landscape of a country, including education policies, a country's technological absorptive capacity, its general institutional base to promote domestic research and development (R&D), and legal and economic incentives particularly in terms of adequate intellectual property and investment regimes.[86] Interestingly

---

84 A Cooray, 'Oriental and Occidental Laws in Harmonious Co-existence: The Case of Trusts in Sri Lanka' (2008) May 12/1 Electronic Journal of Comparative Law 1,1, available at: <http://www.ejcl.org/121/art121-5.pdf> (accessed 20 January 2012).

85 AS Gamage, 'Small and Medium Enterprise Development in Sri Lanka: A Review.' Meijo University, Faculty of Business Management, Nagoya, Japan. 134, available at: <http://202.11.2.113/SEBM/ronso/no3_4/aruna.pdf> or <http://wwwbiz.meijo-u.ac.jp/SEBM/ronso/no3_4/aruna. pdf (2003)> (accessed 25 January 2012).

86 U Suthersanen, 'Utility Models and Innovation in Developing Countries' (2006) UNCTAD-ICTSD Issue Paper No. 13 Project on IPRs and Sustainable Development, Foreword provided by R Meléndez-Ortiz and S Panitchpakdi vii-viii, avail-

though, the principal argument favoring the introduction of an STP system is based on the specific characteristics of the innovation landscape of Sri Lanka.

1.3.1. Specific Characteristics of the Sri Lankan Innovation Landscape

As observed by commentators, there seems to be a shortage of home-grown creativity in Sri Lanka.[87] As interpreted through the lens of global innovation indicators, the country's performance is not encouraging. Sri Lanka stands in the 94th position out of 141 in the Global Innovation Index 2012.[88] Most notably, Sri Lanka has been sliding in the index from the 82nd position in 2011 and the 79th position in 2010. Moreover, in the Global Competitiveness Index,[89] the Sri Lankan economy was ranked 68th out of 144 countries. According to both innovation measurements, the country lags behind in realizing its innovation potentials. These international benchmarks offer useful insights into the areas in which more improvement is needed, and of the top of this is undoubtedly innovation.

Another striking feature of the Sri Lankan innovation landscape is the large presence of the SME sector. The most frequent type of innovation activity of SMEs is generally characterized by minor or incremental changes, together with innovative applications of existing products or processes.[90] They are technically less complex (easy to copy simple products) and quite often have a short commercial life. Moreover, both large and small industries more often than not use less advanced technology. This might be one of the reasons for a large number of minor and incremental

---

able at: <http://unctad.org/en/docs/iteipc20066_en.pdf> (accessed 15 March 2012).

87 D Llewelyn, Invisible Gold in Asia: Creating Wealth through Intellectual Property (Marshall Cavendish 2010) 241.

88 WIPO, 'Global Innovation Index 2012' (2012) WIPO & INSEAD, available at: <http://www.globalinnovationindex.org/gii/main/fullreport/index.html> (accessed 30 August 2012).

89 K Schwab (ed), 'The Global Competitiveness Report' (2012-2013) World Economic Forum- Insight Report, available at: <http://reports.weforum.org/global-competitiveness-report-2012-2013/> (accessed 10 November 2012).

90 See OECD/Eurostat, *OSLO MANUAL: Guidelines for Using and Interpreting Innovation Data* (3rd edn, The Measurement of Scientific and Technological Activities, OECD Publishing 2005) 138.

technical advances to have a lower level of inventiveness. The country is still in the initial stage of the technological ladder and the industrial sector in general and SME sector in particular has suffered over years due to marginal technological capability.

Even though Sri Lanka is a country well-endowed with natural and remarkable human resources (with a high literacy rate of 92 percent), the country is an exporter of low-value added products and raw materials. According to recent statistics, Sri Lanka's export consists only of 2 percent of high-tech products. This high concentration on low-tech products is evidenced by 43 percent export of garments, 16 percent Tea, 5 percent of rubber products and 3 percent of food and beverages.[91] Looking analytically into industrial geography, the country has, by and large, remained in the stage of value adding rather than value creation.

Sri Lankan is a heavy IP importing country as opposed to IP exporting countries in East Asia such as Japan, South Korea, China and Malaysia, though the country has significantly been transformed from an agrarian economy to a low-industry based economy. Last but not the least, traditional knowledge-based innovation and grassroots innovations have also occupied a significant place in the innovation landscape of the country. Viewed from a comparative perspective of other emerging economies in the Asian region, one can reasonably conclude that the Sri Lankan industrial sector is less innovative, weak and far less satisfactory. An STP may be viewed as a step towards addressing above issues.

1.3.2. The Statistical Story

As adopted by global benchmarks of innovation such as OECD's Oslo Manual,[92] "the number of patent applications filed per year is a good metric of measuring the innovation potential of a country".[93] And it is consid-

---

91 See Ministry of Finance and Planning, *The Emerging Wonder of Asia: Mahinda Chintana Vision for the Future* (2010) 69. These statistics are considered as of 2009.

92 See JWM van Leuven, 'Patent Statistics as Indicators for Innovation' (1996) November/December, Patent World 20, 20.

93 A Aggrawal and B Rawat, 'The Indian Patent System should grant Utility Model Patents' (2011) India Business Review, available at: <http://www.entrepreneurswebsite.com/2011/09/08/the-indian-patent-system-should-grant-utility-model-patents/?goback=%2Egde_3297732_member_69774577> (accessed 3 May 2012).

ered to be a proxy for innovation. Analysing the innovation landscape through the prism of patent statistics of well over a decade suggests that Sri Lanka is a patent granting country as opposed to a patent producing. This empirical evidence as such paints a picture of weak innovation character of the country. As is seen from the figures below, the poor patent filing is perhaps the single most indication of a shortage of home-grown creativity. In recent years, the patent applications filed remain dominated mostly by foreign patent applications.

Table 1.1: Industrial Property Statistics for Patents

Year	Resident Applications	Non Resident Applications	Total Applications	Resident Registrations	Non Resident Registrations	Total Registrations
1999	119	248	367	78	101	179
2000	71	250	321	59	169	228
2001	120	236	356	71	109	175
2002	123	202	325	59	54	113
2003	95	189	284	63	52	115
2004	120	195	315	103	85	188
2005	149	211	360	64	116	180
2006	153	270	423	68	69	137
2007	151	279	430	54	37	91
2008	209	241	450	89	70	159
2009	202	200	402	11	254	365
2010	225	235	220	220	284	504
2011	196	233	429	48	224	272
2012	328	188	516	71	165	236
2013	365	29	394	60	28	88

(Source: National Intellectual Property Office data)[94]

Empirical evidence from these statistics suggests that the gap between foreign patent and domestic ownership is widening yearly. It can also be observed that Sri Lanka has made relatively low level of use of the patent system. Therefore, the important question is, what are the factors that have contributed to this situation? There may be several possible reasons for this. One can of course argue that there have been insufficient patentable innovations and the lack of awareness from the part of individual innova-

94 NIPO, Statistics -National Intellectual Property Office of Sri Lanka (2012) Official website – National Intellectual Property Office of Sri Lanka, available at: <http://www.nipo.gov.lk/about.htm> (accessed 2 November 2012).

tors and firms as the key-factors for this scenario. It is argued that the local markets in developing countries like Sri Lanka tend to be small, sometimes as a result of a less-developed infrastructure, and this reduces the scope of the enterprise's actions and the relevance of actual innovations.[95]

On balance, the Sri Lankan situation is far from satisfactory when compared to the volumes of applications annually filed in other fast-developing countries in the South East Asian region such as Malaysia. A closer analysis of these statistics further reveals that the existing patent regimes have a marginal impact on domestic innovations. This does not, however, imply that Sri Lankan people are less innovative or creative. This can be further exemplified by a comparison of patent statistics between China and Europe. In China, more patents are granted than the European Patent Office. This does not necessarily mean that the Chinese are more innovative than Europeans. As mentioned before, there may be a problem of access to patent protection as a large part of innovation falls short of patent protection on one hand, and on the other hand due to high transaction costs which may be well beyond the means of SMEs making patent protection less attractive. In hindsight, it seems that the architects of IP legislation evidently have paid scant attention to this scenario. IP laws in the country have been shaped viewed through the lens of UK and US models. Thus, the current legislation does not go far enough to incentivise incremental or minor innovations.

One of other possible explanations, Sri Lanka being less innovative evident by low investment in the R&D.[96] According to available statistics it is not more than 0.17 percent (on average) of the GDP.[97] This is of course

---

95 See OECD/Eurostat, *OSLO MANUAL: Guidelines for Using and Interpreting Innovation Data* (3rd edn, The Measurement of Scientific and Technological Activities, OECD Publishing 2005) 137.

96 Ibid. The Oslo Manual notes that the R&D is defined by including the followings: (i) The firm can engage in basic and applied research to acquire new knowledge and direct research towards specific inventions or modifications of existing techniques. (ii) It can develop new product or process concepts or other new methods to assess whether they are feasible and viable, a stage which may involve: (ii-a) development and testing; and (ii-b) further research to modify designs or technical functions.

97 The total expenditure for R&D remains low at less than 0.2 percent of the GDP in Sri Lanka in comparison with nearly 4 percent of the GDP in South Korea and over 2 percent in Singapore. See SS Colombage, 'Sri Lanka is not yet ready for knowledge-driven economic growth' *Sunday Times* (Colombo, 20 July 2014), available at <http://www.sundaytimes.lk/140720/business-times/sri-lanka-not-yet-

grossly inadequate level of investment and is among the lowest in the region which stands at just 0.1 percent (2008) of GDP in Sri Lanka, as compared to 0.8 percent (2008) of GDP in India and 0.67 percent (2008) of GDP in Pakistan.

Table 1.2: A Comparative View of R&D Expenditure of GDP in Selected Countries

Rank	Country	R&D Expenditure (% GDP)	Year
1	Israel	4.74%	2007
4	Japan	3.45%	2007
7	United Sates	2.67%	2007
10	Germany	2.55%	2007
12	Australia	2.17%	2006
21	China	1.49%	2007
38	India	0.8%	2007
41	Pakistan	0.67%	2007
43	Malaysia	0.64%	2006
80	Sri Lanka	0.17%	2006

(Source: United Nations Educational, Scientific, and Cultural Organisation (UNESCO)- Institute for Statistics)[98]

According to the above available empirical evidence, most strikingly, fewer resources are devoted to innovation activities across all industries in Sri Lanka, thereby reducing the innovation potential of enterprises. The government has been a major player in R&D execution and funding, mainly owing to a low level of resources devoted to R&D by businesses.[99] It

ready-for-knowledge-driven-economic-growth-107301.html> (accessed 22 July 2014). PRMP Dilrukshi, 'Science and Technology Indicators of Sri Lanka' (2008), Science and Technology Policy Research Division-National Science Foundation, Colombo, available at: <www.nsf.ac.lk> (accessed 2 May 2012).

98 UNESCO Institute for Statistics, available at: <http://www.nationmaster.com/graph/eco_res_and_dev_exp_of_gdp-economy-research-development-expenditure-gdp> (accessed 30 June 2012).

99 OECD/Eurostat, *OSLO MANUAL: Guidelines for Using and Interpreting Innovation Data* (3rd edn, The Measurement of Scientific and Technological Activities, OECD Publishing 2005) 138.

should nevertheless be mentioned that speculation beyond the limits of the available data would inevitably turn out to be an exercise in futility. In fact, Sri Lanka is not an industrial country and much innovation happens in the agricultural sector and rural hinterland. In terms of industrial structure of the country, the technology level of innovations generated in the country is not very advanced. Besides, at least one economist, based on the latest Economic Complexity Index, has argued that almost 100 percent of products that Sri Lanka produces are simple products which can easily be copied by other competitors. Hence, year after year, Sri Lanka is facing the problem of maintaining and retaining high economic growth.[100] In response, Sri Lanka needs to bring an incentive mechanism to acquire enhanced levels of innovation.

Therefore, it is necessary to reconsider whether the existing IP regimes have served their primary objective of promoting innovations in the country. Given a large part of innovation derive from incremental and TK-based innovations, the current protective measures for minor and incremental innovations are deemed inadequate. It can be argued that neither the patent system nor the design right system can reasonably be viewed as an appropriate method of protecting such innovations. In essence, it may be correct to argue that Sri Lanka is lagging far behind in fostering valuable domestic innovations.

1.3.3. A Lack of Incentives for Innovation?

As Lon Fuller has observed, man is an 'economic animal' constantly seeking his own advantages.[101] Then, the decisive question we need to ask is whether there is a lack of incentives for innovations in Sri Lanka. Un-

---

100 WA Wijewardena, 'Sri Lanka's Future: Convert the Simple Economy into a High-Tech based Complex Economy' *Daily FT* (Colombo, 17 September 2012), available at: <http://www.ft.lk/2012/09/17/sls-future-convert-the-simple-economy-into-a-high-tech-based-complex-economy/> (accessed 3 March 2013). This author has argued quoting Jack Welch's statement 'produce what others cannot copy'. The Economic Complexity Index takes into consideration whether county's production base is composed of complex products. According to this ranking 2010, Japan tops the list followed by Germany and Switzerland. Singapore ranks at No. 7 while China ranked at No. 29. Sri Lanka's ranking in the index is No. 71.

101 LL Fuller, *Legal Fictions* (Stanford University Press 1967) 98.

doubtedly, in the Sri Lankan context, there has been a long-felt need to create a mechanism that would provide adequate incentives for minor and incremental innovations. As interpreted through the lens of the innovation landscape, one can conclude that there may be a lack of rewards and encouragement for innovations in the country. First and foremost, under the current one-size-fits-all patent regime, the patent office and the courts have to make the reward an all-or-nothing proposition where the innovator either receives a certain term of exclusive rights for his invention or if it is of the required standard or he receives nothing.[102] There is no middle path for innovations falling through the protection net of the current single-tier patent system. Arguably, an STP regime may fill this gap in protection making the lesser inventions to receive a lesser form of protection. On the other hand, the one-size-fits-all patent regime may not be able to accommodate the differing needs of the industries of a country like Sri Lanka.

Moreover, the incentive theory advances the argument that the *homo economicus*[103] will tend not to engage in economically valuable creativity and innovation without external rewards.[104] According to basic human sense, external motivational factors such as rewards would also create a psychological effect resulting in intrinsic motivation for further innovations. It is certainly true that there is a system of incentives via current IP paradigms. But the more important question is whether the existing incentive mechanism is adequate, efficient and effective for the kind of innovations that are generated in the country and for all industrial sectors involved in innovation. The answer to this question is probably negative and Sri Lanka would further improve its business climate to attract more investment in innovation if the existing set of incentives is modified to accommodate small and incremental innovations. When there is no appropriate legal framework for providing incentives for innovations, it would lead to discourage innovation.

Secondly, apart from the above incentive-based argument, a growing body of empirical evidence suggests that most innovations generated by SMEs result from adaptation of imported equipments and raw materials to

102 LH Gee, 'The Long March-National Laws Travel the Tortuous Route Towards Utility Protection' (1993) May, Managing Intellectual Property 41, 42.

103 The term refers to the concept of a rational, economic-utility-maximizing actor.

104 EE Johnson, 'Intellectual Property and the Incentive Fallacy' (2011) 39 Florida State University Law Review 623, 640.

local conditions.[105] It is indeed undeniable that in many sectors, SME innovations are mainly of an informal nature, without formal R&D investments, R&D laboratories or R&D personnel.[106] In that case, a large part of innovations of SMEs, in spite of being new, may be obvious and fall short of patent protection. Put differently, the absence of other appropriate protection system would lead to create disincentives to local innovators because such innovations are often the prime candidates for free-riding activities by competitors.[107] This argument has been reinforced by the findings of a recent WIPO study, according to which, a large variety of innovations of SMEs may lack the inventive step to be protectable under the patent system or because process innovations or innovations in certain low-technology sectors are less likely to be patented.[108] From an industrial point of view, a firm anticipates a substantial economic return from an investment and when there is no protection it would encourage free-riding resulting in market failures. As has been observed in recent scholarship, one of the main reasons that has been attributed to the technological underdevelopment of SMEs in Sri Lanka are market failures.[109] In such cases, other intellectual property rights (such as utility models) may play a bigger role than patents to recoup investments in innovation, while providing a competitive edge to SMEs.[110]

Thirdly, there is a need to explore an additional strategy to increase access to the patent system, especially for the SME sector. The costs related

---

105 S Chandrasiri, 'Technological Issues of Small and Medium Scale Enterprises in Sri Lanka' (2003) 4/1 Sri Lanka Economic Journal 59, 60.

106 WIPO, 'Intellectual Property (IP) Rights and Innovation in Small and Medium-sized Enterprises' (2004) WIPO Working Paper August 10/2004, 9 available at: <http://www.wipo.int/export/sites/www/sme/en/documents/pdf/iprs_innovation.pdf> (accessed 10 June 2011).

107 U Suthersanen, G Dutfield and KB Chow (eds), Innovation Without Patents: Harnessing the Creative Spirit in a Diverse World (Edward Elgar 2007) 68.

108 WIPO, 'Intellectual Property (IP) Rights and Innovation in Small and Medium-sized Enterprises' (2004) WIPO Working Paper August 10/2004, 5-6, available at: <http://www.wipo.int/export/sites/www/sme/en/documents/pdf/iprs_innovation.pdf> (accessed 10 June 2011).

109 S Chandrasiri, 'Technological Issues of Small and Medium Scale Enterprises in Sri Lanka' (2003) 4/1 Sri Lanka Economic Journal 59, 60.

110 WIPO, 'Intellectual Property (IP) Rights and Innovation in Small and Medium-sized Enterprises' (2004) WIPO Working Paper August 10/2004, 9, available at: <http://www.wipo.int/export/sites/www/sme/en/documents/pdf/iprs_innovation.pdf> (accessed 10 June 2011).

to patent protection will act as a disincentive to patenting whenever firms do not expect to obtain sufficient benefits to cover the expenditure related to patent protection.[111] One of the major challenges for innovators and SMEs is to find a protection system that they can afford. A more accessible IP system would, of course, bring the concept of innovation closer to rural-based enterprises located in the periphery. In fact, Sri Lankan SMEs are at the low end of technological development. What is even more disturbing to learn is that even such marginal technological capacities are limited to Colombo and suburbs fail to reach SMEs operating outside main cities.[112] It is therefore urgently required to promote access to an affordable protection mechanism not only for the formal sector, but also for creative solutions of rural hinterland mainly developed by informal sectors. It would help new technologies and industries to emerge. From a policy perspective, it can be argued that intellectual creations at all levels should be encouraged and rewarded by creating more access to the protection mechanism.[113]

Furthermore, many critics argue that the current patent regime is an inefficient and ineffective means of achieving its desired end; hence it appears appropriate to consider an alternative incentive mechanism with the right checks and balances, in addition to the regular patent system in place in the country. It is undeniable that Sri Lanka needs to re-energize its R&D activities through incentivising minor and incremental innovations. Sri Lanka needs to explore an alternative philosophy in this regard. There is certainly a need to raise the local technological capacity which is still in the initial stage of the technological ladder. As a result, a paradigm shift in technological and incentive mechanism is urgently needed. There is a need to revisit the prevailing wisdom on IP policies in the country. It is certainly true that squeezing today's innovations into yesterday's system simply does not work.[114] And the IP system should be designed to cater to the needs of the country. Obviously, Sri Lanka needs to improve the legal environment in order to remedy the deficiencies of the incentive paradigm.

111 Ibid.

112 S Chandrasiri, 'Technological Issues of Small and Medium Scale Enterprises in Sri Lanka' (2003) 4/1 Sri Lanka Economic Journal 59, 91.

113 M Crinson, 'Is Some Novel Protection of Invention Needed in Canada' (1997) 12 Intellectual Property Journal 25, 52.

114 LC Thurow, 'Needed: A New System of Intellectual Property Rights' (1997) 75 Harvard Business Review 95, 95.

1.4. TK-based Innovation

Intellectual creations at all levels should be nurtured so as to develop an innovation culture in a country.[115] TK-based innovation, however, has only received little attention. At least, in the Sri Lankan context, it is high time for Sri Lanka to increase the role of traditional innovators in its development strategy. TK-based innovations are generally characterized by value addition and incremental steps. The incentive theory informs us that, by affording an appropriate intellectual property protection, a society can encourage and promote such innovation. Since the question of protecting TK as an IP right has extensively been dealt with in academic and policy circles, this study is not the place to discuss the same highly controversial issue. For purposes of this research, TK-based or TK-inspired innovations are only address insofar as they meet the general standards of a utility model or a petty patent regime. AN STP is by no means any substitutes for protection of TK as such, and the issue of TK protection is independent from what we discuss in this research.

Figure 1.1: TK-based Innovation

115 Federation of Indian Chamber of Commerce and Industry/Luthra & Luthra, 'FICCI's Suggestions on Proposed National Intellectual Property Policy' (2011) Report – Federation of Indian Chamber of Commerce and Industry (FICCI), available at: <http://www.ficci.com/Sedocument/20170/ip-policy.pdf> (accessed 2 June 2012).

1.4.1. What is it?

Sri Lanka is a country with a rich endowment of TK. Today, as elsewhere in the region, misappropriation of TK has become one of the hottest issues in public discourse in Sri Lanka. In other words, the issue of protecting traditional knowledge is extremely controversial and it produces more heat than light. Before embarking on a further discussion, it is important to outline what TK-based innovations mean. The term 'traditional knowledge' refers to the know-how, skills, innovations, practices, teachings and learning, resulting from intellectual activity and developed within a traditional context.[116] Thus, any new step ahead or improvement on existing TK resulting in a new or valued-added product or process should be considered as a TK-based innovation. For instance, clove oil has been used in TK to help fight germs and prevent tooth decay for ages and an SME trading in TK wants to develop and commercialize a quality enhanced herbal toothpaste that may be considered as an innovation under such definition. As another example, *Kothala Himbatu* (*Salacia reticulate)* is used to reduce diabetes in indigenous medicine and a traditional healer wants to put modern technology touches on TK and develop a user-friendly form of a new capsule or tablet replacing the earlier way of using dried leaves, seeds or roots of the plant. Here the specific improvement through the blending of traditional wisdom with formal science can result in enhancing efficacy, quality and safety of a product and should be rewarded.

1.4.2. A particular Need for Protection?

It is quite often argued that Sri Lanka should be able to reap greater benefit from its rich TK base. At present, such knowledge is not being properly utilized and its potentials remain untapped. However, it is possible to make out a strong case for the protection of TK-based innovations by refashioning the IP system to take advantage of its incentive philosophy. As it has already been observed, the conventional patent regime may find it

---

116 This definition is adopted by WIPO. See, WIPO, 'Intergovernmental Committee on Intellectual Property and Genetic Resources, Traditional Knowledge and Folklore on the Protection of Traditional Knowledge: Draft Articles' (April 2012) Document prepared by the Secretariat to the WIPO IPO/GRTKF/IC/21/4, available at: <http://www.wipo.int/tk/en> (accessed 2 June 2012).

difficult to accord any protection for minor incremental innovation. The same is certainly true for TK-based innovations because such innovations build upon exiting innovations, and are often without much original contribution though such products may have huge market potentials.[117] In the absence of an effective protection there would be no incentives for innovation on one hand, and on the other such innovation like a crop in an unfenced field would become vulnerable for free-riding activities by competitors once the product appears on the market. In that case, an STP regime would afford short-term protection through low transaction costs that would go a long way in incentivising R&D in local TK-based industries.

Such a regime would, at least, give a window of opportunity for protection or an option for TK innovators to choose if they so decide. Exclusive reliance on the patent regime may create not only substantive legal hurdles, but also practical problems in acquiring a legal right. On the other hand, protection under unfair competition law is not effective as it does not provide a legal title that can be used as a negotiating instrument in licensing etc. Nevertheless, there are many arguments against affording protection for TK-based innovations. This study observes that there are reasonable concerns over creating of IP rights on what would be in public domain. It can further be argued that such a system is prone to be abused by large and multi-national companies. On balance, there is always the possibility that such a system is being abused, and it is important to have safeguards against potential abuses. In sum, Sri Lanka needs innovative ways of preventing erosion of TK by enthusing younger members of communities to remain and contribute to TK-based innovations. Mashelkar argues that "to achieve this goal we [the South Asia] need innovation in the IP system itself".[118]

---

117 KR Srinivas, 'Traditional Knowledge and Intellectual Property Rights: A Note on Issues, Some Solutions and some Suggestions' (2008) 3/1 Asian Journal of WTO & International Health Law and Policy 81, 100-101.

118 RA Mashelkar, 'The New Millennium Challenges for Indian Science and Technology' (CMS Communication Colloquium National Lecture, Centre for Media Studies New Delhi, 23 July 1999), available at: <http://www.hks.harvard.edu/sustsci/ists/TWAS_0202/mashelkar_230799.pdf> (accessed 15 January 2011).

1.5. The South Asian Scenario

As stated earlier, harnessing innovation to generate wealth is a huge challenge for many countries. This task is particularly daunting for the developing economies in South Asian region where a large part of innovation tends to be based on improvements or derived from traditional knowledge and mostly subpatentable. Theoretically, the patent system is conceived as an important tool to stimulate indigenous technological development, promote domestic inventive activity and enhance the exploitation of patented inventions.[119] However, those expectations seem to be far from being realised in many, if not all South Asian countries. The strict patentability criteria (with worldwide novelty and greater degree of inventiveness) in these countries are in line with global standards as defined by TRIPS Agreement and other international IP conventions. It is nevertheless argued that the South Asian region has failed to address the issue of improvement innovations and falls short in providing them with an adequate protection mechanism. Incremental and minor innovations can, even if they are below the level of patentability, contribute significantly to the development of the economy in developing countries. In the absence of a lower level protection system, such innovations would not be recognized and rewarded. Accordingly, there would be no incentives for small and medium-sized enterprises (SMEs) and individual innovators to make sufficient investments in such innovations. Most interestingly, no country in the South Asian region has an STP regime.

A closer look at the innovation climate in the Asian region reveals an innovation gap between South Asian countries on the one hand, and the East and Southeast Asian countries on the other. This situation mirrors a protection gap in the existing patent laws and policies in the region. Not surprisingly, the R&D activities in most countries in the South Asian region are far from satisfactory and fall much below the level of innovation in emerging economies in East Asia. It is barely imaginable as to why such a low level of innovation prevails in the region. As aptly observed by scholars, in most developing countries the innovation systems are fragmented and weak and they overwhelmingly depend on innovations made

---

119 G Mengistie, 'The patent system in Africa: its contribution and potential in stimulating innovation, technology transfer and fostering science and technology: Part 2' in *International Trade Law and Regulation* (Sweet and Maxwell 2010) 1-2.

abroad.[120] This is certainly true for many South Asian countries with certain exceptions, especially in case of India. Different types of patent statistics and other measurements of innovation can be used to analyse the innovation landscape of the South Asian region. "First and foremost, the statistics on the first patent applications filed after an invention are reliable indications for innovation".[121]

Table 1.3: Comparison of IP Statistics of South & East Asian Countries, 2009-2010

Type of IP	India	Pakistan	Bangladesh	China	Malaysia	S. Korea
Patents						
Applications	34287	1208	330	391177	6464	170101
Registrations	6168	252	130	135110	2177	68843
Utility Models						
Applications	NA	NA	NA	409836	84	13661
Registrations	NA	NA	NA	344472	-	4301
Designs						
Applications	6092	389	992	421273	16677	57187
Registrations	6025	359	394	335243	1598	33136

(Source: Databases of National IP offices and WIPO IP Statistics/Country Profiles)[122]

120 C Correa, 'Designing Patent Policies suited to Developing Countries Needs' (2008) 10/2 Econômica, Rio de Janeiro 82, 89.

121 JWM van Leuven, 'Patent Statistics as Indicators for Innovation' (1996) November/December, Patent World 20, 20.

122 Controller General of Patents Designs and Trademarks/Government of India, 'Annual Reports of Office of CGPDTM' (2009 to 2010) CGPDT official website, available at: <http://ipindia.nic.in/ipr/patent/patents.htm> (accessed 15 April 2012). Intellectual Property Organisation of Pakistan, 'Patents – List of Patents Granted'(2009 to 2010) IPO official website, available at: <http://ipo.gov.pk/Patent/PatentGranted.aspx> (accessed 15 April 2012). State Intellectual Property of the People's Republic of China, 'Grants for Three Kinds of Patents Received from Home and Abroad' (2009 to 2010) SIPO official website, available at: <http://english.sipo.gov.cn/statistics/gnwsqnb/2010/201101/t20110125_570600.html>(accessed 15 April 2012). Intellectual Property Cooperation of Malaysia (MyIPO), 'Application and Granted Patents and Utility Innovations From 1986 –

As this table indicates, South Asian countries have far less number of patent applications when compared to East and Southeast Asian countries. The data suggests that China has as many as 10 times more patent applications per capita (number of patent applications per 1 million people) as India, given its population of 1.2 billion when compared to Chinese population of 1.3 billion in 2010. Similarly, it is also evident that there is a gap between South Asian countries and East Asian countries in terms of patent ownership. When it comes to other South Asian countries such as Pakistan and Bangladesh, the situation is even worse. On the other hand, the R&D spending in many South Asian countries is less than 1 percent of GDP, with India 0.8 percent of GDP and Pakistan 0.67 percent of GDP in 2008 whereas emerging market countries (for example, South Korea 3.39 percent of GDP and China 1.47 percent of GDP) invest relatively more resourses for the R&D than their South Asian counterparts.[123] The following statistics in Table 1.5 give an idea of the current situation of patents landscape in India.

2014' (2009 to 2010) MyIPO official website, available at: < http://www.myipo.gov.my/web/guest/paten-statistik> (accessed 15 April 2012). Statistics of Korean and Bangladesh are available at WIPO – Statistical Country Profiles, available at: <http://www.wipo.int/ipstats/en/statistics/country_profile/> (accessed 15 April 2012).

123 The World Bank, 'Science and Technology-World Development Indicators' (2012) The World Bank official website, available at: <http://data.worldbank.org/topic/science-and-technology> (accessed 15 April 2012).

Table 1.4: Trends in Patent Applications and Grants in India

Year	Filed	Examined	Granted
2003/4	12613	10709	2469
2004/5	17466	14813	1911
2005/6	24505	11569	4320
2006/7	28940	14119	7539
2007/8	35218	11751	15316
2008/9	36812	10296	16061
2009/10	34287	6069	6168
2010/11	39400	11208	7509

(Source: Based on data from Annual Reports of Office of the CGPDTM of India)[124]

According to Annual Reports of IP India, the number of patent applications filed by domestic applicants is between 20-25 percent and in 2010-2011 alone it is 20.46 percent.[125] A vast majority of patent applications and grants are represented by foreign applicants, and thus India can be viewed as a patent granting rather than patent producing nation. This picture is not much different in the case of Pakistan. The following statistics in Table 1.6 provide a glimpse of what the innovation landscape in Pakistan looks like.

124 Controller General of Patents Designs and Trademarks/Government of India, 'Annual Reports of Office of CGPDTM' (2009 to 2011) CGPDT official website, available at: <http://ipindia.nic.in/ipr/patent/patents.htm> (accessed 30 January 2012).

125 Ibid.

Table 1.5: Trends in Patent Applications and Grants in Pakistan

Year	Filed	Granted
2004-05	493	484
2005-06	1406	256
2006-07	1790	299
2007-08	1535	152
2008-09	1365	162
2009-10	1208	252

(Source: Based on data from Annual Reports-IPO Pakistan)[126]

What are we to conclude from all these statistics? One possible and most likely conclusion is that the patent system is not robustly used by local innovators. This conclusion is consistent with recent empirical studies. Most importantly, a recent study by Kardam observes that, "although India has put in place very modern patent and design laws recently, the small scale industry sector and small innovators are still unable to take full advantage of this legislation as under this legislation, the requirements of patenting and registration are very stringent in nature and at the same time, take a lot of time and very expensive. Due to these reasons, these small innovators and small industry sector seem to have lost interest".[127] Moreover, a recent WIPO study finds that a low number of annual patent applications in Pakistan shows a clear disconnect between domestic economic/industrial activity and the corresponding IP protection.[128] This may be due to the fact

126 Intellectual Property Organisation of Pakistan, 'Patents – List of Patents Granted' (2009 to 2010) IPO official website, available at: <http://ipo.gov.pk/Patent/Patent Granted.aspx> (accessed 15 April 2012).

127 KS Kardam, 'Utility Model –A Tool for Economic and Technological Development: A Case Study of Japan' (2007) Final Report in Fulfillment of the Long-term Fellowship Sponsored by World Intellectual Property Office (WIPO) in Collaboration with the Japan Patent Office (from April 2, 2007 to September 28, 2007), 16-17, available at: <http://www.ipindia.nic.in/research_studies/FinalReport_April2007.pdf> (accessed 15 April 2012).

128 HG Ruse-Khan, 'Utility Model Protection in Pakistan-A Feasible Option for Incentivising Incremental Innovation?' (2012), Study conducted for the World Intellectual Property Organisation 77 (copy on file with author).

that patent applications involve very high standards of invention and not many innovative activities would qualify for such protection.[129] In essence, both studies have found that the existing IP regimes are not an adequate and effective means of protecting most innovation that are generated in the region.

From a different perspective, one can of course argue that India is more advanced than most of Southeast Asian countries in terms of technology and innovation. It is certainly true that India has certainly made some impressive strides in the global software market as well as in the pharmaceutical and chemical sector.[130] Even though India has developed its capabilities considerably in certain industrial sectors, engineering industries and others have suffered from not having a mechanism for encouraging minor adaptations made by domestic firms.[131] As Kumar has observed, this difference could perhaps explain the not so encouraging performance of Indian enterprises in other industries.[132] According to some scholars, the time has come for South Asian to revisit their IP regimes and policies. Therefore, we need innovations in the intellectual property system itself.[133] New models and new thinking on IP will have to be envisioned to accomplish this.[134] There is a rising tide of opinion in the South Asian region in favour of adopting an STP, such as that of a UM regime. India has pioneered in this regard by introducing a Discussion Paper on UM in May 2011. Similar situation are being considered in Pakistan and Sri Lanka. It

---

129 Ibid.

130 RA Mashelkar, 'The New Millennium Challenges for Indian Science and Technology'(1999) CMS Communication Colloquium National Lecture-Centre for Media Studies, New Delhi, 23 July 1999, 3-6, available at: <http://www.hks.harvard.edu/sustsci/ists/TWAS_0202/mashelkar_230799.pdf> (accessed 15 April 2012).

131 N Kumar, 'Technology and Economic development: Experiences of Asian Countries' (2002) Commission of Intellectual Property Rights- Study Paper 1b, 6 and 26, available at: <http://www.twnside.org.sg/title2/FTAs/Intellectual_Property/IP_and_Development/IPR_TechnologyandEconomicDevelopment-Nagesh_Kumar.pdf> (accessed 10 January 2011).

132 Ibid.

133 See generally RA Mashelkar, 'Intellectual Property Rights and The Third World' (2001) October -18/8 Current Science 955, para 40, available at: <http://www.sristi.org/material/1.2intellectual%20property%20and%20the%20third%20world.pdf> (accessed 11 January 2011).

134 Ibid.

is encouraging to see that South Asian countries are paying attention to this largely unexplored option for incentivising local innovation.

1.6. Overview of Second-Tier Protection

Second-tier protection (STP) has been considered a backwater of intellectual property law.[135] Seen from a different perspective, patent, copyright and trademark laws are the three accepted bastions of the intellectual property world, with their respective legal satellites of utility models, design and unfair competition laws.[136] As used elsewhere in this paper, the terms STP and utility models are synonymous. As noted above, there is no global acceptance of the term 'utility model' due to there being fundamentally different concepts from one country to another.[137] If one examines national laws, one finds that utility model protection is referred to in Australia as 'innovation patent', in Malaysia as 'utility innovation', in Thailand 'petty patent' and in Belgium as 'short-term patent'. These terms simply refer to a title of protection for certain innovations, in particular devices, articles or other engineering products which are technically less complex and have short product life cycles in order to foster local innovations.[138] As commentators argue, the utility model is not an accepted or clearly defined legal concept within the intellectual property paradigm but it is a generic term which refers to subject-matter that hinges between that protectable under patent law and design law.[139] Policy makers, legislatures and legal scholars refer to a second-tier patent system, which offers a cheap, no-ex-

---

135 MD Janis, 'Second Tier Protection' (1999) 40/1 Harvard International Law Journal 151, 152.

136 U Suthersanen, 'Breaking Down the Intellectual property Barriers' (1998) 3 Intellectual Property Quarterly 267, 267.

137 U Suthersanen, 'Utility Models and Innovation in Developing Countries' (2006) UNCTAD-ICTSD Issue Paper No. 13 Project on IPRs and Sustainable Development 1-2, available at: <http://unctad.org/en/docs/iteipc20066_en.pdf> (accessed 15 March 2012).

138 HG Ruse-Khan, 'Utility Model Protection in Pakistan-A Feasible Option for Incentivising Incremental Innovation?' (2012), Study conducted for the World Intellectual Property Organisation 22 (copy on file with author).

139 U Suthersanen, 'Utility Models and Innovation in Developing Countries' (2006) UNCTAD-ICTSD Issue Paper No. 13 Project on IPRs and Sustainable Development 1, available at: <http://unctad.org/en/docs/iteipc20066_en.pdf> (accessed 15 March 2012).

amination protection regime for technical inventions which would not usually fulfil the strict patentability criteria.[140] Interestingly though, ten of the world's 14 trillion dollar economies alone with South Korea have some form of UM. These are Japan, China, Germany, Japan, France, Italy, Russia, Brazil, Mexico and Australia. The major economies that do not have a similar protection are the USA, the UK, Canada and India.[141]

1.6.1. Common Elements and Divergence

According to Suthersanen, from a global perspective, there are common elements amongst different national STP regimes.[142] They are: (1) all utility model laws confer exclusive rights on the proprietor of the right; (2) novelty is a criterion in all utility model systems, though the standard of novelty varies widely; (3) registration is a requirement but usually there is no substantive examination of applications; (4) most utility model laws protect the technical character of the invention, as opposed to the ornamental function or the appearance of the product.

Even more significantly, there are more differences than similarities in national approaches to STP regimes due to the policy space that countries enjoyed in the implementation of such systems.[143] Such areas of divergence may be summarized as follows:

- *Subject matter under protection:* Some utility model laws protect only the three-dimensional form, while others extend the umbrella of protection to cover technical inventions and processes. In most countries it is narrower than regular patents. A majority of utility model laws sim-

---

140 NAO Boztosun, 'Exploring the Utility of Utility Models for Fostering Innovation' (2010) 15 Journal of Intellectual Property Rights 429, 434-435.

141 C Thompson and L Dumbrell, 'A really Useful Utility Model' (2010) Issue 220 Patent World 28, 28.

142 U Suthersanen, 'Utility Models and Innovation in Developing Countries' (2006) UNCTAD-ICTSD Issue Paper No. 13 Project on IPRs and Sustainable Development 1, available at: <http://unctad.org/en/docs/iteipc20066_en.pdf> (accessed 15 March 2012).

143 WIPO-CDIP, 'Patent related Flexibilities in the Multilateral Legal Framework and their Legislative Implementation at the National and Regional Level' (2010) The Document prepared by the Secretariat to the WIPO-CDIP/5/4, 1st March 2010, 26-27.

ply adopt the domestic patent law definition of protectable subject matter.[144]

- *Conditions for protection*: While the novelty requirement as such is used by all countries with a system of utility model protection, the level of novelty required ranges from ranges from universal novelty, to relative novelty, to domestic novelty.[145]

When it comes to inventive step requirement, there is huge variation between different countries. In some countries an inventive step is not a requirement for protection, while many other countries need a lower level of inventiveness. A few countries still insists on the same level of inventive step as that is for patents. Moreover, industrial applicability is generally applicable under every system.

- *Granting procedure:* Many systems adopt a simple registration procedure with cursory examination; while a few implement a detailed examination process.[146]
- *Duration of protection:* The term of protection varies from four years (Somalia) to twenty five years.
- The following table offers a bird's eye view of second-tier protection systems in place in different jurisdictions in the world.

---

144 U Suthersanen, 'Utility Models and Innovation in Developing Countries' (2006) UNCTAD-ICTSD Issue Paper No. 13 Project on IPRs and Sustainable Development 1-2. available at: <http://unctad.org/en/docs/iteipc20066_en.pdf> (accessed 15 March 2012).

145 HG Ruse-Khan, 'Utility Model Protection in Pakistan-A Feasible Option for Incentivising Incremental Innovation?' (2012), Study conducted for the World Intellectual Property Organisation 24 (copy on file with author).

146 U Suthersanen, 'Utility Models and Innovation in Developing Countries' (2006) UNCTAD-ICTSD Issue Paper No. 13 Project on IPRs and Sustainable Development 1-2, available at: <http://unctad.org/en/docs/iteipc20066_en.pdf> (accessed 15 March 2012).

Table 1.6: Comparison of Second-Tier Protection Regimes in Selected Countries

Country	Name of right	Novelty	Inventive step	Subject matter of protection	Substantive examination	Max. term (yrs)
Australia	Innovation patent	same as patents	lower standard than patents	Same as patents	No	8
China	Utility model	same as patents	lower standard than patents	shape or structure of product	No	10
Germany	Utility model (Gebrauch-smuster)	relative novelty	lower standard than patents	all inventions except processes & methods	No	10
Japan	Utility model	same as patents	lower standard than patents	shape, construction etc. of an article	No	10
Kenya	Utility model	similar to patents	not required	form, configuration utensil, tool and herbal formulations	Yes	10
Malaysia	Utility innovation	same as patents	not required	similar to patents	Yes	20
Philippines	Utility model	local novelty only	not required	any technical solution of a problem in any field of human activity	No	7
Russia	Utility model	relative novelty	not required	any technical solution relating to an apparatus	No	8
Republic of Korea	Utility model	same as patents	inventive step required	shape, construction etc.	Yes	10

(Table is created based on information provided in different publications and personal communication.)[147]

---

147 Based on, U Suthersanen, G Dutfield and KBB Chow (eds), *Innovation Without Patents: Harnessing the Creative Spirit in a Diverse World* (Edward Elgar 2007) 34. Australian Government's Advisory Council on Intellectual Property, 'Review of the Innovation Patent System' (2011) Issues Paper -August 2011, 7, available at: <http://www.acip.gov.au> (accessed 10 February 2012). Department of Industrial Policy and Promotion/India, 'Utility Models' (2011) Discussion Paper-23 May 2011, para 41, available at: <http://dipp.gov.in/English/Discuss_paper/Utility_Models_13May2011.pdf> (accessed 30 December 2011). J Richards, 'Utility

Viewing through the characteristics of the law, commentators have also classified the national STP systems into two groups (prototypes), namely, *patent-like regimes* and three-*dimensional regime*. According to patent prototype, UM laws mimic the domestic patent law, under which absolute or international novelty and the full inventive step are required.[148] Moreover, there is no three-dimensional or form limitation within the definition.[149] The main difference between the patent and utility model system lies in the fact that the latter provides a shorter period of protection and a quick examination (instead of the normal substantive examination of patents).[150] The STP systems that operate in France and Belgium represent this model. To the contrary, however, the *three-dimensional regime* requires that the protectable innovation must be embodied in three-dimensional form. Usually, the inventive step required is smaller than for patents (a diminished inventive step requirement) though there can be differing standards of novelty), which allows protection to be extended to minor inventions. Nevertheless, within this group, important differences exist from one country to another regarding substantive examination.[151] Countries such as Germany, Italy, Spain, Japan, and China as well as Scandinavian countries use this type of regime. In reality though, many countries use a mixed-strategy drawing experiences from 'best practices' or common elements of other countries to design the most appropriate STP regimes in ac-

---

Model Protection throughout the World' (2010) Internet Publication, available at: <http://www.ipo.org/AM/Template.cfm?Template=/CM/ContentDisplay.cfm&ContentID=25244> (accessed 30 December 2011). Personal communication with Kenyan Intellectual Property Institute (11 September 2012).

148 U Suthersanan, 'A Brief Tour of "Utility Model" Law' (1998) 2 European Intellectual Property Review 44, 45.

149 Ibid.

150 WIPO-CDIP, 'Patent related Flexibilities in the Multilateral Legal Framework and their Legislative Implementation at the National and Regional Level' (2010) Document prepared by the Secretariat (CDIP/5/4, 1st March 2010) para 85.

151 Ibid.

cordance with their domestic needs; for example, Australia, Philippine and Thailand to name but a few.

1.6.2. The Rationale for STP Systems

The accepted rationale for the introduction of the STP is to encourage innovative activity by providing an alternative system of protecting innovations which could not be protected by standard patent system because they fall short of the inventive step and/or novelty bars.[152] Without this protection, innovators who come out with new products involving innovations of smaller importance and lesser technological advance would find rampant copying and competition without any remedy.[153] As a general matter, the STP is to protect modest improvements in technical inventions that may not merit the cost of a patent application, and in so doing encourage innovation in the field of technology to which STP systems apply.[154] One of the other rationales behind STP systems is that such systems improve access to patent protection for individuals and small and medium-sized enterprises (SMEs).[155] Such protection is particularly useful where the lifespan of the product is shorter than the time it takes to obtain a patent. In order to further accelerate the grant the IP right, most countries are dispensing with substantive examination for these patents. However, the protection conferred is less secured.[156] When it comes to dealing with the innovations of developing countries with marginal technological capacities,

---

152 LH Gee, 'The Long March-Utility Model Protection for Minor Inventions' (1993) Managing Intellectual Property 42. U Suthersanen, G Dutfield and KBB Chow (eds), *Innovation Without Patents: Harnessing the Creative Spirit in a Diverse World* (Edward Elgar 2007) 17.

153 LH Gee, 'The Long March-Utility Model Protection for Minor Inventions' (1993) Managing Intellectual Property 42.

154 Advisory Council on Intellectual Property (ACIP) of Australia, Should Plant and Animal subject Matter be excluded from the Protection by Innovation Patent? (2004) 7.

155 AF Christie and SL Morritz, 'Australia's Second-Tier Protection System: A Preliminary Review' (2005) Intellectual Property Research Institute of Australia (IPRIA) Report No. 02/04, 7, available at: <http://www.ipria.org/publications/reports/AU_2nd-tier_Report-revised.pdf> (accessed 30 December 2011).

156 Advisory Council on Intellectual Property (ACIP) of Australia, Should Plant and Animal subject Matter be excluded from the Protection by Innovation Patent? (2004)7.

the utility models are particularly useful for inventions, that have only incremental improvements over prior art. From an economic perspective, most individual innovators and SMEs have limited financial resources and IPR protection becomes a hurdle for them as they are unable to secure IP rights at a cost they can afford. This, in effect, creates a barrier in terms of accessibility to the protection. It can well be argued that an STP could benefit individual innovators and SMEs, if a country could sufficiently focus the STP on industries that should be promoted.

1.6.3. Pros and Cons of an STP Regime

There are a number of arguments that strongly speak in favour of UM regime. The main advantages are: (1) Such regimes serve as an incentive mechanism encouraging local and indigenous innovation; (2) it would provide a solution to the problem of unfair copying and prevent free-riding activities on the achievements of others competitors; (3) a utility model right can be used as a bargaining tool in the hands of the right-holder for negotiation and litigation; (4) UMs can provide an easily accessible means of protection for SMEs and individual innovators which can be considered as a 'low-cost entry point into the IP system; (5) such a system can address the perceived protection gap that exists between patent and design regimes by providing protection for innovations falling from the safety net of IP system; (6) it serves the interests of cash-strapped SMEs in gaining access to finance through licensing, venture capitalism and granting security/collaterals for credits; (7) a UM right confers to the holder a psychological advantage over competitors by creating an (illusory) effect that imitation by competitors will be delayed due to the exclusive right.[157]

There are also several downsides of a UM system. The main disadvantages are: (1) Since UM rights are granted without substantive examination, it would increase business risk and do more harm than good for enterprises, and on the other hand, it would lead to proliferation of unstable rights; (2) generally, there could be an increase of spurious and wasteful

157 U Suthersanen, G Dutfield and KBB Chow (eds), *Innovation Without Patents: Harnessing the Creative Spirit in a Diverse World* (Edward Elgar 2007) 42. HG Ruse-Khan, 'Utility Model Protection in Pakistan-A Feasible Option for Incentivising Incremental Innovation?' (2012), Study conducted for the World Intellectual Property Organisation, 28 (copy on file with author).

litigation; (3) there are also concerns that UM system is prone to be easily abused large companies and create problems for small businesses; (4) such a system would also lead to create a mountain of worthless patents and they may not be worth the papers they were written on;[158] (5) a UM can be a dangerous device as they are like 'minefield' for an unsuspecting manufacturer which is hidden from the view until it explodes;[159] (6) moreover, creating a new right would cause an erosion of public domain and would detrimentally affect downstream innovations.

1.6.4. Policy Considerations to be applied by Legislators

Intellectual property systems are more than just pieces of legislation, and may best be viewed as public policy regulatory institutions.[160] Thus, any policy considerations in relation to an STP regime should mirror domestic needs and circumstances of individual countries. Most importantly, the policymakers in developing countries need to pay attention to the following factors in designing an appropriate IP policy framework for protecting and promoting small and incremental innovations. First and foremost, innovation landscape of the country and the level of domestic innovation. More significantly, whether there is a large part of innovation emanates from SME sector and if such innovations are of lower standards of inventiveness. Secondly, level of the technological development of the country. For instance, the regular patent system may not be of much use for countries that are in the initial stage of technological ladder. Thirdly, whether unfair copying and imitation is a real problem for those who want to develop and commercialize small scale innovation. Fourthly, the availability of alternative IP regimes such as unfair competition, trade secrets and design protection. This is because the creation of new IP right may cause undue social costs. Last but not the least, domestic IP infrastructure is of vital importance for successful implementation any incentive mechanism in

158 P Leith, 'Software Utility Models and SMEs' (2000) 2 Journal of Information Law and Technology 6.

159 Ibid.

160 U Suthersanen, 'Utility Models and Innovation in Developing Countries' (2006) UNCTAD-ICTSD Issue Paper No. 13 Project on IPRs and Sustainable Development 7, available at: <http://unctad.org/en/docs/iteipc20066_en.pdf> (accessed 15 March 2012).

a country. In this regard, strengths and weaknesses of administrative and enforcement agencies need to be properly assessed.

1.7. International Legal Framework

The internationalisation of IP law, regulation and policy began in the eighteenth and nineteenth century, when IPRs appeared in Friendship, Commerce and Navigation (FCN) treaties.[161] Interestingly, the multilateralisation of international IP quickly followed in the latter part of the nineteenth century through the negotiation and adoption of two important treaties; namely, the Paris and the Berne Conventions.[162] Most significantly, in 1994 the TRIPS Agreement established universal minimum standards of IP protection by creating another milestone in the history of IP law. International IP treaties cover various IP rights in varying degrees of detail and comprehensiveness. Hence the treaty obligations that the contracting parties must adhere to equally vary.[163] As is well known, UM or petty patent systems have remained in the backwater of international IP system ignored by major IP treaties. For utility models, international IP law so far contains relatively few provisions and consequently few relevant treaty obligations the contracting States must comply with.[164] As a result, most remarkably, there are no independent and self-standing obligations flowing from leading international treaties leaving a quite broad policy space for countries in crafting their STP regimes suited to domestic needs and objectives.[165] Nevertheless, according to commentators, this policy space is being eroded to some extent due to TRIPS-Plus provisions that now appears in many comprehensive Free Trade Agreements (FTAs) and other

161 B Mercurio, 'Reconceptualising the Debate on Intellectual Property Rights and Economic Development' (2010) 3/1 The Law and Development Review 65, 71.

162 Ibid.

163 HG Ruse-Khan, 'Utility Model Protection in Pakistan-A Feasible Option for Incentivising Incremental Innovation?' (2012), Study conducted for the World Intellectual Property Organisation, 7. (copy on file with author).

164 Ibid.

165 WIPO-CDIP, 'Patent related Flexibilities in the Multilateral Legal Framework and their Legislative Implementation at the National and Regional Level' (2010) The Document prepared by the Secretariat to the WIPO-CDIP/5/4, 1st March 2010, 26.

Bilateral Investment Treaties (BITs) negotiated by some countries.[166] In this context, it is worth analyzing the relevant provisions with regard to STP in major international IP conventions.

1.7.1. Obligations under the Paris Convention

The utility model was internationally recognized by the Paris Convention as *modèle d'utilité* by the Revision Conference of Washington on 2nd June 1911.[167] Since then the concept of utility model has gained some legitimacy in intellectual property arena though the Paris Convention which does not explain what a utility model might be. It is also true that, in the international context, the concept of utility models has been enshrined in the Paris Convention, but the Paris Convention seems to be more associated with patents, trademarks and industrial designs.[168] An analysis of provisions of the Paris Convention shows that utility models are recognised as industrial property by virtue of Article 1(2) which states that 'the protection of industrial property has as its object patents, utility models, industrial designs, trademarks, service marks, trade names, indications of source or appellations of origin, and the repression of unfair competition'. Resulting from this definition of industrial property, contracting States, includ-

166 Sri Lanka has entered into Free Trade Agreements (FTAs) with both India and Pakistan and Bilateral Investment Protection Agreements (BITs) with 27 countries. According to communication with the Director/Research at the Board of Investment in Sri Lanka, FTAs do not have provision on IP protection but BITs do have a general clause for the protection of IP rights. Most likely, the future agreements which are still under negotiation would containing obligation to protect IP rights but certainly would not go beyond TRIPS standards. See C Correa, 'Designing Patent Policies suited to Developing Countries Needs' (2008) 10/2 Econômica, Rio de Janeiro 82, 95.

167 K Königer, 'Registration without Examination: The Utility Model-A Useful Model?' in W Prinz zu Waldeck und Pyrmont and others (eds), *Patents and Technological Progress in a Globalized World: Liber Amicorum Joseph Straus* (Springer 2009) 17.

168 W Weeraworawit, 'Utility Models in Thailand' in C Heath and A Kamperman Sanders (eds), *Industrial property in the Bio-Medical Age: Challenges for Asia* (Kluwer Law 2003) 269, 269.

ing Sri Lanka,[169] and other and other South Asian countries,[170] are bound by national treatment obligation under Article 2 and right of priority principle under Article 4 of the Convention. As a fact though, other than the inclusion of these two principles, Paris Convention is silent as to the definition and scope of the UM protection.

The national treatment principle is a rule of non-discrimination enshrined in the Paris Convention, ensuring that foreign IP owners will enjoy in the protecting country, at least the same treatment as the protecting country give to its own nationals, without the condition of reciprocity.[171] Pursuant to Article 2(1), each Member States requires to grant nationals of the other member countries states the same protection and same remedies against infringement as available to their own nationals with regard to the protection of industrial property as referred to in Article 1(2). Therefore, a national system of utility model protection may not discriminate against foreign right holders in terms of protection and enforcement.[172] According to scholars, this national treatment obligation, however, does not create an obligation for Paris Union countries to introduce utility model protection in their national laws; nor does it require any specific minimum scope or substance of protection if such a system is established.[173] Undoubtedly, Member States such as Sri Lanka remain free not to introduce such a system into their domestic law. If they decide to foresee utility model protection in their national law, they can freely determine the conditions for it; as well as the scope, substance, limitations and duration of utility model

169 Sri Lanka acceded to the most recent Stockholm Act (1967) of the Paris Convention on 20 June 1978.

170 For instance, India acceded to the most recent Stockholm Act (1967) of the Paris Convention on 7 September 1998 while Pakistan acceded on 22 April 2004.

171 Y Li, International and Comparative Intellectual Property: Law, Policy and Practice (Butterworths 2005) 17.

172 HG Ruse-Khan, 'Utility Model Protection in Pakistan-A Feasible Option for Incentivising Incremental Innovation?' (2012), Study conducted for the World Intellectual Property Organisation, 8. (copy on file with author). See also GHC Bodenhausen, *Guide to the Application of the Paris Convention for the Protection of Industrial Property* (BIRPI 1968) 27-29. (Bodenhausen observes that the principle of 'national treatment' or 'assimilation with nationals' embodied in this provision is one of the basic rules of the convention.

173 HG Ruse-Khan, 'Utility Model Protection in Pakistan-A Feasible Option for Incentivising Incremental Innovation?' (2012), Study conducted for the World Intellectual Property Organisation, 7-8. (copy on file with author).

protection.[174] Predictably, this absence of any substantive minimum standards is one of the main reasons for the diversity in the design of national utility model systems around the world.[175]

Probably, the other most important provision that creates obligation on its Member States in relation to UM protection is the right of priority embodied in Article 4 of the Paris Convention. According to this Article, 'any person who has duly filed an application for a patent, or for the registration of a utility model, or of an industrial design, or of a trademark, in one of the countries of the Union, or his successor in title, shall enjoy, for the purpose of filing in the other countries, a right of priority during the periods hereinafter fixed'.[176] As a general rule, an application duly filed in one of the countries of the Union (first application) creates a right of priority as regards any subsequent filings in the other countries of the Union.[177] Therefore, Paris Union countries which foresee a system of utility model protection have to allow a grace period of 12 months from the date of the first filing of a utility model registration in one of the Union countries within which the right holder may register the utility model in other Union countries.[178] Logically, a period of priority can be secured for an application for an industrial design based[179] on the filing date of a utility model; and a period of priority can be secured for a utility model application by virtue of a right of priority based on a patent application (and *vice versa*).[180]

In addition to the above mentioned obligations, Article 5(A) of the Convention sets certain limits and restrictions to national legislatures providing for the grant of compulsory licenses and the forfeiture of patent rights

---

174 Ibid.

175 Ibid 8.

176 See Article 4(A)(1) of the Paris Convention.

177 T Cottier and P Véron, Concise International and European IP Law: TRIPS, Paris Convention, European Enforcement and Transfer of Technology (Kluwer Law 2008) 195.

178 HG Ruse-Khan, 'Utility Model Protection in Pakistan-A Feasible Option for Incentivising Incremental Innovation?' (2012), Study conducted for the World Intellectual Property Organisation, 8. (copy on file with author).

179 Compared to patent, industrial designs enjoy a shorter period of 6 months in terms of priority.

180 U Suthersanen, 'Utility Models and Innovation in Developing Countries' (2006) UNCTAD-ICTSD Issue Paper No. 13 Project on IPRs and Sustainable Development 3, available at: <http://unctad.org/en/docs/iteipc20066_en.pdf> (accessed 15 March 2012.).

which is applicable, mutatis mutandis, to utility models by Article 5(A) (5).[181] A plain reading of the provision reveals that there are obligations relating to forfeiture or revocation patents or introduction compulsory licenses, especially in the case of failure to work. Nevertheless, scholars argue that these provisions are primarily relevant in the context of importing protected products and their local working, whereas utility model protection, in all jurisdictions, is primarily utilised by local residents. Thus, the obligations contained in Article 5(A) are most unlikely to play an important role in the practice of utility model protection.[182] The question that arises is whether a Member State who decides to introduce an STP regime is barred by this provision from introducing some form of compulsory licensing if it considers this necessary. The answer to this question lies in Article 5A(2) which explicitly allows 'the grant of compulsory licenses to prevent the abuses which might result from the exercise of the exclusive rights conferred by the patent'.

Scholars argue that the failure to work is mentioned as an example and it is not exhaustive and other forms of abuse can also be addressed by compulsory licensing system.[183] Put differently, it will primarily be relevant for compulsory licenses addressing failure to work a scenario which does not seem to have practical significance for utility models or petty patents. Most importantly, the obligations in Article 5(A) (2)-(4) do not apply to measures other than those whose purpose is to prevent abuses.[184] As a result, Member States are free to introduce compulsory licenses (or other limitations to utility model protection) for other reasons such as to promote public interest or to allow the utilisation of utility models necessary for follow-on innovation.[185] In that sense, one can reasonably argue that Article 5(A) of the Paris Convention allows its Member considerable leeway in crafting exceptions and limitations to utility model protection. In the light of the above, one can conclude that under Paris Convention a

181 T Cottier and P Véron, Concise International and European IP Law: TRIPS, Paris Convention, European Enforcement and Transfer of Technology (Kluwer Law 2008) 210.

182 HG Ruse-Khan, 'Utility Model Protection in Pakistan-A Feasible Option for Incentivising Incremental Innovation?' (2012), Study conducted for the World Intellectual Property Organisation, 8. (copy on file with author).

183 Ibid.

184 Ibid.

185 Ibid.

domestic lawmaker enjoys a considerable flexibility to carefully design an STP system to address the goals and concerns of the domestic innovators.

1.7.2. Obligations under TRIPS Agreement

Many, indeed, consider the TRIPS Agreement[186] a 'sea change' or a 'tectonic shift' in international intellectual property law. The TRIPS Agreement establishes minimum substantive standards for each of the major intellectual property regimes, but fails explicitly to mention second tier or utility model protection, thus leaving WTO member countries free to formulate or reject second-tier protection regimes as they see fit.[187] Most strikingly, the substantive scope of TRIPS is defined in its Article 1(2), whereby the term 'intellectual property' refers to all categories of intellectual property that are the subject of Sections 1 through 7 of Part II of the Agreement and do not in any way refer to utility models.[188] Nevertheless, pursuant to Article 2(1), WTO Members are obliged to 'comply with Articles 1 through 12, and Article 19, of the Paris Convention (1967)'. Arguably, the substantive obligations of the Paris Convention, including those on utility models described above, are made part of TRIPS and hence are obligations under the WTO Agreements.[189] This point has been made clear by the Appellate Body Report in *US Omnibus Appropriations Act* case.[190] According to the WTO panel's finding in this case, the scope of the application with respect to the subject matter extends to those forms of protection covered by the conventions that have been incorporated by

186 Agreement on Trade-Related Aspects of Intellectual Property Rights, 15 April, 1994, Marrakesh Agreement Establishing the World Trade Organization, Annex 1C, Legal Instruments-Results of the Uruguay Round, 33 I.L.M. 1197 (1994) (TRIPS Agreement).

187 U Suthersanen, 'Utility Models and Innovation in Developing Countries' (2006) UNCTAD-ICTSD Issue Paper No. 13 Project on IPRs and Sustainable Development 3, available at: <http://unctad.org/en/docs/iteipc20066_en.pdf> (accessed 15 March 2012).

188 HG Ruse-Khan, 'Utility Model Protection in Pakistan-A Feasible Option for Incentivising Incremental Innovation?' (2012), Study conducted for the World Intellectual Property Organisation, 10. (copy on file with author).

189 Ibid.

190 See *US-Sec 211 Omnibus Appropriations Act of 1998*, Appellate Body Report (WT/DS/176/AB/R.).

reference in the TRIPS Agreement according to Article 2(1).[191] Thus, compliance with these provisions of the Paris Convention can be tested under the World Trade Organization (WTO) dispute settlement system. For the protection and enforcement of utility models or petty patents, this arguably means that compliance with the core national treatment obligation in Article 2(1) of the Paris Convention can be challenged by a WTO Member in front of a dispute settlement panel established under the Dispute Settlement Understanding (DSU).[192] Sri Lanka ratified the Marrakesh Agreement establishing the WTO in June 1994 and is bound by legal obligations imposed under the TRIPS Agreement.[193] Arguably, the TRIPS Agreement has not really created new obligations on Sri Lanka in relation to UM protection, but confirms the existing obligations it has already undertaken. In other words, as a member of the WTO, Sri Lanka is under obligation to provide national treatments and right of priority for foreign applications for UM or petty patents.

1.7.3. Other Patent Treaties and Agreements

Apart from the above mentioned leading multilateral treaties IP treaties, the Strasbourg Agreement for the International Patent Classification[194] and the Patent Cooperation Treaty (PCT)[195] refer to utility models, without providing any substantive minimum standard of protection. In particular, national utility model systems tend to adopt the International Patent Classification (IPC) as provided by the Strasbourg Agreement concerning the International Patent Classification, which facilitates the retrieval of

191 T Cottier and P Véron, Concise International and European IP Law: TRIPS, Paris Convention, European Enforcement and Transfer of Technology (Kluwer Law 2008)13.

192 HG Ruse-Khan, 'Utility Model Protection in Pakistan-A Feasible Option for Incentivising Incremental Innovation?' (2012), Study conducted for the World Intellectual Property Organisation, 10. (copy on file with author).

193 Agreement on Trade-Related Aspects of Intellectual Property Rights, 15 April, 1994, Marrakesh Agreement Establishing the World Trade Organization, Annex 1C, Legal Instruments-Results of the Uruguay Round, 33 I.L.M. 1197 (1994) (TRIPS Agreement).

194 Strasbourg Agreement Concerning the International Patent Classification on 24 March 1971 as amended on 28 September 1979.

195 The Patent Cooperation Treaty was concluded in Washington on 19 June 1970 and has been amended in 1979, 1984 and 2001.

patent documents in order to conduct effective novelty searches and determine the state of the art.[196] The other significant agreement is the PCT which facilitates patent applications in more than one country. By simplifying and cheapening the process, the treaty encourages patentees to secure protection over a broader geographical range.[197] Instead of filing separately in all countries where protection is desired, applicants may file a single application in one language with a national patent office. By virtue of Article 2, the PCT clarifies that 'application' means an application for the protection of an invention which can be interpreted to include an application for UM or petty patent.[198] Using this route, nationals of Member States can make international applications not only for standard patents but also for second-tier patents such as UMs. Nevertheless, both treaties do not contain any substantive minimum standard of protection. All in all, compared with other IP rights, there remains a great deal of flexibility for a country in designing an appropriate utility model system.

1.7.4. Flexibilities and Policy Space

According to commentators, flexibilities include a range of rights, safeguards and options that WTO Members can exploit in their implementation of the TRIPS Agreement.[199] As we have seen, the policy space that countries enjoy under international IP treaties in the implementation of STP is quite broad. In other words, unlike densely regulated patent protec-

196 U Suthersanen, 'Utility Models and Innovation in Developing Countries' (2006) UNCTAD-ICTSD Issue Paper No. 13 Project on IPRs and Sustainable Development 3, available at: <http://unctad.org/en/docs/iteipc20066_en.pdf> (accessed 15 March 2012). Strasbourg Agreement Concerning the International Patent Classification on 24 March 1971 as amended on 28 September 1979. Article 1 states: the countries to which this Agreement applies constitute a Special Union and adopt a common classification for patents for invention, inventors' certificates, utility models and utility certificates, to be known as the "International Patent Classification" that the IPC covers not just 'patents for invention', but also 'inventors' certificates, utility models and utility certificates'.

197 U Suthersanen, 'Utility Models and Innovation in Developing Countries' (2006) UNCTAD-ICTSD Issue Paper No. 13 Project on IPRs and Sustainable Development 3 available at: <http://unctad.org/en/docs/iteipc20066_en.pdf> (accessed 15 March 2012).

198 Ibid.

199 C Deere, *The Implementation Game* (Oxford University Press 2009) 68.

tion, this policy space is almost unlimited.[200] Thus, Sri Lanka and other South Asian countries may be able to use these key flexibilities in line with their domestic economic needs. In evaluating the policy space and flexibilities, it is evident that a country that foresees a UM regime in its domestic law can freely regulate the subject matter it wants to protect, conditions must be attached for a grant of such protection, the exceptions and limitations, term of protection as well as enforcement measures. The obligations multinational legal framework only requires member States to make available the same rights and remedies to nationals of the other WTO members and does not discriminate against foreign nationals or firms. Viewed through the perspectives of these flexibilities, there is a range of options on the table for consideration in designing an appropriate STP regime. Nevertheless, from a practical point of view, one can reasonably argue that, through national treatment obligation and principle against non-discrimination, foreign firms and big players in the market can considerably reduce the benefit that domestic firms can reap under such system. All in all, however, developing countries should be able to better utilize these flexibilities by crafting laws which promote the objectives, including the transfer of technology.[201]

1.8. Conclusion

In sum, a utility model or petty patent system may be viewed as one of the options available within the IP system to promote incremental and minor innovations. Such a system is intended to provide an IP right for innovations whose technical advances are not as great as that should be required for the grant of a regular patent, but there is an improvement over art. From a policy perspective, it is argued that this legal tool would be of an importance for a developing country whose technological capacities are marginal. Indeed, innovation at all level should be encouraged in order to

---

200 HG Ruse-Khan, 'Utility Model Protection in Pakistan-A Feasible Option for Incentivising Incremental Innovation?' (2012), Study conducted for the World Intellectual Property Organisation, 21-22. (copy on file with author).

201 See also, KE Maskus and JH Reichman (eds), *International Public Goods and Transfer of Technology Under a Globalized Intellectual Property Regime* (Cambridge University Press 2005). RE Evenson and LE Westphal, 'Technological Change and Technology Strategy' in H Chenery and TN Srinivasan (eds), *Handbook of Development Economics* (1988) 2209-2299.

build an innovative culture in a country. Incentive-base theory informs us that without adequate protection, minor and incremental innovations would not be rewarded. In fact, an STP system can be tailored to suit local need and concerns of local industries, especially for those of the SME sector. There is evidence that a UM regime may be more suitable for Sri Lanka, given the specific characteristics of its innovation landscape. Moreover, it is argued that an STP regime is more suitable and comprehensive enough to be used by TK-based innovators because such innovations are made without much original contribution. Perhaps most encouragingly, the policy space left by the multinational legal framework can be used to design a most appropriate form of a second-tier protection that suits the specific needs of an individual country. Countries in the region should be able to experiment this alternative legal approach since one 'size fit for all patent system' has not lived up to its expectation in terms of promoting innovation and inventions. Although, the idea of an STP regime has been in the backwater of IP law for decades in South Asian countries, there is a rising tide of opinion in favour of such as system in recent years. Most notably, the momentum has of course picked up sooner the Indian government introduced the Discussion paper on UM. In light of the above, it seems logical to argue that Sri Lanka and other developing economies in the South Asian region should carefully consider this largely unexplored option of STP in order to stimulate domestic innovations.

2. Incremental Innovations and the Existing IPR System in Sri Lanka

'A nation that does not invent and produce new things cannot prosper in this world, but will lie lamenting, being unable to beg'.
Munidasa Kumaratunga[202]

2.1. Introduction

Innovation has paved the way for many countries to succeed in becoming globally competitive. Today, human creativity is the cutting edge factor for success.[203] Viewed through the lens of a well-respected Sri Lankan intellectual and poet, Munidasa Kumaratunga, a country, an enterprise or an individual who does not look for new things and innovative ways cannot rise in a competitive world.[204] The same is certainly true for many developed and developing counties, especially in the face of current global economic slowdown. Invention and innovation are no doubt the driver of economic growth and development of a country. Their protection lies at the heart of intellectual property which emanates from the need to reward innovation and creativity. Intellectual property (IP) is a form of knowledge which societies have decided can be assigned specific property rights.[205] IP rights are becoming an increasingly essential foundation for innovation

---

202 M Kumarathunga, *Virith Wakiya* (Godage Publishers 2000) i.

203 A Dharmasiri, 'The Triple 'I' for Transformation' *Daily FT* (Colombo 20 June 2011), available at: <http://www.ft.lk/2011/06/20/the-triple-%E2%80%98i%E2%80%99s-for-transformation/> (accessed 30 August 2011).

204 M Kumarathunga, *Virith Wakiya* (Godage Publishers 2000) i. See also, DM Karunaratna, 'Copyright – Current System in Sri Lanka' *The Daily News* (Colombo, 30 October 2004), available at: <http://archives.dailynews.lk/2004/10/30/fea13.html> (accessed 20 May 2011).

205 Commission on Intellectual Property Rights, *Integrating Intellectual Property Rights and Development Policy* (London 2002) 11-12 (The Commission's definition, Intellectual property (IP) rights are the rights awarded by society to individuals or organisations principally over creative works: inventions, literary and artistic works, and symbols, names, images, and designs used in commerce).

and economic growth in the 21st century.[206] The concept of 'intellectual property rights' embraces a set of legally enforceable rights resulting from intellectual activity in the industrial, scientific, literary or artistic field.[207] The term 'intellectual property' has been used for almost one hundred and fifty years to refer to the general area of law that encompasses copyright, patents, designs, and trademarks, as well as a host of related rights.[208]

In brief, intellectual property covers a range of personal property rights attached to various products of the human mind.[209] It is intangible (i.e. not attached to any physical object in which creation may be embodied) and as a result IP rights are not enforceable by possession, but by law.[210] In the eyes of economists, the subject matter of IP rights by their nature are 'non-rivalrous' and non-excludable. Non-rivalrous means one person's enjoyment of the good does not prevent another's ability to enjoy it. Similarly, the subject matter of protection is non-excludable because one person cannot prevent other persons enjoying the good. In this sense, unlike physical property, knowledge, ideas and creations are considered as a 'public good'. This does not mean they are funded with public money. It means that, as soon as they are created, they instantly inure to the benefit of the general public.[211] In other words, everyone can take a free ride on the labour of persons who create public goods.[212] Most notably, IP rights exist as instruments of legal and economic policy of an individual country.[213]

206 Business and Industry Advisory Committee (BIAC) to OECD, Discussion Paper on 'Creativity, Innovation and Economic Growth in the 21st Century: An Affirmative Case for Intellectual property Rights (Paris, December 2003) 6.

207 DM Karunaratna, *Elements of the Law of Intellectual Property in Sri Lanka* (Sarasavi Publishers 2010) 15.

208 L Benlty and B Sherman, *Intellectual Property Law* (3rd edn, OUP 2008) 1.

209 M Coulter, Protection in Ideas: The Patent Question in Mid-Victorian Britain (Thomas Jefferson University Press 1991) 2-3.

210 M Elmslie and S Portman, *Intellectual Property: The Lifeblood of Your Company* (Chandos Publishing 2006) 13.

211 EE Johnson, 'Intellectual Property and the Incentive Fallacy' (2012) 39 Florida State University Law Review 623, 629.

212 Ibid. See also, RG Bone, 'A New Look at Trade Secret Law: Doctrine in Search of Justification' (1998) 86/2 California Law Review 243, 263. RH Coase, 'The Lighthouse in Economics' (1974) 17/2 Journal of Law and Economics 357, 359-360. A classic example of public good is a lighthouse. It is extremely difficult to exclude ships from the navigational benefits a lighthouse provides, and all ships can enjoy this benefit without reducing its availability to others).

213 WR Cornish, 'The International Relations of Intellectual Property' (1993) 52/1 Cambridge Law Journal 46, 46-47.

Nevertheless, creating exclusive rights over information through IP rights has its own downsides. In hindsight, IP rights can of course generate social costs that would exceed perceived benefits. One of the vehement critics on IP rights, C.G. Weeramantry, has listed IP in scientific knowledge as a source of possible denigration of the right to share in scientific advancement and benefit.[214] Thus, one needs to recognize that, despite its importance, IP is not a sacred cow; it is merely a body of law which is intended to act as a measure of achieving a particular set of ends.[215]

2.1.1. Philosophical Underpinnings of IP

This section also merits a brief understanding of philosophical roots of IP protection. The philosophical richness of the justification of IP rights can be viewed through economic, moral, cultural and political dimensions.[216] Interestingly, the importance of innovation in economic thinking can be traced as far back as 1776. In his famous treatise on the *Wealth of Nations*, Adam Smith notes that 'the invention of all those machines by which labour is so much facilitated and abridged seems to have been originally owing to the division of labour'.[217] Although IP is not rooted in conventional property rights, it does not lack philosophical underpinnings. Several theories have been advanced to explain why society needs to grant IP rights. According to a leading study by Fritz Machlup, there are four well-known justifications for IP protection.[218] They are, namely, the 'natural-law' thesis, the 'reward-by-monopoly' thesis, the 'monopoly-profit-incen-

---

214 J Phillips and A Firth, *Introduction to Intellectual Property Law* (4th edn, Butterworths 2001) 7. (CG Weeramantry, one of the renowned academics from Sri Lanka and former vice-president of ICJ made his remarks in *The Slumbering Sentinels* (1983).

215 J Phillips and A Firth, *Introduction to Intellectual Property Law* (4th edn, Butterworths 2001) 9.

216 W Davies and K Withers, 'Public Innovation: Intellectual Property in a Digital Age' (Institute for Public Policy Research 2006)13-14.

217 WIPO, World Intellectual Property Report: The Changing Face of Innovation (2011) 77.

218 F Machlup, *An Economic Review of the Patent System* (1958) Study No. 15 of the Subcommittee on Patent, Trademarks and Copyrights of the Senate Committee on the Judiciary 20.

tive' thesis, and the 'exchange-for-secrets' thesis. Interestingly, natural right and moral reward theories are based on non-economic arguments.

Even more significantly, different jurisprudential approaches offer different rationales to justify IP protection.[219] The 'natural-rights' school of thinking assumes that the creator or inventor has a 'natural' property right in his intellectual achievement and society is morally obliged to recognize and implement his property right.[220] It has also been argued that everyone has a natural right to the results of his or her creative labour. This argument is founded on the Lockean 'labour desert theory'. John Lock, in his famous *The Second Treaties on Government*, has advanced the argument that everyone has a property right in the labour of his own body.[221] However, to the contrary, the utilitarian school of thought focuses less on how IP is created but more on its consequences. According to the utilitarian justification, IP rights are necessary because they contribute to general economic welfare.[222] In order to achieve this goal, property rights are granted to authors and inventors as an incentive to create and innovate, but some aspects must remain in the public domain to preserve future creations and innovations.[223]

Most significantly, according to some commentators, this utilitarian approach to IP is echoed quite clearly in the United States (US) Constitution,[224] which gives the US congress the power 'to promote the progress of science and useful arts, by securing for limited times to authors and inventors, the exclusive right to their respective writings and discoveries'.[225] This ideology is reinforced by the 'reward-by-monopoly' thesis, according

219 See generally, T Cottier and C Germann, 'Teaching Intellectual property, Unfair Competition and Anti-trust law' in Y Takagi, L Alliman and MA Sinjela (eds), *Teaching Intellectual Property: Principles and Methods* (WIPO 2008) 130, 134.

220 Ibid.

221 See C Colston and J Galloway, *Modern Intellectual Property Law* (3rd edn, Routledge 2010) 45.

222 E Derclaye, 'Intellectual Property Rights and Human Rights: Coinciding and Cooperating' in Paul LC Torremans (ed), *Intellectual Property and Human Rights: Enhanced Edition of Copyright and Human Rights* (Wolters Kluwer 2008) 136.

223 Ibid.

224 See Article 1, para 8, Section 8, *The Constitution of the United States of America (U.S.A)*, adopted in 1787. However, it might also be argued that the Constitutional IP clause mirrors natural right theory influenced by John Locke's social contract theory.

225 W Davies and K Withers, 'Public Innovation: Intellectual Property in a Digital Age' (Institute for Public Policy Research 2006) 14.

to which a creator or an inventor should receive a reward for his or her services in proportion to their usefulness to society.[226] Apart from these traditional justifications, more recently, the 'incentive-to-commercialize' or the 'incentive-to-invest in further development' thesis or so-called 'prospect theory' has attracted considerable attention to rationalize granting exclusive rights over the fruits of human intellectual effort and ingenuity. In essence, though, the incentive theory remains the dominant view of IP rights and it can also be traced as the 'engine of IP policy'. The incentive theory, in fact, holds that legal protection in the form of exclusive rights is granted by society to creative people as an economic incentive to engage in creative efforts.[227]

As is known, intellectual property is traditionally divided into two branches; namely, 'industrial property' and 'copyright'. In the strict sense, industrial property covers inventions and industrial designs, though it can possibly include trademarks, geographical indications and protection against unfair competition etc. But in the latter, the aspect of intellectual creation, although existent, is less prominent.[228] For the purposes of this chapter, industrial property will be considered with regard to patent and design regimes in Sri Lanka. Thus, the following analysis is limited in scope to ascertain whether and to what extent each system offers protection for incremental and minor innovations.

2.2. Patent Protection in Sri Lanka

2.2.1. A Brief Overview

The term 'patent' derives from the Latin verb *patere*. Patent, the adjective, means 'open', and patent, the noun, is the customary abbreviation of 'open letter'.[229] The official name is 'letters patent', a literal translation of the

---

226 T Cottier and C Germann, 'Teaching Intellectual property, Unfair Competition and Anti-trust law' in Y Takagi, L Alliman and M Sinjela (eds), *Teaching Intellectual Property: Principles and Methods* (WIPO 2008) 130, 134.

227 Kinney and PA Lange, *Intellectual Property Law for Business Lawyers* (2010-2011 edn, West Publishers 2010) para1:1.

228 WIPO, Intellectual Property Handbook: Policy, Law and Use (WIPO, 2004) 3.

229 F Machlup, *An Economic Review of the Patent System* (1958) Study No. 15 of the Subcommittee on Patent, Trademarks and Copyrights of the Senate Committee on the Judiciary 1.

Latin *litterae patentes*. Letters patent are official documents by which certain rights, privileges, ranks, or titles are conferred.[230] Patents are legal instruments used in economic life.[231] Economists view patents as a policy tool aimed at fostering innovation and diffusion of technology which would result in economic growth.[232] In the eyes of law, a patent is a legal title protecting an invention.[233] Defined more accurately, a patent confers the right to secure the enforcement power of the State in excluding unauthorized persons, for a specified number of years, from making commercial use of a clearly identified invention.[234] Patents grant their owner a set of rights of exclusivity over an invention (a product or process that is new, involves an inventive step and is susceptible of industrial application) as defined by the 'claims'.[235]

The legal protection conferred by a patent gives its owner the right to exclude others from making, using, selling, offering for sale or importing the patented invention for the term of the patent, which is usually 20 years from the filing date, and in the country or countries concerned by the protection.[236] The rationale underlying the patent system is to encourage invention and technical progress by providing a temporary period of exclusivity over the invention in exchange for its disclosure.[237] This *quid pro quo* rewards the patentee for investing, in most circumstances, substantial time and recourses in researching and developing an invention, by awarding the most powerful IP right.[238] Moreover, under the disclosure theory,

---

230 Ibid.

231 Organisation for Economic Co-operation and Development (OECD), *Patent Statistics Manual* (OECD 2009) 18.

232 See D Encaoua and D Guellec and C Martínez, 'Patent Systems for Encouraging Innovation: Lessons from Economic Analysis' (2006) 35/9 Research Policy 1423, 1423.

233 See, Article 28 of the Trade-Related Intellectual Property Rights (TRIPS) Agreement.

234 F Machlup, *An Economic Review of the Patent System* (1958) Study No. 15 of the Subcommittee on Patent, Trademarks and Copyrights of the Senate Committee on the Judiciary 1.

235 A claim form part of the specification. The specification is essentially a description of the invention and the best method of performing it.

236 Organisation for Economic Co-operation and Development (OECD), *Patent Statistics Manual* (OECD 2009) 18, 18.

237 Ibid 21.

238 J Henderson, 'Is the Application of Science and Technology a Necessary requirement for Patentability' (2009) IP Forum 29. According to Elizebeth Pesses, the

patents are considered as a contract between two parties: society and the inventor. Each party has its rights and obligations.[239] According to commentators, without patents, ideas have little protection. As soon as a product implementing a new idea hits the market, anybody can copy it and compete with the original producer without incurring the initial costs of invention and product development.[240] A patent thus gives its holder a lengthy breathing-space to enable the invention to be developed and marketed without competition, except from non-infringing substitutes. In this way, the patent holder can recoup his investment. The economic theory holds that the introduction of patent protection into a country will entail sacrifices in static efficiency, to the extent that it stimulates innovation, it may in the long term improve dynamic efficiency.[241]

2.2.2. The Origin of the Patent System

Although the modern patent system originated in the Renaissance city of Venice in the fifteenth century, the earliest form of patents might have existed in 500 BC in Sybaris, a Greek colony in southern Italy where monopolies were granted to new dishes for a period of one year.[242] What is

patent system is often viewed as 'a carefully crafted bargain that encourages both the creation and the public disclosure of new and useful advances in technology, in return for exclusive rights for a limited period of time. This exchange is the '*quid pro quo*' of patent law.

239 P Weiss, *Patent Policy* (Rautledge 2010) 28.

240 D Vaver, 'Sprucing up Patent Law' (2011) 23 Intellectual Property Law Journal 64, 64-65.

241 See UNCTAD-ICTSD, *Resource Book on TRIPS and Development* (Cambridge University Press 2005) 364-365. Static efficiency, is achieved when there is an optimum utilization of existing resources at the lowest possible cost. Dynamic efficiency is the optimal introduction of new products or products of superior quality, more efficient production processes and organization, and (eventually) lower prices over time.

242 JN Adams, 'History of the Patent System' in Toshiko Takenaka (ed), *Patent Law and Theory* (Edward Elgar 2008) 101. See also, GA Nord, *The Law of Patents* (Kluwer Law 2008) 4-5 (Quoting from the historian Phylarcus, the Greek writer Athenaeus states: "The Sybarites, having given loose to their luxury, made a law that... if any confectioner or cook invented any peculiar and excellent dish, no other artist was allowed to make this for a year; but he alone who invented it was entitled to all the profits to be derived from the manufacture of it for that time; in order that others might be induced to labour as excelling in such pursuits").

remarkable is that the very idea of an incentive-based system has prevailed for over 2000 years and it has been closely tied to human civilization. Nevertheless, the patent system in the modern sense has its origin in Venice. Under the ground-breaking Venetian Statute of 1474 'men of great genius, apt to invent and discover ingenious devices' were encouraged and rewarded by the grant of a monopoly right for ten years over any 'new and ingenious device' which they invented and disclosed.[243] Thereafter, the British Statute of Monopolies in 1624 marked another milestone in the patent history of Common Law countries. Last, but certainly not least, the US Patent Act of 1790 established the US patent system with a constitutional mandate. According to Abraham Lincoln, the only United States President to ever issue a patent, 'the patent law added the fuel of interest to the fire of genius, in the discovery and production of new and useful things'.[244] Not surprisingly, by the second half of the 19th century, many countries had recognized the value of the patent system as a tool for technological and economic development; consequently, several systems for the protection of inventions were established.[245] In the realm of ancient Asia, though, exclusive rights of inventors were unknown.[246] Nevertheless, inventors were not forgotten and they were often held in high honor. In countries like China and Persia, periodic prize awards (for Chinese silk and Persian rugs) had been granted.[247]

2.2.3. The Introduction of Patent Law in Sri Lanka

Like any other IP right, a patent is a territorial right. Historically, the concept of patents, and consequently of IP rights, came into existence in Sri Lanka during the British colonial period, when the British Inventors' Ordi-

---

243 A Fitzgerald, *LBC Nutshell Intellectual Property* (2nd edn, Lawbook 2002) 144.

244 Abraham Lincoln, Second Lecture on Discoveries and Inventions (11 February 1859).

245 WIPO-Committee on Development and Intellectual Property (CDIP), Patent Related Flexibilities in the Multilateral Legal Framework and their Legislative Implementation at the National and Regional Level- Document prepared by the Secretariat (CDIP/5/4, 1st March 2010) 4.

246 FD Prager, 'The Early Growth and Influence of Intellectual Property' (1950) 34/2 Journal of Patent Office Society 110.

247 Ibid.

nance of 1859 became applicable to Sri Lanka (then Ceylon).[248] Perhaps even more significantly, the first Sri Lankan patent had been granted to a British engineer in January 1861 for the invention of a coffee pulping machine.[249] That law was replaced by the Patent Ordinance of 1906 which was based exclusively on the English Patent Law and was in force until the enactment of the Code of Intellectual Property Act No. 52 of 1979.[250] After the introduction of new economic policy, namely, the free market economy in 1977, the patent regime gained significance in the country's new industrial, technological and agricultural strategies. Thus, the Code of Intellectual Property Act marked a turning point in the evolution of the intellectual property system in Sri Lanka and it enacted, among others, the law relating to patents.[251] The Intellectual Property Act No. 36 of 2003 replaced the Code of Intellectual Property Act No 52 of 1979.[252]

The new Act was introduced to bring the Sri Lankan IP regime in compliance with TRIPS obligations. The rationale underlying its introduction has been spelt out in Parliament during the debate on the Bill as the promotion of national creativity, the protection of creative efforts, the enhancement of the integration of the national economy into the knowledge driven global economy, the attraction of more investment and the protection of consumer interests.[253] More importantly, the current law relating to patents is governed by the Intellectual Property Act No. 36 of 2003 and the regulations made thereunder. More specifically, Part IV of the Act deals with patent protection. Besides, Sri Lankan patent law follows the 'first to file' system as oppose to 'first to invent' system.[254] Viewed from a user perspective, the Sri Lankan patent regime has, however, come un-

248 RMW Amaradasa, MAT de Silva and RP Pathirage, 'Patents in a Small Developing Economy: A Case Study of Sri Lanka' (2002) 17 Journal of Intellectual Property Rights 395.

249 Ibid.

250 DM Karunaratna, *Elements of the Law of Intellectual Property in Sri Lanka* (Sarasavi Publishers 2010) 19.

251 DM Karunaratna, 'Issues Related to the Enforcement of IP Rights: National Efforts to Improve Awareness of Decision Makers and Education of Consumers' (WIPO Advisory Committee on Enforcement, Third Session, Geneva May 2006) (The 1979 Code was based on the 'model laws' prepared by the World Intellectual Property Organization (WIPO), which was intended to improve a development friendly environment in the country.

252 Ibid.

253 Ibid.

254 See Section 64 (2)(a) of the IP Act of Sri Lanka No 36, 2003.

der heavy criticism for being less attractive to domestic industries, especially for SMEs. Despite its comparatively long history, there are only a few cases available in the area of patent law and they hardly deal with any substantive patent law issues such as treatment of novelty and inventive step.

2.2.4. Which Inventions are Patentable?

Patents are granted in Sri Lanka in relation to an invention. An invention is defined by the Act as an idea of an inventor which permits in practice the solution of a specific problem in the field of technology.[255] Sri Lanka's IP Act provides protection for inventions relating to products as well as processes.[256] The followings are not regarded as inventions within the meaning of an invention in the Act and are thus excluded from patent eligibility:[257]

- discoveries, scientific theories and mathematical methods;
- plants, animals and other microorganism other than transgenic microorganism and an essentially biological process for the production of plants and animals other than non-biological and microbiological processes;[258]
- schemes, rules, or methods for doing business, performing purely mental acts or playing games;
- methods for the treatment of the human or animal body by surgery or therapy, and diagnostic methods practiced on the human or animal body; Provided however, any product used in any such method shall be patentable;
- an invention which is useful in the utilization of special nuclear material or atomic energy in an atomic weapon;

---

255 See Section 62 (1) of the IP Act of Sri Lanka No 36, 2003. The 'word' technology may be understood as the systematic knowledge essentially required for the manufacture of a product.

256 See Section 62 (2) the IP Act of Sri Lanka No 36, 2003, the process patents are those patents which are for inventions which perform a function.

257 See Section 62 (3) of the IP Act of Sri Lanka No 36, 2003.

258 The clause in the IP Bill was scrutinized by the Supreme Court and the words *'other micro- organism other than transgenic micro organism'* were added after the word animal. See SC Special determination Nos. 14/2003 and 16/2003-the Supreme Court of Sri Lanka.

- any invention, the prevention within Sri Lanka of the commercial exploitation of which is necessary to protect the public order and morality including the protection of human, animal or plant life or health or the avoidance of serious prejudice to the environment.

As interpreted through the lens of TRIPS obligations, Sri Lanka being a contracting party is bound to provide protection for both product and process patents in all fields of technology whether products are imported or locally produced.[259]

2.2.5. Conditions of Patentability

Article 27(1) of the TRIPS Agreement requires that 'patents shall be available for any invention that is new, involves an inventive step and is capable of industrial application'. Although the TRIPS Agreement requires WTO members to implement and enforce a comprehensive set of minimum standards in the protection of IP rights, it does not however define the term 'invention', nor does it specify how the three criteria for patentability are to be treated.[260] When it comes to Sri Lankan Law, an invention is patentable if it is new, involves an inventive step and is industrially applicable.[261] Obviously, the Sri Lankan IP law has adopted a similar approach taken by the TRIPS Agreement, in deciding the criteria of patentability; namely, novelty, inventive step/non-obviousness and industrial applicability.

2.2.6. The Concept of Novelty

In the eyes of patent law, the concept of novelty has been evolved from the word 'new'.[262] Perhaps more importantly, 'novelty' is one of the essential conditions for an invention to qualify for patent protection. As per this requirement, a patent application for an invention needs to be 'novel'

---

259 See Article 27 (1) of the TRIPS Agreement.

260 See also, CM Correa, *A Guide to Pharmaceutical Patents* (vol I, South Centre 2008) 26-27.

261 See Section 63 of the Act which deals with protectable inventions.

262 In practical terms, novelty is opposite to anticipation. For example, an invention is 'anticipated' if it was disclosed in a prior art reference or a prior publication.

or new before the date of filing of a patent application.[263] Pursuant to Article 27(1) of the TRIPS Agreement, an invention needs to be 'new'. The Sri Lankan IP Act does not provide a definition as such, for what novelty means, rather it provides that an invention is new if it is not anticipated by prior art.[264] Everything made available to the public, anywhere in the world, by means of written publication, oral disclosure, use or in any other way (i.e. exhibition or other non-written means) shall be considered as prior art provided that such disclosure occurred before the date of filing of the patent application claiming the invention.[265] It is, however, evident from the plain reading of this provision that Sri Lankan patent law requires an invention to meet the 'absolute' or 'universal' novelty standard as the first prerequisite of patentability.[266] Moreover, the idea of 'grace period' has also been recognized under Sri Lankan law, but in a restricted way. Section 64(3) of the IP Act provides an inventor with a grace period during which such disclosures will not destroy novelty.[267] In other words, inventions disclosed during that period would be eligible for protection, despite that they would have been deemed in the prior art in accordance with the general rule on novelty.[268] This one year grace period aims at ensuring that any disclosure of the invention by the inventor, his predecessor in title, or third parties (in which case six months) or who have abused the

263 CM Correa, *A Guide to Pharmaceutical Patents* (vol I, South Centre 2008)1-2.

264 See Section 64(1) of the IP Act of Sri Lanka No 36, 2003.

265 See Section 64(2) of the IP Act of Sri Lanka No 36, 2003.

266 There are three kinds of novelty standards followed by different jurisdictions in the world, namely, absolute or universal novelty, relative novelty and local or domestic novelty. Absolute novelty means that invention is new throughout the world and thus all material made available to the public anywhere in the world forms part of the state of the art (i.e. UK and EPC). On the other hand, relative novelty means a publication available in any country will destroy novelty but use of the invention outside the country will not (i.e. USA). Moreover, local novelty is usually restricted to within the country, where only local knowledge and use can destroy such novelty.(i.e. New Zealand). CM Correa, *A Guide to Pharmaceutical Patents* (vol I, South Centre 2008) 2-4.

267 According to Section 64(3) any disclosure under Section 64(1) would not affect a patent application 'if such disclosure occurred within one year preceding the date of the patent application by reason or consequence of acts committed by the applicant or his predecessor in title' and if such disclosure occurred within six months preceding the date of the patent application and if such disclosure was by reason or in consequence of any abuse of the rights of the applicant or his predecessor in title.

268 CM Correa, *A Guide to Pharmaceutical Patents* (vol I, South Centre 2008)18-19.

rights (i.e. who have stolen the invention) of the applicant or his predecessor in title would not become prior art resulting in destroying the novelty of the claimed invention.

Novelty generally requires that the information must not have been available to the public prior to the original application date (the priority date).[269] Since the inventor is granted a patent for disclosing something new, it follows that if the invention has already been disclosed to the public, the applicant (the 'inventor') can disclose nothing new in return for the grant, and is either not entitled to be granted a patent, or if one has been granted, is liable to have it revoked.[270] The disclosure may have taken place within the jurisdiction or elsewhere in the world.[271] When assessing novelty, the disclosure of a particular item of prior art always has to be considered in isolation (test of comparison in isolation). In other words, it is not admissible to combine separate items of prior art, for example several documents.[272] To put it differently, only a single document of prior art that contains all elements of the claimed invention can destroy novelty. However, if in one document there is an explicit reference to another document, then the part or the entire second document is to be considered as a part of the disclosure of the first document. The same is true with regard to several different sections within one document of prior art.[273] According to commentators, in practice, the concept of novelty is narrowly construed by patent offices, requiring an almost 'photographic' disclosure of the invention in a single prior document in order to consider that novelty does not exist.[274] Viewed from a different angle, novelty exists in an invention if there is any difference between the invention and the known prior art.[275] In other words, an invention will be new if it differs from the prior art. In

269 UNCTAD-ICTSD, *Resource Book on TRIPS and Development* (Cambridge University Press 2005) 359.

270 Ibid.

271 Ibid.

272 M Philipp, 'Novelty and Inventive Step under the European Patent Convention' (Boehmert & Boehmert 2001) 4.

273 Ibid.

274 CM Correa, 'Designing Patent Policies Suited to Developing Countries Needs' (2008) 10/2 Econômica, Rio de Janeiro 88.

275 MJ Davison, AL Monotti and L Wiseman (eds), *Australian Intellectual property Law* (Cambridge University Press 2008) 65.

fact, not much difference is required; a simple difference is sufficient.[276] An examination with respect to novelty functions as a filter before the examination of the inventive step and in many cases is not considered as a major hurdle for inventors.[277]

2.2.7. Inventive Step

The terms 'inventive step' and 'non-obviousness' are interchangeably used to mean the level of inventiveness required from an invention. While under patent law in Europe and in many other countries this is generally described as an 'inventive step', in the United States the requirement is defined as 'non-obviousness'.[278] The word 'obvious' comes from the Latin term *ob via*, meaning 'on the road'.[279] In the eyes of patent law, it means that what is now being claimed for the patent was something which 'lay on the road' of those who were developing the art. In other words, it means something that would be the next logical step along the path from the problem to the solution.[280] The philosophy behind the doctrine of obviousness is that the public should not be prevented from doing anything which was merely an obvious extension or workshop variation of what was already known at the priority date.[281] It means that an invention must

---

276 M Franzosi, 'Novelty and Non-obviousness-The Relevant Prior Art' (2001) Training Course Materials on Obtaining, Enforcing and Evaluating Intellectual Property Rights in Europe, conducted by Boehmert & Boehmert – Munich, 2-6 July 2001, 1.

277 See, M Philipp, 'Novelty and Inventive Step under the European Patent Convention' (2001) Training Course Materials on Obtaining, Enforcing and Evaluating Intellectual Property Rights in Europe, conducted by Boehmert & Boehmert – Munich, 2-6 July 2001, 3-4.

278 UNCTAD-ICTSD, *Resource Book on TRIPS and Development* (Cambridge University Press 2005) 359-360.

279 JR Thomas and others, 'Panel I: KSR v. Teleflex: The Nonobviousness Requirement of Patentability' (2007) 17 Fordham Intellectual Property, Media and Entertainment Law Journal 875, 880.

280 Ibid. See also, J Richards, 'Obviousness and Inventive Step-New Differences?' [2009] Ladas and Perry LLP 3.

281 The UK Patent office (UKPO), The Inventive Step Requirement in United Kingdom Patent Law and Practice (2006) UKPO official website, 12, available at: <http://www.ipo.gov.uk/pro-policy/consult/consult-closed/consult-closed-2006/consult-2006-inventive.htm> (accessed 12 April 2012).

not merely be something new; it must represent a development over prior art.[282] The TRIPS Agreement, in fact, permits its members to consider 'inventive step' as synonymous with 'non-obvious'.[283] Moreover, the TRIPS Agreement does not define the concept of inventive step, but only requires members to grant patents for inventions which 'involve an inventive step'. It is undeniable that inventive step is one of the most critical aspects of a patent regime, as it determines the level of technical contribution required to obtain a patent.[284] Under Sri Lankan law "an invention is considered as involving an inventive step if, having regard to the state of the art relevant to the patent application, it is not obvious to a person having ordinary skills in the art".[285] This statutory language of the IP Act is the same as in many other jurisdictions and term 'inventive step' is used in the Act.

The inventive step is often evaluated by considering the 'unexpected' or 'surprising' effect of the claimed invention.[286] The claimed invention must have some inventive aspect to it. In other words, the invention must be something which is not only new but possessed of an inventive element, a quality which will be recognized by someone experienced in the field as being a real step forward in the area.[287] The inventive step requirement is intended to prevent exclusive rights forming barriers to normal and routine development.[288] Thus, it serves the function of a gatekeeper to patent protection. Determining whether or not the invention involves an inventive step depends on the specific details of each patent application and in particular the subject-matter of each claim.[289] More significantly, an inven-

---

282 UNCTAD-ICTSD, *Resource Book on TRIPS and Development* (Cambridge University Press 2005) 359-360.

283 Ibid. See footnote 5 to art 27 (1) of the TRIPS.

284 CM Correa, 'Designing Patent Policies Suited to Developing Countries Needs' (2008) 10/2 Econômica, Rio de Janeiro 89.

285 Section 65 of the IP Act of Sri Lanka No 36, 2003. In the Sri Lankan context, the 'inventive step' requirement has been examined in 'Rigid T-Sack' case by the Commercial High Court. See, Amarasekare J in *Caderamanpulle v Mohamed Haniffa Ajmal* (CHC Case No: 33/2004/03, 22-23 decided on 18 February 2014).

286 UNCTAD-ICTSD, *Resource Book on TRIPS and Development* (Cambridge University Press 2005) 359-360.

287 M Elmslie and S Portman, *Intellectual Property:The Lifeblood of your Company* (Chandos Publishing 2006) 13.

288 TL Bittner, 'EPO Procedure' (2001) Training Course Materials on Obtaining, Enforcing and Evaluating Intellectual Property Rights in Europe, conducted by Boehmert & Boehmert – Munich, 2-6 July 2001, 2.

289 Ibid.

tion is non-obvious when it is sufficiently different from prior art.[290] Here lies the difficulty because a certain degree of difference is required and a simple difference is not sufficient. An invention is therefore non-obvious when it is significantly different from the prior art.[291] Most importantly, in contrast to novelty examination, the inventive step is assessed by comparing the invention as a whole against the state of art as a whole ('mosaicing') and thus it is permitted to combine any of the prior art (whether published documents, instances of prior use or common knowledge) in order to argue that an inventive step is lacking.[292] Not surprisingly, of all three conditions of patentability set out in the Sri Lankan IP Act, the inventive step is, in effect, the most difficult hurdle to overcome by inventors, especially for small and adaptive innovations.

Sri Lankan patent regime under the current IP Act is relatively young and very little exists in the form of case-law to clarify the provision of the Act in relation to inventive step. According to the author's knowledge, there has so far been no reported decision from the Supreme Court of Sri Lanka on the issue of interpretation of the inventive step. Nevertheless, the Commercial High Court of Sri Lanka, in one of the few cases on the subject, has emphasized the need to have access to expert evidence in assessing the inventive step.[293] As such, the principles and case-law from other jurisdiction may provide much needed guidance for the Sri Lankan judiciary. Besides, Sri Lankan court decisions are highly influenced by IP jurisprudence of Common Law countries, especially from the UK.[294]

---

290 M Franzosi, 'Novelty and Non-obviousness-The Relevant Prior Art' (2001) Training Course Materials on Obtaining, Enforcing and Evaluating Intellectual Property Rights in Europe, conducted by Boehmert & Boehmert – Munich, 2-6 July 2001, 1.

291 Ibid.

292 United Kingdom Patent Office (UKPO), *Manual of Patent Practice: Inventive Step* (2012) UKPO official website, 13, available at:<http://www.ipo.gov.uk/> (accessed 12 April 2012).

293 See the observation of Chitrasiri J in *Michael Laurents Cyrille Chanderampulle v Mohamed Haniffa Mohamed Ajmal & Brothers* (CHC Case No: 33/2004 (03) 5-6), where he stated that 'I should state with humility that I do not posses such knowledge and expertise in the field of engineering to decide on novelty and inventive step…Therefore I am of the view that this court may come to an incorrect decision, if the court decides on novelty and inventive step…, without considering expert opinion on the subject.

294 See also, IN Abeyesekere, 'Copyright Law and Practice in Sri Lanka' (1998) 29/1 International Review of Intellectual Property and Competition Law 27, 31.

In the UK, the current test and the guiding principles in assessing the inventive step have emerged in the leading case of *Windsurfing International v. Tabur Marine*.[295] In this case, the Court of Appeal adopted a four steps inquiry in examining the inventive step: (1) to identify the inventive concept; (2) to assume the mantle of the normally skilled but unimaginative addressee and to impute to him 'the common general knowledge of the art'; (3) to identify the differences between that and the invention; (4) to ask whether it is obvious or not.[296] The Court of Appeal has further held that "the question of obviousness (inventive step) 'has to be answered, not by looking with the benefit of hindsight at what is known now and what was known at the priority date and asking whether the former flows naturally and obviously from the latter, but by hypothesizing what would have been obvious at the priority date to a person skilled in the art to which the patent in suit relates'".[297] Moreover, the 'person having ordinary skill in the art' (PHOSITA) is not a highly skilled expert or a Nobel prize winner, nor is he some form of lowest common denominator and to a large degree the capacities of the skilled person will be determined by the nature of the common general knowledge identified as being 'relevant'.[298] Perhaps, the notion of common general knowledge can be summarized as a part of the mental equipment or mental toolkit needed so as to be competent in the art concerned and a set of industry standards may be considered to be part of the common general knowledge.[299]

She argues that when deciding a case on copyright Sri Lankan judges still tend to follow UK law decided from 1911 onwards.

295 (1985) RPC 59.

296 JR Thomas and others, 'Panel I: KSR v. Teleflex: The Nonobviousness Requirement of Patentability' (2007) 17 Fordham Intellectual Property, Media and Entertainment Law Journal 875, 885.

297 The UK Patent office (UKPO), The Inventive Step Requirement in United Kingdom Patent Law and Practice (2006) UKPO official website, 8, available at: <http://www.ipo.gov.uk/pro-policy/consult/consult-closed/consult-closed-2006/consult-2006-inventive.htm> (accessed 12 April 2012).

298 United Kingdom Patent Office (UKPO), *Manual of Patent Practice: Inventive Step* (2012) UKPO official website, 5-6, available at:<http://www.ipo.gov.uk/> (accessed 12 April 2012).

299 Ibid 7.

The current British law position regarding the inventive step was succinctly stated in a leading case by Lord Justice Jacob as follows:[300]

> 'One can, of course, postulate a different policy under which a monopoly might make sense. There are old or obvious ideas which take a lot of work, expense and time to develop and turn into something practical and successful. Without the incentive of a monopoly, people may not do that work or spend the time and money. (The present case) is an example of an obvious invention which costs lots to bring to market. But patent law provided no protection for all that investment because the basic invention was obvious. The courts' job is not, however, to uphold any claim to a monopoly for an idea which requires investment and risk to bring to market, only those for ideas which are new, non-obvious and enabled'.

The above British decision from one of the leading Common Law patent jurists makes it very clear that the UK patent system does not reward all types of inventions, though they create value. In particular, the inventions that are new but obvious. Thus, this high patentability standard is now well-settled law in the British legal system.[301]

In US practice, courts applying the non-obviousness standard undertake a three-step factual inquiry, examining: (1) the scope and content of the prior art to which the invention pertains; (2) the differences between the prior art and the claims at issue; (3) the level of ordinary skill in the pertinent art.[302] The examiner then makes a final determination of non-obviousness by deciding whether a person of ordinary skill could bridge the differences between the prior art and the claims at issue given the relevant prior art.[303] The landmark case under the US law on the nonobviousness standard is the Supreme Court decision of *KSR International Co. v Teleflex Inc.* in 2007.[304] In *KSR*, the Supreme Court authoritatively held that 'a

---

300 *Angiotech Pharm., Inc. v. Conor MedSystems Inc.*, [2007] EWCA Civ 5 para. 50. (Judgment of Lord Justice Jacob with whom Lord Justice Tuckey and Lord Justice Mummery agreed).

301 This position of the courts has been criticized for 'looking at from the point of view of Einstein, and then everything is obvious'.

302 CM Correa, *A Guide to Pharmaceutical Patents* (vol I, South Centre 2008) 39-40.

303 Ibid.

304 (2007) 127 S.Ct. 1727. In this case, the US Supreme Court unanimously held that the Court of Appeals erred in rigidly applying the 'teaching-suggestion-motivation' (TSM). Under the TSM test, a patent claim is considered obvious, and thus unpatentable, if some teaching, suggestion, or motivation to combine the prior art can be found in the prior art by a person having ordinary skill in the art.

person of ordinary skill is also a person of ordinary creativity, not an automaton' and raised the threshold for assessing non-obviousness.[305] Arguably, after the unanimous decision of the Supreme Court in *KSR*, US law is moving towards a tougher and higher standard of nonobviousness. Taken together, the *Windsurfing* and the *KSR* decisions can be viewed as 'traveling jurisprudence' which would certainly influence courts across jurisdictions in many parts of the Common Law world.

In determining inventive step, the European Patent Office has adopted a *problem-solution* approach.[306] The leading decision in this regard has emerged from COMVIK case.[307] According to the technical board of appeal of the European Patent Office, "for the purpose of the problem-and-solution approach, the problem must be a technical problem, it must actually be solved by the solution claimed, all the features in the claim should contribute to the solution, and the problem must be one that the skilled person in the particular technical field might be asked to solve at the priority date. In this context "problem" is used merely to indicate that the skilled person is to be considered as faced with some task (German "Aufgabe"), not that its solution need necessarily involve any great difficulty".[308]

In Europe, the goal of the method is to determine whether a claimed invention would be obvious to a skilled person based on a three-step test by: (1) determining the closest prior art; (2) determining the objective problem to be resolved in relation to this prior art by a comparison of the results; (3) determining the obviousness of the claimed solution in regard to further prior art and general technical knowledge.[309] Apart from that, the Indian Patent Act and the Patent Office Manual define 'inventive step' as a feature of an invention that involves technical advance as compared to the existing knowledge or having economic significance or both and that makes the invention not obvious to a person skilled in the art.[310] It is evi-

---

305 CM Correa, *A Guide to Pharmaceutical Patents* (vol I, South Centre 2008) 57.

306 See Article 56 EPC reads with Regulations of the EPC: Rule 27 (1) (c).

307 Case T 0641100, *COMVIK GSM AB v. DeTeMobile Deutsche Telekom MobileNet. GmbH* (Technical Bd. of Appeal Sep. 26, 2002), available at:http://www.epo.org/law-practice/case-law-appeals/pdf/t000641ep1.pdf (accessed on 20 May 2012).

308 Ibid 7.

309 CM Correa, *A Guide to Pharmaceutical Patents* (vol I, South Centre 2008) 40.

310 See Section 2(f) Patents (Amendment) Act 2005. Indian Patent, Office *Manual of Patent Practice and Procedure* (Indian Patent Office Mumbai 2005). The recent

dent from the wording of the Indian Patent Act and recent judicial pronouncements[311] that Indian law also follows a high-degree of non-obviousness standard. From an economic perspective, increasing the standard of non-obviousness increases the expected value of patents, but it decreases the probability that a given invention will be protected.[312] Economists argue that the increase in the value of patents is the *dynamic* effect and the reduction in the probability of obtaining protection the *static* effect, of raising the standard of nonobviousness.[313] Thus, increasing the patentability standard weakens the static effect of the patent system and strengthens the dynamic effect.[314]

2.2.8. Industrial Applicability

Industrial applicability is the third criterion of patentability. In patent law, the term 'industrial applicability' or 'utility' may perhaps be used synonymously, but 'utility' could give a wider sense than 'industrial'. The underlying rationale is that patent protection should not be available for abstract ideas or purely intellectual creations that cannot be put to any use.[315] A patentable invention has to be concrete and should have a technical character. The term 'industrial' is used in a very wide sense, irrespective of the for-profit or not-for-profit nature of the industry.[316] Comparatively speaking, the threshold of industrial applicability is rather low in many jurisdictions. Under Sri Lankan Law, an invention shall be considered industrially applicable if it can be made or used in any kind of industry.[317] Since Sri

---

changes in definition of inventive step has been embraced by Indian courts in *Mariappan v. A.R. Safiullah* (17) 2008-(Madras HC).

311 See the decision of the Supreme Court of India on 1 April 2013 in *Novartis AG v Union of India and Others* (2013) Civil Appeal Nos. 2706-2716 of 2013, available at: <http://supremecourtofindia.nic.in/outtoday/patent.pdf> (accessed 2 February 2014).

312 RM Hunt, 'Nonobviousness and the Incentive to Innovate: An Economic Analysis of Intellectual Property Reform' (1999) Working Paper No. 99-3, Federal Reserve Bank of Philadelphia 3.

313 Ibid.

314 JH Barton, 'Non-Obviousness' (2003) 43 IDEA:The Journal of Law and Technology 475, 494.

315 CM Correa, *A Guide to Pharmaceutical Patents* (vol I, South Centre 2008) 81.

316 Ibid.

317 See Section 66 of the IP Act of Sri Lanka No 36, 2003.

Lankan superior courts have so far not had an opportunity to interpret the concept of industrial applicability, it is worth considering how other major patent jurisdictions deal with this requirement.

According to commentators, the term 'industry' is generally understood in its broad sense as including any physical activity of 'technical character' and it also includes commerce and is extended to extractive industries and any type of manufacture.[318] The situation under the European Patent Convention (EPC) is that there is no need to prove that the invention can actually be applied in the industry. All that is needed is that it should be susceptible to or capable of industrial application.[319] In US law, the concept applied is 'utility'. Hence, certain developments that do not lead to an industrial product may be patented in the US: an invention only needs to be operable and capable of satisfying some function of benefit to humanity (i.e. be useful). This concept is broader than the industrial applicability required in Europe and other countries.[320] All in all, however, according to the approaches taken by the US, Europe and other leading jurisdiction, there is no need to prove that it can be put to use in the industry; it is enough if it is demonstrated that it is capable of being put to use in industry.[321]

2.2.9. The Rights of the Owner of a Patent

Under Sri Lankan law, the statutory life of a patent is 20 years from the date of application for its registration.[322] From a legal perspective, a patent is not a right to practice, but to a right to exclude.[323] In that sense, patent is

318 According to Article 1(3) of the Paris Convention, industrial property shall be understood in the broadest sense and shall apply not only to industry and commerce proper, but likewise to agricultural and extractive industries and to all manufactured or natural products, for example, wines, grain, tobacco leaf, fruit, cattle, minerals, mineral waters, beer, flowers, and flour. See also CM Correa, *A Guide to Pharmaceutical Patents* (vol I, South Centre 2008) 84.

319 CM Correa, *A Guide to Pharmaceutical Patents* (vol I, South Centre 2008) 81.

320 UNCTAD-ICTSD, *Resource Book on TRIPS and Development* (Cambridge University Press 2005) 361.

321 See CM Correa, *A Guide to Pharmaceutical Patents* (vol I, South Centre 2008) 81.

322 See Section 83 of the IP Act of Sri Lanka No 36, 2003.

323 Kinney and PA Lange, *Intellectual Property Law for Business Lawyers* (2010-2011edn, West Publishers 2010) para 2:1.

a negative right as opposed to an affirmative right. Pursuant to Section 84 of the IP Act, a patent confers its owner a bundle of exclusive rights to exploit the invention. Such rights include preventing third parties not having the owner's consent from the acts of making, using, importing, offering for sale, selling, and exporting the patented invention. Moreover, patent owners shall also have the right to assign, transfer or to conclude licensing contracts with regard to the rights conferred by the patent. This does not, however, mean that the exclusive rights granted by law for patent owners are without limitations.[324] Perhaps more importantly, the patent owner has a powerful weapon in his hands namely, the right to enforce his rights against any act of infringement. Most strikingly, in Sri Lankan context, there is no settled position of law regarding patent claim interpretation and infringement analysis so far. It is unclear whether Sri Lankan courts embrace the 'doctrine of equivalents' which is followed by other countries and thus Sri Lankan courts may need to look into principles and tests laid down by other jurisdictions such as the UK, the US, Europe and India.[325] As a general matter, in cases of violation of IP rights, Sri Lankan courts grant injunctions and award damages. The active use of the judiciary for patent litigation is an important aspect in enforcing patent rights. Although there are very few cases dealing with patent rights, the Sri Lankan Supreme Court in *St. Regis Packing (Pvt) Ltd v. Ceylon Paper Sacks Ltd.*, which is considered to be a progressive judgment, held that an infringement of an intellectual property is a continuous act giving a recurring cause of action.[326] Moreover, the current IP enforcement mechanism

---

324 The possibility of granting compulsory licenses is provided for in the IP Act of Sri Lanka No 36, 2003 under Section 86 and it may operate as a limitation of the owner's right. Another possible exception on the rights of the owner of a patent is the prior user right recognized under Section 87 of the IP Act of Sri Lanka No 36, 2003.

325 There are two approaches in assessing a patent infringement: (1) literal infringement (2) the doctrine of equivalents (DOE). Historically, UK courts have followed the literal infringement analysis under which courts examine whether the allegedly infringing device falls exactly within the literal scope of the patent. Taking a different approach, however, the US courts have adopted (in *Graver v Linde* 339 US 605 (1950) 609) and developed over the years the DOE, which analyses whether the two devices perform substantively the same function in substantively the same way to obtain the same result. Arguably, DOE offers fair protection to a patent owner.

326 (2001) 1 Sri LR 36, 38 (as per Banaranayake J) This case involved the right of assignee of a registered patent. This patent was granted for a product called

in Sri Lanka has also been strengthened with criminal sanctions which allows for the imposition of fine and imprisonment or both.

2.2.10. Empirical Analysis of Sri Lankan Patent System

The analysis in this section paints a picture on the use of the patent system in the Sri Lankan context, viewed through the lens of empirical evidence. The country's current patent system under the new IP Act came into existence in 2003. Since then, for almost the last 10 years, there has been a general increase in patent applications, with a marginal decrease in year 2009 and 2011. When compared with other fast-growing East Asian economies, the patent applications in Sri Lanka have not only remained low, but also recorded a slow growth. As mentioned before, the number of patent applications is an indicator of innovation activities of the country, on the one hand, and on the other, it is a measure of technological strengths of a nation.

"SAFE T PACK" a container used for packing tea as a cost effective alternative to plywood chest.

Figure 2.1: Trends in Patent Filings

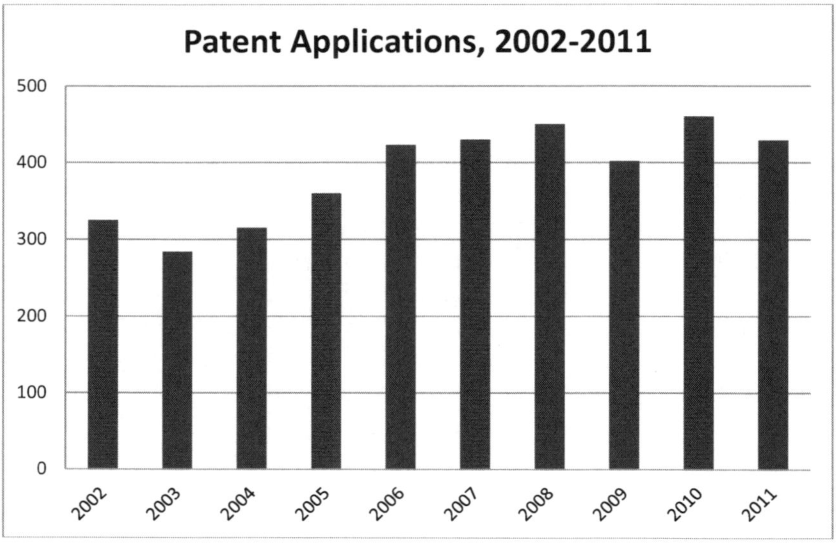

(Source: Based on data from the National Intellectual Property Office of Sri Lanka)

As indicated in Figure 2.1, the number of patent filings has increased gradually from 284 in 2003 to 429 in 2011 over the last 10 years. This increase is more apparent in years 2008 with 450 and 2010 with 460 applications. More interestingly, these are the highest figures that Sri Lanka has achieved in its recent history. Nevertheless, patent flings have slightly declined in 2011 to 429 applications. This may be attributed to the general economic slowdown which swept across every region in the world. Comparatively speaking, these numbers are almost negligible and are far from satisfactory. When compared with emerging market economies such as South Korea, China, and Malaysia, Sri Lanka has only less than 500 patent applications annually. It is evident from this data that the country's patent system has been under-utilized and it should, in fact, be a cause for concern. Perhaps a beter explanation for this phenomenon is that Sri Lanka is a country with a comparatively small market. Therefore, not even many foreign firms are interested in filing patent applications. Conversely, if that might have been case, then it may be equally applicable to relatively small market ecomomies in East Asia, where patent statistics prove otherwise. Nevertheless, it might still be argued that, although there is a modern legal framework, there is no aggressive enforcement of patent rights in Sri

Lanka which could increase the number of patent filings. There have been very few cases of infringement law-suits so far and the active use of the judiciary for patent litigation is not evident. Thus, there is plenty of evidence to conclude that inventors, industries and research institutions are not interested in enforcing their patent rights. Probably, this may also be a reason why there is a general lack of patenting in Sri Lanka.

Figure 2.2: Trends in Patent Filings: Resident and Non-Resident

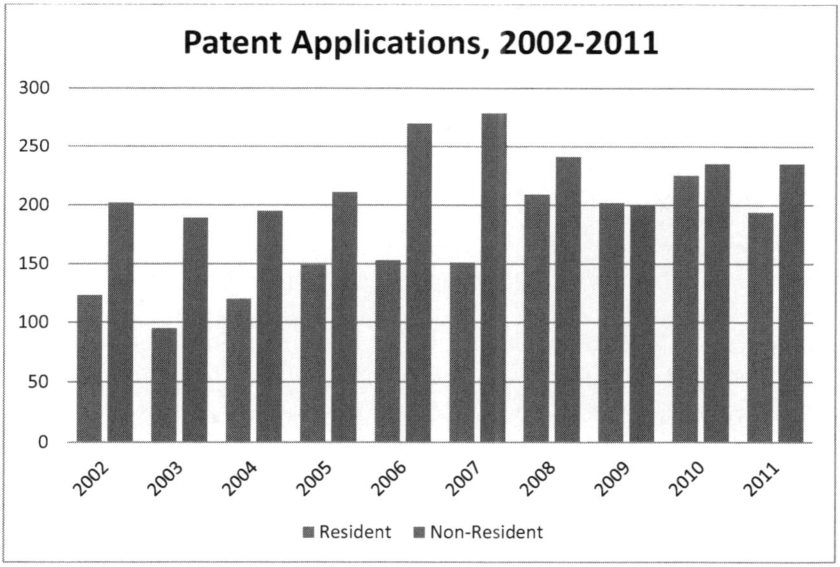

(Source: Based on data from the National Intellectual Property Office of Sri Lanka)

It is evident from Figure 2.2 that the majority of patent applications in Sri Lanka are filed by foreign applicants. This may be a cause for concern, but on the positive side, it can also be interpreted as a signal that the Sri Lankan market is becoming attractive for exploitation of foreign inventions. Non-resident patent filings can, in one way, be interpreted as defensive patenting to prevent possible infringements by local firms. Even more significantly, there has been a gradual increase of domestic applications over the last ten years, with a marginal decrease in 2003, 2009 and 2011. From an analytical perspective, only the number of domestic patent applications can be taken as a proxy of innovative activities of the country as non-resident applications do not emanate from local R&D activities.

Figure 2.3: Trends in Patent Grants

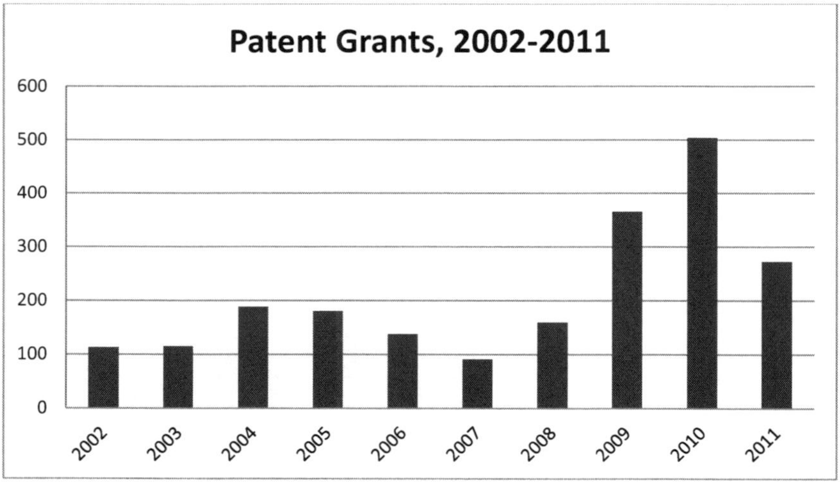

(Source: Based on data from the National Intellectual Property Office of Sri Lanka)

As shown in Figure 2.3, patent grants, in general, have seen a slow growth from year 2002 to 2008. Most notably, from 2009 to 2010, there seems to have been a considerable increase in total granted patents by the Sri Lankan IP office. One of the reasons for this development, as we can speculate, is the increase in foregn applications and grants, with the dawn of peace after ending the three-decades-long civil war which would have enhanced business confidence among foreign investers.

Figure 2.4: Trends in Patent Grants: Resident and Non-Resident

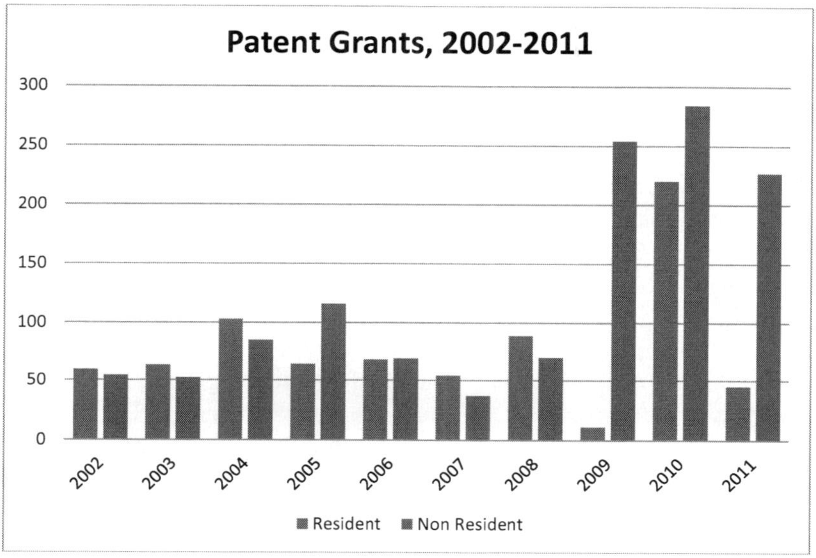

(Source: Based on data from the National Intellectual Property Office of Sri Lanka)

As evident in Figure 2.4, foreign patent grants are much higher than domestic patents in Sri Lanka. It is argued, however, that foreign patent filings and grants are an indication of the attractiveness of the market. Most significanlty, forein patents can be an instrument of technology transfer to the country. Viewed from the international technology transfer perspectives, if an inventor in one country files a patent application in another country it signals willingness to deploy that technology in the recipient country.[327] In that sense, a patent provides a direct (i.e. licensing) as well as indirect (i.e. data in patent application) source technology transfer. It must be noted, however, that the gap between resident and non-resident

327 KE Maskus, *Encouraging International Technology Transfer* (2003) Report for ICTSD/UNCTAD 9-23 (Technology transfer refers to any process by which one party gains access to a second party's information and successfully learns and absorbs it into his production function. Technology may be defined as the information necessary to achieve a certain production outcome from a particular means of combining or processing selected inputs).

patent grants is very wide in certain years, i.e. 2009 and 2011, with more than 80 percent being constituted of foreign grants. Alarmingly, the level of innovative activities has not been advanced enough to result in patents being granted. Not surprisingly, the rejection rate of patent application is considerably high, and in 2011 alone, it is more than 75 percent of the total domestic patent applications filed. Most notably, a large majority of applications, according to the Sri Lankan IP office, is basic inventions that are obvious and cannot be patented as they do not satisfy the test of inventive step as applied under the IP Act

As shown in Figure 2.5 below, a total of 82 percent of granted patents by NIPO in 2011 are owned by foreign entities. Most strikingly, only 18 percent of total granted patents is owned by Sri Lankan nationals. Interestingly, the patent grants for residents is very small in comparison with patents granted to foreigners. Probably, this data suggests that the patent system does not appeal to domestic industries, 80 percent of which are SMEs. In terms of the profile of domestic users, private individual inventors consist of the biggest share of 83 percent, followed by private sector commercial organisations with 10 percent of granted domestic patents. Moreover, the use of the patent system by public research institutons such as universities remains minimal in the Sri Lankan context. Interestingly, it was also demonstrated during our interviews with NIPO officials that most of domestic industries tend to file individual patent applications due to the application fee structure which is double the amount when it is filed by a company. Perhaps, this may be the reason why individual applications and grants are dominent with regard to patent grants to Sri Lankan residents.

Figure 2.5: Who owns Sri Lankan Patents?

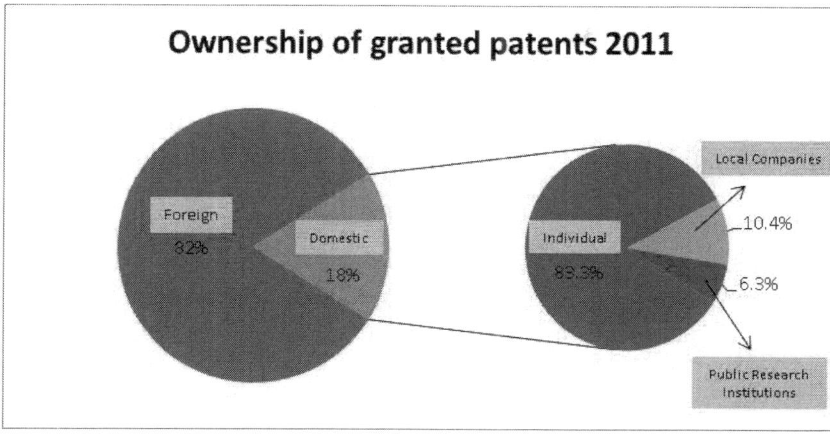

(Source: Based on data from the National Intellectual Property Office of Sri Lanka)

2.2.11. Use of the Patent System

As seen in the previous discussion, the statistical indicators shed light on the functioning of the patent system in the country. It is rather disappointing to learn that the use of the patent system has been and is still very low in the Sri Lankan context. Significantly, the number of domestic patent applications and grants is not encouraging. No doubt there are possible explanations for this situation. One possible and most likely reason is that Sri Lankan inventors and firms do not generate enough patentable innovations. Another reason is the relatively small size of the market that might not provide adequate incentives for R&D activities. Moreover, Sri Lanka has a large presence of SMEs in its industrial sector and the SME sector is mainly confined to the simple end of technology. For these reasons, not many patents are annually added to the patent landscape of the country. As analysed by scholars, the prime motives for patenting include direct exploitation of patented inventions, prevention of copying, prevention of other firm's attempts to patent a related invention('patent blocking'), earning license revenue, use in negotiation, prevention of law-suits and enhancement of the firm's reputation.[328] Apparently, most of these motives have not been given due consideration by Sri Lankan individual inventors and firms despite the fact that a patent is a business tool which can be used to secure a commercial advantage for its owner. There is hardly any rigorous patent enforcement in courts with only a handful of decided cases for more than a century and a half. This shows a low rate of use and enforcement of patent law in Sri Lanka.

Moreover, the patent system might be called 'direct means' of technology transfer to the country and serves as a vehicle for bringing technology to the rural industrial base which mostly consists of SMEs.[329] Nevertheless, probably due to the lack of awareness on the part of domestic industries, the technology transfer aspect of the patent regime has poorly been grasped. Conversely, it might still be argued that even though technology is transferred through the importation of patented goods and patent licensing, the industrial sector in the country does not have the ability to absorb foreign technologies and engage in progressive imitation and adaptations. There is no reliable evidence that such transferred technology is used for technology learning and as a basis for further follow-on innovation. As evident from statistics, Sri Lanka has limited patent filing high-tech industries.[330] In fact, most of the products are still simple products such as tea and garments and that there are very few high-tech products. Not surprisingly, the majority of patents granted in Sri Lanka to domestic applicants are in low-tech areas such as mechanical, electronics, agricultural tools and equipments, domestic appliances, as well as food and beverages. It is also interesting to note that neither individual inventors and SMEs nor large domestic companies have made good use of patent information such as granted patents. Seen through Sir Isaac Newton's metaphor, inventors can see further by standing on the sholders of the giants and undoubtedly, such information is a valuble source of up to date scientific and technical information, which can be used to avoid duplication of work already done

328 WM Cohen, RR Nelson and JP Walsh, 'Protecting Their Intellectual Assets: Appropriability Conditions and Why US Manufacturing Firms Patent (or Not)' (2000) Working Paper No.7552, National Bureau of Economic Research 17.

329 Article 7 of the TRIPS Agreement states that transfer of technology is one of the fundamental objectives of the global IPR regime.

330 According to OECD definition, high-tech industries are characterized by technical products of which the manufacturing involves high intensity of R&D, i.e. computers, photo-copying apparatus.

elsewhere.[331] It may partly be attributed to the lack of awareness and the practical dificulties in accessing such information as evidenced by our survey.

It is also important to consider factors that discourage the use of the patent mechanism by Sri Lankans. Most notably, the type of innovations produced in the country does not qualify for patent protection. Simply put, most of the innovations are not obvious over prior art and do not possess an inventiveness step. Thus, new but obvious improvements are not rewarded by the current patent regime which follows stringent global standards of novelty and inventive step. This typical developing country scenario has rightly been observed by commentators. According to them, domestic firms generally follow 'imitative' or 'dependent' technological strategies, usually relying on external sources of innovation, such as suppliers, customers and competitors.[332] These are successive improvements upon existing products and processes which bring about increases in technical efficiency or/and improvements in quality.[333] Thus, in most cases, Sri Lankan firms mostly rely on alternative appropriation mechanisms such as secrecy even though their effectiveness is subject to debate. Another reason why patent system has neither become attractive to individuals nor companies is the cost factor. Enormous costs associated with acquisition, maintenance and enforcement of patent rights is a greater deterrence for applicants. Moreover, TK-based industries such as the cosmetics industry occupy an important place in the Sri Lankan industrial economy, and according to our findings, such industries are hesitant to use the patent system mainly because they do not want to disclose valuable information to competitors and face delays in the granting process as their product lifecycle is relatively short. They also fear that TK-based innovations generally lack novelty and inventive step.

The effectiveness of patents as an incentive to invest in R&D depends not just on what the patent system can and does provide, but also on what

331 A Fitzgerald, *LBC Nutshell Intellectual Property* (2nd edn, Lawbook 2002) 144. See also, S Richetson, 'The Future of Australian Intellectual Property Reform and Administration' (1992) 3 Australian Intellectual Property Journal 3, 3-5.

332 C Correa, 'Designing Patent Policies suited to Developing Countries Needs' (2008) 10/2 Econômica, Rio de Janeiro 82, 89.

333 RM Galhardi, Small High Technology Firms in Developing Countries: The case of biotechnology (Avebury Press, 1994) 49.

investors think or perceive that it provides.[334] During our interviews, a number of firms confirmed that they more often than not use alternative appropriation mechanisms (non-IP strategies) such as lead-time advantage, secrecy and complementary sales. When it comes to IP mechanisms, they mostly rely on trademark protection. Due to the level of innovations they rarely apply for patents. The majority of small firms do not consider that patent protection is something that is important or necessary for their businesses. The following figure captures a snapshot view on the awareness and use of the patent system by the Sri Lankan SME sector. It needs to be interpreted with caution as there is a need for further rigorous research on the issue.

Figure 2.6: Use of Patent System by SMEs

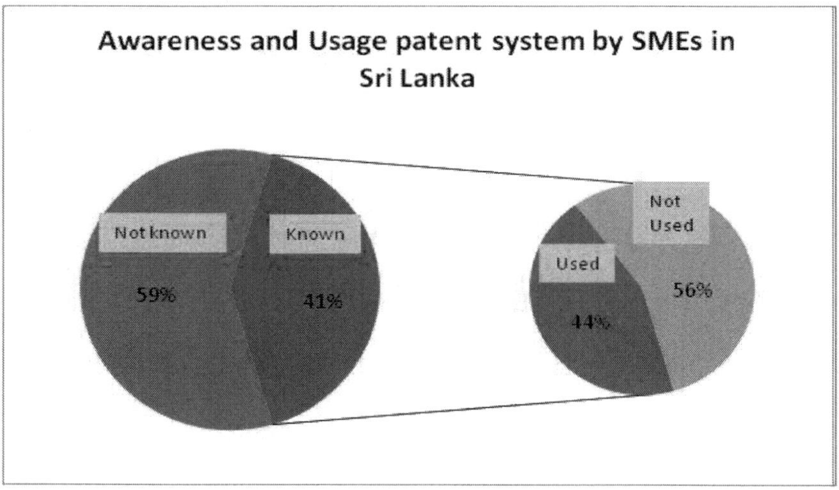

(Source: Survey evidence gathered from personal and telephone Interviews)[335]

334 The UK Patent Office (UKPO), *The UK Intellectual Property Awareness Survey 2006*. The Report was prepared by R Pitkethly (2007) 11, available at: <http://www.ipo.gov.uk/ipsurvey.pdf> (accessed 20 June 2012).

335 The methodology employed to gather information was to conduct face to face interviews and detailed telephone interviews with owners and managers of randomly selected 25 representatives of SMEs in Sri Lanka, whose contact details were obtained from the Ministry of Productivity Promotion and other industrial sector organizations of Sri Lanka. These interviews were carried out in 2011 and 2012.

Fugure 2.6 suggests that nearly 60 percent of SMEs in Sri Lanka are not aware of the importance of the patent system as an appropriation mechanism. Perhaps more importantly, firms that are aware of patent system are not inclined to seek patent protection. As evident from the data, not many firms in SME sector are enthusiastic about filing patents. Our survey evidence shows that patenting propensity among Sri Lankan SMEs is relatively low.[336] The SME sector is still unable to reap the benefit from the patent system. In other words, SMEs are kept away from using the patent system. They seem to favour informal ways of protection such as lead-time advantages and secrecy. The survey evidence suggests that awareness about the patent mechanism is a major issue in Sri Lanka. It was also observed that the level of awareness is higher among individual inventors and large companies than the SME sector. As a result, propensity to patents is far fewer among the SME sector. This by no means explains that the propensity to patent is high among large firms. Survey evidence from large firms supports the view that there is a general lack of confidence in the legal mechanism for obtaining protection in Sri Lanka.[337] Moreover, individual inventors are also discouraged to apply for patents due to practical difficulties such as getting access to qualified persons for legal advice and for drafting patent applications. Most of the professional service providers are lawyers and they charge relatively high fees from their clients. In hindsight, it can be argued that Sri Lankan SMEs have not made productive use of the patent system in place in the country. In other words, the patent regime has not worked well for a vast majority of local industries creating a disconnection between patent mechnism and industrial landscape. Our survey provides ample evidence to prove the proposition that the role of the patent system in the innovation process is poorly grasped by local industries in their research and development activities. As interpreted through the lens of patent jurisprudence, neither the message of incentive rationale nor the prospect theory of patent law has been well re-

336 Propensity to patent refers to probability/tendency to apply for and/or to obtain a patent, given a patentable invention. Put differently, the percentage of patentable innovations that are patented. Propensity to patent depends on, among other things, market, size of the firm, and level of innovation. See E Mansfield, 'Patents and Innovation: An Empirical Study' (1986) 32/2 Management Science 173, 176.

337 For example, several legal officers from leading companies in Sri Lanka pointed out that they do not wish to apply for patent due to long delays in granting process, in some cases more than 3-4 years.

ceived by the relevant sectors in the industrial landscape of Sri Lanka.[338] In essence, the Sri Lankan patent system remains under-appreciated and under-utilized.

2.2.12. Adequacy of the Existing Patent Regime

The basic motivation of the legislature in support of the new IP legislation in 2003 is best illustrated by the wordings of Ravi Karunanayake, the former Minister of Commerce and Consumer Affairs (2003) when it was introduced in the parliament.[339] He emphasized that 'in a knowledge-based economy, one of the biggest aspects and one of the biggest intrinsic advantages is the knowledge of our people. There are hidden talents in people. Creativity is there. That is what we want to protect. We feel that this type of thing will certainly help our very creative minded people to get a foothold into the globalized world'.[340] Despite these optimistic words, the reality is very different and little substantive progress has been so far made in the creation of innovation in the country. In hindsight, however, the current patent regime falls far short of the potential benefits envisioned by lawmakers, namely, promotion of the innovation potential and to create an innovative culture in the country. As evident from previous analysis, the current patent regime has become almost unsuitable for protecting creative efforts of the country because the Sri Lankan innovation landscape is dominated by subpatentable innovations. Thus, the patent system is disassociated with industries, especially the SME sector whose use of the patent mechanism is disappointingly low. Moreover, the statistical data depicts that the technological landscape of the economy is still at the initial stage of the technological ladder. There remains a question whether technology transfer and technological learning really occurs in Sri Lanka. Based on our survey evidence, the catch-all-patent system has proved to

---

338 The 'incentive theory' argues that granting legal protection encourages innovations, while 'prospect theory' holds that patent system brings an array of prospects associated with cost and returns. See EW Kitch, 'The Nature and Function of the Patent System' (1977) 20 Journal of Law & Economics 265, 266.

339 R Karunanayake – the former Minister of Commerce and Consumer Affairs (2003), *Hansard Report-23 July 2003* (The Parliament of Sri Lanka 2003) 1048, 1049-1050. He made this statement in the second reading of the Code of Intellectual Property Law Bill in Parliament.

340 Ibid.

be ineffective and much less attractive for the SME sector which is considered to be the engine of growth in the country.

Contrary to the generally held view, the patent system has failed to deliver worthwhile protection for the industrial sector in Sri Lanka. In reality, we face a paradox: the patent regime, which was introduced to help boost domestic industries and creative minds to get a foothold into the globalized world, is increasingly becoming an obstacle to gain protection for the kind of innovations that Sri Lankans produce. This is clearly evident from the number of patent applications filed and granted. When asked, why there is a high rate of rejection, relevant officials revealed that most inventions that are filed with the National Intellectual Property Office (NIPO) are very basic and cannot fulfill the patentability requirements as provided in the Act. That is of course only an aspect of this problem. The truth is, however, that a large majority of innovations of domestic industries do not find their way to the patent registry in the capital city. As aptly observed by Carlos Correa, in most developing countries the innovation systems are fragmented and weak and they overwhelmingly depend on innovations made abroad.[341] Furthermore, a large part of firms have confirmed that they do not regard patents as a significant factor in their decisions to invest time and resources for development. Not only is there a clear lack of interest in patents in the SME sector, there is also an impression that the patent system is ineffective and unimportant for them. This may not be the case for large companies though we found mixed evidence. The patent regime does appeal to certain industries like large corporations. One of the major problems faced by small firms is the accessibility of the patent system because patents are simply too expensive for them. Viewed against the backdrop of the intention of the legislature, the main objectives of the patent law was to promote national creativity and the protection of the creative efforts of the nation. Unfortunately, the implementation of the current patent regime has probably not furthered this policy goal.

As pointed out in our interviews with the honorable members[342] of the Sri Lankan judiciary, without diluting the patentability standard, Sri Lankans should consider adopting an STP system of protecting incremental types of innovations that would not qualify for patent protection. As

---

341 C Correa, 'Designing Patent Policies suited to Developing Countries Needs' (2008) 10/2 Econômica, Rio de Janeiro 82, 90.

342 Interview with, Justice KT Chitrasiri/The Court of Appeal of Sri Lanka and Justice Saleem Marsoof/The Supreme Court of Sri Lanka. (20 and 29 August 2012).

our survey evidence suggests, the SME sector may be better served by such a regime as their innovative activities are characterized by relatively small incremental improvements to existing products rather than the development of completely new products. Such innovations should be promoted although, they have received little attention so far. From a policy perspective, it is neither logical nor practical to lower standards of patentability as they are interpreted in a global manner. Sri Lanka should continue to follow a similar line with the EPC, USPTO, PCT, JPO and many other jurisdictions in order in order to comply with international standards and developments. What may be more appropriate to consider is a different regime to deal with incremental innovations which have largely remained unnoticed by policy makers in Sri Lanka so far.

2.3. Design Protection in Sri Lanka

2.3.1. Introduction

The industrial design regime, which is one of the four pillars of industrial property protection, plays an important role in the market place today. It is needless to mention that the appeal of consumer goods of everyday life is influenced by the appearance of products. The more appealing such products are, the more likely it is that they will be bought by consumers.[343] Designs make a product attractive and appealing; hence they may add significantly to the commercial value of a product and increase its marketability. Design protection is wide enough to encapsulate designs of three-dimensional patterns such as toys, shoes, perfume bottles, cutlery, and even domestic furniture on the one hand, and two-dimensional patterns such as textiles and wallpapers, on the other hand. Industrial design protection worldwide has developed slowly, following a different path in each country, and even today, there are significant differences in various jurisdictions.[344] While a patent protects the technical solution or the inventive technical improvement in a product or a process, the new and original shape and external appearance of a useful object is protected by an indus-

343 Y Takagi and others (eds), *Teaching of Intellectual property* (WIPO and CUP 2008) 85.

344 D Musker, Community Design Law: Principles and Practice (Sweet & Maxwell 2002) viii.

trial design right.[345] Interestingly, industrial design protection suffers jurisdictional encroachments under copyright, patent, utility model, trademark and unfair competition law.[346] According to Article 25(1) of the TRIPS Agreement, WTO members have an obligation to provide for the protection of independently created industrial designs that are new or original. Nevertheless, the TRIPS Agreement does not provide a definition of novelty or originality. An industrial design may be defined as the (outward) appearance of a product or a part of a product which results from the lines, contours, colours, shape, texture, materials and its ornamentation.[347] Even though the protection of industrial designs is of vital importance to the promotion of trade and innovation, it remains a less harmonized aspect in the global IP arena.

2.3.2. Overview of Sri Lankan Law

The current legal protection of industrial designs in Sri Lanka is governed by Part III of IP Act No. 36 of 2003. It appears from the statutory language that industrial designs can also be protected under other IP regimes such as copyright, trademarks and unfair competition[348] and arguably, like in other jurisdictions such as European and US, the overlap of rights makes cumulative protection possible in the area of design rights in Sri Lanka. According to the Act, "any composition of lines or colours or any three dimensional form, whether or not associated with lines or colours, that gives a special appearance to a product of industry or handicraft and is capable of serving as a pattern for a product of industry or handicraft, shall be deemed to be an industrial design".[349] However, pursuant to Section 30 of the Act, anything in an industrial design which serves solely to obtain a technical result shall not be protected as an industrial design in Sri Lanka. From an IP law perspective, the exclusion of functional features of a prod-

---

345 S Alikhan and RA Masshelkar, Intellectual Property and Competitive Strategies in the 21st Century (Kluwer Law 2004) 8-9.

346 U Suthersanen, *Design Law in Europe* (2nd edn, Sweet & Maxwell 2010) 1.

347 See art 3 of the Council Regulation (EC) No. 6/2002 of December 12, 2001 on Community Designs (Community Designs Regulation-CDR).

348 See Section 28 of the IP Act; "The protection of industrial designs provided under this Part shall be in addition to and not in derogation of any other protection provided under any other written law".

349 See Section 30 of the IP Act of Sri Lanka No 36, 2003.

uct from the design protection arises from the policy consideration that the protection of function of an article should be left for patent and utility model protection. Moreover, even though there is no definition of the term 'product', it can be interpreted from the wording of Section 30 that a 'product' would mean an industrial or a handicraft item. In order to be eligible for protection under Sri Lankan law, any registerable design has to be new and must not be anti-social in the sense that it does not consists of any scandalous design or that it is contrary to morality or public order or public interest or is likely to offend the religious or racial susceptibilities of any community.[350] The Act does not provide any guidance as to what 'public order or morality' means, and arguably, it has to be understood in the light of the moral and socio-cultural climate of the country.

As stipulated in the Act, "an industrial design is new when it had not been made available to the public anywhere in the world and at any time whatsoever through description, use or in any other manner before the date of an application for registration of such industrial design or before the priority date validly claimed in respect thereof".[351] It is clear from the wording of the Act that Sri Lankan law imposes a high threshold of novelty or absolute novelty for design protection. Taken together, the emphasis on absolute novelty and exclusion of functional aspects of course creates difficult hurdles for designers.

Under Sri Lankan law, an owner of a registered industrial design can enjoy his exclusive rights to exploit by preventing others from unauthorized making, selling, importing, or using of any product that is protected by the design law.[352] The registration of an industrial design lasts for five years from the date of application and it can be renewed for two consecutive periods of five years. Thus, the statutory life of a registered design lasts for 15 years from the date of application.[353] Moreover, in order to further strengthen the position and the rights of the design owner, Sri

---

350 See Section 29 of the IP Act of Sri Lanka No 36, 2003. See also DM Karunaratna, *Elements of the Law of IP in Sri Lanka* (Sarasavi Publisher 2010) 116.

351 See Section 31, and as per this Section 31(2), a restrictive grace period of 6 months if provided, the design is displayed at an official or officially recognized, international exhibition. Moreover, according to Section 31 (3) an industrial design shall not be considered a new industrial design solely by reason of the fact that *it differs from an earlier industrial design in minor respects or that it concerns a type of product different from a product* (*emphasis added*).

352 See Section 47 of the IP Act of Sri Lanka No 36, 2003.

353 See Sections 45 and 46 of the IP Act of Sri Lanka No 36, 2003.

Lankan law has implemented the legal presumption according to which the person who makes the first application for a design is presumed to be its owner. In principle, Sri Lankan industries such as textiles and garments, toys, cottage industries like handicrafts, as well as the producers of gem and jewelry should have been prime candidates for design protection. Nevertheless, the relatively high novelty standard and non-protection of technical features prevent most incremental and minor innovations from receiving protection under this mechanism.

2.3.3. Empirical Analysis

Table 2.1: Industrial Design Applications and Registrations

Year	Applications			Registrations		
	Resident	Non Resident	Total	Resident	Non Resident	Total
2002	345	40	385	253	13	266
2003	386	42	428	365	23	388
2004	254	50	304	224	40	264
2005	257	47	304	269	88	357
2006	477	39	516	422	45	467
2007	328	24	352	8	6	14
2008	333	56	389	85	4	89
2009	273	40	313	238	36	274
2010	233	51	284	228	37	265
2011	387	56	443	88	21	109

(Source: National Intellectual Property Office of Sri Lanka data)

The statistical evidence from the NIPO demonstrates that the application and registration of design rights in Sri Lanka has recorded a slow growth over the last 10 years with fluctuating numbers in certain years. As presented in Table 2.1, filings of design applications have recorded a small increase from 345 in 2002 to 385 in 2011. Notably, there has been a considerable increase in filing and registration in year 2006. Nevertheless, the increase has not remained constant in the following years. Significantly, in recent years such as 2007, 2008 and 2011, there has been a decline in the number of registered designs. In other words, the rate of rejection seems to be very high. Most strikingly, over the last decade, the recorded design applications remain less than 500 per year. One conclusion that we can draw from this data is that the design regime has not been very attractive for domestic industries in Sri Lanka.

Figure 2.7: Trends in Design Applications

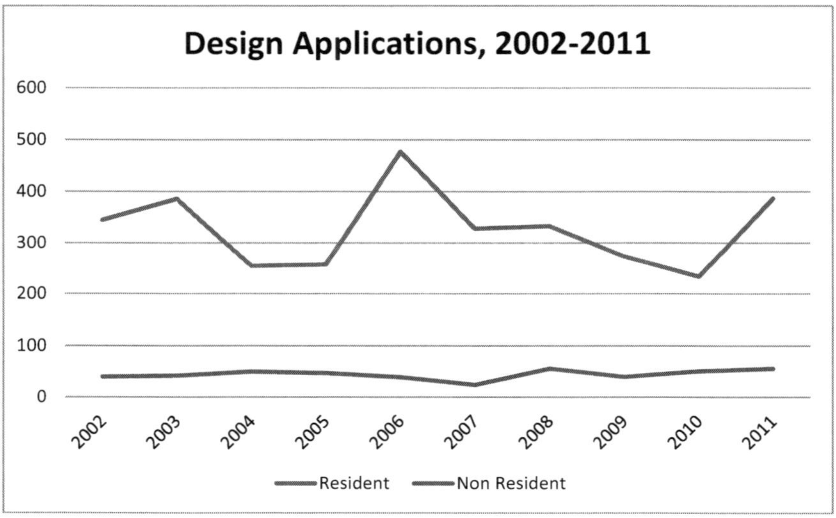

(Source: Based on data from the National Intellectual Property Office of Sri Lanka)

Figure 2.8, shows that resident applications constitute a large share of total design applications between the years 2002 to 2011 and it is more than 85 percent in 2011 alone. In stark contrast to patent applications, foreign applications for design protection remains low. Different conclusions are possible. One possible and most likely explanation is that, since Sri Lanka has a relatively small market, not many foreign applicants are willing to or interested in exploiting their design in Sri Lanka. Moreover, foreign design applications have remained more or less constant, with a marginal increase.

Figure 2.8: Trends in Design Applications and Registration

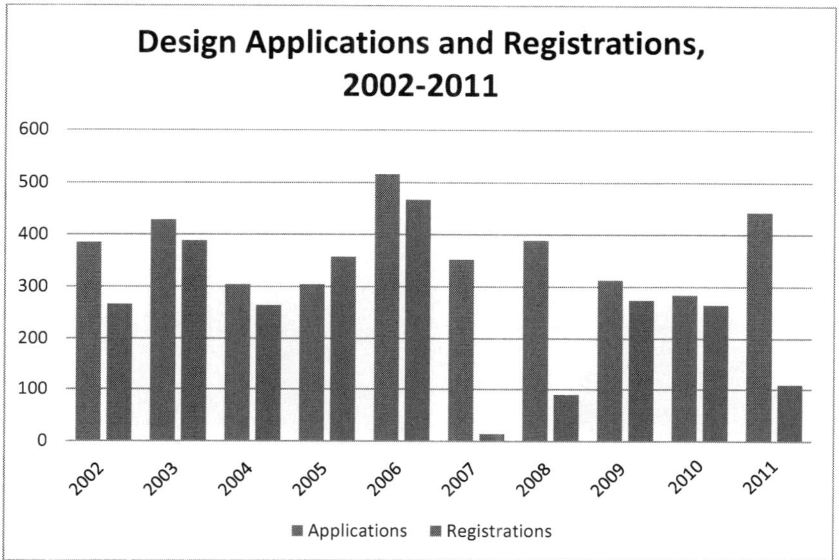

(Source: Based on data from the National Intellectual Property Office of Sri Lanka)

As shown in figure 2.9, even though the design regime has not created significant growth in terms of applications, the available data suggests that the system in place is working quite well in Sri Lanka. Nevertheless, it is rather disappointing to learn that there is a considerable gap between the design applications and registrations, most notably in 2007, 2008 and 2011, where the registered designs are as low as less than 100 annually. One possible explanation for this decrease in registrations would be that the high threshold of novelty filters out many applications for designs that were not universally new. There is yet another reason that might have been attributed to this situation. Probably, many design applications might have fallen into the exclusion clause for being functional and become unprotectable. As a fact, the scope of design protection is limited to the appearance of the product. Moreover, when visual features of the design serve only a functional purpose, such a design would not qualify for protection under the design regime. Furthermore, the survey evidence suggests that, due to the lack of awareness among industries, the number of application files for design protection is limited. Most strikingly, it was also revealed that design protection was not very attractive for fast-moving industries (of short product life cycle) such as fashion designers and manufacturers due to delays in the granting procedure. In particular, novelty examination for industrial designs applications is carried out by the National Intellectual Property Office (NIPO) of Sri Lanka and it generally takes quite a long time. Nevertheless, according to NIPO, design protection is mainly sought to protect items such as toys, garment hangers, bottles shapes and jewellery. Apparently, the relevant industrial sectors in Sri Lanka have not made very effective use of the protection mechanism available under design regime for their businesses.

2.3.4. Is Design Protection an Alternative to a Second-Tier Protection Regime?

An industrial design constitutes the ornamental or aesthetic aspect of an article.[354] From an economic perspective, the design right is a marketing tool which can incentivise innovation and support its commercialization.[355] Comparatively speaking, industrial design protection in Sri Lanka does not have to survive rigorous obviousness scrutiny as in US law or prove individual character requirement as in Europe. As a result, the available protection mechanism does probably not cause serious difficulties for designers in Sri Lanka. Nevertheless, in order to serve as an effective alternative to an STP regime, the industrial designs application and registration system in Sri Lanka would need to be made simpler and faster without insisting on rigorous standards for protection. In that sense, enforcing a very strict worldwide novelty requirement would create a hurdle which can dissuade and discourage the design industry from using the system. However, the major fault in obtaining protection for minor and incremental innovations under design law is that the scope of protection may be limited to the 'overall impression' of the design.[356] In other words, the law will not protect the underlying function or principle but rather the appear-

354 WIPO, 'What is an Industrial Design?' (2012) Official website of WIPO, available at: <http://www.wipo.int/designs/en/> (accessed 2 May 2012).

355 U Suthersanen, *Design Law in Europe* (2nd edn, Sweet & Maxwell 2010) 23.

356 U Suthersanen, 'Utility Models and Innovation in Developing Countries' (2006) ICTSD Issue Paper No.13, 32, available at: <http://unctad.org/en/docs/iteipc20066_en.pdf> (accessed 15 March 2012).

ance of the product. The problem that arises here is that minor innovations will not qualify for design protection.[357]

Under the 'functionality doctrine' design protection will not be available for features of a product which are solely dictated by its technical function. In other words, the functions that are necessary for a product to work effectively are generally defined as 'primarily functional' or 'solely functional'.[358] Arguably, the design regime is not there to grant rights for technical effect circumventing the underpinning rationale of the patent law. For this reason, technical innovation does not attract design protection and needs to be treated under a different regime. Thus, it may be argued that design protection does not amount to an alternative protection for an STP system. It may be true that design protection can be used in some circumstances, but certainly not in all circumstances; and such use will usually require using design protection for a purpose other than its intended use.[359] In principle, different forms of IP rights have been created to serve different underlying objectives, and when one right is used for another purpose for which it was not created, the objective of that regime can easily be undermined resulting in an imbalance in the entire legal framework. All in all, the industrial design regime does not offer the same benefits as an STP regime does. Conversely, in some cases, the design regime may be adequate, but arguably it will rarely be ideal.[360]

---

357 Ibid 30-32.

358 Y Takagi and others (eds), *Teaching of Intellectual property* (WIPO and CUP 2008) 85.

359 M Crinson, 'Is Some Novel Protection of Invention Needed in Canada' (1998) 12 Intellectual Property Journal 25, 49.

360 Ibid 49-50.

2.4. Comparative view of Different IPRs in Sri Lanka

Figure 2.9: Trends in Patent, Design and Trademark Applications

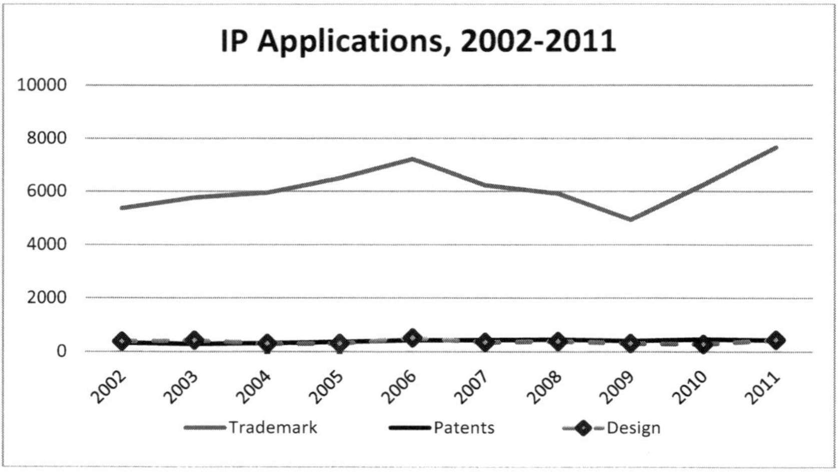

(Source: Based on data from the National Intellectual Property Office of Sri Lanka)

Even though an analysis of the trademark regime is well beyond the scope of this research, a comparative view on the disparate development of different industrial property regimes seems appropriate. As shown in Figure 2.9, trademark protection is the most commonly used IP instrument in the industrial landscape of Sri Lanka. Statistical evidence from 2002 to 2011 demonstrates that, on average, the number of annual filings of trademark applications remains more than ten times higher than that of patents and industrial design applications. Even more significantly, the gap between trademarks and patent applications is widening. The increased use of the trademark regime mirrors the socio-economic realities and the level of technological development of the country. Sri Lanka is still making simple products such as tea and garments and very few hi-tech complex products.[361] Moreover, it can be labeled as a raw material exporting country as opposed to a value-creating nation. Understandably, Sri Lankan firms in

361 WA Wijewardene, 'How Sri Lanka can move up' *Lanka Business Online* (Colombo, 20 October 2012), available at: <http://www.lankabusinessonline.com /> (accessed 1 January 2013).

low-tech sectors are more prone to rely on trademark protection as the most appropriate means of protecting their investments. The limited importance of patents and design rights for SMEs received further confirmation in our interviews with the industrial organizations. Thus, it comes as no surprise that the majority of registered industrial property belongs to trademark rights. The same is also evident from case law jurisprudence in IP law that only a handful of cases reported in the other areas, especially of patent and industrial designs, is making it difficult to develop the law in these areas. The Courts have apparently not had adequate opportunities to deal with the subject in a constructive way.[362] According to commentators, the unencouraging economic environment and lack of creative activity have largely contributed to this situation.[363]

2.5. Conclusion

IP law encompasses a range of property rights attached to various products of the human mind and is traditionally divided into industrial property and copyright. Not surprisingly, granting of IP rights is based on sound theoretical and philosophical justifications. In this chapter, only patent and design regimes have been dealt with especially from a Sri Lankan perspective insofar as to ascertain the adequacy of the existing IP framework to incentivise incremental and minor innovations in the industrial landscape of Sri Lanka.

Viewed from an innovation perspective, a patent is a policy instrument aimed at encouraging inventors to invest in R&D activities and their commercialization through securing exclusive rights. Moreover, it is hoped that the patent system stimulates indigenous technological development, promotes domestic inventive activity and facilitates technology transfer as well as technology learning. Sri Lanka being a commonwealth country inherited its patent system from the UK but gradually developed its own independent system. Despite the fact that the country's patent system is more than one and a half centuries old, its contribution to science and technological development has been minimal. It is observed that the strict requirements of global novelty and inventive step as implemented in the

---

362 DM Karunaratna, *A Guide to the Law of Trademarks and Service Marks in Sri Lanka* (2nd edn, Sarvodaya Vishva Lekha Publishers 2007) 3.

363 Ibid.

current patent law has created roadblocks in protecting the kind of innovation that emanates from domestic industries, especially for SMEs. Patent law jurisprudence, on the other hand, has not been adequately advanced as there are only a handful of cases that have gone up to the appeal level.

It is, of course, true that Sri Lanka has a smaller market and a less technologically advanced economy. The country is still in the initial stage of technological ladder, and needs to move into the rank of technological innovative nation through innovation. Empirical evidence has confirmed that the current patent regime, in most cases, does not provide suitable means of protecting the type of innovations that are generated in domestic industries. Patent protection will not be available for most of that type of innovation because of its high inventive step requirement. As confirmed by empirical evidence, for SMEs, patent protection is 'too demanding, too time-consuming, and too complex to handle. A relatively low number of resident patent filings and registrations provide ample evidence to prove this fact. There are also growing concerns that a uniform patent system may not be the right tool for incentivising local innovations in developing countries. Viewed through the patent landscape of the country, the country's patent system does not positively encourage domestic inventive activities. The government should also have a policy to enhance the use of the patent system and Sri Lanka needs to move from the labour-intensive garment industry to knowledge-intensive products. There is evidence that the state of IP awareness among large firms is much higher than in the SME sector in Sri Lanka. In sum, when judged by the policymakers' objectives, the Sri Lankan patent system has failed to live up to its expectations. There is compelling evidence to conclude that most SMEs in Sri Lanka are proceeding largely in ignorance of their IP entitlements. Without diluting standard for patenting, it may be appropriate to consider the introduction of an STP to capture incremental types of innovation which may fit the needs of SMEs in the country. There is, therefore, a need for an STP regime to protect innovation that falls into the gap at the interface of patent and design rights.

In contrast to the patent regime, the design regime has its objective of protecting the overall appearance of a product. Due to the lack of international consensus for harmonization, design laws in different countries vary in terms of criteria of protection. In the Sri Lankan context, industrial design must meet the standard of worldwide novelty. Perhaps even more importantly, based on policy reasons, the exclusion of functional aspects of a product makes it difficult, if not impossible, to protect incremental innovations through design protection. Thus, innovations relating to mechanical or technical devices may not be served by the design regime. Put differently, design law in Sri Lanka cannot protect functional innovations. This brings us to the question of whether design protection is an alternative to an STP system. The answer is no. Nevertheless, in some cases, where the features of the product that serve to improve the product appearance and do not perform primarily functions of the product, such products would attract design protection under Sri Lankan law. When compared with the patent regime, the usage of industrial design protection has remained modest in recent years. As evidenced by empirical data, the majority of design applications are filed by domestic applicants. It does not, however, mean that the design regime has made some encouraging steps in terms of application and registration of designs. Most importantly, an urgent effort is needed to enable the country to move up the technological ladder. In the final analysis, a paradigm shift will be necessary if Sri Lanka wants to enter the ranks of emerging economies and beyond.

3. Incentive Mechanisms for Incremental and Minor Innovations under Unfair Competition Law and Trade Secrets Law in Sri Lanka

'He who has no hope that he shall reap will not take the trouble to sow'. Jeremy Bentham[364]

In the preceding Chapter, I have attempted to explore the possibility of protecting minor and incremental innovations under the existing IP paradigms; namely, patent and designs. The remit of this Chapter is, therefore, to consider whether and to what extent unfair competition and trade secret regimes can be used to protect innovative achievements of enterprises, especially those of SMEs in the Sri Lankan context. Generally speaking, while the rules against unfair competition supplements in some cases IP protection, trade secrets protection is an alternative to other IP rights such as patents. As a caveat, however, it should be borne in mind that unfair competition law does not grant exclusive rights as in the case of patent or design, rather it prohibits and provides remedies against specific acts of misappropriation. Perhaps more importantly, even though the trade secret regime would come under the umbrella of unfair competition law, for the purposes of this Chapter, it is treated separately given its increasing importance in incentivising innovation in the current business environment in Sri Lanka.

3.1. Unfair Competition Law

As Lord Justice Peterson has stated 'what is worth copying is worth of protecting',[365] and the underpinning idea of unfair competition law is to prevent someone reaping where he has not sown. In the realm of IP law, the protection against unfair competition falls outside the hard-core IP themes and is considered to be the 'fallback protection', especially when

364 J Bowring, *The Works of Jeremy Bentham* (vol 3 -part 1, William Tait 1839) 71.

365 *University of London Press Ltd v. University Tutorial Press Ltd* (1916) 2 Ch. 601, 610.

there is no other specific IP right available. Arguably, one can of course make a strong case for developing a misappropriation-based unfair competition regime as a third IP paradigm for the protection of products that fall through the crack between patent and copyright.[366] Indeed, from an innovation perspective, mostly though not necessarily, an unfair competition law regime ensures fair play in the market and reduces the risk of an economic injury to a business, thereby creating incentives to invest in innovation. Significantly, the rational basis for protection against unfair competition can be traced as to protect competitors by ensuring trade values to be observed in the market on one hand, and to safeguard the interests of consumers, as well as public at large, on the other.

3.1.1. Introduction

The concept of unfair competition, *concurrence déloyale,* emerged in France around 1850.[367] According to scholars, "it is not known who originated the use of this widely-adopted legal concept. It is known, however, who provided the impetus for creating a law of competition: the businessmen, the honorable merchants who under the new free competitive system saw no other means of protecting themselves from unlawful competition. In order to satisfy their needs, the French courts, working from the Code Napoléon, developed a law against unfair competition".[368] Over the years, unfair competition law has developed to remedy the *lacunae* between rights and it provides an alternative approach to avoiding situations deserving of protection falling into the 'gap' which lies between the specifically defined IP right and public domain, in particular, in guarding the interests at stake when new ideas are developed.[369] Conversely, one might still argue that the habit of relying on unfair competition regimes to protect innovations carries many drawbacks.

---

366 See DS Karjala, 'Misappropriation as a Third Intellectual Property Paradigm' (1994) 94 Columbia Law Review 2594, 2604-2605.

367 G Schricker, 'Unfair Competition and Consumer Protection in Western Europe' (1970) 1 International Review of Intellectual Property and Competition Law 415, 415.

368 Ibid.

369 C Colston and K Middleton, *Modern Intellectual Property* (2nd edn, Cavendish Publishing 2005) 37-38.

Viewed from an economic perspective, a free market economy implies competition. Competition is the 'great regulative force' which establishes control over economic activities.[370] The freedom to engage in business and to compete for the patronage of prospective customers is the fundamental premise of the free enterprise system. Competition in the marketing of goods and services creates an incentive to offer quality products at reasonable prices and foster general welfare by promoting the efficient allocation of economic resources.[371] Most notably, competition encourages innovation in two ways. First, it pressures companies to introduce new or improved products or services that win them additional customers, or to keep up with the innovations introduced by their competitors.[372] Second, competition creates pressure to reduce costs or improve the quality of existing products.[373] The law of course favours the doctrine of free competition; but where there is competition; there is also the likelihood of unfair competition. In today's global market, safeguarding free but fair competition in the market has become even more important.[374]

Unfair competition law is one of the most important areas of law in the face of increasing globalization and free market economy, even as it remains an elusive area of law. A recent study by the World Intellectual Property Organisation (WIPO) has revealed that the many different national legal systems which offer protection against unfair competition throughout the world have many common elements, but also employs the diversity of norms in use throughout the world.[375] It is certainly true that terms such as 'honest practices', 'good customs', 'good faith' and 'professional correctness' escape clear-cut universal definitions. Very broadly, an act of unfair competition may be defined as 'any act that a competitor or

---

370 A Terry, 'Unfair Competition and the Misappropriation of a Competitor's Trade Values' (1988) 51 Modern Law Review 296.

371 JC Ginsburge, J Litman, ML Kevlin, *Trademark and Unfair Competition Law: Cases and Materials* (4th edn, Foundation Press 2007) 1.

372 Economic Commission for Europe-The Committee on Economic Cooperation and Integration, 'Good Practices and Policy Recommendations: Intellectual Property and Competition Policy as Drivers of Innovation' (Economic and Social Council of the United Nations, Geneva, 26 September 2012, document prepared by the Secretariat) 2-3.

373 Ibid 2.

374 A Kamperman-Sanders, Unfair Competition Law: The Protection of Intellectual Property and Industrial Creativity (Clarendon Press Oxford 1997) 1.

375 Ibid 56.

another market participant undertakes with the intention of directly exploiting another person's industrial or commercial achievement for his own business purposes without substantially departing from the original achievement'.[376]

3.1.2. The International Dimension

As commentators have pointed out, it is quite difficult to determine what is meant by the term 'unfair competition'. The very term 'unfair competition' is paradoxical, and therefore it is very difficult to define.[377] There is certainly no international consensus on the meaning of the term, and neither is there anything like an international unfair competition convention. As a result, there is no real starting point for an understanding of unfair competition either in Europe, the US or any other part of the world. One possible starting point is the Paris Convention.[378] The original Convention of 1883 (Paris Convention) did not carry any specific provision concerning the repression of unfair competition and the Article 10*bis* which postulated the principle of unfair competition was newly inserted by the Revision Conference of Brussels in 1900.[379] Then the Revision Conference in Washington in 1911 went further by introducing an obligation for all States adhering to this revision to provide effective protection against unfair competition.[380] Most importantly, the definition and examples of acts of unfair competition were introduced at the Hague Conference in 1925 and the Lisbon Conference in 1958.[381] Article 10*bis* of the Paris Convention contains the law against unfair competition in a nutshell, or rather part of such a law, since that article contains no provisions concerning the legal

---

376 UNCTAD-ICTSD, *Resource Book on TRIPS and Development* (Cambridge University Press 2005) 521.

377 G Dworkin, 'Unfair Competition: Is the Common Law Developing a New Tort?' (1978/9) 1 European Intellectual Property Law Review 241.

378 Paris Convention for the Protection of Industrial Property of March 20, 1883 as last revised in 1978.

379 GHC Bodenhausen, Guide to the Application of the Paris Convention for the Protection of Industrial Property (BIRPI 1968) 142.

380 Ibid.

381 Ibid 142-143.

consequences of violation of the principles of unfair competition.[382] Most notably, the repression of unfair competition, according to Article 1(2) of the Paris Convention, is treated as a part of the protection of industrial property. As a result, the landscape of international unfair competition law has considerably changed in the last few decades.

Unfair competition is defined in the second paragraph of Article 10*bis* as 'any act of competition contrary to honest practices in industrial or commercial matters'.[383] In other words, any act of competition will have to be considered unfair if it is contrary to *honest practices in industrial or commercial matters*.[384] As argued by scholars, this criterion is not limited to honest practices existing in the country where protection against unfair competition is sought.[385] Of course, the term 'honest' is a flexible one, and arguably, courts should adopt a purposive interpretation in order to achieve the underlying objectives of the provision. Moreover, three types of behaviour are explicitly prohibited in Article 10*bis* (3), creating the risk of confusion, discrediting or denigrating competitors through false allegations, and making misleading indications or allegations about one's own goods. However, this list of examples is not enumerative, so other dishonest competitive acts can also be covered by the general clause.[386] For example, the act of unfair free riding on the back of other competitors' achievements (case of unfair coat-tail riding), misappropriation or violation of others' trade secrets, comparative advertising, touting such as offering bonuses and many other acts, although not expressly mentioned, would arguably come into this catalogue. The general clause (the second paragraph of Article 10*bis*) can be considered the heart of every law on unfair competition. Most significantly, such a general clause seems necessary in order to accommodate ever-changing market practices. Moreover,

---

382 G Schricker, 'Twenty-Five Years of Protection against Unfair Competition' (1995) 26/4 International Review of Intellectual Property and Competition Law 782, 782.

383 See also F Henning-Bodewig, and Gerhard Schricker 'New Initiatives for the Harmonization of Unfair Competition Law in Europe' (2002) 24/5 European Intellectual Property Law Review 271, 272.

384 GHC Bodenhausen, Guide to the Application of the Paris Convention for the Protection of Industrial Property (BIRPI 1968) 144.

385 Ibid.

386 F Henning-Bodewig, 'International Protection Against Unfair Competition – Article 10bis Paris Convention, TRIPS and WIPO Model Provisions' (1999) 30/2 International Review of Intellectual Property and Competition Law 166, 173.

it may also be assessed as a 'gate of entry' for consumer protection in the Paris Convention.[387] Most national courts, however, have tended to construe this wide provision *ejusdem generis* with specified activities, and not as the catch-all provision that a literal reading of the article might suggest.[388]

Furthermore, the TRIPS Agreement refers to Article 10*bis* of the Paris Convention within the framework of the protection of geographical indications[389] and undisclosed information.[390] In particular, unfair competition law as such is not mentioned in Part II of the TRIPS Agreement and there is nothing in the language of TRIPS that would lead one to conclude that unfair competition law should be put on an equal footing with patent, trademark, copyright and design law.[391] Cornish argues that the TRIPS Agreement itself contains no substantial provisions on unfair competition, save for Article 39, when it is mentioned in relation to undisclosed information. The TRIPS Agreement therefore 'reinforces' the Paris Convention's Article 10*bis* only by making the existence of that article binding on WTO states.[392] Arguably, Article 10*bis* should be viewed as the minimum threshold of protection against unfair competition. Compared with other disciplines of industrial property law, in particular, patent and trademark laws, the law of unfair competition is far less strongly developed in many countries of the world. In international law as well, the rules against unfair competition were recognized as part of the protection of industrial property relatively recently.[393]

---

387 G Dworkin, 'Unfair Competition: Is the Common Law Developing a New Tort?' (1978/9) 1 European Intellectual Property Law Review 241, 242-243.

388 Ibid.

389 Articles 22-24 of the TRIPS Agreement.

390 Article 39 of the TRIPS Agreement.

391 F Henning-Bodewig, 'International Protection Against Unfair Competition – Article 10bis Paris Convention, TRIPS and WIPO Model Provisions' (1999) 30/2 International Review of Intellectual Property and Competition Law 166, 178-179.

392 WR Cornish, 'Genevan Bootstraps' (1997) 7 European Intellectual Property Law Review 336.

393 G Schricker, 'Twenty-Five Years of Protection against Unfair Competition' (1995) 26/4 International Review of Intellectual Property and Competition Law 782, 782.

3.1.3. Current Legal Regime against Unfair Competition in Sri Lanka

Sri Lanka's IP Act of 2003 contains specific provisions on the protection against unfair competition. At first glance, the statutory scheme in section 160 first deals with the general clause followed by a list of non-exhaustive specific acts. Pursuant to section 160(1) of the Act, the term 'unfair competition' is defined as 'any act or practice carried out or engaged in, in the course of industrial or commercial activities, that is contrary to honest practices'. This broad definition is comparable with the basic principle postulated in Article 10*bis* (2) of the Paris Convention and it has reinforced the general clause. The basic elements of unfair competition under Sri Lankan law are: (1) any act or practice; (2) contrary to honest practices; (3) carried out or engaged in, in the course of industrial or commercial activities. According to commentators, the law refers to both 'act and practices' and the word 'practices' is used in addition to 'act' in order to avoid a strict interpretation of the word 'act' which can also include 'omissions'.[394] In view of the WIPO Model Provisions, 'failure to correct or supplement information concerning a product test published in a consumer magazine, thereby giving a wrong impression of the quality of the product offered on the market, or failure to give sufficient information concerning the correct operation of a product or concerning possible side-effects of a product' can also be considered an act of unfair competition.[395] Moreover, the phrase 'industrial and commercial activities' should be broadly construed so as to include not only the activities of enterprises providing goods and services, but also activities of professionals such as medical or legal practitioners.[396] The meaning of 'contrary to honest practices' will be dealt with in the next section in the light of judicial pronouncements on the subject by Sri Lankan courts. Moreover, Section 160 embraces a wide spectrum of specific acts with much-detailed examples of instances of unfair competition. This includes acts of causing confusion or being likely to cause confusion with respect to competitors' goods or ser-

394 DM Karunaratna, *Elements of the Law of Intellectual Property in Sri Lanka* (Sarasavi Publishers 2010) 324.

395 WIPO, *Model Provisions on Protection against Unfair Competition: Articles and Notes* (WIPO 1996) 9.

396 Ibid. DM Karunaratna, *Elements of the Law of Intellectual Property in Sri Lanka* (Sarasavi Publishers 2010) 324.

vices,[397] causing damage to goodwill or reputation including acts of dilution,[398] acts that are misleading such as advertisements, any false or unjustifiable allegations, discrediting or denigration of competitors, etc.[399] Most notably, the wordings of the provision indicate that the above acts are examples and not exhaustive. At first sight, it appears that Sri Lankan law has given wide and comprehensive protection for unfair competition in compliance with its international obligations.

3.1.4. Development of the Case-Law

Apart from the statutory provisions, the ramification of the case-law is of vital importance to understand unfair competition law in practice. Thus, an examination of evolving case-law of the superior courts in defining the boundaries of unfair competition law in Sri Lanka is warranted. The statutory law more often than not is far from perfect and the concepts that we read in IP law acquire better clarity when understood in the context of the application of the law by the courts to a set of facts in a real life dispute.[400] Recent judicial decisions have perceivably recognized the importance of purposive interpretation of provisions relating to unfair competition. In particular, the decision of the Supreme Court in *Sumeet Research and Holdings Ltd. v. Elite Radio & Engineering Co. Ltd.,*[401] deserves a special notice in this regard. Most notably, the decision of Justice Mark Fernando in this case is a step in the right direction. In this case, for the first time, the Sri Lankan judiciary enthusiastically came out with an authoritative interpretation of the meaning of unfair competition embodied in Section 142 of the Code of Intellectual Property Act, No.52 of 1979,[402] (Section 160 of present Act). Arguably, the case also illustrates the court's willingness to expand the scope of protection in order to achieve the desired objectives

---

397 See Section 160(2); this sub-section in particular deals confusion caused by look-alike products and appearance of a product (get-up/trade dress).

398 See Section 160(3); significantly, anti-dilution protection has been introduced via this provision. Dilution can lessen the distinctive character of a trademark by blurring or tarnishment.

399 See Section 160(4) and (5).

400 Z Thomas, 'Intellectual Property Case Law Development' (2009) 14 Journal of Intellectual Property Rights 153.

401 (1997) 2 Sri LR 393.

402 Code of Intellectual Property Act No. 52 of 1979.

of the law. This case, of course, could have important and far-reaching implications in relation to unfair competition as applied in Sri Lanka. In expounding the phrase 'contrary to honest practices in industrial or commercial matters', Justice Fernando, in the *Sumeet Research & Holdings* case, gave a broad definition to include higher standards of conduct, norms of business ethics that do not merely restate existing legal obligations and the determination of such standards of conduct is a matter for the trial judge.[403] Commendably, the *Post*-Sumeet Research and Holdings case law development suggests that Sri Lankan law is moving towards a broad and flexible concept of unfair competition. Perhaps more encouragingly, in *Viocom International Inc v The Maharaja Organization Ltd*, another landmark judgment of the Sri Lankan Supreme Court, recently recognized that unfair competition law safeguards not only the interests of the traders and service providers but also of the consumers.[404]

Perhaps more significantly, in *James Finlay and Company Ltd. v. Stassen Exports Ltd,*[405] Justice CV Wigneswaran highlighted the importance of Sri Lankan law moving from the narrow passing off principle to a broader understanding of unfair competition law. As his Lordship rightly pointed out, there is no need for us to conclude that English law principles were introduced to Sri Lanka through the Code of Intellectual Property Act. The Act itself is based on the model of the United International Bureaus for the Protection of Intellectual Property (BIRPI). The Act must be interpreted as is, and any attempt to read into its provisions the principles and traditions peculiar to English law might do harm to the Act.[406] Though this statement refers to the earlier Code, the importance of this judicial pronouncement is great. It is hoped that future decisions would follow the same path with this consistent pattern. There is absolutely no need to go back to the narrow scope of the passing off tort. One of the most significant changes that has occurred in the unfair competition law landscape in Sri Lanka in recent years is the move from the traditional English Common Law approach to a broader international concept of unfair competition. This trend has been amply demonstrated by the developments of the statutory regime and its approval by the judiciary in subsequent decisions. This positive development is more in line with the continental European

403 (1997) vol 2 Sri LR 393, 402.
404 As per Justice R Fernando (2006) vol 1 Sri LR 140, 150.
405 (2001) 3 Sri LR 336.
406 Ibid.

approach to unfair competition, which has found its way to set international norms through the Paris Convention and the TRIPS Agreement. Besides, the international unfair competition law anchored in Article 10*bis* has further been developed by WIPO Model Provisions on protection against unfair competition that has gone beyond these two key international instruments.[407] In fact, the WIPO Model provisions are an extremely useful tool for countries wishing to adopt or improve their legislation on unfair competition. This progressive development no doubt, is useful for the Sri Lankan context in terms of interpretation of provisions set out in section 160 of the Act.

3.1.5. How Effective is Unfair Competition Law to Protect Sub-patentable Innovation?

Broadly speaking, an unfair competition regime provides protection for technical and non-technical achievements of business entities in Sri Lanka. Interestingly, as evidenced from relatively high numbers of reported and unreported cases, the protection against unfair competition has been popularly used by industrial and commercial sectors in the country, especially the competitors in the tea industry. The evidence gathered from interviews with large, medium and small enterprises suggests that there is a serious issue in relation to imitation and copying of new products in Sri Lankan markets. The survey evidence from judges, legal academics and lawyers in Sri Lanka has further confirmed that the unfair competition regime is one of the most used mechanisms in both trial and appellate courts. Little is known, however, about the effectiveness of the unfair competition regime as an instrument in protecting small incremental improvement from the exploitation of existing technologies by the SME sector. At first sight, unfair competition regime should be able to accord a reasonable protection for innovation that falls through the safety net of patent and design regimes. In reality, as earlier observed, unfair competition law has become a platform to introduce protection for all sorts of

---

407 WIPO, *Model Provisions on Protection Against Unfair Competition* (WIPO 1996). This model law is a type of guidelines and no binding effect under Public International Law.

achievements which IP laws cannot properly accommodate.[408] But then again the question would arise as to whether such protection is appropriate and desirable from IP law policy perspectives. There lies a danger that the over-stretching of the unfair competition regime to accommodate sub-patentable innovation would undermine the delicate balance between the other IP regime on the one hand, and unfair competition on the other. Similarly, it might also be argued that the unfair competition law would have an adverse impact on the freedom of imitation. Cornish makes trenchant criticism of too carefree an adoption of wide-ranging unfair competition emphasizing the potential danger of such as a remedy.[409] Perhaps more importantly, unfair competition rules supplement in some cases the protection of industrial property rights, such as patents and trademarks. Unlike the latter, however, the protection against unfair competition does not entail the granting of exclusive rights, thus a granting of license is not possible.[410] Another possible downside of relying on unfair competition to protect subpatentable innovations is that such protection relates to the conduct of an imitator, rather than what is imitated. Therefore, it is submitted that an unfair competition regime cannot be viewed as an effective protection mechanism as such.

3.1.6. Passing-off Action

In Sri Lanka, the passing off action is quite often pursued in infringement actions as the second or alternative course of action in a context where unfair competition is available. Arguably, this is an undesirable practice from a legal policy perspective. Since Sri Lankan law has been heavily influenced by English Common Law, the legal profession is inclined to use English legal principles. As a fact, English law remains skeptical about the

---

408 C Heath, *Intellectual Property Law in Asia* (vol 5, Kluwer Law 2003) Max Planck Series on Asian IP Law 155.

409 C Colsten and K Middleton, *Modern intellectual Property law* (2nd edn, Cavendish Publishing 2005) 39 (Cornish argues that such a remedy can all too easily become a weapon by which first entrants on the market can engage in legalistic bullying of those who would subsequently seek to compete with them).

410 UNCTAD-ICTSD, *Resource Book on TRIPS and Development* (Cambridge University Press 2005) 551.

value of a law of unfair competition.[411] It traditionally refused to deal with concepts such as fairness or good faith in business, leaving the marketplace to determine its own morality without the force of legal sanction.[412] The tort of passing off is a judge-made law that evolved through judicial precedent. The essence of the passing off action, as enunciated in the House of Lords decision of *Reddaway v Banham* by Lord Halsbury, is that 'nobody has any right to represent his goods as the goods of somebody else'.[413] The tort of passing off is concerned with misappropriation by misrepresentation. It offers protection of goodwill against misrepresentations that would mislead the public as to the origin or quality of goods and services. In recent years, the passing off action has mostly been used in the context of trademark actions. As has been authoritatively established in *Reckitt & Colman v Bolden*, the case which has become a 'traveling jurisprudence' in many Common Law countries, the essential ingredients of passing off have now been reduced to three elements.[414] To establish the right of action, one must prove the 'so-called classic trinity': goodwill or reputation, misappropriation and damage. Goodwill has been defined as the 'attractive force which brings in customers'.[415] Moreover, in a passing off action, the defendant must represent his goods or services to be those of the claimant,[416] and the claimant should have suffered damages due to the defendant's conduct.

---

411 A Roberson and A Horton, 'Does the United Kingdom or the European Community Need an Unfair Competition Law?'(1995) 12 European Intellectual Property Law Review 568.

412 Ibid 569.

413 *Reddaway v Banham* (1896) AC 199, 204. See also WR Cornish and D Llewelyn, *Intellectual Property: Patents, Copyrights & Trade Marks and Allied Rights* (6th edn, Sweet & Maxwell 2007) 627.

414 As per Lord Oliver in *Reckit & Colman v Bolden (Jif Lemon case)* (1990) RPC341. Previously in *Erven Warnink* case (1979) AC 731, another leading case Lord Diplock has set out a five factor test to establish a passing off claim, namely: (1) misrepresentation; (2) made by a trader in the course of trade; (3) to prospective customers of his or ultimate consumers of goods or services supplied by him; (4) which is calculated to injure the business or goodwill of another trader; (5) and which causes actual damage to the business or goodwill of the trader bringing the action.

415 RM Hilty and F Henning-Bodewig, *Law of Unfair Competition: Towards a New Paradigm in Europe?* (Springer 2007) 190.

416 P Torremans, *Holyoak and Torremans Intellectal Property Law* (4th edn, OUP 2005) 446-467.

In this context, it is important to understand the meaning of the words 'misrepresentation' and 'misappropriation' along with their conceptual underpinnings. The phrase 'misrepresentation' means saying something which is wrong or not true, while 'misappropriation' is taking away someone else's trade values. In many continental European jurisdictions, protection is available against misappropriation of trade values as such. In contrast, English law only provides for misappropriation carried out by misrepresentation, that is, by saying something which is wrong. As a result English law provides for a limited scope of protection, despite the attempt by the House of Lords' to liberalize the range of actionable misappropriation in the *Advocaat* case, a leading case on the issue.[417] Undoubtedly, the English law approach is much narrower in comparison to other continental European jurisdictions with regard to misappropriation of trade values. This difference is amply highlighted in the Privy Council decision of *Cadbury-Schweppes v. Pub Squash*.[418] In *Pub Squash* case, there was no misrepresentation whatsoever and no confusion caused between the drinks of the respective parties, which means that there is nothing wrong in that respect. The *Pub Squash* decision of the Privy Council is a clear case of misappropriation, because the defendant company had tried to take away the goodwill that the plaintiff company had built up with significant financial investment.

Unfortunately, the attempt to persuade the Privy Council to develop a concept similar to that which exists in continental Europe with regard to the right to restrain unfair competition by protecting trade values in the *Pub Squash* case was not welcomed by the Law Lords. The reluctance on the part of judiciary to expand the scope of passing off was demonstrated by the decision of Lord Scarman.[419] In hindsight, it very much depends on judicial creativity and the willingness of judges to stretch the boundaries of law. Perhaps Lord Denning said it best when he wrote that the develop-

---

417 As per Lord Diplock in *Even Warnink Besloten Vennootschap v. J. Towned & Sons (Hull) Ltd. and Other Respondents* (1979) AC 731. Most notably, this decision of House of Lord shows a high point in a gradual extension of passing off.

418 The decision of Privy Council (1981) RPC 429, in this Australian case, the plaintiff intensively promoted a lemon squash using various slogans and themes. The defendant launched his own squash and employed similar marketing and advertising themes. The Privy Council concluded that unfair competition is based upon misappropriation and there is no cause of action for misappropriation as such.

419 *Cadbury-Schweppes v. Pub Squash* (1981) RPC 429.

ment of law depends on 'bold spirits and timorous souls'.[420] According to Andrew Terry, 'reaping without sowing' will continue to haunt the intellectual property jurisdiction until one of Lord Denning's 'bold spirits' pushes back the perceived limits of judicial doctrine and formalities in the judiciary's sphere of influence, or the legislature intervenes.[421] The current status of English law relating to unfair competition is without critics. For instance, Gerald Dworkin states that unless it can be protected by one of the recognized IP or other 'property rights' reaping without sowing may escape liability.[422]

Nevertheless, Cornish argues that the fundamental British skepticism towards the expansion of unfair competition law is due to excessive protection. In England, consumers are protected by both criminal law and public authorities, with the result that there is no need for competitors' actions to protect the consumer.[423] There is no doubt that English law's argumentation is based on the premise that too much protection would restrict free competition. The rationale of this argument would be that the world needs to keep a strict rein on the spread of unfair competition liability, for it can all too easily become a weapon by which first entrants on the successful market can engage in legislative bullying of those who would subsequently seek to compete with them.[424] This English law approach with regard to passing off action has been followed by many Commonwealth jurisdictions including India, Pakistan, Sri Lanka and even Malaysia.

---

420 See the dissenting judgment of Lord Denning in *Candler v. Crane, Christmas and Co* [1951] 2 KB 164, 178 (the occasional victories of the 'bold spirits' over the 'timorous souls').

421 A Terry, 'Unfair Competition and the Misappropriation of a Competitor's Trade Values' (1988) 51 Modern Law Review 296, 322.

422 G Dworkin, 'Unfair Competition: Is the Common Law Developing a New Tort?' (1978/9) 1 European Intellectual Property Law Review 241, 246.

423 RM Hilty and F Henning-Bodewig, *Law of Unfair Competition: Towards a New Paradigm in Europe?* (Springer 2007) 263.

424 WR Cornish, 'Genevan Bootstraps' (1997) 7 European Intellectual Property Law Review 336, 337.

3.1.7. Current Status of Passing-off Action in Sri Lanka

As the Sri Lankan legal framework is based on Common Law legal principles, their influence cannot easily be disregarded. Before the introduction of the Code of IP Act of 1979, the protection against acts of unfair competition was provided by the general concept of passing-off. Thus, one can reasonably argue that the passing of action is well established in the domestic legal system. Then a question that arises today is whether or not the action for passing off has, in view of the provisions relating to unfair competition embodied in the Act (formerly the Code of 1979), ceased to exist in the Sri Lankan legal system.[425] There are two lines of argument on this point. It was pointed out by several members of the Sri Lankan judiciary (during our interviews with them) that there is absolutely no need to look for passing off action as it only protects just one form of unfair competition, namely, the protection of reputation or goodwill which is covered by the broad scope of an unfair competition regime. Thus, judges should not allow passing off action to be claimed and maintained in an action for infringement. Nevertheless, Karunaratna, one of the leading scholars in the field of IP in Sri Lanka, counter-argues this point and maintains that this question is yet to receive the attention of an authoritative court.

> 'It is arguable that the statutory provisions on unfair competition cover the acts of passing off and consequently, the law of passing off has become irrelevant and redundant. On the contrary, it may also be arguable that the action for passing off is a remedy available in Common Law and it continues its presence in the law of Sri Lanka despite the statutory provisions relating to unfair competition. The Code of Intellectual Property Act or the IP Act of 2003 has not expressly abolished the action for passing off. Consequently, it appears that both the Common Law remedy and as well as the statutory remedy co-exist'.[426]

Even an analysis of earlier case-law would suggest a similar kind of conclusion that the passing off action remains unaffected, though the IP Act has not specifically provided for it.[427] In light of the above, it seems logi-

---

425 DM Karunaratna, *Law of Trademarks and Service Marks in Sri Lanka* (Sarvodaya Vishva Lekha Publishers 1997) 145.

426 DM Karunaratna, *Elements of the Law of Intellectual Property in Sri Lanka* (Sarasavi Publishers 2010) 344.

427 Case law such as *Kapadia v. Mohamad* (1918) 22 NLR 314 and *Liver Brothers v. R. M. Renganathan Pillai* (1937) 39 NLR 332 provide argument for the above proposition.

cal to argue that the passing off action has been recognized by implication. Although the current IP Act has not explicitly preserved the passing-off action as a separate cause of action, the ramifications of case law supports the retention of the same. This argument can be buttressed by recourse to Justice Shaw's decision in *Kapadiya v Mohamed*, where the court held that even though passing-off actions are not specifically reserved in our trade mark Ordinance, such an action can be maintained under Sri Lankan law.[428] Furthermore, our survey evidence suggests that there is a tendency of Sri Lankan legal practitioners to file actions based on passing off action. One possible explanation would be that they are more familiar with English Law principles than the IP Act. Yet another reason for this would be that the legal community is less familiar with the modern concept of unfair competition. This development is neither encouraging nor desirable as the concept of unfair competition attracts broader protection than the action for passing off. There is an uncertainty, however, as to the correct legal position. Understandably, the opinions are divided and some judges and academics consider that passing off action is still available in spite of the comprehensive protection scheme provided in IP Act. The question then arises, should there still be any role for the passing-off action in Sri Lanka? The answer is probably no. This answer follows logically from the provisions of the current IP Act which has a broader scope of protection though both unfair competition law and passing-off closely overlap. In short, the protection afforded by unfair competition law inevitably diminishes the role of passing-off action.[429] Since there has been so far no decision on this issue under the new Act, one has to wait until Sri Lankan the Supreme Court is confronted with this issue in the future. But for the sake of argument, one can still highlight the importance of passing-off action as a gap-filler of trademark law as used in England.

3.1.8. Conclusion

In essence, unfair competition law regulates the behaviour of the competitors in the market and ensures that competition is fairly and properly carried on. The great strength of unfair competition is that it can extend pro-

---

428 *Kapadiya v. Mohamed* (1918) 20 NLR 314.

429 P Torremans, *Holyoak and Torremans Intellectal Property Law* (4th edn, OUP 2005) 446.

tection for subject matters that other IP rights cannot reach and tackles the problem of free riding and promotes innovation without creating unnecessary barriers for free competition. As noted before, however, the biggest weakness of unfair competition is that the concept is vague, difficult to define and imprecise. As commentators have pointed out, if the courts stretch the arm of protection too far to catch the areas previously unprotected, it would reach an undesirable destination by limiting the vigorous competition on which a market economy is based on. Paradoxically, unfair competition law would create a negative impact on free competition in the market. What is needed is a law to promote responsible business conduct without undermining the delicate balance between unfair competition on one hand, and other branches of IP law on the other. Viewed from a policy perspective, if the unfair competition regime is broadly interpreted to offer protection for incremental innovation, there would also be an allegation that it is creating protection through the back door. Moreover, protection against unfair competition does not entail exclusive rights such as to grant a license in the case of a utility model or petty patent systems.

In the Sri Lankan context, it is especially disappointing that despite the fact that the current IP Act provides broad protection for unfair competition the passing off action is still invoked in many cases of unfair competition probably due to the lack of awareness on the part of legal practitioners and the familiarity of Common Law principles practiced among the legal community for centuries. The case law development in recent years is rather encouraging and Sri Lankan law can be further developed by recourse to international jurisprudence, in particular, learning from the continental European experiences.[430] Furthermore, in defining the boundaries of unfair competition law, it is essential that a balance is struck between, on one hand, the interests of competitors, and, on the other, the interests of consumers and the general public as a whole. Moreover, Sri Lankan courts should closely follow international developments and legislative patterns in order to meet new situations and circumstances. Only this type of approach will allow the future of unfair competition law of Sri Lanka to support one of the fundamental goals of a free market economy: fair competition in the market. Last but not the least, minor and incremental innovations may indirectly be protected under the existing unfair competition

430 For example, Germany-Act Against Unfair Competition 2004 (as last amended 1October 2013) available at WIPO Official website: <http://www.wipo.int/wipolex/en/details.jsp?id=14027> (accessed 12 March 2013).

regime in Sri Lanka, but such protection may not be real or an ideal protection that would incentivise such innovations.

3.2. Trade Secrets Protection

> *'He who has received information in confidence shall not take unfair advantage of it'.*
> *Lord Denning*[431]

3.2.1. Background and the Emergence of Trade Secret Law

As succinctly illustrated by Lord Denning, the legal concept of breach of confidence in Common Law jurisdictions emanated from the Chancery Courts in the nineteenth century.[432] Trade secrets law is a relative latecomer to the IP pantheon,[433] and in many ways, trade secrets law is the 'Cinderella' of the IP law field, the forgotten step-daughter who toils in the shadow of her more privileged siblings: patent, copyright and trademark law.[434] Even though trade secret law in its modern form in Anglo-American jurisprudence is a Common Law creation, there were forms of trade secret protection in Europe dating perhaps as far back as Roman times.[435] In the world of IP, the legal protection of trade secrets (often referred to as undisclosed information) is considered to be 'soft intellectual property' which lies on the periphery of hardcore IP such as patent and copyright.[436] According to Posner, IP rights tend to be limited in time, but there are forms of IP or quasi-IP that do not have durational limitation.[437] One of the prominent exemptions to durational limitation of IP is trade se-

---

431 *Seager v. Copydex Ltd* (1967) 1 WLR 923, 931.

432 Ibid.

433 MA Lemley, 'The Surprising Virtues of Treating Trade Secrets as IP Rights' (2008) 61/2 Stanford Law Review 311, 315.

434 PK Yu (ed), *Intellectual Property and Information Wealth: Patents and Trade Secrets* (Praeger 2007) 399.

435 MA Lemley, 'The Surprising Virtues of Treating Trade Secrets as IP Rights' (2008) 61/2 Stanford Law Review 311, 325.

436 See also, Justice Raynor Asher, 'Breach of Confidence' (2009) March, IP Forum 3, 4.

437 RA Posner, 'Do We Have Too Many Intellectual Property Rights?'(2005) 9 Intellectual Property Review 173, 174-175.

crets protection. Posner further argues that trade secrets are IP in only a special sense because the main trade secret law only allows its owner to enforce tort law and contract law against efforts to appropriate some secret process or methods that he has. As long as copiers and imitators avoid violating tort law or contract law they can make use of other firms' secrets after disclosing them through legal means such as reverse engineering.[438] Nevertheless, today, trade secrets are among the most valuable assets that enterprises own and the ability of companies to compete in any market depends on their ability to acquire and maintain a competitive advantage.[439] Companies carefully guard essential and sensitive information that has an impact on a company's strength to compete. Protecting this sensitive information as a trade secret is one legal mechanism that companies generally use to this end.[440] From a historical perspective, trade secrets laws developed as a substitute for the physical and contractual restrictions those companies would otherwise impose in an effort to prevent a competitor from acquiring their information.[441] Therefore, it appears that trade secret protection is a key aspect of creating a favourable investment climate for businesses in any country. Moreover, some commentators argue that trade secrets law is a useful supplement to patent law because it allows inventors to internalize more of the social benefit of their inventions.[442]

3.2.2. What is a Trade Secret?

Defining the term 'trade secret' is not an easy task, but, very broadly, a trade secret may include 'any information that can be used in the operation of a business or other enterprise and that is sufficiently valuable and secret to afford an actual or potential economic advantage over others'.[443] Obviously, trade secrets are proprietary information that would include cus-

---

438 Ibid 175.

439 BH Malkawi, 'A Critical Look at Trade Secrets Protection in Jordan' (2012) 1 Intellectual Property Quarterly 123, 123.

440 Ibid.

441 MA Lemley, 'The Surprising Virtues of Treating Trade Secrets as IP Rights' (2008) 61/2 Stanford Law Review 311, 336.

442 D Friedman, W Landes and R Posner, 'Some Economics of Trade Secret Law' (1991) 5/1 Journal of Economic Perspectives 61, 64.

443 The American Law Institute, Restatement of the Law (Third) of Unfair Competition (1994) Section 39.

tomer lists, formulas, practices, manufacturing processes, designs and even business plans etc. Even though the TRIPS Agreement, by virtue of Article 2(1) has recognised 'undisclosed information' or trade secret as one of the categories of IP rights, it does not give a specific definition as to what undisclosed information means. Nevertheless, pursuant to Article 39(2), the TRIPS Agreement specifies what conditions that such information needs to meet in order to be protected as trade secrets. It is obvious from the wording of the article that such information should be secret, possess a commercial value and be subject to reasonable steps, under the circumstances, to be kept secret.[444] From an innovation perspective, by creating a right to protect information, trade secrets (from European terminology, secret know-how) act as an incentive for investment in technological development.[445] Moreover, trade secrets law provides the means to exclude third parties from misusing valuable knowledge and thus increases the competitive advantage and the expected returns of innovation. And it also provides a basis for technology transfer.[446] Significantly, the theoretical underpinning of the protection for trade secrets may be traced primarily to two main theories. The first counts in its utilitarian justification, according to which the protection against the theft of proprietary information encourages investment in such information.[447] The second is a duty-based theory which emphasizes the maintenance of commercial morality and thus the aim of trade secret law is to punish and prevent illicit behavior, and even to uphold reasonable standards of commercial behavior.[448] Arguably, the trade secret regime provides an additional incentive to innovate beyond what may be possible under other IP rights, especially patents.

---

444 See also UNCTAD-ICTSD, *Resource Book on TRIPS and Development* (Cambridge University Press 2005) 521.

445 H Lovells-International LLP, Report on Trade Secrets for the European Commission (2012) 5.

446 Ibid.

447 MA Lemley, 'The Surprising Virtues of Treating Trade Secrets as IP Rights' (2008) 61/2 Stanford Law Review 311, 320.

448 Ibid.

3.2.3. Current Protection of Trade Secrets in the IP Act

Like in some other jurisdictions, even under Sri Lankan IP law, trade secrets are referred to as confidential information. The key provisions of the Sri Lankan trade secret law are found in the section for unfair competition. In other words, trade secret provisions are incorporated into the section dealing with the unfair competition. Presumably, the reason for not addressing trade secrets in a separate provision may be due to the legislature's thinking that trade secrets should be treated as a part or subset of unfair competition. Nevertheless, more encouragingly, by virtue of Section 160(6) of the IP Act of 2003, in the history of IP law has attempted to grant statutory protection for undisclosed information for the first time. Pursuant to Section 160(6)(a) any act or practice, in the course of industrial or commercial activities, that results in the disclosure, acquisition or use by others, of undisclosed information without the consent of the person lawfully in control of that information and in a manner contrary to honest commercial practices shall constitute an act of unfair competition. At a glance, this provision covers a large array of instances of disclosure, acquisition or use of trade secrets. More significantly, even though the Act does not define what undisclosed information means, it sets out what conditions that information needs to fulfill in order to qualify for protection as undisclosed information. Accordingly, information shall be considered 'undisclosed information' if: (i) it is not, generally known among, or readily accessible to, persons within the circles that normally deal with the kind of information in question; (ii) it has actual or potential commercial value because it is secret; and (iii) it has been subject to reasonable steps under the circumstances by the rightful holder to keep it secret.[449] In fact, this provision corresponds to Article 39 of the TRIPS Agreement. Moreover, the wording of the provision reveals that such information shall include technical information, as well as business information. Arguably, it needs to be interpreted broadly and not as limitative.[450]

By following the approach of footnote 10 of the TRIPS Agreement, Section 160(6)(b) of the Act provides certain examples of disclosure, acquisition and use of undisclosed information 'contrary to honest commercial practices' including, industrial espionage, breach of contract, induce-

---

449 See Section 160 (6)(c) of the IP Act of Sri Lanka No 36, 2003.
450 See Section 160 (6)(e).

ment to breach of contract, and includes the acquisition of undisclosed information by third parties who knew, or were grossly negligent in failing to know, that such practices were involved in the acquisition of such information.[451] It is also evident that the IP Act has imposed legal obligations, by virtue of Section 160(6)(d), upon public authorities regarding the information coming to their possession. In particular, this provision provides protection for secret test data or other data that is submitted for approval from relevant regulatory authorities. Moreover, not only civil remedies, even criminal sanctions may be invoked against a person who willfully or without lawful authority discloses any undisclosed information.[452] As another important matter, Section 160(9) has expressly provided that, unlike in the case of unfair competition, provisions relating to undisclosed information in the Act exist in addition to the Common Law rights. It means that the Common Law action for breach of confidence remains unaffected by the provisions in the IP Act. Last but certainly not the least, the protection of undisclosed information under the provisions of the IP Act has been relied upon, before the Commercial High Court of Sri Lanka, at least, in several cases so far.[453]

3.2.4. Common Law Action for Breach of Confidence

The breach of confidence action is rooted in the law of equity and developed through principles and rules laid down by Chancery and Common Law courts. Sri Lanka being a Commonwealth country has long followed Common Law jurisprudence. Before the introduction of the New IP Act 2003, the breach of confidence action was the principle means of protecting trade secrets in Sri Lanka. As noted above, the current IP Act has specifically stated that the Common Law rights are unaffected by the pro-

---

451 TRIPS Agreement's footnote 10: 'For the purpose of this provision, 'a manner contrary to honest commercial practices' shall mean at least practices such as breach of contract, breach of confidence and inducement to breach, and includes the acquisition of undisclosed information by third parties who knew, or were grossly negligent in failing to know, that such practices were involved in the acquisition.

452 See Section 160 (8), if convicted, such a person may be liable to a fine or to imprisonment or for both.

453 See *Mackwoods Ltd v. Manoj Wickramatunga & Another* (CHC/Case No: 37/2003(3).

visions of section 160(6) relating to undisclosed information. Thus, it is obvious that the protection of trade secrets can be sought under principles of Common Law and equity as followed by Sri Lankan courts. One of the major advantages of the breach of confidence action is that, irrespective of the existence of contractual obligations, courts can grant remedies for breach of confidence by relying on the broad equitable doctrine that 'he who has received information in confidence shall not take undue advantage of it'.[454] In cases of misuse of trade secrets, as they are more familiar with the Common Law rights, Sri Lankan legal practitioners are often inclined to file such cases based on the breach of confidence claim in the District Court (the first instance court on civil matters) instead of going to commercial high court on the basis of the provisions of IP Act. Bringing the action in the Commercial High Court, which is the specialized court for IP matters, would however have the advantage of getting the case heard by judges who are better aware of IP issues.

As enunciated by Megarry J in *Coco v. AN Clark (Engineers) Ltd*, a landmark case in Common Law jurisprudence, the main elements of breach of confidence action are: (1) information should have the necessary quality of confidence; (2) it should be imparted in confidence; and (3) the person who received the information must have misused it.[455] Today, these elements of a breach of confidence action have become the general requirements and are followed in Common Law jurisdictions, including Sri Lanka. Moreover, as a result of further judicial developments of law in this area, the 'springboard' doctrine has emerged to prevent a person who is in breach of a confidentiality obligation from obtaining an unfair advantage, even when information is in the public domain. According to this doctrine, a person who has obtained information in confidence is not allowed to use it as a springboard for activities detrimental to the person who made the communication.[456] Consequently, a person who has used the information in breach of confidence may still be under an obligation not to compete with the owner of the trade secret for a certain period of time even after the information ceases to be confidential. In a breach of confidence action, Common Law remedies of injunctions and damages are generally granted by the courts and a number of superior

---

454 As per Lord Denning in *Seager v. Copydex Ltd* (1967) 2 All ER 415.

455 (1969) RPC 41.

456 As per Roxburgh J in *Terrapin Ltd v. Builder's Supply Co.* (Hayes) Ltd (1967) RPC 375.

court decisions[457] in recent years suggest that the beach of confidence action is fairly used by the Sri Lankan industrial sectors in protecting their valuable trade secrets. Nevertheless, the reliance on the Common Law action has its own downside because the judicial decisions in this area depend very much on the particular facts and circumstances of each case and the court has to decide on a case by case basis whether the information is qualified for protection or not. Of course, this task involves judicial anthropology, an endeavor at which the judges may not be particularly skilled and the judge, after all, is on the outside, looking in.[458] Arguably, this would create clouds of uncertainty for the business sector that primarily rely on such protection. Nevertheless, it might still be argued whether there is a need for a separate trade secrets provisions in the IP Act when the Common Law principle would suffice.

3.2.5. Other Legal Regimes: Contract and Labour Law

The area of trade secrets law has a fascinating interface with other branches of law. Thus, courts, lawyers, scholars, and treatise writers argue over whether trade secrets are a creature of contract, tort, property, labour, or even criminal law. In that sense, trade secrets law is simply a compilation of bits and pieces of other laws.[459] From a labour law perspective, the Common Law master and servant relationship imposes a duty of loyalty and fidelity upon all employees. As judicial pronouncements have further illuminated, such a fiduciary obligation is implied by the contract of employment.[460] Most significantly, in many cases, business firms in Sri Lanka rely on contractual liability to prevent unauthorized disclosure of secret information and to stop employees walking out with trade secrets and join-

457 *Coats Thread Lanka (Pvt) Ltd v. Samarasundara* 2011 BLR 37, *Hently Garments Ltd v. JSA Fernando* (1980) 2 Sri LR 145. *Finlay Rentokil Ltd v. Vivekananda* (1995) 2 Sri LR 346. *Caldera v. John Keels Holdings Ltd (*1986) 1 CALR 575.

458 SL Carter, 'Custom Adjudication, and Petrushevsky's Watch: Some Notes from the Intellectual Property Front' (1992) 72 Virginia Law Review 129.

459 MA Lemley, 'The Surprising Virtues of Treating Trade Secrets as IP Rights' (2008) 61/2 Stanford Law Review 311, 312.

460 See *Robb v. Green* (1895) 2 QB 315.

ing other competitors.[461] These contractual arrangements can generally take the form of either non-disclosure or non-compete covenants. As many other Common Law courts, Sri Lanka, has been very reluctant to enforce such contracts in restraint of trade, especially post-contractual obligations involving ex-employees, citing public policy reasons. Critics point out that these covenants impose draconian limits on the mobility of employees in the ever-changing employment market. Thus, it might still be argued that an ex-employee is free to use the skill and knowledge acquired during employment in exercising his or her profession.

An analysis of the latest case-law of the Sri Lankan Supreme Court shows that the courts engage in a two-step inquiry into post-employment obligations. Whenever the employer tries to enforce such restrictive clauses, courts first examine whether the contract is so restrictive of the employee's liberty, and if so, the agreement is considered to be *prima facie* void.[462] Then it is up to the employer to show that the covenant can be justified as being reasonable in the light of the interests of both parties and the public.[463] Sri Lankan courts have adopted the test of reasonability in ascertaining the validity of any covenant of restraint of trade.[464] In analyzing reasonableness, the court needs to investigate whether the post-employment restrictions are justifiable in terms of scope, geography and time to protect the legitimate interests of the employer in view of employee's freedom of employment. Arguably, courts have to achieve a reasonable balance between economic incentives for employers on the one hand and the employee's interests in maintaining his employment option on the other. Nevertheless, the law in this area is neither clear nor well-settled and the outcome of the case depends on the particular facts and circumstances of each individual case. Sri Lankan court decisions are highly influenced by Common Law case-law developments in this area of law. Viewed from a different perspective, the legal regimes under the trade secrets law and

---

461 WADJ Sumanadasa, 'The Intersection of Contract Law with IP Law in the Protection of Undisclosed Information: A Sri Lankan Perspective' ((2012) Annual Research Symposium of the University of Colombo, Sri Lanka 160-162.

462 *Finlay Renckotill (Ceylon) Limited v. Viveknanthan* (1995) 2 Sri LR 345.

463 As per Ranasinghe J in *Hentley Garments v. GSA Fernando* (1980) 2 Sri LR 145.

464 See JAN de Silva CJ in *Coats Thread Lanka (Pvt) Ltd v. Samarasundara* (2011) BLR 37.

restraint of trade agreements are not mutually exclusive, but overlapping.[465] On the other hand, trade secrets law goes beyond contract law and reaches where contract law alone cannot.[466] However, the most serious concern with contract law is that its protection is limited to privity of contract. It means that, whenever an outsider or third party is involved in the act of misappropriation of trade secrets, contract law has no satisfactory remedy.

3.2.6. Empirical Evidence

The survey evidence gathered from large and SME sectors suggests that the use of trade secrets protection in the Sri Lankan industry is quite encouraging.[467] The information obtained through telephone interviews with the Sri Lankan SME sector has confirmed that many firms (more than 60 percent) use at least informal means of secrecy to protect their products and processes. Most of them utilize access restrictions to control valuable information getting into the hands of their competitors. Nevertheless, firms in the SME sector hardly use legal advice in protecting their trade secrets. Almost none of the respondent firms had any in-house lawyers or counsels to provide necessary assistance to deal with trade secrets issues. Most notably, at least several SMEs in the TK-based product sector (i.e. herbal beauty-care products and its herbal medicine industry) have employed legal officers to deal with undisclosed information and issues relating to employment contracts with employees. Thus, it is evident that the TK-based industrial sectors especially use trade secret protection as an ap-

465 WADJ Sumanadasa, 'The Intersection of Contract Law with IP Law in the Protection of Undisclosed Information: A Sri Lankan Perspective' ((2012) Annual Research Symposium of the University of Colombo, Sri Lanka 160-162.

466 MA Lemley, 'The Surprising Virtues of Treating Trade Secrets as IP Rights' (2008) 61/2 Stanford Law Review 311, 331-332.

467 Information gathered through conducting face to face interviews and detailed telephone interviews with the owners, managers, and legal officers of large, small and medium sized enterprises consisting of 5 large and 25 SMEs in Sri Lanka. These respondent-firms were selected from a list of SMEs in Sri Lanka, whose contact details were obtained from the government Ministry of Productivity Promotion and 5 other large companies were selected representing different industrial and commercial sectors in Sri Lanka. These interviews were carried out in 2011 and 2012.

propriate means of protecting their innovative products and processes. Moreover, a large part of TK-based enterprises belong to so-called 'family businesses' and it is observed that such firms keep their traditional recipes and formulas within family boundaries. As a general matter, expenses and costs involved in securing patent or other IP rights have encouraged SMEs to use secrecy in their innovative activities. It is notable, when asked about the reasons for not using the patent system to protect innovation, not only the SMEs sector but also large firms answered that they have serious concerns about the disclosure requirement and they did not want their competitors to see their valuable information. Significantly, there is both logical and evidentiary reason to believe that, even though trade secrets protection may not be very effective to protect innovative achievements of firms, many enterprises use such protection mainly due to the lack of awareness of other IP regimes, procedural impediments (difficulties) in acquiring IP rights and various costs involved in maintaining and enforcing IP rights. As commentators have rightly pointed out, SMEs often use trade secrets protection by default, i.e. as a way of avoiding the expenditure and administrative procedures involved in patent protection, without taking adequate measures that need to be in place in order to ensure that confidential information is considered a legally protectable trade secret.[468]

3.2.7. Why is Trade Secrets Protection so Attractive?

Probably, due to the strategic importance of trade secrets protection, many firms rely heavily on such protection, irrespective of being big or small. According to scholars, keeping an innovation as a trade secret offers its owners some significant advantages over other forms of IP rights.[469] It is cheaper and quicker to obtain, since it does not require government approval, and it extends the protection to types of business and process information that are unlikely to be patentable.[470] Interestingly, there is a growing number of innovators who do not wish to apply for patent protection due to the disclosure requirement and they fear that, if the relevant infor-

---

468 WIPO, *Intellectual Property Rights and Innovation in Small and Medium-Sized Enterprises* (WIPO 2004) 9.

469 MA Lemley, 'The Surprising Virtues of Treating Trade Secrets as IP Rights' (2008) 61/2 Stanford Law Review 311, 313.

470 Ibid.

mation is disclosed, their products would easily be copied by competitors. Moreover, unlike other IP rights, a trade secret can be protected for an indefinite period of time as long as it remains secret. Globally, the food and beverages industries have a keen interest in keeping their proprietary information secret for example Coca Cola's secret formula. Most significantly, trade secrets laws protect types of information that do not qualify for protection under the patent regime and this may be one of the reasons why it is more attractive for many SMEs. As noted in the previous Chapter, the innovations made by SMEs are often characterized by minor adaptation of existing products and emanate from the informal sector making them rely on secrecy. It is obvious that any kind of invention that confers a competitive advantage on its owner may be protected under a trade secrets regime. In that sense, trade secrets protection gives firms additional incentives for innovation.[471]

As argued by scholars, "another reason for choosing the trade secret route is that it gives the developer of new and valuable information, a right to restrict others from using it, and therefore the prospect of deriving profits from the information".[472] This may be true of business as well as technical secrets, since some protection for business ideas helps ensure a first-mover advantage for those who take risks on untested business models.[473] Perhaps more interestingly, one of the great strengths of trade secrets protection is protecting technical information of 'easy to invent/design around' products for which trade secrets protection is far more satisfactory than patents. Furthermore, trade secrets protection can coexist with contractual obligations in order to extend protection beyond the privity of contract. As noted above, trade secrets protection can be a valuable alternative which can supplement and/or complement other IP rights. As survey evidence suggests, from a practical perspective, immediate protection compared to patent or trademark rights which usually require several years of waiting for registration (at least four years waiting in the case of patents), is more effective and appropriate for fast-moving consumer goods industries that need quick protection. When compared to other IP rights, of course with the exception of trademark cases, trade secret litigations are a relatively frequent phenomenon in the Sri Lankan context. This

471 See *Kewanee Oil Co. v. Bicron Corp* (1974) 416 US 470, 481-485.

472 MA Lemley, 'The Surprising Virtues of Treating Trade Secrets as IP Rights' (2008) 61/2 Stanford Law Review 311, 330.

473 Ibid.

is no surprise given that costs involved in acquiring; maintaining and enforcing patent rights makes such a protection mechanism unattractive for many SMEs. Sri Lankan case-law also shows that many cases have been filed based on breach of confidence premised on contractual obligation.

3.2.8. Difficulties and Challenges for SMEs

Even though trade secrets protection provides incentives for innovators by protecting valuable investment in technological progress, there may also be considerable disadvantages and risks associated with such a protection mechanism. One of the major concerns in this regard relates to the enforcement aspect of trade secrets protection in Sri Lanka. As in many other jurisdictions, there is always a risk that court proceedings might lead to possible further disclosure of a trade secret.[474] Arguably, there should be clear legal provisions against such public disclosure of trade secrets during and after litigations. The current IP Act of Sri Lanka does not contain any legal provision specifically designed to address this issue. Nor is there any case-law dealing with such a situation. Survey evidence obtained from legal practitioners in Sri Lanka confirmed that, in many cases that involve misappropriation of trade secrets, the plaintiff has to describe his trade secret in the pleadings supported by other relevant documents, and also in the event of leading evidence in open court, such court proceedings would further jeopardize the interests of the trade secret owner. One possible solution to this problem is to allow 'in camera' hearing (hearing that excludes the public from court proceedings) and to make confidential schedules to pleadings in trade secret cases.[475] It is clear that Section 160 of the IP Act does not provide for any kind of such protection.

Moreover, Article 106(1) of the Constitution of Sri Lanka provides that all sittings of every court shall be held in public, and all persons shall be entitled freely to attend such sittings. There are exceptions to this constitutional rule in cases such as proceedings relating to family relations, sexual offences and issues relating to national security, but arguably such excep-

474 Hogan Lovells International LLP, *Report on Trade Secrets for the European Commission* (2012) 44. In the Sri Lankan context, the decision of the Commercial High Court in *Link Natural Products Ltd v Tropical Herbs Ltd* (CHC Case No: 25/2001/03 decided on 1 February 2013) illustrates this point.

475 Ibid.

tions would probably not include the protection of trade secrets.[476] The correct legal position under Sri Lankan law is far from clear, but as pointed out by an eminent member of the judiciary and a legal academic in Sri Lanka, the Court can hold proceedings in camera under exceptional circumstances, though the general rule is that the court proceedings must be open to the public. Section 839 of the Civil Procedure Code will provide discretion to the Judge if holding the proceedings in public would defeats the ends of justice; then the Judge can decide to hold it in camera. Pursuant to Section 839 of the Civil Procedure Code, the court has the power to make an order to conduct the proceedings in camera or in an appropriate manner that is necessary for the ends of justice by making use of its inherent powers.[477] However, it is purely a matter that is laft to the discretion of Court. Therefore it depends on the circumstances of each application and one cannot draw a line to identify the area covered under that Section of the Civil Procedure Code.[478] On the most general level, any relief under judicial discretion depends on the skills of the trial lawyer and most importantly the lawyer needs to invite the judiciary to use its inherent discretionary powers to prevent further disclosure of trade secrets. Arguably, due to limited awareness of the lawyers, in many cases the above provision would hardly be used. In view of the above, it can reasonably be argued that the trade secrets regime may not be of any real assistance in practice for SMEs in Sri Lanka as long as it does not provide effective procedural tools to prevent further disclosure of trade secrets in the course of litigation. Understandably, this may be one of the reasons for many firms to avoid going to courts in case of trade secrets violations and, in fact, there could be very little to gain by recourse to legal means of protection. Moreover, not only court proceedings, but also the handling of the case by lawyers (when a case involves technical information lawyers need to consult experts) and a judgment of the court can be a possible source of further disclosure of a trade secret.

476 See Article 106 (2) of the Constitution of Sri Lanka of 1978 as amended.

477 According to Section 839 of the Civil Procedure Code Ordinance No. 2 of 1889 as amended Section 839, nothing in this Ordinance shall be deemed to limit or otherwise affect the inherent power of the court to make such orders as may be necessary for the ends of justice or to prevent abuse of the process of the court.

478 Personal communication with a senior members of Sri Lankan judiciary (email received on 11Februray 2013and a senior legal academic in IP law (email received on 15 February 2013).

Among other concerns, gathering information of misuse would also be a serious issue in the enforcement of trade secrets law by industrial sectors, especially for SMEs. Most notably, in order to be protected, the information should be kept secret. The secrecy requirement, therefore, serves as a gatekeeper function and once the control of access to information is lost there is no protection available.[479] Moreover, when a third party receives a trade secret in good faith, there is no possible remedy. Trade secrets protection has several other downsides. In general, detection of trade secret theft is likely to be very difficult. Unlike tangible property, information can be stolen without depriving the owner of anything observable and without leaving any physical trace of the deed whatsoever.[480] Moreover, the simple fact that a competitor eventually acquired the information is not in itself a sign of stealing; a competitor may properly acquire such information through independent discovery or reverse engineering.[481] Furthermore, the potentially high direct and indirect enforcement costs involved in trade secret law-suits discourage many firms from bringing trade secret suits. One reason for the high costs is the large number of complex factual issues in a trade secret case. For example, plaintiffs must prove that they took reasonable precautions to protect the secret and that the defendant acquired the information from the plaintiff and did so unlawfully.[482] Given the likelihood of concurrent innovation in the technology field, it can often be very difficult to show that the defendant obtained the information improperly. This difficulty is only compounded when a secret is susceptible to lawful reverse engineering.[483] For this reason, the likelihood of success in a trade secret lawsuit is relatively low. Significantly, as scholars pointed out, the uncertain scope and the vague concept of 'commercial morality' of trade secret law create incentives for frivolous litigation designed to harass competitors rather than to obtain relief for trade secret misappropriation.[484] This problem is also aggravated when a company

479 MA Lemley, 'The Surprising Virtues of Treating Trade Secrets as IP Rights' (2008) 61/2 Stanford Law Review 311, 313.

480 RG Bone, 'A New Look at Trade Secret Law: Doctrine in Search of Justification' (1998) 86 /2 California Law Review 241, 278.

481 Ibid.

482 Ibid.

483 BH Malkawi, 'A Critical Look at Trade Secrets Protection in Jordan' (2012) 2 Intellectual Property Quarterly 123, 127.

484 RG Bone, 'A New Look at Trade Secret Law: Doctrine in Search of Justification' (1998) 86 /2 California Law Review 241, 278.

sues ex-employees who leave to start a competing firm in order to hinder their ability to raise capital during the start-up phase. Frivolous suits of this sort not only add to litigation costs, they also chill competition.[485]

A survey of the cases reported in Sri Lanka shows that the majority of trade secrets cases involve disloyal employees who use or disclose their employers' secrets in violation of a duty of confidence stemming from the employment contract. Not many cases have come to courts over improperly acquiring trade secret by theft. But the possibility of espionage or stealing cannot be ruled out as a potential risk, given the increasing use of modern technology in the industry. There has been a number of incidents of computer hacking and other forms of corporate espionage in recent years. In an era of information technology, this may be cause for concern in view of the fact that documents and data can be downloaded, stored and transmitted electronically. As lucidly illustrated by Robert G Bone:

> 'Ideas were like wild animals ferae naturae, common property free for all to enjoy until captured. An idea could be captured by "discovering" it and then excluding others through secrecy. Secrecy required constant vigilance, however, since ideas, like wild animals, had a tendency to escape. Once gone, they returned to the commons as public property'. [486]

According to critics, trade secrets law is in a muddle today. Thus, from a policy perspective, Sri Lankan courts should also need to be very cautious when defining the boundaries of the scope of trade secrets protection because such protection may encroach upon things that are in the public domain which would ultimately defeat the purpose of the law. As has been argued by commentators, an over-generous protection could undermine the objectives of IP regimes, such as copyright and patent law, and have harmful effects on competition.[487]

---

485 Ibid.

486 Ibid 255.

487 See H Carty, 'An Analysis of the Modern Action for Breach of Commercial Confidence: When a Protection is Merited' (2008) 4 Intellectual Property Quarterly 416, 433. See also Lord Hoffmann's statement in *Douglas v Hello!* (2007) UKHL 21, 292. Lord Hoffmann argued that unorthodox forms of IP should not be created by a manipulation of the action for breach of confidence. Furthermore, in the same case, Lord Walker warned that 'uncontrolled growth of the law of confidence… tends to bring incoherence into the law of IP'.

3.2.9. Conclusion

Today, the protection of trade secrets or undisclosed information has a profound impact on the innovation climate of a country. A trade secrets regime primarily deals with the protection of commercially valuable information that is maintained secret. Article 39 of the TRIPS has laid the foundation for international harmonization of such protection. In the Sri Lankan context, apart from the protection under the IP Act, different layers of protection are available such as the Common Law action for breach of confidence and protection under the law of contract. What may be striking is that the statutory protection of undisclosed information is a part of the section that deals with unfair competition law. There may be a need in the future for specific and comprehensive legislation dealing with trade secret protection in order to create a better legal environment. Perhaps more interestingly, trade secrets are more prevalent than ever before among Sri Lankan business enterprises, especially within TK-based firms. There are several reasons for this trend including the disclosure requirement under patent law and the costs involved in acquiring, maintaining and enforcing other IP rights. There are both logical and evidentiary reasons to conclude that a large number of enterprises in Sri Lanka use or have used informal means of secrecy in their businesses. Even though trade secrets protection may, in some cases, supplement or even complement other IP rights, there are practical concerns regarding the enforcement of trade secret rights. In particular, legal proceedings in trade secrets may lead to possible further disclosure. Obviously, there seems to have been no satisfactory answer on this issue at least in the Sri Lankan context.

All in all however, both unfair competition law and trade secret law have an inherent flexibility to extend the protective arm to a number of corners that patent and other IP rights cannot reach. However, herein lies a danger that flexibility may be replaced by incoherence. As noted above, there is always a policy argument that trying to create protection from the back door is undesirable. Viewed from policy perspectives, neither unfair competition law nor trade secrets protection provides a precise form of protection with adequate legal certainty. In that sense, it might still be argued that both regimes would not provide sufficient alternatives to a second-tier protection regime. Conversely, by providing a reasonable protection for simple and obvious innovations that fall through patent and design regimes and by preventing misappropriation of undisclosed information, the trade secrets regime may provide some protection for minor and incremental innovations in the industrial geography of Sri Lanka.

4. Second-Tier Patent Protection in other Jurisdictions: Legislative Examples from outside South Asia

'If I have seen far, it is by standing on the shoulders of giants'.
Sir Isaac Newton[488]

As Sir Isaac Newton himself acknowledged, most innovators stand on the shoulders of giants, and never more so than in the current evolution of high technologies, where almost all technical progress builds on the foundation provided by earlier innovators.[489] It goes without saying that there is no need to reinvent the wheel. The idea behind this statement is that 'the more knowledge that is available, the more can be developed by others'.[490] The same can certainly be applied to countries that need to make innovations in their IP law systems. In that sense, Sri Lanka and other developing countries in the South Asian region, especially those who foresee an STP system in their domestic laws can benefit from reflection on the rich experiences of other jurisdictions. The question is whether such models can serve as blueprints in crafting new STP regimes. This Chapter presents experiences of STP systems in selected developed and developing countries. Each country experience is analysed along the lines of historical development, current legal framework, and economic impact on the basis of empirical data on the use of the system and policy implications. In this study, the German *Gebrauchsmuster* (UM) system and Australian innovation patent system from the developed countries and the experiences of China, Malaysia and Kenya from the developing world will be analysed from critical and comparative perspectives.

488 S Scotchmer, 'Standing on the Shoulders of Giants: Cumulative Research and the Patent Law' (1991) 5/1 Journal of Economic Perspectives 29, 29.

489 Ibid.

490 British Government, *Gowers Riview of Intellectual Property* (HMSO Norwich 2006) 12.

4.1. Experience from Developed Countries

4.1.1. Germany

4.1.1.1. A Brief Historical Overview

> 'The utility model, the 'little brother' of the patent, offers fast and low cost protection for technical inventions'
> *DMPA Annual Report 2011*[491]

From a historical perspective, even though the United Kingdom had a short-lived Utility Designs Act of 1843,[492] Germany was the first country in the world to introduce a specific form of secondary protection for sub-patentable innovations in the late 19th century. Specifically, Germany has used the UM regime in its IP landscape since 1891. According to commentators, the utility model system, initially a German invention was later enthusiastically followed by many other jurisdictions, including a number of Asian countries such as Japan, Korea, China, Taiwan, and Vietnam.[493] In that sense, the German utility model has always been the source of inspiration for many countries that have virtually followed the provisions of the German utility model law in enacting their own laws to protect the small innovations as utility models.[494] Historical evidence suggests that Germany developed a system of second-tier protection as a response to the perceived inadequacies and the protection gap which existed between the patent and the design regimes.

Prior to the enactment of the German Utility Model Act (*Gebrauchsmustergesetz*, GebrMG) of 1 June 1891, IP protection for innova-

491 German Patent and Trade Mark Office (DPMA), *Annual Report* (2011) Official website- DPMA 18, available at: <http://www.dpma.de/docs/service/veroeffentlichungen/jahresberichte_en/dpma-annualreport2011_barrierefrei.pdf> (accessed 2 May 2012).

492 See L Bently and B Sherman, 'The United Kingdom's Forgotten Utility Model: The Utility Designs Act 1843' (1997) 1/3 Intellectual Property Quarterly 265.

493 See C Heath, 'Utility Models in East and West' in Current Problems of Intellectual Property Law-Writings in honour of Nobuo Monya (Tokyo, 1998) 47-72.

494 KS Kardam, 'Utility Model –A Tool for Economic and Technological Development: A Case Study of Japan' (2007) Final Report In Fulfillment of the Long-term Fellowship Sponsored by World Intellectual Property Office (WIPO) in Collaboration with the Japan Patent Office (from April 2, 2007 to September 28, 2007), 67, available at: <http://www.ipindia.nic.in/research_studies/FinalReport_April2007.pdf> (accessed 15 April 2012).

tive goods was generally available in accordance with the two traditional branches of exclusive rights: either under the Patent Act or under the Act on Copyright Protection for Designs (*Gesetz betreffend das Urheberrecht an Mustern und Modellen*) of 11 January 1876.[495] Soon after the enactment of these laws the question arose whether the Act on Copyright Protection for Designs would extend protection also to technical and/or functional features of products of practical use or whether it merely covers aesthetical features of designs. In a far-reaching decision, the highest German Commercial Court of that time, the Reichsoberhandelsgericht (ROHG), denied protection under the Act on Copyright Protection for Designs.[496] Moreover, due to the stringent patentability threshold under the German Patent Act which required a *technischer Fortschritt*, or 'technical step forward in the art', minor inventions and technical improvements could not receive legal protection under the patent regime.[497] Hardest hit by this lack of protection were small and medium-sized enterprises, traditionally a forte of the German economy ('Mittelstand').[498] Thus, the UM system was introduced with a lower standard of inventiveness, a non-examination system and a short period of protection.[499] Scholars have described the main features of the first German Utility Model Act as follows:[500]

- Protection of models of working tools and objects of utilitarian use or parts of those, insofar as these were meant for working or utilitarian purposes by a new design, arrangement or contraction;
- Utility model applications were only checked for the formalities, without any substantial examination;
- The protection period was six years in total, divided into two periods of three years each;

495 HG Ruse-Khan, *Utility Model Protection-A Feasible Option for Incentivising Incremental Innovation?* (2012) Study conducted for the World Intellectual Property Organisation 40-49 (copy on file with the author).

496 Ibid 41. See also Decision of 3 September 1878 – ROHG 24, 109.

497 See U Suthersanen, G Dutfield and KB Chow (eds), *Innovation Without Patents* (Edward Elgar 2007) 28.

498 C Heath, 'Utility Models in East and West' in *Current Problems of Intellectual Property Law-Writings in honour of Nobuo Monya* (Tokyo, 1998) 47- 48.

499 U Suthersanen, G Dutfield and KB Chow (eds), *Innovation Without Patents* (Edward Elgar 2007) 28-29.

500 C Heath, 'Utility Models in East and West' in *Current Problems of Intellectual Property Law-Writings in honour of Nobuo Monya* (Tokyo, 1998) 48.

- Fees were 15 German marks for the first period, and 60 marks for the extension;
- Novelty was limited to publications or domestic use.

Even though the German UM regime was initially limited to 'working tools, implements, utensils and articles of everyday use' which contained a three-dimensional form (*Raumform*), the protected subject matter has gradually been enlarged to a much broader scope of protection. After the revision of the UM law in 1986 and 1990, which abolished three-dimensional form requirement, the German UM system is no longer considered to be a classical three-dimensional model.

4.1.1.2. Main Features of the Current UM System

In spite of the repeated legislative changes since 1891, the legislative rationale of the German UM system has remained the same which is mirrored by the following wording of the law.[501] As stated in the policy document *"the utility model is mainly to quickly and inexpensively make available a manageable (easy to handle) industrial property right for sole inventors and small and medium sized enterprises for their everyday life inventions"*.[502] This approach was endorsed and supported by the Max Planck Institute in 1986 by arguing that "there will still be a need for a minor industrial property right for individual inventors, small and medium-sized industry, and for short-lived inventions which need immediate protection against imitation. This must be an entitlement which can be acquired simply and cheaply, for which a costly and lengthy preliminary examination of protectability would be prohibitive".[503] Today, the German UM regime is governed by the Utility Model Act (GebrMG), last amended

---

501 For further information see, W Prinz zu Waldeck und Pyrmont, 'Secondary protection for innovations in Germany- What are the Advantages?'(2013) January, Journal of Intellectual Property and Practice/Weblog, available at: <http://jiplp.blogspot.com/2013/01/secondary-protection-for-innovation-in.html> (accessed 13 February 2013).

502 K Königer, 'Registration without Examination: The Utility Model-A Useful Model?' in Wolrad Prinz zu Waldeck und Pyrmont and others (eds), *Patent and Technological Progress in a Globalized World* (Springer 2009) 23.

503 Ibid.

in 2011.[504] According to Section 1 of the Act, utility model protection shall be afforded to inventions that are new, involve an inventive step and are susceptible of industrial application. Moreover, the eligible subject matter for UM protection is nearly identical to that of patent law. In other words, the German UM system protects a broad range of subject matter including electrical inventions, chemical substances, and pharmaceuticals in addition to basic mechanical inventions.[505] Significantly, according to the recent case-law of the German Federal Supreme Court, UM protection is also available for second medical use inventions.[506] Nevertheless, pursuant to Sections 1 and 2 of the Act, methods and processes, computer programs, and biological inventions discoveries, scientific theories, aesthetic creations, as well as plants and animal varieties are specifically excluded from the scope of UM protection.

In terms of conditions for protection, UM law demands a lower threshold compared to patent law. The first criterion of eligiblity for protection is the novelty requirement. Pursuant to Section 3 of the UM Act, a utility model shall be considered to be new if it does not form part of the state of the art. The state of the art comprises any knowledge made available to the public by means of a *written description* (anywhere in the world) or by *use within the territory of the Republic of Germany*. It is obvious from this wording that neither oral disclosure, nor public use abroad can destroy novelty. Thus, this novelty requirement can be interpreted as 'relative novelty' standard. Unlike in the case of patents, the UM Act provides a six months grace period of novelty for prior publications by the applicant or his predecessor in title. Perhaps more significantly, an invention must meet a certain inventive threshold in order to gain protection under the German UM regime. The Act does not define what inventive step means. According to commentators, the 1986 reform codified for the first time the 'inventive step' (*erfinderischer Schritt*) requirement by Section 1 of the

---

504 The text of 1936 Act was fundamentally revised by Utility Model Law of August 28, 1986 and was most recently amended in November 24, 2011.

505 PA Cummings, 'From Germany to Australia: Opportunity for a Second Tier Patent System in the United States' (2010) 18/2 Michigan State Journal of International Law 297, 304.

506 A von Uexküll and N Hölder, 'A Clever Move: Utility models for Second Medical Use Inventions in Germany' (2006) June Patent World 22-23. Second Medical use claims relate to the use of a known compound for a new purpose, generally for treating a new specified disease.

Utility Model Act, but the requirement has always existed.[507] In using the wording 'inventive step' the legislature sought to distinguish utility model law's lower inventive level from 'inventive activity' (*erfinderische Tätigkeit*) requirement under the German patent Act.[508] An analysis of the case-law before 2006 shows that a lower degree of inventiveness or slightly lower inventive step was sufficient for a grant of a UM right. Nevertheless, in a landmark ruling of the German Federal Supreme Court in *Demonstrationsschrank* case has changed the landscape of UM law in Germany.[509]

In this leading case, the German Supreme Court, in 2006, held that the inventive step required for utility models is the same as in the case of a patent. In other words, there is now no longer a distinction between the threshold for inventiveness in German patent and utility model law resulting in that there is no more a lower degree of inventiveness under the Utility Model Act.[510] The Court stated that it could not find a capable criterion for (utility model) protectability that lies between non-obviousness in the sense of patent law and novelty.[511] In its reasoning, the German Supreme Court observed that the objective of making UM right easily available for small and medium-sized enterprises is already achieved by the lower requirements for novelty.[512] Moreover, the German Supreme Court explicitly stated that UM must increase the requirements for inventiveness in order to prevent the utility model from transitioning into a 'fall back option for non-patentable subject matter'.[513] This ruling is certainly not without its critics. From a policy perspective, the German Supreme Court ruling has changed the primary objectives the UM system. The crucial question

507 R Liesegang, 'German Utility Models after the 1990 Reform Act' (1992) 1 American Intellectual Property Law Association 5.

508 Ibid.

509 The decision of German Federal Supreme Court (Bundesgerichtshof BGH) June 20, 2006 GRUR 2006, 842- *Demonstrationsschrank.*

510 HG Ruse-Khan, *Utility Model Protection-A Feasible Option for Incentivising Incremental Innovation?* (2012) Study conducted for the World Intellectual Property Organisation 43 (copy on file with the author).

511 K Königer, 'Registration without Examination: The Utility Model-A Useful Model?' in Wolrad Prinz zu Waldeck und Pyrmont and others (eds), *Patent and Technological Progress in a Globalized World* (Springer 2009) 24.

512 TT Moga, *China's Utility Model Patent System: Innovation Driver or Deterrent* (Research Paper, US Chamber of Commerce 2012) Forward and Commentary provided by T Pattloch, 3.

513 Ibid.

that arises here is whether there is any need to protect 'trivial' or minor improvements to the state of art. Arguably, the fear of the UM system becoming a 'dumping ground for sub-patentable inventions' has probably created two systems of patent rights, namely one which is examined and the other (UM) unexamined one. Conversely, one can still argue that there is considerable difference between UM and patent threshold in view of the definition of novelty for which the prior art base is limited (oral description, prior use outside Germany would not be considered). The elimination of a lower inventive step threshold has not been unanimously approved by the legal community in Germany. The ruling of the Supreme Court has, however, left many IP scholars, as well as practitioners with more questions and uncertainties than answers. One commentator in his metaphor has even suggested that we would not have this 'Schrank' (cupboard) and let us forget it quickly.[514] There is no doubt that the abandonment of the lower threshold doctrine would have far-reaching repercussions on the use of the UM system in Germany.

Another key aspect of the German system is that UM applications are registered after formality examination (without substantive examination) and the granting process at the German Patent and Trademark Office (GPTO) generally takes about two to three months. Similar to patents, a UM application needs to include claims, description and drawings.[515] Moreover, the filing fee (€40, or €30 if filed online) and maintenance costs are considerably less compared to patents. The maximum term of protection for a UM is ten years from the date of application. Upon registration, the holder of UM is granted exclusive rights similar to that of patents. According to Section 11 of the UM Act, such rights includes the right to exclude third parties from making, offering, putting on the market or using a product which is the subject matter of the utility model, or importing or stocking the product for these purposes. This by no means explains that the UM right is without exceptions and limitations. As stipulated in Section 12 of the UM Act, acts of private and non-commercial nature acts done for experimental purposes, prior user's right etc. are not affected by a UM right. More importantly, according to Section 20, a registered UM may be subject to compulsory licenses in case of public interest. In terms of remedies

514 G Eisenführ, 'Heraus aus dem Domonstrationsschrank' (2009) 4 Mitteilungen 169.

515 See Section 4 (3) GebrMG.

against UM infringements, the Act provides for the same remedies (injunctive relief and damages) that are granted in patent infringement cases.

One of the other most important features of the German UM system is the option of branching off (*Abzweigung*) a utility model application from a pending patent application. According to Section 5 of the UM Act, every inventor, seeking patent protection, is entitled to file a UM application within two months after his patent application has been decided upon (by final grant, final rejection or withdrawal) and before the lapse of ten years from the date of patent application, if the patent and UM application cover the same invention.[516] A branched-off UM application has the advantage of claiming the priority date from the first filing. According to the latest statistics, in 2011 alone, 739 applications that were branched off, which is equal to 4.8 percent of the total UM applications filed.[517] The option of branching off is often used as a strategic tool to immediately enforce the applicant's rights in a case of an infringement. Last, but certainly not least, the German UM system has built-in safeguards in place against possible abuses of UM rights. Most importantly, pursuant to Section 15 of the Act, anyone can file invalidation proceedings to test the validity of an issued UM. As per the most recent data available, there have been 104 cancellation proceedings concluded in 2011, from which more than 75 percent resulted in a restriction or cancellation.[518] Moreover, validity of registered patents is also examined as an integral part of infringement proceedings. Besides, everyone has the right to apply for a search report for any registered utility model. Significantly, in 2011 there have been about 3,000 such applications (compared with 15,486 utility model applications) for such reports.[519]

---

516 C Einem and J Bartmann, 'The Rise of the Utility Model in Germany' [1995] Managing Intellectual Property 44.

517 W Prinz zu Waldeck und Pyrmont, 'Secondary protection for innovations in Germany- What are the Advantages?'(2013) January, Journal of Intellectual Property and Practice/Weblog, available at: <http://jiplp.blogspot.com/2013/01/secondary-protection-for-innovation-in.html> (accessed 13 February 2013).

518 Ibid.

519 TT Moga, *China's Utility Model Patent System: Innovation Driver or Deterrent* (Research Paper, US Chamber of Commerce 2012) Forward and Commentary provided by T Pattloch, 3.

4.1.1.3. Empirical Analysis and Policy Implications

The empirical evidence paints a picture that the German UM system continues to be an attractive protection mechanism for industrial and commercial sectors. According to the *World IP Indicators 2012*, Germany has recorded the second-greatest number of utility model applications after China in 2011.[520] The following statistical data of the users of both patents and UM regimes offers a revealing glimpse of the effectiveness of the system. As presented in Table 4.1, Germany remains an innovative economy in the global innovation arena with a growing number of patent applications every year. In fact, Germany is a leading producer and an exporter of high-tech goods in the world market which may also be evident from the patent statistics. Most notably, there is also an increase in the number of patent applications from abroad since recent years. It is obvious that the German economy has been an attractive market for foreign technologies and inventions. Another possible explanation for this increase is the rigorous enforcement of patent rights in Germany.

---

520 Germany has received around 16,000 utility model applications in 2011, See WIPO, *World IP Indicators* (2012 edn, WIPO 2012) 90, available at: <http://www.wipo.int/export/sites/www/freepublications/en/intproperty/941/wipo_pub_941_2012.pdf> (accessed 15 February 2013).

Table 4.1: Patent Applications, 2000-2010

Patent Applications				
Year	Resident	Non-Resident	Abroad	Total
2000	51736	10406	42795	104937
2001	49989	10486	44903	105378
2002	47598	10589	42866	101053
2003	47818	10663	41382	99863
2004	48448	10786	50201	109435
2005	48367	11855	55549	115771
2006	48012	12573	59987	120572
2007	47853	13139	62518	123510
2008	49240	13177	65904	128321
2009	47859	11724	61180	120763
2010	47047	12198	63800	123045

(Source: Based on data from WIPO statistics database)

Figure 4.1: Trends in Patent Applications, 2000-2010

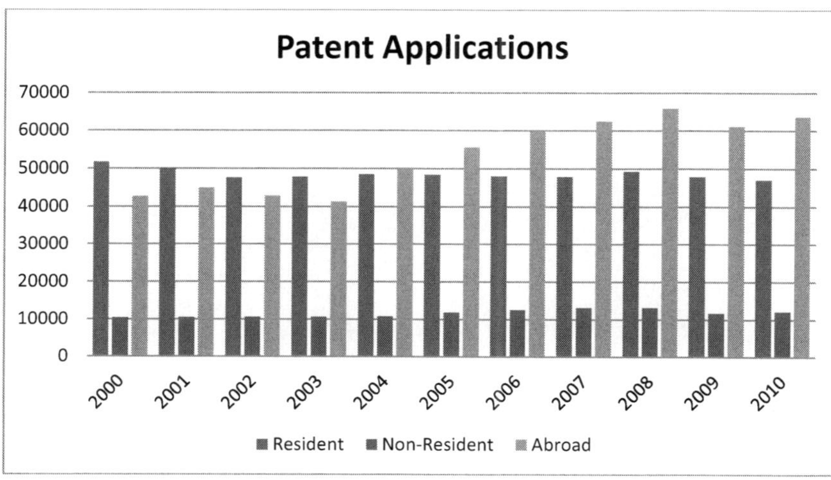

(Source: Based on data from WIPO statistics database)

When compared with the annual number of patent filings, the UM system is predominantly utilized by German firms and individuals. As shown in Table 4.1.and Figure 4.1 even though the foreign patent applications accounted for more than 50 percent of foreign applicants, only about 20 percent of total UM applications in Germany come from abroad. In 2010, foreign applications have mainly originated from Taiwan (6.5 percent), Austria (2.4 percent), Switzerland (1.9 percent), and USA (1.3 percent). This indicates that domestic UM filings are still the vast majority; this supports the claim that utility models are (still) primarily a tool for domestic innovators.[521] From the data above, it can be concluded that a strong and vibrant use of the utility model system exists in the country. Presumably, German industrial sectors and individuals are more aware of the importance of UM rights and enforcement. Moreover, according to the latest figures an estimated 10 percent of all litigations related to innovations in Germany each year are related to utility models.[522]

---

521 HG Ruse-Khan, *Utility Model Protection-A Feasible Option for Incentivising Incremental Innovation?* (2012) Study conducted for the World Intellectual Property Organisation 53 (copy on file with the author).

522 TT Moga, *China's Utility Model Patent System: Innovation Driver or Deterrent* (Research Paper, US Chamber of Commerce 2012) Forward and Commentary provided by T Pattloch, 3.

Table 4.2: Utility Model Applications, 2000-2010

Utility Model Applications				
Year	Resident	Non-Resident	Abroad	Total
2000	18899	3411	257	22567
2001	17126	3159	250	20535
2002	17363	6065	109	23537
2003	16945	6463	123	23531
2004	17053	3233	113	20399
2005	17021	3397	289	20707
2006	16406	3360	283	20049
2007	14834	3249	345	18428
2008	14047	3020	391	17458
2009	14242	3064	492	17798
2010	13694	3311	483	17488

(Source: Based on data from WIPO statistic database)

Figure 4.2: Trends in Utility Model Applications, 2000-2010

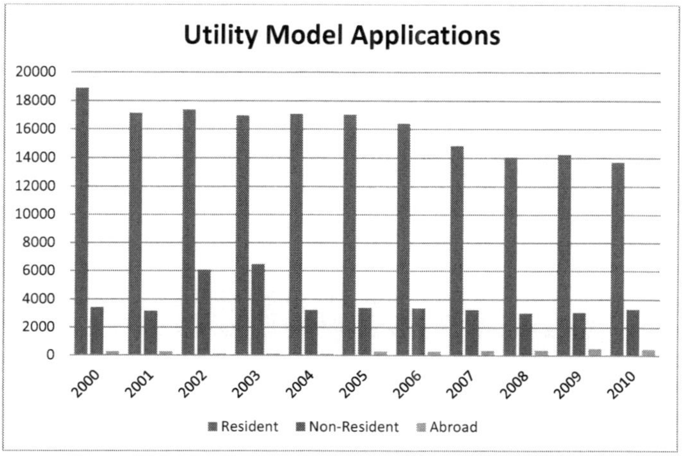

(Source: Based on data from WIPO statistics database)

It is obvious from the empirical evidence that the utility model system is an integral part of the German industrial geography, even though the numbers of applications in the recent years have slightly trended downward. Most notably, as shown in Table 4.2 and Figure 4.2, the overall number of utility model applications has seen a gradual decline in recent years resulting in a drop of the total number of UM in force in the last five years from 104,117 in 2006 to 96,096 in 2011. Perhaps more importantly, the main technology group represented in UM applications in 2011 are as follows:[523]

- Household goods (2052)
- Construction (1597)
- Vehicles, ships, planes (1345)
- Hoisting, lifting, upholstery (1114)
- Electrical engineering (1052)
- Illumination, heating (960)
- Medical supplies, hygiene (877)
- Machine construction (898)
- Grinding, pressing, tools (756)
- Agriculture (503).

In contrast, the top 5 technology groups for patents in 2011 are vehicles, ships and planes (7752), electronic engineering (7142), machine constructions (4899), medical supplies and hygiene (2485), illuminating and heating (2455).[524] This comes as no surprise, given that the UM system aims at different groups of users and the level of novelty and inventiveness required for UM is rather low.

Viewed from legislative goals, the German UM system was designed to provide: (1) protection for technical inventions which involves only a small inventive step; (2) protection that is easily obtainable; (3) protection to be inexpensive; and (4) protection to be rapidly obtainable.[525] Since there is a higher percentage of domestic users in Germany, one can rea-

523 See W Prinz zu Waldeck und Pyrmont, 'Secondary protection for innovations in Germany- What are the Advantages?'(2013) January, Journal of Intellectual Property and Practice/Weblog, available at: <http://jiplp.blogspot.com/2013/01/secondary-protection-for-innovation-in.html> (accessed 13 February 2013).

524 Ibid.

525 K Königer, 'Secondary Protection of Innovations in Germany: Is there another Side of the Story? (2013) January, Journal of Intellectual Property and Practice/Weblog, available at: <http://jiplp.blogspot.com/2013/01/secondary-protection-for-innovation-in.html> (accessed 13 February 2013).

sonably argue that the German UM system has successfully advanced the interests of domestic industries sectors. Some critics have, however, argued:

> 'The German utility model does not meet the expectations the German legislator apparently had. Apart from rare exceptions, the German utility model does not provide protection for technical inventions that do not meet the criteria of patentability. The German utility model application is as difficult to handle as a patent application and the utility models cause a lot of legal uncertainty for competitors, especially for SMEs'.[526]

Nevertheless, it is clear that the German courts are well aware of the fact that UM applications are not subject to substantive examinations. Thus, in practice, the lack of examination is taken into account; only about 10 percent of applications for a preliminary injunction are granted in the case of utility models.[527] Judged from policy perspectives, the German UM system is a policy response to the need for a uncomplicated, fast and inexpensive system of protection. Arguably, today the German system may not be serving the primary purpose for which it was introduced as many firms use the UM system as a strategic tool to protect inventions until the time a patent has been granted. On balance, though it would no longer serve the historical function, one cannot underestimate the value of the time-tested German UM regime in incentivising innovations, especially those of SMEs.

4.1.1.4. Lessons from Germany

While the German experience since 1891 provides a great source of reference for many countries, Sri Lanka and other South Asian countries should pay careful consideration to the unintended consequences that have subsequently arisen in the system. As any other protection regime, an STP system might have negative effects although they are not initially thought of, and what may be important is to address such issues. In particular, the

526 See K Königer, 'Registration without Examination: The Utility Model-A Useful Model?' in Wolrad Prinz zu Waldeck and others (eds), *Patent and Technological Progress in a Globalized World* (Springer 2009) 29.

527 TT Moga, *China's Utility Model Patent System: Innovation Driver or Deterrent* (Research Paper, US Chamber of Commerce 2012) Forward and Commentary provided by T Pattloch, 3.

strategic use of the regime by big players or large companies in the market would undermine the primary purpose of adopting such a regime. In that respect, the German mechanism against abuses of the system sheds some light on how to mitigate potential misuse of the system. As a caveat, the success of the system would also depend, at least in part, on the judicial and other administrative infrastructure of the country. Arguably, the abandonment of the lower threshold for inventive step would not be emulated by other countries. From a policy perspective, when the inventive step for UM is identical to that of patents, there would be little reasons to apply for an STP. Moreover, beyond Germany's borders, the successful experience of the German UM system has greatly influenced the European Commission to consider the adoption of a European wide harmonized UM regime since 1995.[528] These proposals of the European Commission also would no doubt be worth considering in designing a model that is best suited to the needs of the country. Most encouragingly, many East Asian countries have learned and benefited from the German UM experience and it is fascinating to examine the German UM regime as the first point of reference.

4.1.2. Australia

> *'IP laws provide a protective barrier against free-riders without which innovation is like a crop in an unfenced field, free to be grazed by competitors who have made no contribution to its cultivation'.*
> *PMSEC Report, 1993*[529]

When compared with Germany and some other jurisdictions, Australia has a relatively young STP regime. Perhaps most encouragingly, Australia is one of the leading countries in the Common Law world to experiment with an alternative approach for incentivising sub-patentable innovations. Therefore, the Australian experience of the STP system provides useful insights for many Common Law countries such as Sri Lanka which foresee an STP system in their IP law landscape. At present, the Australian IP le-

528 See European Commission, 'Green Paper on the Protection of Utility Models in the Single Market Document' COM (95) 370 final. European Commission, 'Proposal for a European Directive approximating the legal arrangements for the protection of inventions by utility model Document' COM (97) 691 final. The European Commission amended this proposal on 28 June 1999.

529 Australian Prime Minister's Science and Engineering Council (PMSEC), 'Report – The Role of Intellectual Property in Innovation' (1993) 2 Perspectives 61.

gal framework provides two types of patents; one is the traditional 'standard patent' and the other is the 'innovation patent' which is unique to Australia. Before introducing the innovation patent regime, Australia had experienced a 'petty patent' system from 1979 to 2000. The innovation patent system, the successor of the petty patent system, was introduced in Australia by an Amendment to the *Patent Act 1990* (Cth) in 2000 which came into effect on 24 May 2001.[530] The development of the Australian second-tier patent protection system has responded to perceived deficiencies in the existing patent and design regime.[531] Significantly, one of the main objectives of implementing an innovation patent system is to stimulate innovation in Australian small and medium-sized enterprises (SMEs) by providing IP protection for minor and incremental inventions.[532] From a historical perspective, the main reason for introducing an STP system in Australia was the findings of the Design Law Review Committee ('the Franki Committee') in its *Report Relating to Utility Models* in 1973.[533] Based on the recommendations of the Franki Committee report, the petty patent system was introduced in 1979.

The objective of the petty patent system was to create a form of protection that was less expensive, more easily obtained and more quickly granted than standard patent protection, and that would accordingly be used for inventions with a relatively short lifespan.[534] The other main features of

530 AL Monotti, 'Innovation Patents: The Concept of a Manner of New Manufacture and Assessment of Inventive Step: Dura-Post (Aust) Pty Ltd v Delnorth Pty Ltd' (2010) 32 European Intellectual Property Review 93, 94. See also, PA Cummings, 'From Germany to Australia: Opportunity for a Second Tier Patent System in the United States' (2010) 19 Michigan State Journal of International Law 297, 331.

531 A Christie and S Moritz, 'Australia' in U Suthersanen and others (eds), *Innovation Without Patents: Harnessing The Creative Spirit In A Diverse World* (Edward Elgar 2007) 119.

532 See Explanatory Memorandum for the Patents Amendment (Innovation Patents) Bill 2000.

533 The Parliament of the Commonwealth of Australia, 'Design Law Review Committee (Franki Report), The Law Relating to Utility Models' (1973) Parliamentary paper No. 121. The Franki Committee compiled a report analyzing whether Australia needed a form of intellectual property protection for lesser technological developments in addition to patent and design law.

534 SL Moritz and AF Christie, 'Second-Tier Patent System: The Australian Experience' [2006] European Intellectual Property Review 230, 231.

the petty patent system were:[535] primarily intended for Australian industry; subject matter permitted was identical to standard patents; whilst not intended by the legislation, petty patents underwent examination prior to grant; maximum term of protection was six years; convertibility to a standard within certain time limits; only one claim was permitted; there was no opposition prior to grant; and the prior art base was limited to documents published in Australia. Nevertheless, the petty patent system was heavily criticized for not serving the people for whom it was intended and, moreover, the system was rarely used as evident from the filing of an average of 300 applications annually.[536] One of the major problems with the petty patent system resulted from its requirement that only one claim could be made for each petty patent and the single claim made it difficult to enforce.[537] Another problem was that the costs associated with petty patents were comparably same as standard patents. Moreover, the six year term was criticized for being too short to provide an incentive for a potential manufacturer to invest.[538] In 1995, the Advisory Council on Intellectual Property (ACIP) undertook an extensive review of the petty patent system.[539] In its report, the ACIP identified that the system was being underused, with one of the key problems being the level of invention required to obtain a petty patent.[540] The ACIP concluded that there was a gap between the protection afforded under the registered designs regime and that which was available under the patent system, so that what it called 'functional innovations' were unable to be protected.[541] The various reviews of the petty patent system led to the introduction of the new innovation patent system in July 2001.

---

535 L McCaffery, 'Key Features: Patents and Utility Models Protection' (WIPO Regional Seminar on the Legislative, Economic and Policy Aspects of Utility Models Protection System, Kuala Lumpur, Malaysia, September 3 to September 4, 2012).

536 SL Moritz and AF Christie, 'Second-Tier Patent System: The Australian Experience' [2006] European Intellectual Property Review 230, 232.

537 Ibid.

538 Ibid.

539 R Gay, 'Editorial: The Innovative Step Conundrum' (2009) April, Managing IP 98.

540 Ibid.

541 Ibid.

4.1.2.1. Main Features of Current Innovation Patents

The primary objective of the innovation patent regime is to fill the 'gap' that existed with regard to minor and incremental innovations and secondly, it offers a quick, less expensive and simple form of protection to encourage individuals and SMEs to realise their good ideas.[542] To be eligible for innovation patent protection, an invention must be new, involve an innovative step and be useful as stipulated in Section 18 (1A) of the Australian Patent Act. The same prior art criterion, as in the case of standard patent, is taken into consideration when assessing the novelty standard under the innovation patent regime. The Patent Amendment Act 2001 (Cth) for the first time imposed an absolute novelty standard for Australian patents.[543] According to the current law, the prior art base for novelty is comprised of information made publicly available anywhere in the world before the priority date through either a document or an act.[544] Thus, the test applied for novelty is the same in both standard and innovation patents. Most notably, the inventive threshold for patentability in the case of innovation patent is significantly different from that of the standard patent. Pursuant to Section 7(4), an innovation patent requires an 'innovative step' rather than an 'inventive step'. As articulated in the Act, an invention involves an innovative step when compared with the prior art base 'unless the invention would, to a person skilled in the relevant art, in the light of the common general knowledge as it existed in the patent area[545] before the priority date of the relevant claim, only vary from the kinds of information set out in subsection (5) in ways that make no substantial con-

---

542 U Suthersanen and others (eds), *Innovation Without Patents* (Edward Elgar 2007) 125.

543 C Bodkin, *Patent Law in Australia* (Thomson Reuters 2008) 113. At its commencement, the *Patent Act 1990* imposed a 'relative novelty' standard by *excluding* information made publicly available by doing an act outside the patent area from the prior art base. The change to 'absolute novelty' was achieved by changing part (a)(ii) of the definition of 'prior art base' by replacing the words 'in the patent area', which had appeared previously, with the words 'whether in or out of the patent area which now appear there').

544 See the definition of 'prior art base' in the Schedule 1 of the Patent Act. See also Bill Bennet, *A Reference Guide to the Australian Patent System* (2008) 12.

545 Intellectual Property Laws Amendment (*Raising the Bar*) Act No. 35, 2012 has now changed the wording of this section. Under its Part 1-Main amendments, Section 7(4) replaces 'whether in or out of the patent area' instead of 'in the patent area'. This Act came into force on 15 April 2013.

tribution to the working of the invention'. The legislative intention of providing protection to incremental technological advances with a lower level of inventive step has also been made clear by the Explanatory Memorandum to the Patents Amendment (Innovations Patents) Act. The test requires that the invention is not only new, but also differs from what was already known in a way that is not merely superficial or peripheral to the invention.[546] The variation must be of practical significance to the way that the invention works.[547] Unlike for patents, there is, however, no requirement that an innovation must be non-obvious. The key features of the innovation patents system summarized by commentators are as follows:[548]

- Patentable subject matter for the purpose of innovation patent is the same subject matter for which standard patent protection is available, with the exception of inventions concerning plants, animals and biological processes. Innovation patents can be obtained for products as well as processes;
- Maximum eight year term of protection;
- Applications for an innovation patent should be limited to a maximum of five claims;
- Same prior art base as for standard patents (absolute novelty)
- Prior art base applicable to an innovation patent is that of a standard patent;
- Lower standard of inventiveness (innovative step);
- Innovation patents do not undergo a substantive examination before the grant. Nevertheless, an innovation patent needs to be examined and certified before an infringement action can be brought against a third party. Otherwise, the substantive examination is optional and if certification of an innovation patent is requested, the patent office will conduct a substantive examination to determine whether the innovation patent meets threshold requirements such as novelty and inventive step;[549]

546 R Gay, 'Editorial: The Innovative Step Conundrum' (2009) April, Managing IP 98-99.

547 Ibid.

548 U Suthersanen and others (eds), *Innovation Without Patents* (Edward Elgar 2007) 126. See also Australian Government's Advisory Council on Intellectual Property, Review of the Innovation Patent System: Issues Paper (August 2011).

549 See W Hird and DC Cave, 'Protect Your Rights with Utility Model Patents' (2009) July/August Managing Intellectual Property 68.

- There is no opposition prior to grant;
- An application for a standard patent can be converted to an innovation patent application.[550] This can be done simply by filing a divisional innovation patent from the parent patent application at any time before the patent is granted;[551]
- In case of infringement, available remedies are identical to those of for standard patents (the injunctive relief, award of damage etc).

Unlike many other jurisdictions, the Australian innovation patent system offers protection for processes and methods. Thus, it is viewed as a unique feature of the STP regime.

Even though the innovation patent regime is relatively young, there exists a considerable body of case-law with regard to innovation patents in Australia. In fact, judgments of Australian courts have further illuminated the provisions relating to innovation patent under the current Patent Act, in particular, the court decisions dealing with the test of 'innovative step'. According to scholars, the innovative step requirement remained less clear until recent years.[552] In 2008, the innovative step test was first judicially evaluated in the decision of *Delnorth Pty Ltd v Dura- Post (Australia) Pty Ltd*,[553] by Justice Gyles. The invention claimed in *Delnorth* was a roadside marker post made of sheet spring steel as seen below.[554]

550 See Sections 79(B) and (C) of the Patent Act 1990.

551 See C Thompson and L Dumbrell, 'A Really Useful Utility Model' (2010) March/220 Patent World 31.

552 See R Gay, 'Editorial: The Innovative Step Conundrum' (2009) April, Managing IP 99.

553 (2008) 78 IPR 463. The case involved three separate innovation patents of Delnorth relating to 'Roadside Post', which were filed as divisional applications from a standard patent. Delnorth brought the case against Dura-Post for allegedly having infringed its innovation patents. Dura-Post challenged arguing that the innovation patents obviously lacked any innovative step.

554 DC Cave, 'The Test for Innovative Step confirmed *Dura-Post (Australia) Pty Ltd v. Delnorth Pty Ltd* [2009] FCAFC 81 (30 June 2009)' (2009) September DCC Intellectual Property, available at: <http://www.davies.com.au/pub/detail/225/the-test-for-innovative-step-confirmed> (accessed 10 May 2012). M Summerfield, 'Re-examination Limits Rights to Flexible Roadside Post' (2011) July, Patentology, available at: <Patentologyhttp://blog.patentology.com.au/2011/07/re-examination-limits-rights-to.html> (accessed 10 May 2012).

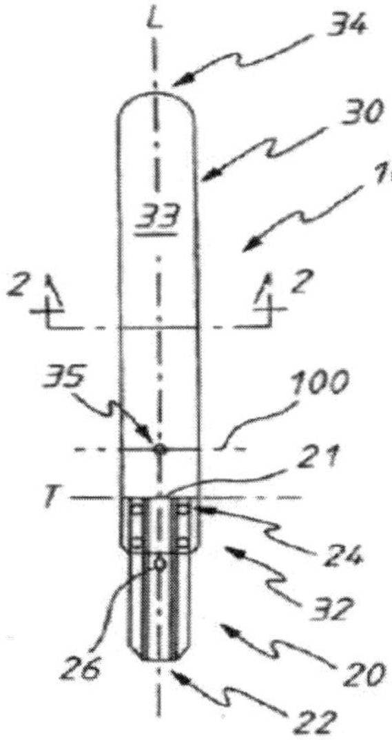

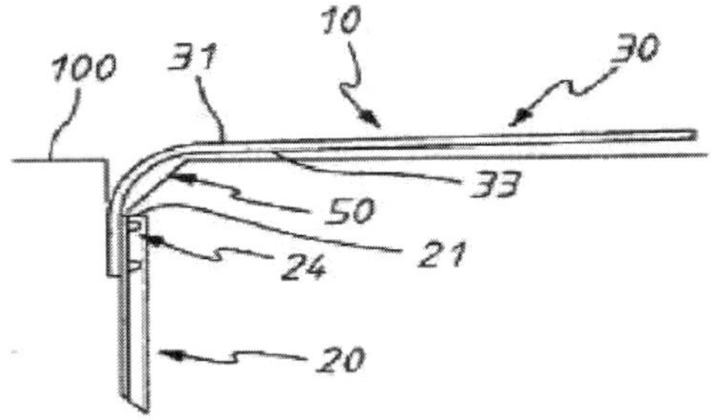

Even though the post included features known from existing plastic roadside marker post, the court found that a number of obvious combinations claimed in the invention satisfied the innovative step as the new features contributed substantially to the working of the roadside post claimed.[555] This decision of a single judge of the Federal Court of Australia was affirmed on appeal by the Full Court on 30 June 2009.[556] In this judgment, the term 'substantial' in the Act was judicially evaluated and the court further interpreted that 'make no substantial contribution to the working of the invention', does not mean 'great' or 'weighty'. Instead, it must be taken to mean 'real' or 'of substance' as contrasted with distinctions without real difference.[557] Obviously, through a 'purposive interpretation', the

555 C Thompson and L Dumbrell, 'A Really Useful Utility Model' (2010) March/220 Patent World 28, 29.

556 See *Dura-Post (Aust) Pty v. Delnorth Pty Ltd Pty* Ltd (2009) 177 FCR 239. See also C Thompson and L Dumbrell, 'A Really Useful Utility Model' (2010) March/ 220 Patent World 28, 30.

557 See R Gay, 'Editorial: The Innovative Step Conundrum' (2009) April, Managing IP 100. The Court confirmed that, in accordance with subsections 7(4) and 7(5) of the Patent Act 1990 the following elements should be identified and considered: (a) the invention so far as claimed in any claim; (b) the 'person skilled in the relevant art'; (c) the common general knowledge as it existed in Australia be-

Australian courts have in effect given life to the legislative intention as manifested in the Act. Viewed through the lens of the *Delnorth* decision, it is clear that an innovation that only differs from prior art and makes a substantial contribution to the working of the invention may well be protected under the current innovation patent regime in Australia. From a practical perspective, an invention can quite easily satisfy the innovative step requirement, even if the claimed invention is rather obvious in view of the totality of prior art. This is because, in the evaluation of innovative step, the patent office makes only a comparison of a claim against each single item of prior art and the law does not allow any 'mosaicing' or a combined prior art reference. More recently, the jurisprudence advanced by the *Delnorth* ruling has received further consideration from the Australian courts in the *Seafood Innovations Pty Ltd* case.[558]

Some commentators have, however, disapproved of the current treatment of the innovative step by the Australian courts. They argue that the innovative step enquiry is no more than a modified novelty test requiring nothing more than the presence of at least one meaningfully functional novel feature, when a claim is compared to each individual item of prior art separately. Whether or not the novel feature has any inventive merit is completely irrelevant to the test.[559] Moreover, in the recent years, the frequent abuse and strategic use of the innovation patent system has worried Australian policymakers. As a result, the Australian Government (IP Australia) released a consultation paper proposing to raise the patentability threshold for Innovation Patents to the same level of inventiveness as required for standard patents.[560] The Australian Government's Intellectual Property Office (IP Australia) has observed that the current innovative step threshold is too low and there may be a case for policy reform. Concerns have also been raised in the Consultation Paper regarding the com-

---

fore the priority date; and, (d) whether the invention only varied from the prior art information in ways that make no substantial contribution to the working of the invention.

558 Spender J in *Seafood Innovations Pty Ltd v. Richard Bass Pty Ltd* [2010] FCA 723.

559 M Summerfield, 'Innovation Patents Flop like Stunned Mullet' (2010) July, Patentology, available at: <http://blog.patentology.com.au/2010/07/innovation-patents-flop-like-stunned.html> (accessed 10 May 2012).

560 See IP Australia, Innovation Patents-Raising the Step: Consultation Paper announced on 24th September 2012. The public consultation was closed on 25th October 2012.

parative ease of obtaining innovation patents may lead to the creation of patent thickets (patent trolls) and patent evergreening in the area of pharmaceutical patents. Most problematically, according to IP Australia, many firms are using the innovation patent system to obtain quick protection for most inventions that should be protected under the standard patents regime. Interestingly, even though Germany, Japan, and Korea have excluded computer-implemented inventions (computer software) from the STP regimes, the Australian innovation patent system currently grants protection for such inventions. In a number of most recent patent litigations in Australia (i.e. as a part of global battle between Apple and Samsung), innovations patents have been asserted and enforced. In fact, Apple has become the single largest user of the innovation patent system in Australia.[561] Nevertheless, the importance of the innovation patent regime as a useful alternative to standard patents cannot be downplayed by the increased number of abuses. The strategic use of the system to gain a rapidly enforceable right is a common phenomenon in many jurisdictions, if not all. Of course, future reforms would certainly need to address many of the above concerns, but raising the innovative step to the level of inventive step that is applied for standard patents would inevitably result in the innovation patent system becoming obsolete and ineffective, as was the case for the petty patent system.

561 See M Summerfield, 'Apple's 'Innovative' Australian Patent Strategy' (2012) August, IPWatchdog, available at: <http://www.ipwatchdog.com/2012/08/15/apples-innovative-australian-patent-strategy/id=27378/> (accessed 10 December 2012).

Table 4.3: A Snapshot View of Standard, Petty and Innovation Patents

	Standard Patent	Petty Patent	Innovation Patent
Objective	To encourage greater inventive activity through the grant of exclusive rights	To provide less expensive, quicker patent protection, encourage inventions of a short lifespan	To provide less expensive, simpler and quicker protection, to encourage minor and incremental innovations of SMEs
Initial legislation	Patents Act 1903 (Cth)	Patents Amendment Act 1979 (Cth)	Patents Amendment (Innovation Patent) Act 2000 (Cth)
Novelty	Originally domestic, currently absolute novelty	Domestic	Absolute novelty (Same prior art base as for the standard patents)
Inventiveness	Inventive step	Inventive step	Innovative step
Granting Procedure	Substantive examination	Substantive examination	Preliminary examination
Number of claims	Multiple	One claim only	Up to 5 claims
Divisional application	Yes	Yes	Yes
Opposition proceedings	Yes	No	Only post-grant
Subject matter	No express exclusions, except human beings, and the biological processes for their generation	As for standard patents	Identical to standard patents, additionally excluded plants, animals, and biological process
Average time for grant	2-4 years	90 percent granted within 3 months	2-3 months from filing
Term	20 years	6 years	8 years

(Source: Based on Australia's Second-Tier Patent System: A Preliminary Review (2004)

4.1.2.2. Empirical Analysis and Policy Implications

As noted above, one of the primary objectives of the Australian innovation patent regime is to provide protection for small and incremental innovations of Australian individuals and SMEs. The empirical data on the use of both standard and innovation patent systems would probably offer credible evidence on whether the innovation patent system works well in the Australian context. As presented in Table 4.4, Australian standard patent applications have significantly increased in the recent years. Nevertheless, the lion's share of Australian standard patent applications has been made by foreign companies and individuals. On average, Australian applications consisted of about 10 percent of total standard patent applications filed in the last ten years. From these statistics, it can reasonably be concluded that the Australian standard patent system is predominantly used by foreign interests. From an analytical perspective, domestic patent filing is an indication of the technology strength of the nation. Obviously, the standard patent system is less used by Australian applicants.

Table 4.4: Patent Applications, 2000-2010

Patent applications				
Year	**Resident**	**Non-resident**	**Abroad**	**Total**
2000	1928	20073	3399	25400
2001	2187	20548	3868	26603
2002	2364	20181	4128	26673
2003	2418	19176	4714	26308
2004	2559	20274	6524	29357
2005	2555	21302	6988	30845
2006	2837	23166	7342	33345
2007	2718	24122	7914	34754
2008	2821	23525	7955	34301
2009	2494	21187	711	24392
2010	2409	22478	7408	32295

(Source: Based on data from WIPO statistic database)

Figure 4.3: Trends in Patent Applications, 2000-2010

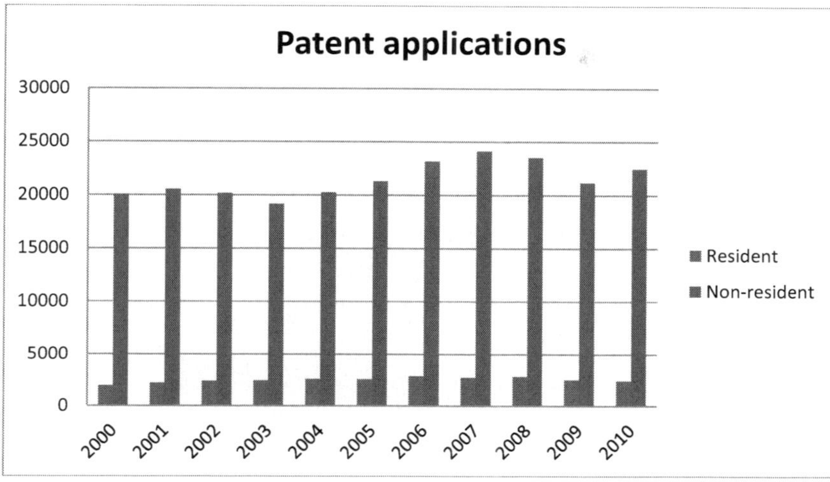

(Source: Based on data from WIPO statistic database)

In stark contrast to applications for standard patents, the majority of innovation patent applications are made by Australians, though the share of innovation patent applications as against the total number of standard patent applications is small (around 6 percent). Perhaps more encouragingly, even though the petty patent system (1979-2001), the predecessor of innovation patents was not well-utilized by domestic applicants, with an average of 300 petty patent filings each year, the empirical data supports the view that Australian applicants have made relatively good use of the current innovation patent system. As evident from Table 4.5, the number of innovation patent applications has considerably increased in the last ten years, since its introduction in 2001.

Table 4.5: Innovation Patent Applications, 2000-2010

Year	Resident	Non-resident	Total
2000	528	126	654
2001	762	136	898
2002	868	121	989
2003	901	139	1040
2004	956	137	1093
2005	925	134	1059
2006	917	159	1076
2007	1036	193	1229
2008	1024	231	1255
2009	1110	210	1320
2010	1126	339	1465

(Source: Based on data from WIPO statistic database)

Figure 4.4: Trends in Innovation Patent Applications, 2000-2010

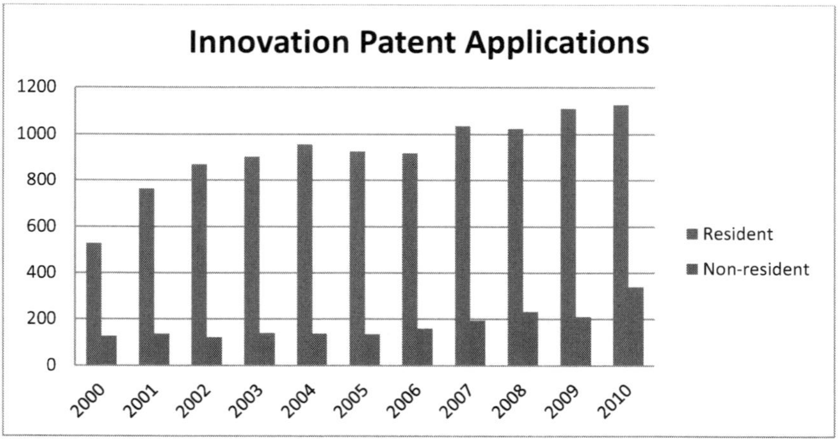

(Source: Based on data from WIPO statistic database)

As noted above, the Australian innovation patent system was intended to appeal to domestic innovators and SMEs. As Figure 4.4 shows, both resident and non-resident innovation patent applications have trended upward. Arguably, the increase may reflect the reduced level of inventiveness required for innovation patents. One other possible reason is that there has been a significant rise in innovation patent applications within certain high-tech technologies in the recent years, in particular, electrical devices and engineering (with an increase of 350 percent), information technology (with an increase of 390 percent), and pharmaceuticals (with an increase of 560 percent).[562] According to IP Australia, this compares to a rise in applications of 150 percent averaged over all technologies.[563] The annual number of Innovation Patent applications for these technologies has increased from 82 applications in 2001 to 401 in 2011, amounting to nearly a quarter of all Innovation Patent applications filed in 2011.[564]

An analysis of the latest statistics shows that, even though the majority of innovation patent applications are made by Australian individuals and companies, the proportion of domestic applications has significantly declined from 85 percent in 2001 to 65 percent in 2011.[565] Probably, this may be attributed to the increase in innovation patent application from abroad, especially from high technology industries such as computer software. Nevertheless, the technology groups represented in standard patent applications are different from that of innovation patents. According to recent studies,[566] the top five technology groups for standard patents are: (1) organic fine chemicals (9 percent); (2) pharmaceuticals, cosmetics (6 percent); (3) medical engineering (5 percent); (4) telecommunications (5 percent); (5) analysis, measurement, control (5 percent). When compared with standard patent applications, the applications for innovation patents are largely made in relation to: (1) consumer goods and equipment (22 percent); (2) civil engineering, building, mining (13 percent); 3) transport (9 percent); (4) information technology (9 percent); (5) handling and print-

562 IP Australia, 'Innovation Patents-Raising the Step: Consultation Paper- 24 September 2012' (2012) IP Australia/Australian Government, available at: <www.ipaustralia. gov.au> (accessed 10 December 2012).

563 Ibid.

564 Ibid.

565 Ibid.

566 SL Moritz and AF Christie, 'Second-Tier Patent System: The Australian Experience' (2006) 4 European Intellectual Property Review 230, 236.

ing (6 percent).[567] Furthermore, the following Table provides a glimpse of innovation patents granted by IP Australia since 2001.

Table 4.6: Innovation Patents Granted by Calendar Year

Years	2001	2002	2003	2004	2005	2006	2007	2008	2009	2010	Totals
Innovation patents granted	660	1026	1036	1104	1068	1085	1241	1272	1326	1469	**11,287**
Granted to foreign applicants	83	136	145	146	146	167	207	244	217	342	**1,833**
Percentage of foreign applicants	13%	13%	14%	13%	14%	15%	17%	19%	16%	23%	**16%**
Granted to Australian (Aus) applicants	577	890	891	958	922	918	1034	1028	1109	1127	**9,454**
Percentage of Aus applicants	87%	87%	86%	87%	86%	85%	83%	81%	84%	77%	**84%**
Granted to Aus individuals	428	644	674	667	626	566	682	686	676	697	**6,346**
Overall percentage of Aus individual applicants	65%	63%	65%	60%	59%	52%	55%	54%	51%	47%	**56%**
Granted to Aus companies/ firms	149	246	217	291	296	352	352	342	433	430	**3,108**
Overall percentage of Aus companies/ firms	23%	24%	21%	26%	28%	32%	28%	27%	33%	29%	**28%**

(Source: Australian Government's Advisory Council on Intellectual Property, 'Review of the Innovation Patent System: Issue Paper', 2011)

As indicated by Table 4.6, the total number of innovation patents granted has doubled over the period 2001 to 2011. This can be interpreted as an indication of the fact that more Australian nationals than before are interested in using the incentive mechanism accorded by the innovation patent regime. Nevertheless, it might still be argued that this increase in granted innovation patent is an inevitable result of a large number of divisional in-

567 Ibid.

novation patent applications filed from pending standard patent applications for strategic purposes. In that sense, this does not reflect the real increase in incremental innovations in Australia. Moreover, as can be seen from the above Table, a vast majority of innovation patents are granted to Australian applicants, while on average, only about 1 in 6 innovation patents are granted to foreign applicants.[568] Last but not the least, of all granted innovation patents, only about 20 percent of innovation patents are substantively examined and certified each year. As noted, the certification of an innovation patent is mandatory before initiating any legal action against a third party.

4.1.2.3. Lessons from Australia

Australia has lived with an STP system (petty patent and innovation patent regimes) since 1979 and the Australian experience could well serve as a model for Sri Lanka and other South Asian countries. Most importantly, various reviews and previous studies have confirmed that the Australian STP system has generally met and continues to meet the objectives for which it was introduced.[569] Undeniably, the Australian system suggests an interesting way of advancing the interests of domestic innovators and SMEs by providing quick, less expensive and more easily obtainable protection for minor and incremental innovations. To that extent, the reflections on the Australian experience can provide an impetus to many countries to provide for an STP regime in their legal systems. One other important lesson that can be learned from Australia is to undertake periodical reviews on the working of the system once it has been introduced. The strength of the system such as its ability to protect almost every novel and useful product or process, lower threshold for inventiveness, quick and low-cost granting procedure and the need of certification before enforcing the rights are worth emulating by other countries. Nevertheless, the system

568 Australian Government's Advisory Council on Intellectual Property, 'Review of the Innovation Patent System: Issue Paper' (2011) Official Website of Australian Government/Advisory Council on Intellectual Property 8, available at: <http://www.acip.gov.au/reviews/all-reviews/review-innovation-patent-system/> (accessed 12 August 2012).

569 SL Moritz and AF Christie, 'Second-Tier Patent System: The Australian Experience' (2006) 4 European Intellectual Property Review 230, 238.

is certainly not without its critics. Even though the innovation system offers unique advantages for the domestic industrial sectors, it is often used as a strategic tool to gain rapidly enforceable right by filing an innovation patent divisional from a pending standard patent application by large domestic and foreign companies. This practice, along with patent evergreening and patent thickets, has raised serious concerns about the Australian innovation patent system today. To overcome such abuses, Sri Lanka would have to tailor the scope of the protected subject-matter narrowly; reduce the scope for strategic use, and exclude computer software from the design of a future STP regime. Moreover, relatively shorter term protection would also help to reduce the threat of pharmaceutical patent evergreening. Most significantly, even though the low innovative step threshold may be a concern for Australia as it is a more technologically advanced country, it should not be an issue for a developing country like Sri Lanka where most innovations by SMEs consist of minor adaptations and improvements for existing products. In conclusion, the Australian system provides valuable insights for countries where an STP regime is under consideration.

4.2. Experience from Emerging and Developing Economies

4.2.1. China

> *'Core technology cannot be bought. Only by strong capacity of science and technological innovation, and by obtaining our own IP rights, can we promote China's competitiveness and win respect in the international society'.*
> *Former Chinese Premier Wen Jiabao*[570]

While becoming an economic powerhouse in Asia, China has recorded awe-inspiring economic growth in the last three decades. From a negligible poor economy based on agriculture and manufacturing in the 1970s, China has moved towards an innovation-based economy, thanks to science and technology policies that have been implemented to encourage indigenous innovations. Thus, China has attracted much attention from South Asian policymakers as a successful growth model. With the 'Open Door Polices' in 1979, it has implemented an export-oriented economic strate-

570 Quoted by E Zhou and B Stembridge, Patented in China-The Present and Future State of Innovation in China (Thomson Reuters 2010) 16.

gy. Today, China has emerged as the world's second-largest economy with an annual GDP growth close to ten percent. Even more encouragingly, China has championed the world from another front, namely, innovations and patents. In 2011 alone, the Chinese State Intellectual Property Office (SIPO) has received 585,467 utility model (UM) applications, ranking number 1 and securing 87 percent of the world total UM patent filings.[571] Not surprisingly, China has recorded an exploding number of patent filings in the recent years. Moreover, in 2001, China became a member of the World Trade Organization (WTO), turning a new leaf in the country's history of IP law.[572] Admittedly, the most recent developments in IP have occurred as a result of China's legal obligations under the TRIPS Agreement. Even though Japan (as the first country in Asia), following the German experience, introduced a UM regime in 1905, China did not have such a regime until 1984. While enacting its first modern patent law in 1984, China brought the idea of an STP regime into its IP legal landscape. As a result, under the current Patent Act of China, there are three types of patents, namely, invention patents, utility models and design patents. Like many other countries, one of the main objectives of the Chinese UM system is to encourage domestic innovative activities by protecting small and incremental innovations.

4.2.1.1. Current System of Utility Model Protection

The utility model patent system constitutes an important part of the Chinese patent system and the purpose of the system is to protect small inventions and creations which play a unique role in China's patent protection system.[573] According to commentators, "throughout the drafting of the Patent Act, there had been a strong debate regarding the adoption of a UM law (*shiyong xinxing*), with the legislators' fearing that the patent office

---

571 WIPO, World Intellectual Property Indicators (WIPO 2012) 90.

572 The World Trade Organization successfully concluded negotiations on China's terms of membership of the WTO, paving the way for the text of the agreement to be adopted formally at the WTO Ministerial Conference in Doha, Qatar, in November 2001.

573 State Intellectual Property Office of People's Republic of China (SIPO), 'Development of China's Utility Model System' (2013) Report released on 5 January 2013, SIPO-Official website, available at: <http://english.sipo.gov.cn/news/official/201301/t20130105_782325.html> (accessed 10 January 2013).

would be flooded by minor inventions from foreign corporations, especially those from Japan".[574] The current UM system in China is governed by the Chinese Patent Act and its implementing regulations.[575] Since its adoption in 1985, the Patent Act has been revised three times in 1992, 2000 and 2009. Most importantly, the third revision in 2009 introduced the requirement of 'absolute novelty' and 'evaluation report' into the UM regime. Under Chinese patent law, a utility model is defined as 'any new *technical solution* relating to the shape, structure, or the combination of a product, which is fit for practical use'.[576] Thus, the subject-matter protectable as a utility model is limited to product-related technological solutions, excluding processes as well as methods, chemical compositions and computer software etc.[577] Viewed through the lens of protectable subject-matter, the Chinese UM regime can be viewed as a three-dimensional model. Pursuant to Article 22(1) of the patent Act, to be patentable as a utility model, an invention must possess novelty, inventiveness and practical applicability. Like in many other jurisdictions, the Chinese law requires an invention to meet an 'absolute novelty' standard for UM protection.[578]

Nevertheless, the inventiveness standard required for utility models is significantly different from that of invention patent (*faming zhuanli*) in China. According to the wording of Article 22 of the Patent Act, a UM possesses inventiveness when it has '*substantive feature and must represent progress*' which is a lower threshold than for invention patents. Most notably, an invention patent requires a 'prominent (outstanding) substantive feature and represents a notable progress'. Due to frequent confusion as to what level of inventiveness represents, the Examination Guidelines propose that for an invention patent 'an invention is deemed to be non-obvious even to an expert who has conducted a comprehensive search in all

574 U Suthersanen, G Dutfield and Boey (eds), *Innovation Without Patents: Harnessing The Creative Spirit In A Diverse World* (Edward Elgar 2007) 153.

575 See The Patent Law of the People's Republic of China, adopted 12 March 1984, which came into effect on 1 April 1985, as last amended in 2009. See also, Implementing Regulations of the Patent Law, People's Republic of China, adopted 19 January 1985, adopted 1 July 2001 and 2010.

576 See Article 2 (3) of the Patent Act.

577 See also Chinese Patent Examination Guidelines (2010).

578 See Article 22, novelty means that, the invention or utility model does not belong to the prior art; The prior art in this Law referred to any technology known to the public in the country or abroad before the date of filing.

neighboring and related fields,' but for UM patents 'the search should be restricted to the fields to which the technical solution immediately pertains'.[579] Moreover, in the case of a UM application, only two prior art documents may be combined unless the UM results from a simple combination of different pieces of prior art.[580] Whereas for invention patents it is possible to combine more than two prior art documents and attack the inventiveness. As the last condition for protection, practical applicability means that the utility model can be made or used and can produce effective results.[581] Once filed, the application is only subject to *preliminary* examination and this examination includes a review as to formalities only, including a cursory review of the claims to verify appropriate subject-matter for a UM Patent.[582] Once registered, which typically takes seven to ten months after filing, the utility model patent is presumed valid, although the validity of the patent may be challenged by proceedings before the Patent Reexamination Board.[583] This invalidation procedure serves as post-grant protection mechanism against possible abuses of the system because anyone who doubts the patentability of an issued UM patent can make a request for invalidation. Interestingly, there is an increasing concern regarding the validity of issued UM patents. According to the newest data from SIPO, the Patent Reexamination Board of SIPO received 10,044 requests for invalidation of utility model patents between 2010 and 2011. Moreover, from 2002 to 2011, SIPO has closed (decided on) 9,532 requests for invalidation of utility model patents, which has resulted in 35.6 percent invalidations and 11.80 percent partial invalidations respective-

579 PA Cummings, 'From Germany to Australia: Opportunity for a Second Tier Patent System in the United States' (2010) 19 Michigan State Journal of International law 297, 310.

580 T Mak, 'Utility Model and Invalidation in China: Introduction and Practice Notes' (2011) April, Chartered Institute of Patent Agents 231, 233.

581 See Article 22 of the Patent Law of the People's Republic of China.

582 TT Moga, *China's Utility Model Patent System: Innovation Driver or Deterrent* (Research Paper, US Chamber of Commerce 2012) 12.

583 See Article 45 of the Patent Act 1985 as amended. TT Moga, *China's Utility Model Patent System: Innovation Driver or Deterrent* (Research Paper, US Chamber of Commerce 2012) 12.

ly.[584] Generally, the invalidation rate remains as high as 50 to 60 percent.[585]

One other important aspect of the Chinese UM system is the dual filing arrangement as Chinese patent law does not permit conversion from one type of patent to another. Pursuant to Article 9 of the Act, an applicant can file applications for both an invention patent and a UM application for the same invention, but he is required to choose between the two in order to avoid double patenting. In other words, two patents (one invention and one utility patent) cannot exist claiming the same or identical invention.[586] Moreover, in terms of the rights conferred by the Chinese UM regime, an owner of a UM patent is entitled to the same rights as in the case of invention patents. The longest statutory life of a UM patent is ten years from the date of filing. Even more significantly, enforcement of Chinese UM rights has attracted huge interest after the *Schneider v Chint* decision of the Chinese People's Court in 2007 where the highest recorded patent infringement compensation was awarded based on a UM patent.[587] Last but not least, the Chinese UM law also provides enforcement related safeguards against possible abuses of the UM regime. Most importantly, in an infringement dispute involving a UM patent, the people's court or the patent administrative department may require the patentee or the interested parties to provide a patent evaluation report at the beginning of the lawsuit.[588] Given below is an example of UM patent granted by SIPO: UM Patent

584 State Intellectual Property Office of People's Republic of China (SIPO), 'Development of China's Utility Model System' (2013) Report released on 5 January 2013, SIPO – Official website, available at: <http://english.sipo.gov.cn/news/official/201301/t20130105_782325.html> (accessed 10 January 2013).

585 E-mail from a Chinese patent lawyer to author (12 December 2012).

586 TT Moga, China's Utility Model Patent System: Innovation Driver or Deterrent (Research Paper, US Chamber of Commerce 2012) 13.

587 See T Mak, 'Utility Model and Invalidation in China: Introduction and Practice Notes' (2011) April Chartered Institute of Patent Agents 231. Decision WX9744 *Schneider v. Chint*. This case involved an invention for circuit breaker of Chint's UM ZL97248479.5.

588 See Article 61 of the Patent Act. Where any infringement dispute relates to a patent for a utility model… the people's court… ask the patentee or any interested party to furnish an evaluation report of the patent made by SIPO after having conducted search, analysis and evaluation of the relevant utility model, and use it as evidence for hearing or handling the patent infringement dispute. Arguably, such an evaluation report may be viewed as an important supplement to the preliminary examination system.

Number ZL 2006 2 0031103.5 (LCD Display Mercury Free Sphygmomanometer).[589]

4.2.1.2. Empirical Analysis and Policy Implications

The empirical data from SIPO and WIPO provides evidence on how successful the UM system has been in encouraging innovations in China. It also offers very useful insights for the use of the UM patent system by domestic and foreign applicants. Table 4.7 presents some illuminating facts on the latest trends regarding UM, invention and design patent applications and grants by State Intellectual Property Office (SIPO) from 2005 to 2011. Most strikingly, the total number of applications and grants of all three types of patents in China has remarkably increased over this period. According to the newest statistics of SIPO, a total of 1,633,347 patent applications have entered the Chinese patent system in 2011, representing a 33.6 percent increase over 2010. Of the total number, 526,412 (32.2 percent) were applications for inventions, 585,467 (35.8 percent) for utility

589 Department of Industrial Policy and Promotion of India, 'Utility Models' (2011) Discussion Paper-23 May 2011, 28. available at: <http://dipp.gov.in/English/Discuss_paper/Utility_Models_13May2011.pdf> (accessed 30 December 2011).

models, and 521,468 (31.9 percent) for designs.[590] Obviously, more than one third of patent applications received by SIPO are for utility model patents. As shown in Table 4.7, most encouragingly, applications for utility model patents have sharply increased to an extraordinary level by exceeding 200,000 in 2008, 300,000 in 2009, and 400,000 in 2010 and in 2011, its applications reached 585,000, which was a 42.9 percent increase over the previous year.[591]

Table 4.7: Applications and Grants for Three Kinds of Patents by Calendar Year

UMs	2005	2006	2007	2008	2009	2010	2011
Applications	139566	161366	181324	225586	310771	409836	585467
Grants	79349	107655	150036	176675	203802	344472	408110
Invention	2005	2006	2007	2008	2009	2010	2011
Applications	476263	573178	694153	828328	976686	391177	526412
Grants	214003	268002	351782	411982	581992	135110	172113
Design	2005	2006	2007	2008	2009	2010	2011
Applications	163371	201322	267688	312904	351342	421273	521468
Grants	81349	102561	133798	141601	249701	335243	380291

(Source: Based on data collected from SIPO)[592]

590 TT Moga, China's Utility Model Patent System: Innovation Driver or Deterrent (Research Paper, US Chamber of Commerce 2012) 13-14.

591 State Intellectual Property Office of People's Republic of China (SIPO), 'Development of China's Utility Model System' (2013) Report released on 5 January 2013, SIPO-Official website, available at: <http://english.sipo.gov.cn/news/official/201301/t20130105_782325.html> (accessed 10 January 2013).

592 HG Ruse-Khan, *Utility Model Protection-A Feasible Option for Incentivising Incremental Innovation?* (2012) Study conducted for the World Intellectual Property Organisation 43, 60-61 (copy on file with the author).

Figure 4.5: Growth in Patent Applications, 2000-2011

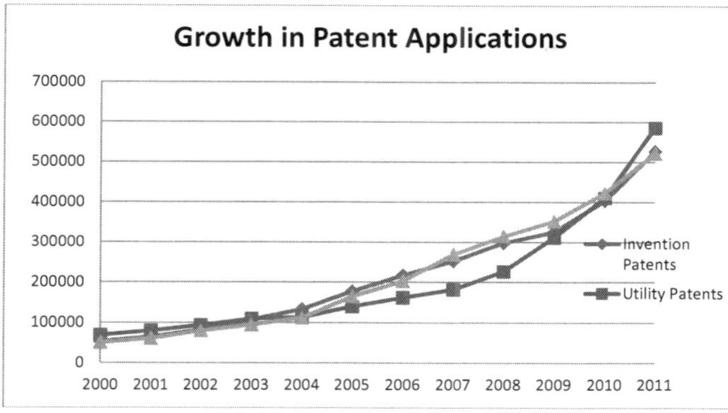

(Source: Based on data from SIPO)

Table 4.8: Chinese Versus Foreign Utility and Invention Patent Applications

	Utility Models			Invention		
	Applications			Applications		
	Domestic	Foreign	Total	Domestic	Foreign	Total
2006	159997	1369	161366	122318	88172	210490
%	99.2%	0.8%	100%	58.1%	41.9%	100%
2007	179999	1325	181324	153060	92101	245160
%	99.3%	0.7%	100%	73.3%	37.6%	100%
2008	223945	1641	225586	194579	95259	289838
%	99.3%	0.7%	100%	67.1%	32.9%	100%
2009	308861	1910	310771	229096	85477	314573
%	99.4%	0.6%	100%	72.8%	27.2%	100%
2010	407238	2598	409836	293066	98111	391177
%	99.4%	0.6%	100%	74.9%	25.1%	100%

(Source: Based on data obtained from SIPO)[593]

593 Ibid 60-62.

Figure 4.6: Invention, Utility and Design Patent Grants, 2011

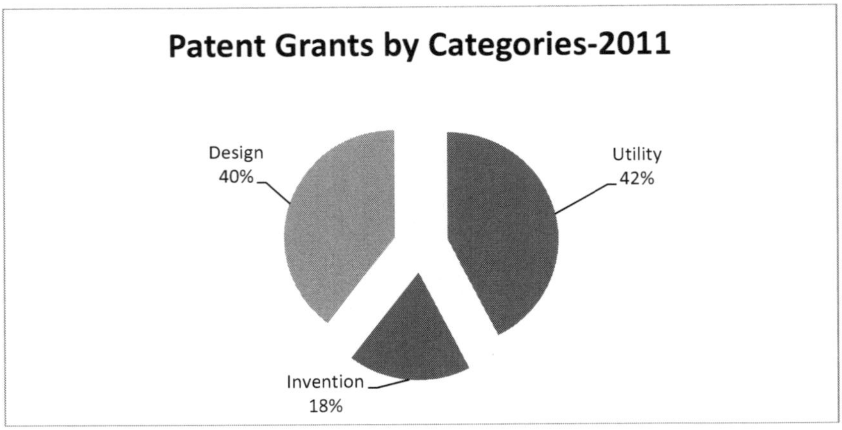

(Source: Based on data obtained from SIPO)

As presented in Table 4.8, domestic applicants make the lion's share of UM applications with more than 99 percent of total applications between 2006 and 2010 in China. Most strikingly, foreign UM applications accounted for less than 1 percent of the total applications filed during this period. In other words, domestic applications dominate the UM system in China. Nevertheless, according to the latest data from SIPO, foreign applications have increased from 2598 (0.6 percent) in 2010 to 4164 (0.71 percent) in 2011. The top five countries represented in foreign UM applications are Japan, the USA, Germany, Korea and Switzerland. On balance, the UM regime has not been attractive for foreign applicants. There may be differing reasons for this phenomenon. One possible explanation is that many Chinese trading partners do not have UM system in their respective countries. Another reason might be the exclusion of processes from UM protection in China. Moreover, many foreign firms are unaware of the benefits of the Chinese UM regime. When compared with UM applications, the share of foreign applications for invention patents is much higher and is accounted for nearly 30 percent in recent years.

According to commentators, the current indicators suggest that the UM system in China has become very popular among domestic users and it is effectively utilized by individuals and firms in securing necessary protection for their investments, in particular by small and medium-sized enterprises (SMEs).[594] The empirical data further suggests that the Chinese UM system has attracted interests of many users from China's industrial landscape. Moreover, according to a recent study, a significant majority of SMEs in China, perhaps as high as 80 percent, believe that a patent is necessary to operate in a certain industry.[595] In terms of the profile of users according to applicant type, our empirical evidence supports the view that individuals and SMEs are the main contributors to the UM applications. According to a recent internal report of SIPO, individuals (around 58 percent) and SMEs (around 26 percent) account for the biggest share of all the UM patents applications. The applications from research institutions, universities and colleges constitute around 16 percent of total UM applications.[596] The main industrial fields for UM applications include inventions relating to human necessities (25 percent), engineering (21 percent), mechanics (13 percent), electronics (11 percent), communications (6 percent).[597] Nevertheless, there is a difference in technology areas of domestic and foreign applications for UM patents. The domestic companies tend to emphasize on mechanical devices, and the foreign companies tend to focus on electrical devices.[598]

4.2.1.3. Critique and New Developments

According to SIPO, the Chinese utility model patent system has made remarkable achievements since its introduction in 1985. It not only promotes the implementation of the patent system, but also the economic, scientific

---

594 See D Wei, 'On the Simultaneous Filing of Patent Application for Invention and Patent Application for Utility Model' (1996) 2 China Patent and Trademark 28, 29.

595 TT Moga, China's Utility Model Patent System: Innovation Driver or Deterrent (Research Paper, US Chamber of Commerce 2012) 17.

596 Disclosed through personal communication with SIPO officials; e-mail from an officer at SIPO to author (20 August 2012).

597 Ibid.

598 See China Science Law Group, 'Characteristics and Best Practices of Utility Model System in China (2011) Website-Chinese Science Law Group 1, 9 available at: <http://www.chinasciencelawgroup.com/documents/Characteristic%20and%20Best%20Practices%20of%20Chinese%20Utility%20Model%20System%20July%2010,%202011.pdf> (accessed 10 May 2012).

and technological development of the country.[599] Although the UM system has provided substantial benefits to local industries, it has also suffered from major criticism. Concerns have been voiced from top IP officials of the government against promoting quantitative metrics over quality of UM patents.[600] Many have expressed doubts regarding the booming number of UM applications. To increase the number of domestic filings, China has introduced an array of incentives. They include cash bonuses, better housing for individual filers and tax breaks for companies that are prolific patent producers.[601] According to critics, China speaks of an innovation-by-the-numbers mentality, much like a student who equates knowledge with scores on standardized tests.[602] On the other hand, the pressure on Chinese entities to file patent applications is enormous, perhaps sometimes overwhelming.[603] Thus, applicants seeking to increase the number of their utility model patents file just about anything, from old technology to unpatentable technology to, in some instances, photocopies of previously issued patents.[604] In at least one province, businesses that do not file patent applications may face closure of their operations.[605] Opponents criticize the UM system for producing a huge number of 'junk patents' that are worthless rights with a high rate of invalidation.[606] Criticism has been leveled against the possibility of double patenting in China. One of the key concerns is that there can be utility model rights that are nothing more

---

599 State Intellectual Property Office of People's Republic of China (SIPO), 'Development of China's Utility Model System' (2013) Report released on 5 January 2013, SIPO – Official website, available at: <http://english.sipo.gov.cn/news/official/201301/t20130105_782325.html> (accessed 10 January 2013).

600 See the comment of M Weiye, The Director General of the State Intellectual Property Office's (SIPO) patent department, who has addressed the issue by saying that 'Our companies should pay much more attention to patent quality instead of only quantity'. M Weiye, 'SIPO: Quality not Numbers, Key to Patent and Innovation' People's Daily (Beijing China, 5 January 2011).

601 S Lohr, 'When Innovation, Too, Is Made in China' *The New York Times* (January 1, 2011) available at: <http://www.nytimes.com/2011/01/02/business/02unboxed.html?r=0> (accessed 10 January 2013).

602 Ibid.

603 TT Moga, China's Utility Model Patent System: Innovation Driver or Deterrent (Research Paper, US Chamber of Commerce 2012) 15.

604 Ibid.

605 Ibid.

606 Z Rongyan, 'The Legislation for Utility Models and Their Examination and Approval: On Improving the System of Patent for Utility Model' (1997) 2 China Patents and Trademark 73.

than an obvious variation of granted patents. There are also fears that the UM system can easily be used for strategic purposes although it is an unexamined right. The unfortunate reputation of utility models of 'easy to get in, hard to get out' is an invitation for free riders and other actors.[607] According to commentators, 'non-practicing entities' (patent trolls) are becoming an increasing threat to the innovation landscape in China.[608] Thus, it comes as no surprise that China's ambitious strategy to move from being the factory floor to being a leader in innovation has attracted huge criticism from many commentators.[609]

4.2.1.4. Lessons from China

The Chinese experience of the STP regime for almost three decades may be a good case study for developing economies such as Sri Lanka. Leaving aside the difference in market size, China can teach the developing countries in South Asia many lessons on encouraging 'indigenous innovation' to improve home-grown creativity. Available empirical evidence supports the view that the Chinese UM system has been a very useful IP tool for SMEs and individual innovators. As explained by SIPO in a recent statement:

> 'When the system was firstly established, China was comparatively weak in capacity for science and technology innovation. The inventions and creations made by many SMEs were technically low, and the majority of the innovative outputs were small inventions and creations. Though these small inventions and creations were not as creative as invention patents in the technological sense, they also contributed to scientific technology advancement, economic and society development of the country and should be given appropriate protection. China's utility model patent system was set up to protect this kind of inventions and creations'.[610]

---

607 TT Moga, China's Utility Model Patent System: Innovation Driver or Deterrent (Research Paper, US Chamber of Commerce 2012) 15.

608 Ibid 21. A 'Non-Practicing Entity' (NPE) is a patent owner that does not produce anything and does not commercialize anything but, instead, uses a patent offensively to extract money through forced licensing or litigation.

609 TT Moga, China's Utility Model Patent System: Innovation Driver or Deterrent (Research Paper, US Chamber of Commerce 2012) 24.

610 State Intellectual Property Office of People's Republic of China (SIPO), 'Development of China's Utility Model System' (2013) Report released on 5 January

There is no doubt that the above observations of SIPO certainly holds true for the Sri Lankan scenario today as the majority of innovations is concentrated on low technology produced by SMEs and individual innovators with less R&D investments. Thus, the Chinese experience could serve as a useful model for Sri Lanka in incentivising such innovation.

Moreover, the Chinese UM regime has been very instrumental in introducing and familiarizing the patent system to local industrial sectors, especially for many SMEs. As noted in Chapter 2, there is a general lack of awareness and a disappointingly low use of the patent system in Sri Lanka. To that extent, Sri Lanka can follow the Chinese example to inculcate the habit of using the IP system by industrial sectors and the general public. Furthermore, the concept of evaluation reports may be worth emulating because such a report would certainly help reduce potential abuses of the system. One other important aspect of the Chinese system that is worth following is the political will and support for promoting innovation in the country which might unfortunately be lacking in many developing countries. Perhaps most encouragingly, the Chinese government's innovation policies are designed to improve innovative capability in science and technology. Of course, through an indigenous innovation approach, the Chinese innovation policy is now directed to move from 'made in China' to 'innovate in China'. However, this by no means explains that the Chinese UM system is perfect. The quality of Chinese UM patents has suffered serious criticism in recent years. Thus, cases of abuse and other concerns regarding the quality need to be addressed in order to further improve the system.

2013, SIPO – Official website, available at: <http://english.sipo.gov.cn/news/official/201301/t20130105_782325.html> (accessed 10 January 2013).

4.2.2. Malaysia

> *'Ignored by many of the world's biggest and lucrative markets, utility model protection continues its long march to respectability and ultimate acceptability'.*
> *Professor Lim Heng Gee*[611]

Malaysia is one of the rapidly developing economies in the Southeast Asian region, with a population over 26.6 million. Like Sri Lanka, Malaysia is a Common Law country which has largely inherited its IP laws from the legal instruments and jurisprudence of the United Kingdom. Since its independence from British colonial rule in 1957, Malaysia has gradually developed its own IP law landscape. In recent decades, Malaysia has transformed its economy from an agricultural to a more industrial economy. Today, the country stands to benefit from its strong growth potential. Perhaps more importantly, Malaysia has a comprehensive UM system in place to protect and to incentivise minor and sub-patentable innovations in the country. The current system of utility innovations in Malaysia is governed by its Patent Act of 1983 (as amended). Given many similarities, among others, relatively small market size and the population, reflection on the Malaysian experience may benefit Sri Lanka in its endeavor to move up the technological ladder by encouraging domestic innovations, especially within the SMEs.

4.2.2.1. Main Features of the UM System

Under the Malaysian Patents Act of 1983, two types of protection are available; the first is through the grant of a patent, and the second is through the issue of a certificate for a utility innovation.[612] The latter system of protection available under the Act aims to protect 'minor inventions', called 'utility innovations' (hereinafter 'UI') in the statute, whereby a lower level of patentability criteria needs to be satisfied.[613] By virtue of

---

611 LH Gee, 'The long March National Laws travel the tortuous route towards utility Model protection' (1993) May, Managing Intellectual property 37, 37.

612 U Suthersanen, 'Utility Models and Innovation in Developing Countries' (2006) ICTSD Issue Paper No.13, 21, available at:<http://unctad.org/en/docs/iteipc 2006 6_en.pdf> (accessed 15 March 2012).

613 Ibid 21.

Section 17, the Act defines a utility innovation as "any innovation which creates a new product or process, or any new improvement of a known product or process, which is capable of industrial application, and includes an invention". According to scholars, the Malaysian utility innovation system may be more aptly described as a 'patent model', as opposed to the 'classical German Model' or the 'intermediate model', where the applicant would have to meet the same or similar substantive requirements as that of a standard patent application and protection is not limited to three-dimensional product or model.[614] The main objective of the introduction of the UI system in Malaysia was to protect inventions which may not be patentable because they do not satisfy the requirement of inventive step.[615] The thinking behind the UI regime has further been explained by the Intellectual Property Corporation of Malaysia (MyIPO) as follows:

> 'Utility innovation in Malaysia is expected to attract the locals and also the small innovators like students, individual inventors and the SMEs. These innovators usually come up with simple but useful everyday life utilities. These innovations might not be able to surpass the threshold of inventive step if applied for patents. Thus, UI incentivizes innovations by giving an easier and better path of protection for this group of innovators'.[616]

To be eligible for UI protection in Malaysia, an innovation must possess novelty and industrial applicability. Significantly, there is no requirement for an inventive step, which is specifically excluded by the Act.[617] Even though the original version of the patent Act carried the local novelty standard up until 1993, the current law, however, pursuant to Section 14, requires UI to satisfy absolute or universal novelty standard.[618] Moreover, other than for some minor modifications specified in the second Schedule, the procedure involved in an application for a certificate for a UI is the same as that is for regular patent.[619] Unlike a normal patent, for which

---

614 LH Gee, 'Second Tier Protection for Minor Inventions in Asia: An Appraisal of the Similarities and Differences' (3rd ASLI Conference Shanghai (China), 25-26 May 2006) 5-6.

615 IMAG Azmi, LH Gee and R Alavi, Intellectual Property System and Industrial Development in Malaysia (IIUM Press 2009) 70.

616 E-mail from MyIPO to author (23 December 2011).

617 See Sections 17 and 17(A) 2 of the Patent Act (as amended). U Suthersanen and others (eds), *Innovation without Patents* (Edward Elgar 2007) 171.

618 See Section 47 (a) (i) of the Patents (Amendment) Act 1993.

619 IMAG Azmi, LH Gee and R Alavi, Intellectual Property System and Industrial Development in Malaysia (IIUM Press 2009) 23.

more than one claim can be applied for, in the case of a UI only one claim is allowed.[620] As in patent law, discoveries, scientific theories, plants and animal varieties other than manmade living micro organisms and their products, methods of doing business and methods of treatment for the human or animal body are excluded from the scope of UI protection.[621]

Most notably, an application for UI is subjected to a substantive examination prior to grant. In that sense, the Malaysian system can be viewed as an examination system as opposed to a simple registration system. Furthermore, even though it is not possible for an applicant to be granted both a patent and a certificate for utility innovation for the same invention, the law allows to convert an application for a patent into an application for a utility innovation and vice versa.[622] The statutory life of a certificate of UI expires 10 years from the filing date of the application. Nevertheless, before the expiration of this 10 year period, an application for extension for two additional five year periods of protection can be made.[623] This means that the total term of protection may be extended to 20 years like in the case of a normal patent. However, before such extensions can be granted, the owner has to show that the utility innovation is in commercial or industrial use in Malaysia.[624] Moreover, pursuant to Section 36 of the Patent Act, the owner of a UI certificate, as in the case of a normal patent, enjoys exclusive rights to exploit the patented invention, to assign or transmit the patent as well as to conclude license agreements. According to the information of the MyIPO, the application fee for a UI is lower (RM 140(US$ 45) than for a normal patent (RM 290 (US$ 93), but the substantive examination fee applicable for both UI and patent remains the same (RM 140(US$ 354). Commentators have summarized the main features of the Malaysian UI regime as follows:[625]

---

620 Ibid 23. See also Section 28 (1) (d), as modified by the Second Schedule.

621 See Section 13 of the Patent Act for non-patentable inventions.

622 U Suthersanen, Utility Models and Innovation in Developing Countries (2006) ICTSD Issue Paper No.13, 22, available at: <http://unctad.org/en/docs/iteipc2006 6_en.pdf> (accessed 15 March 2012).

623 Ibid.

624 See IMAG Azmi, LH Gee and R Alavi, *Intellectual Property System and Industrial Development in Malaysia* (IIUM Press 2009) 23. See also Section 35, as modified by the Second Schedule.

625 See U Suthersanen and others (eds), *Innovation without Patents* (Edward Elgar 2007) 170. HG Ruse-Khan, *Utility Model Protection-A Feasible Option for In-*

- The protectable subject matter for utility innovations is the same as for patents which covers compounds and processes;
- No requirement for inventive step;
- The application can only contain one claim;
- Utility Innovation certificates are subjected to substantive examination before the grant. However, only the criterion of (absolute and universal) novelty is examined during this process;
- The duration of protection is for 20 years;
- Need to show that the invention is in commercial or industrial use in Malaysia for an extension of protection beyond 10 years;
- Not subject to compulsory license;
- Lower registration and maintenance costs.

Given below is an example of a granted UI certificate and its abstract as published by MyIPO. Application No. UI 20002263: Combined toothbrush and tongue cleaner[626]

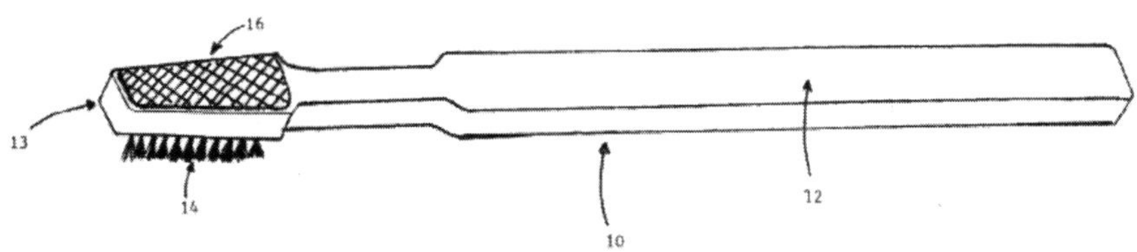

Abstract: "The present invention relates to a tooth brush, particularly one with a tongue cleaner attached at the opposite surface of the bristles at the head section. A toothbrush comprising a handle portion and a head portion at one end thereof, the head portion having a plurality of bristles on one surface as means for brushing the teeth where the improvement lies in the coarse but soft material attached by conventional means to the opposite surface of the said bristles at the head portion for the purpose of cleaning the tongue".[627]

---

centivising Incremental Innovation? 2012) Study conducted for the World Intellectual Property Organisation 65 (copy on file with the author).

626 Received from Industrial Property Division of Intellectual Property Corporation of Malaysia (MyIPO) through personal correspondence (12 July 2012).

627 Ibid.

4.2.2.2. Empirical Analysis of the UI System

The empirical data offers a telling glimpse of how effectively the Malaysian UI system has been used by the industrial sectors in the country. From a broad perspective, the patent landscape of Malaysia is dominated by foreign applications and local applicants represent only around 20 percent of all applications. Interestingly, patent filings from both groups have gone up during the last 10 years and have exceeded 6000 applications in year 2010 and 2011. The statistical evidence from the MyIPO suggests that Malaysia has been and is an attractive market for foreign inventions and technologies though it may be a cause for concern in terms of domestic innovations.

Table 4.9: Patent Applications, 2002-2011

Year	Local	Foreign	Total	Local (%)
2002	325	4609	4934	7
2003	377	4677	5054	8
2004	513	4932	5445	10
2005	514	5769	6283	9
2006	526	4271	4797	12
2007	636	1658	2294	38
2008	832	4473	5305	18
2009	1205	4471	5676	27
2010	1214	5139	6380	24
2011	1075	5373	6448	17

(Source: Based on data collected from MyIPO)

Figure 4.7: Trends in Patent Applications, 2000-2011

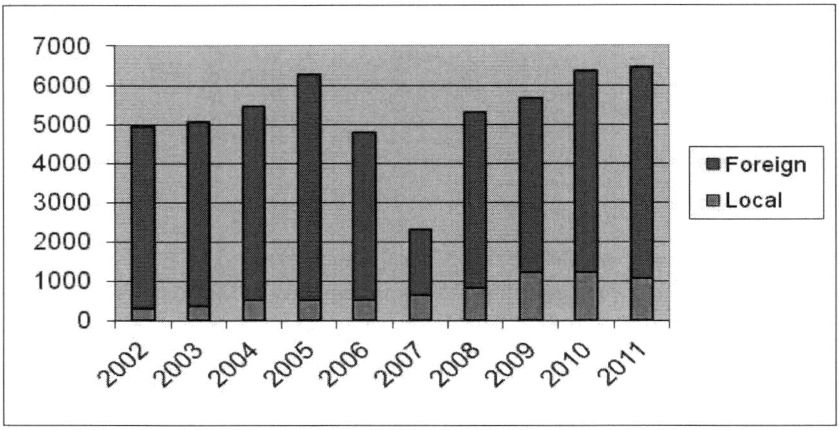

(Source: Based on data obtained from MyIPO)

In contrast to normal patent applications, the number of UI applications has been low and has recorded a slow growth in the recent years. As presented in Table 4.10 below, the foreign applicants have also been dominating UI applications up until year 2010. Most strikingly, since 2010, Malaysian filings have outnumbered foreign applications. According to previous studies, in the initial 10 years after the introduction of the utility innovation system in 1986, there was an overall ten-fold increase in applications (from 15 in 1986 to 152 in 1995) which was quite encouraging.[628] After the change from local to universal novelty in 1995 (The Patents Amendment Act of 1993, which came into force on 1 August 1995, has introduced the concept of absolute novelty for utility innovations),[629] the number of applications have sharply declined to a low of 45 in 1998, from which they then recovered to a range between 70 and 90 applications per

628 See LH Gee, IM Azmi and R Alavi, 'Reform towards Intellectual Property-Based Development in Malaysia' (2009) 12/4 Journal of World Intellectual Property 317, 330. HG Ruse-Khan, *Utility Model Protection-A Feasible Option for Incentivising Incremental Innovation?* (2012) Study conducted for the World Intellectual Property Organisation 66-67 (copy on file with the author).

629 See C Heath (ed), *Intellectual Property in Asia* (Kluwer 2003) 310. See also LH Gee, IM Azmi and R Alavi, 'Reforms Towards Intellectual Property based economic development in Malaysia' (2009) 12 Journal of World Intellectual Property 317, 330.

year.[630] Significantly, the total number of UI applications is less than 2 percent in proportion to annual patent application, except in year 2007. Table 4.11 below indicates the most recent trends in UI applications in Malaysia.

Table 4.10: Utility Innovation Applications, 2003-2011

Utility Innovation Applications				
Year	**Foreign**	**Local**	**Total Application**	**Percentage from total Patent Applications (%)**
2003	40	20	60	1.18
2004	49	48	97	1.78
2005	48	27	75	1.19
2006	46	31	77	1.60
2007	44	34	78	3.28
2008	66	32	98	1.81
2009	32	29	61	1.06
2010	37	47	84	1.30
2011	50	61	111	1.70
Grand Total	412	329	741	1.51

(Source: Based on data collected from MyIPO)

630 See IM Azmi and R Alavi, 'Reforms Towards Intellectual Property based economic development in Malaysia' (2009) 12 Journal of World Intellectual Property 317, 330. HG Ruse-Khan, *Utility Model Protection-A Feasible Option for Incentivising Incremental Innovation?* (2012) Study conducted for the World Intellectual Property Organisation 66 (copy on file with the author).

Figure 4.8: Trends in Utility Innovation Applications, 2000-2011

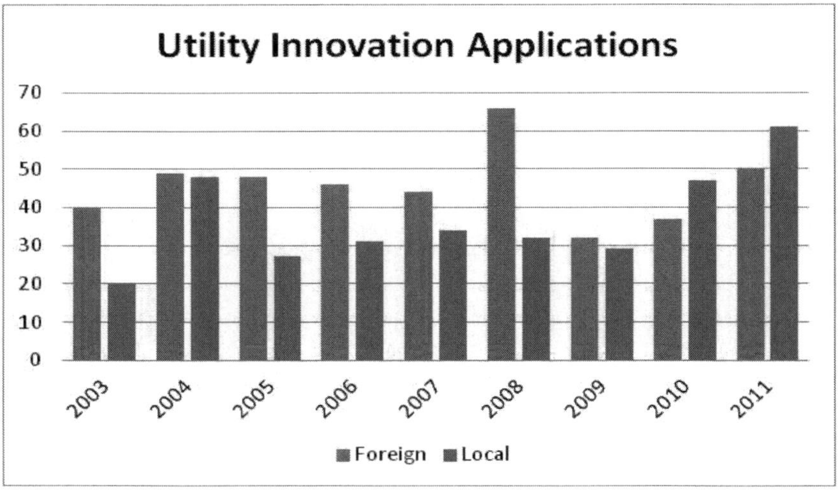

(Source: Based on data collected from MyIPO)

Figure 4.9: Growth in Utility Innovation Applications, 2003-2011

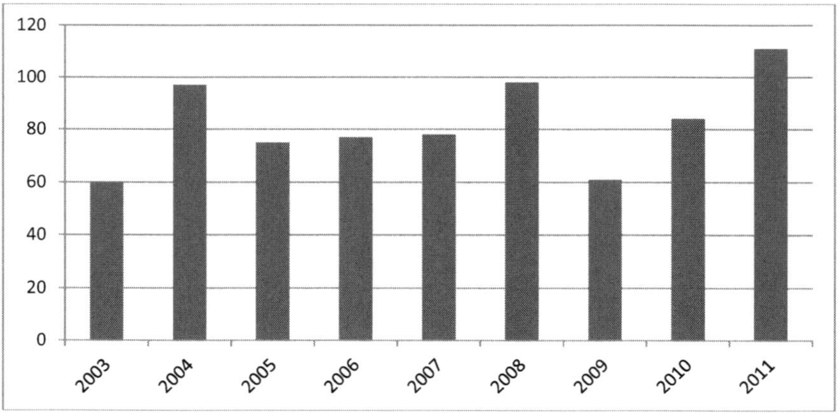

(Source: Based on data collected from MyIPO)

Survey evidence from Malaysian IP scholars also supports the view that low number of applications could be attributed to the change of novelty standard required for utility innovation from local novelty to universal novelty in 1995.[631] One possible explanation for adopting the universal novelty standard is due to the concern of the possibility that an UI may infringe an existing patent. Arguably, a UI claim might well overlap with an existing patent. According to a recent study, the main users of the utility innovation system in the years 1986-2003 come from the region, with 47.3 percent of users from Taiwan Province of China, followed by 38.9 percent of the applications emanating from Malaysia, then from the United States (4.3 percent) and Japan (1.3 percent).[632] As further observed by the same authors, in terms of the proportion of UI applications coming from companies and individuals and comparing the numbers with patents from 1999-2003, 34.2 percent of the utility innovation applications came from companies and institutions, while 65.8 percent came from individuals. When compared with the patent statistics during the same period, the percentages are very different: companies and institutions are responsible for 96.2 percent of applications with only 3.8 percent coming from individuals.[633] Viewed from the field of technology applied, the highest numbers of utility innovations encompasses innovations relating to human necessities such as footwear, furniture, agriculture, jewellery and travelling articles.[634] The second highest category relates to performing operations and transporting, followed by innovations relating to mechanical operations involving physical or chemical processes, machines, apparatus and also transportation such as railways, aircraft and vehicles.[635] According to commentators, these are areas in which individual innovators and SMEs could be involved in the creation of incremental improvements without the use of high technology.[636] All in all, it can be well argued that the Malaysian UI system has not been enthusisatically used by industrial sectors. It may be described as a moderate use. The reasons why the UI system has not been more widely used is perhaps best explained by the MyIPO:

---

631 Telephone interviews with Professor LH Gee, Faculty of Law, Universiti Technologi Mara, Malaysia, (17 November 2011) and the officials of MyIPO.

632 U Suthersanen, G Dutfield and KB Chow (eds), *Innovation without Patents* (Edward Elgar 2007) 176.

633 Ibid.

634 U Suthersanen, Utility Models and Innovation in Developing Countries (2006) ICTSD Issue Paper No.13, 22-23, available at: <http://unctad.org/en/docs/iteipc20066_ en.pdf> (accessed 15 March 2012).

635 Ibid.

636 Ibid.

> 'When these applications are subjected to substantive examination, though omitting the criteria of inventive step, the treatment received will be the same as of patent applications. The earlier applications will be examined first, thus utility innovation (UI) applications will have to wait for its turn to be examined. With UI applications' pendency period being the same as of patent applications, applicants prefer to apply for patents. The scope of protection granted for UIs are often more specific and narrow than patents. Applicants will have to include all features of innovations into the only one claim allowed thus making it easier for others to modify or improvise for further exploitation. Applicants prefer to be granted with a total automatic protection period of 20 years (with yearly renewal fees) without the hassle of providing proof of utilization after the 10th year'.[637]

As interpreted through its objectives, it appears that the Malaysian UI system is not serving the very purpose for which it was introduced, due to the above mentioned reasons. Probably, the potential costs outweigh the perceived benefits of the current system. The policymakers may need to reform the system in order to make it more attractive to local innovators.

4.2.2.3. Lessons from Malaysia

As observed in the above analysis, the current Malaysian UI system is much closer to the normal patent system. Significantly, the requirements of substantive examination of UI application before grant and the emphasis on the absolute novelty standard might have been discouraging factors for domestic industries, even though there is no requirement of inventive step for UI. Viewed through the lens of the underlying rationale of the STP, the Malaysian UI system should be able to provide quick, less expensive and more easily obtainable IP right for domestic industrial sectors. Obviously, the UI system in place is not catering to the needs of the SMEs of the country. It is undeniable that, due to the time-consuming substantive examination procedure, the system cannot meet the demand from the industrial sector for a faster enforceable right for products that have a relatively short commercial life. Moreover, from a practical perspective, the limitation on the number of claims allowed (one claim only) would make the system less attractive. Nevertheless, on the positive side, unlike many other countries such as Germany and China, the Malaysian system offers a broad scope of subject-matter including processes. According to the infor-

637 E-mail from the MyIPO to the author (23 November 2011).

mation from the MyIPO, Malaysia is currently considering an Amendment to the existing UI regime. The proposed amendment aims at changing from the substantive examination before the grant to a non-substantive examination system, providing cheap and fast grant of right, making provisions for a request for substantive examination after grant, allowing more claims, introducing a lower level of inventiveness and a more practical period of protection.[638] In sum, the Malaysian experience would undoubtedly offer motivations and rich insights in designing an appropriate STP regime for Sri Lanka. Nevertheless, emulating the Malaysian model without giving due consideration to the drawbacks of the system would lead to unintended repercussions.

4.2.3. Kenya

> *'The State shall support, promote and protect the intellectual property rights of the people of Kenya'.*
> Article 40 (5) of the 2010 Constitution of Kenya

Like Sri Lanka, Kenya has largely inherited its IP laws from the United Kingdom. Nevertheless, in recent years they were developed independently in view of international IP treaty obligations that Kenya has undertaken. Kenya was one of the first countries in the developing world to introduce a comprehensive system of IP rights and it is one of the leading countries in the African region which provides an effective utility model protection. A unique feature of the Kenyan utility models regime is that it has attempted to provide viable IP protection for traditional herbal medicine through a second-tier protection system. In that respect, the Kenyan system may offer rich insights for countries that consider extending IP protection for traditional knowledge inspired (TK-inspired) innovations. Therefore, the following discussion will mainly focus on that aspect of the Kenyan UM regime. In 2000, the United Nations Conference on Trade and Development has made specific reference to the Kenyan experience by suggesting that TK holders could take advantage of utility model (petty patent) systems that are less expensive to use and have lower inventive step require-

638 FR Dahalan, 'Utility Models protection in Malaysia-Utility Innovation' (2012) WIPO Regional Conference on the Legislative, Economic and Policy Aspects of utility Models Protection System, Kuala Lumpur, 3-4 September 2012.

ments. [639] The Kenya's Industrial Property Act of 1989 allows utility model protection for traditional medicinal knowledge in the form of 'herbal as well as nutritional formulations which give new effects'. Today, the Industrial Property Act of 2001 governs the system of UM protection in Kenya.

4.2.3.1. Protection under the Current System

Under Kenyan IP Law, the certificates of UM are granted for a broad variety of inventions. According to Section 2 of the Industrial Property Act, a 'utility model' is defined as any form, configuration or disposition of element of some appliance, utensil, tool, electrical and electronic circuitry, instrument, handicraft mechanism or other object or any part of the same allowing a better or different functioning, use, or manufacture of the subject-matter or that gives some utility, advantage, environmental benefit, saving or technical effect not available in Kenya before and includes micro-organisms or other self-replicable material, products of genetic resources, herbal as well as nutritional formulations which give new effects. An invention qualifies for a utility model certificate if it is new and industrially applicable.[640] According to the provisions of the Act, the novelty requirement for utility models in Kenya is similar to that required for patents. An invention is new if it is not anticipated by prior art which includes everything made available to the public anywhere in the world by means of written disclosure (including drawings and other illustrations) or, by oral disclosure, use, exhibition or other non-written means shall be considered prior art.[641] It is obvious from this provision that a UM also needs to meet the absolute or universal novelty standard. Perhaps more importantly, unlike for patents, an inventive step is not required for UM protection. Nevertheless, one other striking feature of the Kenyan system is that UM applications are evaluated for novelty and industrial applicability prior to grant of the right. This process impliedly functions as a kind of a

639 United Nations, 'Systems and National Experiences for Protecting Traditional Knowledge, Innovations and Practices' (United Nations Conference on Trade and Development, Geneva, 22 August 2000, the Background Note by the UNCTAD secretariat, TD/B/COM.1/EM.13/2) para 36.

640 See Section 82 (1) of the Industrial Property Act of 2001.

641 See Sections 23(1) and (2) of the Industrial Property Act of 2001.

substantive examination. In response to the author's query an explanation in this regard was offered by the Kenya Industrial Property Institute (KIPI) as follows:

> 'According to current practice, utility models are evaluated for novelty and industrial applicability before registration. The Industrial Property Act 2001 Section 82 seems to prescribe requirements for registration of utility models requiring practice based interpretation since it is not clear how novelty for example may be evaluated without an international type search as stipulated in the Act. The current practice by examiners is to discover prior art by conducting a limited international search based only on what is freely available online or contained in physical records within the Institute, to facilitate the evaluation for novelty; which evaluation is conducted using procedures identical to those adopted to evaluate patents'.[642]

The statutory life of a utility model certificate shall expire at the end of the tenth year after the date of the grant of the utility model, and shall not be renewable. Like patents, UM protection is available for both products and processes in Kenya. Furthermore, pursuant to Section 83(1) of the Act, it is possible to convert an application for patent into a utility model certificate and vice versa.

4.2.3.2. Empirical Analysis

The following data from the KIPI offers a telling glimpse of how patent and utility model regimes have been used in the Kenyan context. Viewed through the lens of statistics, there is a gradual increase in patent applications over the years though the total number of applications remains significantly below 200 per year. As noted before, the number of domestic patent applications is an indication of innovative activities of the country. It is evident that the patent system has been poorly-utilized.

---

642 Personal communication with OJF Omiti, Senior Patent Examiner Kenya Industrial Property Institute facilitated by H Mutai, the Managing Director of KIPI (e-mail from KIPI to author on 17 September 2012).

Table 4.11: Patent Applications, 2003-2010

Year	2003	2004	2005	2006	2007	2008	2009	2010
Residents	22	31	34	41	41	63	48	77
Non residents	3	3	6	2	6	0	6	2
PCT national phase(Non-Residents)	70	50	53	39	85	89	117	118
Total	95	84	93	82	132	97	171	197

(Source: Kenya Industrial Property Institute data)

Figure 4.10: Trends in Patent Applications, 2002-2010

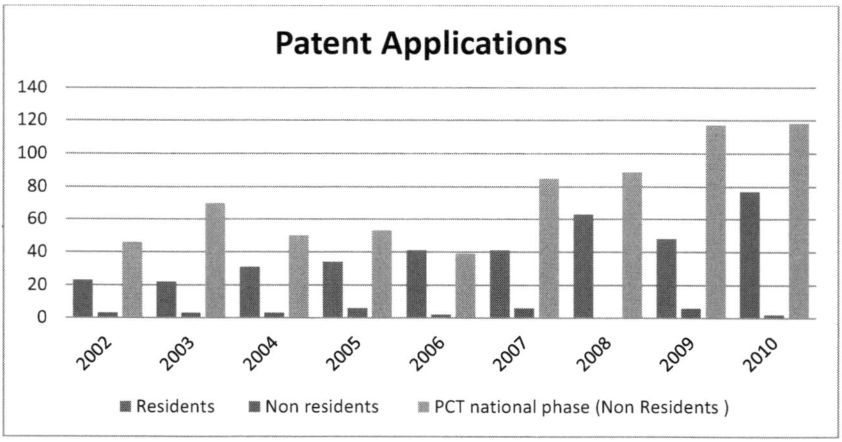

(Source: Based on data collected from Kenya Industrial Property Institute)

As indicated in Figure 4.11, in recent years both resident and non-resident applications have gone up in Kenya. What is clear from these statistics is that the majority of applications are made by non-residents. Most strikingly, the margin between domestic and foreign applications has gotten wider over the last few years and in particular in 2009 and 2010. In stark contrast to the patent applications, the utility model applications are predominantly represented by domestic applicants though the number of applications is small. Notably, as presented in Table 4.13, UM applications have recorded a slow growth since 2002.

Table 4.12: Utility Model Applications, 2002-2010

Utility Model Applications									
Year	2002	2003	2004	2005	2006	2007	2008	2009	2010
Residents	14	12	13	11	19	16	18	29	28
Non residents	0	0	0	0	0	0	1	1	0
Total	**14**	**12**	**13**	**11**	**19**	**16**	**19**	**30**	**28**

(Source: Statistics of Kenya Industrial Property Institute)

Figure 4.11: Trends in Utility Model Applications, 2002-2010

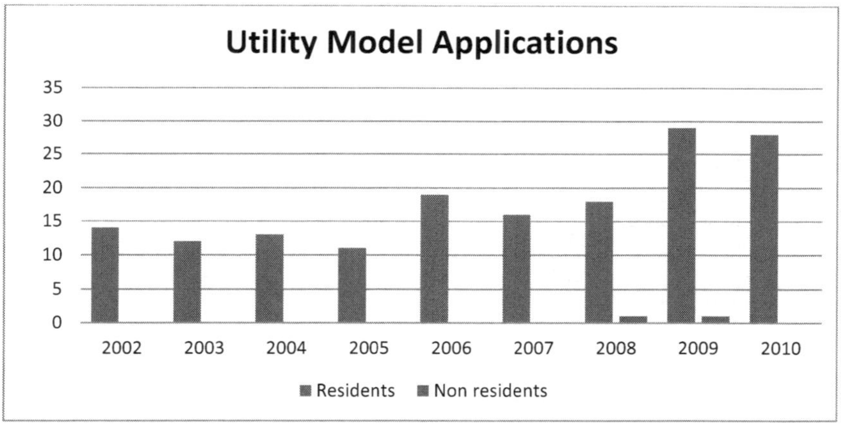

(Source: Based on data collected from Kenya Industrial Property Institute)

From this data, one can reasonably conclude that neither the patent system nor the UM regime has been very attractive for industrial sectors in Kenya. An important question which arises here is whether the objectives of introducing a UM system have not been met in the Kenyan context. From a policy perspective, a UM system aims at promoting indigenous innovation by providing less expensive, quicker to obtain and less complex IP protection. A UM regime is expected to appeal to domestic innovators, and especially to SMEs. Given its unique feature of protecting the traditional herbal medicine, the system should have been attractive for traditional medicine practitioners. The survey evidence from IP practitioners, legal academics and officials at KIPI suggests that the use of the UM system is disappointingly low. There may be several reasons for this situation. According to IP practitioners in Kenya, even though there is an adequate legal framework in place, the level of public awareness on IP remains low.[643] The ignorance on the part of innovators and costs of drafting and other legal services operate as obstacles to the use of the system. It was also revealed during the telephone interviews with officials of KIPI that traditional medicine practitioners are, in most cases, unwilling to disclose their innovations as per the provisions of the Act, and it is not possible to grant UM rights without a full disclosure of the invention. Nevertheless, perhaps more encouragingly, in recent years, there have been at least a few UM applications for TK-inspired innovations. Seen below is one such example.[644]

An example of a granted utility model for herbal formulation[645]

Application type	National Utility Model
Application No	KE/U/2008/000114
Filing date	01/04/2008
Registration date	20/08/2010
Entitlement date	20/08/2010
Expiration date	20/08/2020
Inventor	Antony Mbugua Kamau, P.O. Box 65 Rongai [KE];
Owner(s)	Ambuka Wineries, P.O. Box 65 Rongai [KE];
Title	A Medicinal Alcoholic Drink and Method for its Production.
Abstract	The invention relates to a fermented alcoholic drink with medicinal properties. The alcoholic drink is made by fermenting various ingredients such as maize flour, millet, yeast, water, sugar and juice extracted from the plants stinging nettle, Aloe Vera and Ironweed is added to provide the desired medicinal property. The invention also relates to a method of producing such an alcoholic drink.

643 Disclosed to the author by a interviewed Kenyan IP practitioner.

644 E-mail from KIPI to author (12 November 2012). The above UM example was provided by KIPI at the author's request and more evidence on TK-based innovation (herbal cosmetics) is found in the KIPI Annual Report 2004-2007, 45.

645 E-mail from KIPI to author (12 November 2012). The above UM example was provided by KIPI at the author's request.

Moreover, according to KIPI officials, "herbalists in most cases process their medicine in a traditional non-industrial way. However, if there is any that meets the industrial application as provided in the Industrial Property Act 2001, then such can be protected by a utility model".[646] Much depends on how Section 2 of the Act is interpreted. There are utility models held by innovators in other areas. According to Section 25 of the Industrial Property Act 2001, an invention shall be considered industrially applicable if, according to its nature, it can be made or used (in the technological sense) in any kind of industry, including agriculture, fishery and services.[647]

As observed from the utility model statistics obtained from the KIPI, the utility model system seems to have been under-utilized. The reason for this, according to legal practitioners, is that the target group is not very keen on registering their knowledge as utility models and also the process is lengthy, if subjected to 18 month waiting period. One other possible reason maybe that the law fixes the same novelty standard as for patent for utility models, though there is no requirement for any inventive step. As commentators pointed out, due to the basic similarities in procedure and requirements, the same problems which occurs under patents are experienced when granting utility model rights for indigenous innovations; for example, the substantive examination-like procedure before grant acts as a disincentive for potential users of the system.[648] According to one of the leading IP scholars in Kenya, 'it is true that Kenya has an advanced system of management of utility model. However, it cannot be said surely that this system holds out as the utility model practice system. In Kenya, despite the conditions for grants of utility models being less, the procedure is largely similar to that for grant of patents. Some of the problems of this include, the process is lengthy and technical. Consequently, many applications fail to mature to grant'.[649]

646 E-mail from KIPI to author (12 November 2012).

647 Ibid.

648 See JM Mbeva, 'Experiences and Lessons Learned regarding the Use of Existing Intellectual Property Rights Instruments for Protection of Traditional Knowledge' (UNCTAD Expert Meeting on Systems and National Experiences for Protecting Traditional Knowledge, Innovations and Practices, Geneva, 2000) 8.

649 Explanation of Professor B Sihanya from the University of Nairobi Law School (e-mail communication received on January 21, 2013).

4.2.3.3. Lessons from Kenya

In view of the increasing demand for an appropriate protection mechanism for TK-inspired innovation in TK-rich countries such as Sri Lanka, it is certainly encouraging to observe that Kenya offers a system of UM protection for herbal, as well as nutritional formulations which give new effects. Kenya has extended UM protection system to non-traditional subject matters. As stated by commentators, most of the indigenous knowledge and innovation particularly in herbal medicine may be protected under the UM regime if they are given modern technological touches. Unfortunately, to many of the indigenous people this technology is relatively unavailable.[650] This may also be the case in Sri Lanka. Moreover, it appears quite clear from the available evidence that the Kenyan UM system is under-utilized. There may be several explanations for this. Viewed through the lens of the Kenyan experience, one can well argue that, having an adequate legal framework alone is not enough to promote indigenous innovations, there needs to be a supporting mechanism to help TK-based innovators to turn their innovative ideas to IP rights. The lack of familiarity with the use of the UM system among SMEs may be a discouraging factor to them. Arguably, the low level of public awareness is a major obstacle for the effective use of the system. Most importantly, any STP system needs to be user-friendly and should appeal to the target group of users, especially the individual innovators and the SMEs. The Kenyan experience shows that the granting procedure is rather similar to that of patents and is time consuming. Moreover, the absolute novelty standard may also be a difficult hurdle for local innovators to overcome. As is evident, the disclosure requirement is a serious concern for TK-based industrial sectors. Nevertheless, TK-based innovators need to disclose their innovations if they opt to use the protection mechanism under the UM system. Certainly, secrecy may not be the right path to promote high quality products to meet global demand. Another important lesson from Kenya is that TK-inspired innovators may probably face difficulties in drafting their UM applications in scientific legal language. Like in Kenya, this may be a practical hurdle for potential users in Sri Lanka. In terms of the lessons to be learned from

---

650 See JM Mbeva, 'Experiences and Lessons Learned regarding the Use of Existing Intellectual Property Rights Instruments for Protection of Traditional Knowledge' (UNCTAD Expert Meeting on Systems and National Experiences for Protecting Traditional Knowledge, Innovations and Practices, Geneva, 2000) 8.

Kenya, while some aspects of the UM system may offer useful inspiration for Sri Lanka, other features that make the UM system less attractive for domestic innovators should be treated with caution.

5. South Asian Region and Second-Tier Protection

> *'New models of intellectual property are needed to protect and promote local knowledge in innovations'.*
> *Anil Gupta*[651]

As observed by Anil Gupta, one of the protagonists of the innovation movement in India, we should go beyond conventional models of IP rights to give innovators a true stake in their inventions.[652] The South Asian subcontinent is home to 22 percent of the world's population and is a unique region endowed with rich natural and human resources. Countries in the South Asian region consist of eight middle and low income economies including India, Pakistan, Bangladesh, Afghanistan, Sri Lanka, Nepal, Bhutan and the Maldives. Most strikingly, with the exception of certain technology areas in India (i.e. software and pharmaceutical industries), almost all countries in South Asia are less technologically advanced economies. When compared with the technological and economic development of the Newly Industrializing Countries (NICs) in East Asia, in particular the 'East Asian Tigers', the South Asian countries lag far behind their East Asian counterparts.[653] Experience from East Asia, especially from South Korea and China, has proven that innovation at all levels should be rewarded in order to create an innovation culture in a country. Thus, the time is ripe for developing nations in the South Asian region to create an eco-system for fostering minor and incremental innovation in or-

---

651 A Gupta, 'How to Protect the Inventions of Poor' (2 May 2012) Science and Development Network, available at: <http://www.scidev.net/en/science-and-innovation-policy/supporting-grassroots-innovation/opinions/how-to-protect-the-inventions-of-the-poor.html> (accessed 22 May 2012).

652 Ibid.

653 NICs are countries that have not yet reached the developed country status, but in a microeconomic sense, they have outpaced their developing counterparts. The term 'East Asia Tigers' began to be used in the 1970s for countries which had gained global prominence with rapid economic growth since the 1960s. See BMK Mwiya, 'Trends of Patent and Utility Model Activities in Asia and Africa: A Comparison of Regional Innovation, FDI and Economic Activity' (2012) 3 WIPO Journal 259. The four original 'tiger' economies are Hong Kong, Singapore, South Korea and Taiwan; later Indonesia, Malaysia and Thailand were added to the list.

der to move up the innovation ladder. Interestingly, though, no country in the South Asian region has experienced an STP regime in its IP law landscape.

It may be argued that there exists a protection gap between the patent and industrial design laws for incremental and minor inventions in the region. Obviously, there is no adequate protection for incremental advances in technology and such innovations fall through the protection net of IP law due to their lower level of inventiveness. Without an adequate protection mechanism such innovations may not be properly exploited and appropriated. As various studies have shown, the majority of innovations from developing countries are concentrated on the low level of technologies and often involve minor adaptations or improvements of existing products and processes which mostly emanate from the SME sector.[654] Admittedly, the SME sector in South Asia is affected by this scenario. At least in recent years, a wave of ideological current in favour of an STP regime is sweeping through the Indian sub-continent. And most encouragingly, the concept of utility models or petty patents is under consideration at least in three jurisdictions in the region. It is widely believed that a legal framework for an STP regime would emerge sooner or later from one of these countries. Specifically in 2011, the Indian government introduced a policy document in the form of a Discussion Paper proposing UM protection for India. Further, in the year 2013, the Pakistani government drafted a UM Bill based on a WIPO study carried out in 2012. Even though the strengths and weaknesses of an STP regime may fiercely be contested, the experience from developed and developing countries lends credibility to such a system in encouraging less advanced, but locally useful innovations. Since a detailed analysis of innovation and the legal landscape of all the jurisdiction falls beyond the scope of this research, this chapter only deals with the Indian perspectives of the protection of incremental innovations and a brief account of Pakistani developments in the direction of an STP regime.

---

654 See C Correa, 'Designing Patent Policies suited to Developing Countries Needs' (2008) 10/2 Econômica, Rio de Janeiro 82, 89. See also WIPO, 'Intellectual Property (IP) Rights and Innovation in Small and Medium-sized Enterprises' (2004) WIPO Working Paper August 10/2004, 5-6, available at: <http://www.wipo.int/export/sites/www/sme/en/documents/pdf/iprs_innovation.pdf> (accessed 10 June 2011).

5.1. Indian Perspectives

'Today we [Indians] are a nation that has barely scratched its potential'
Nandan Nilekani [655]

The Republic of India is the largest democracy in the world, consisting of 28 provincial Sates and 7 union territories.[656] Since its economic liberalization in 1991, India has achieved remarkable economic growth. From a global perspective, India is the economic giant in South Asia with a large market. Moreover, India is a leading member of the 'BRICS' group of countries, the world's five major emerging economies in the 21st century.[657] Like other South Asian countries, the Indian legal system has been greatly influenced by the British Common Law tradition. The same is certainly true for the Indian legal framework of IP protection. From a historical perspective, the existence of IP laws in India can be traced back to the mid-nineteenth century when the first patent law was enacted in 1856 to grant certain exclusive privileges to inventors for a period of fourteen years.[658] That law was based on the British Patent Law of 1852.[659] Emerging from British colonial domination, in the last sixty years India h gradually reformed its IP legislation, and in the 1990s, India also attempted to bring its IP regime in conformity with global developments.[660] In that

655 N Nelekani, Advantage India, *The Financial Express* (21 December 2008), available at: <http://www.financialexpress.com/story-print/400976> (accessed accessed 10 June 2011). See generally, N Nelekani, *Imagining India: The Idea of a Renewed Nation* (Penguin 2008). See also D Llewelyn, *Invisible Gold in Asia* (Marshall Cavendish 2010) 188.

656 See S Baldia, 'India' in C Heath (ed), *Intellectual property law in Asia* (Kluwer Law International 2003) 431.

657 The term 'BRIC' was first coined by Jim O'Neill in 2001 to refer Brazil, Russia, India, and China. South Africa was later added to that list. This group represents five emerging world economic powers.

658 VK Unni, 'Indian Patent Law and TRIPS: Redrawing the Flexibility Framework in the Context of Public Policy and Health' (2012) 25 Global Business & Development Law Journal 323, 323-324.

659 NR Subbaram, 'Intellectual Property System in India' (1997) 2 Journal of Intellectual Property Rights 10.

660 S Baldia, 'India' in C Heath (ed), *Intellectual property law in Asia* (Kluwer Law International 2003) 435.

sense, the Indian IP scenario has undergone a sea change in the past decades.[661]

The main legal instruments that govern the protection of inventions are the Patent Act of 1970 (as amended in 1999, 2002 and 2005) and the Design Act of 2000. The underpinning philosophy of the Indian Patent Act, according to the *Ayyangar Report* which led to its introduction, was to accommodate the country's inexperienced industrial sectors and to encourage and reward inventors.[662] The current Indian Patent Act requires an invention to meet the universal novelty standard and a high threshold of inventive step.[663] Pursuant to Section 2(fa), the inventive step is defined as a 'feature of an invention that involves technical advance as compared to the existing knowledge or having economic significance or both and that makes the invention not obvious to a person skilled in the art'. This inventive step criterion needs an invention to fulfill not only 'technical advance', but also 'economic significance'. The global and stringent nature of Indian patent law, in effect, prevents low level inventions receiving patent protection. Moreover, the universal novelty standard and the exclusion of functional innovations from protection exclude technical innovations of incremental nature from protection under the design regime.

Even though some would argue today that India is on the threshold of emerging as an economically and technologically developed nation, most IP scholars from India disapprove of such a claim. As Kumar has observed, 'even though the domestic chemical and pharmaceutical industries have developed in their capabilities considerably over the past three decades, there was no mechanism for encouraging minor adaptations

---

661 S Kumar, 'Does Introduction of a Utility Model Protection Regime make Sense in India' (2011) Intellectual Property Watch, available at: <http://www.ip-watch.org/2011/07/13/does-introduction-of-a-utility-model-protection-regime-make-sense-in-india/> (accessed 2 May 2012). The diverse legislations regarding the different categories of IP in India are: The Patents Act of 1970, The Trade Marks Act of 1999, The Copyright Act of 1957, The Designs Act 2000, The Geographical Indications of Goods Act, 1999, The Protection of Plant Varieties and Farmers' Rights Act 2001, The Semi Conductors Integrated Circuits Layout – Design Act 2000.

662 NR Iyyangar, *Report on the Revision of the Patent Law* (Ministry of Commerce and Industry/India 1959). See also VK Unni, 'Indian Patent Law and TRIPS: Redrawing the Flexibility Framework in the Context of Public Policy and Health' (2012) 25 Pacific McGeorge Global Business & Development Law Journal 323.

663 See The Patents Act of 1970, as last amended in 2005. Section 2(g) for novelty and Section 2(ja) for the inventive step requirement.

through domestic firms. This difference could perhaps explain the not so encouraging performance of Indian enterprises in other industries'.[664] Moreover, despite the fact that India's post-independence technology policies relied heavily on publicly funded research for indigenous technological capacity building and technology development, such publicly funded research has failed to adequately contribute to India's industrial catch up.[665] It is certainly true that India has made some impressive strides since its independence in some areas such as Information Technology (IT), pharmaceuticals, and the agro-chemical industrial sector etc. Most commentators, however, argue that despite India's rapid economic progress and technological proficiency, it has failed to produce any real innovation on its own soil.[666] One possible explanation for this would be that the effectiveness of patent protection varies from industry to industry and inventive activity is sensitive to protection only in a few industries such as the chemical and pharmaceutical industries.[667] Another more likely explanation may be that, unlike in East Asian countries viz. Japan and South Korea, India did not provide encouragement to adaptive and minor inventive activity of domestic enterprises through a utility models system, although the IP regime is only one of the determinants of the technological capability building.[668] In fact, empirical evidence from previous studies suggests that the East Asian economies have greatly benefited from UM regimes at the early stages of their industrial development.[669]

---

664 N Kumar, 'Intellectual Property Rights, Technology and Economic Development: Experiences of Asian Countries' (2003) Commission on Intellectual Property Rights Study Paper-1b, 6.

665 AS Ray and S Saha, 'Patenting Public Funded Research for Technology Transfer: A Conceptual-Empirical Synthesis of US Evidence and Lessons for India' (2011) 14/1 Journal of World Intellectual Property 75, 75.

666 See D Llewelyn, *Invisible Gold in Asia* (Marshall Cavendish 2010) 189.

667 N Kumar, 'Intellectual Property Rights, Technology and Economic Development: Experiences of Asian Countries' (2003) Commission on Intellectual Property Rights Study Paper-1b, 3-6.

668 Ibid.

669 YK Kim and others, 'Appropriate Intellectual Property Protection and Economic Growth in Countries at Different levels of Development' (2012) 1/4 Research Policy 358, available at: <http://www.sciencedirect.com/science/article/pii/S0048733311001715> (accessed 2 June 2012). See also, L Kim, *Technology Transfer and Intellectual property rights: The Korean Experience* (2003) ICTSD-UNCTAD Issue Paper No.2, 9.

5.1.1. Empirical Analysis of the Indian Patent System

The number of patent filings and grants offers a telling glimpse of the use of the current patent system by Indians and foreign applicants. In fact, the number of patent applications filed per year is a good metric of measuring the innovation potential of a country, and as seen below, India fares quite poorly when compared to many other developed and developing countries.[670] Most notably, domestic applications have recorded a slow growth during this period. Does this mean that Indians are less creative? The answer is probably no, but it is true that India is lagging behind many of its East Asian counterparts in terms of the total number of patent applications. An analysis of patent filing trends shows that the majority of patent filers are foreign residents and they make around 80 percent of the total applications every year. One possible reason for such low patenting activities in India may be attributed to the lack of awareness. Nevertheless, it is clear that not many players in the industrial sectors have made good use of the country's patent mechanism.

---

670 A Aggrawal and B Rawat, 'The Indian Patent System Should Grant Utility Model Patents' (2011) Entrepreneurs website, available at : <http://www.entrepreneurswebsite.com/2011/09/08/the-indian-patent-system-should-grant-utility-model-patents/?goback=%2Egde_3297732_member_69774577> (accessed 2 May 2012).

Table 5.1: Patent Applications Received from 2003-2010

	Patent Applications				
Year	**Resident**	**%**	**Non Resident**	**%**	**Total**
2003/4	3218	25,5%	9395	74,5%	12613
2004/5	3630	20,8%	13836	79,2%	17466
2005/6	4521	18,4%	19984	81,6%	24505
2006/7	5314	18,4%	23626	81,6%	28940
2007/8	6040	17,2%	29178	82,8%	35218
2008/9	6161	16,7%	30651	83,3%	36812
2009/10	7044	20,5%	27243	79,5%	34287

(Source: Based on data from Annual Reports of the Controller General of Patents, Designs, Trademarks and Geographical Indication)

Obviously, the total number of patent applications has gradually increased over the years between 2003 and 2010 and it may be seen as almost a three-fold increase from 2003. Viewed from a different perspective, even domestic patent filings are several times less numerous than foreign applications, overall patent activities in India have gradually increased in recent years. As a positive side of this development, the number of patent filings by foreign firms highlights the country's attractiveness as a market for technologies and inventions. It is also a good indication that rapid technological growth is taking place. At the same time, a comparative view with neighboring China shows that these patent filings are far from satisfactory. Arguably, India needs to take some concrete steps to encourage local innovation in order to boost IP creation activities in the country.

Figure 5.1: Trends in Patent Applications, 2003-2010

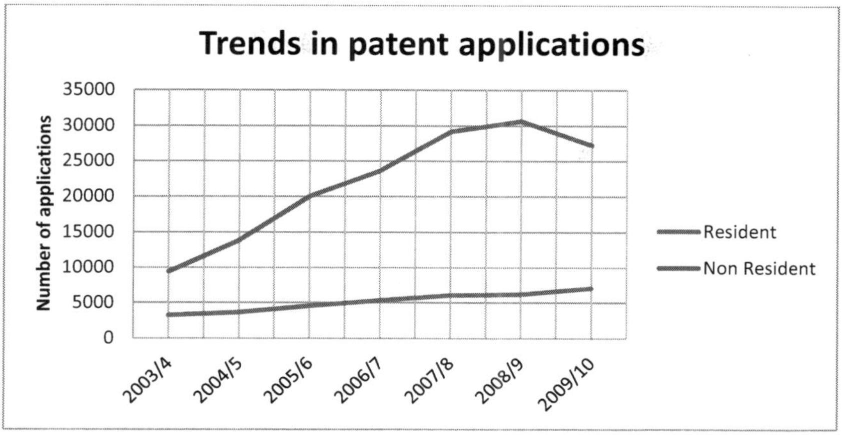

(Source: Based on data from Annual Reports of the Controller General of Patents, Designs, Trademarks and Geographical Indication)

As presented in Table 5.2, the patent system in India is overwhelmingly used by foreign individuals and firms. Obviously, the situation has not changed much from what the *Ayyangar Report* observed as far back as 1959. At that time, the share of patents held by foreign firms accounted for 80-90 percent of all patents issued in India. According to recent data from the IP India, more than 70 percent of all patents granted in India are owned by non-residents. As shown in Table 5.2, the percentage of patents granted to Indian applicants has gradually decreased from 2003 to 2010, except in 2004. Most strikingly, the percentage has fallen to the lowest level in 2008/9, with only 15 percent of patent grants to Indians. Not surprisingly, many commentators have described India as a patent granting country rather than a patent producing one, emphasizing that there is a clear need to encourage more domestic innovations in India.

Table 5.2: Patent Grants from 2003-2010

	Patent Grants				
Year	Resident	%	Non Resident	%	Total
2003/4	945	38,3%	1524	61,7%	2469
2004/5	764	40,0%	1147	60,0%	1911
2005/6	1396	32,3%	2924	67,7%	4320
2006/7	1907	25,3%	5632	74,7%	7539
2007/8	3173	20,8%	12088	79,2%	15261
2008/9	2541	15,8%	13520	84,2%	16061
2009/10	1725	28,0%	4443	72,0%	6168

(Source: Based on data from Annual Reports of the Controller General of Patents, Designs, Trademarks and Geographical Indication)

Figure 5.2: Trends in Patent Grants, 2003-2010

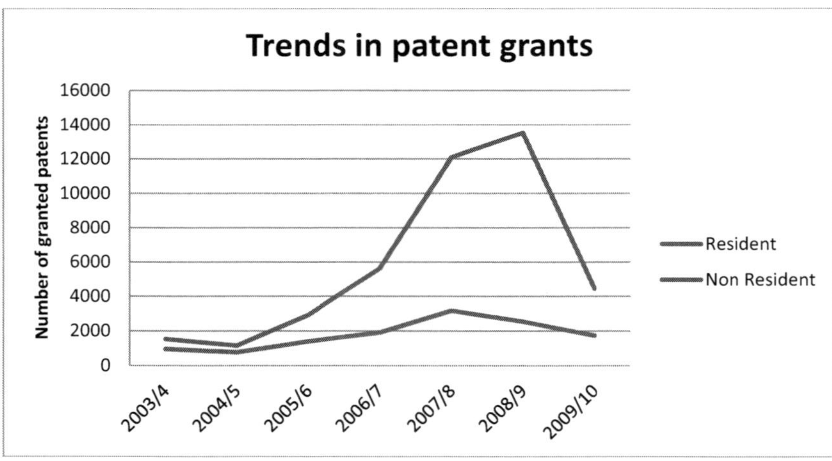

(Source: Based on data from Annual Reports of the Controller General of Patents, Designs, Trademarks and Geographical Indication)

Figure 5.3: A Comparative View on Patent Applications and Grants from 2003-2010

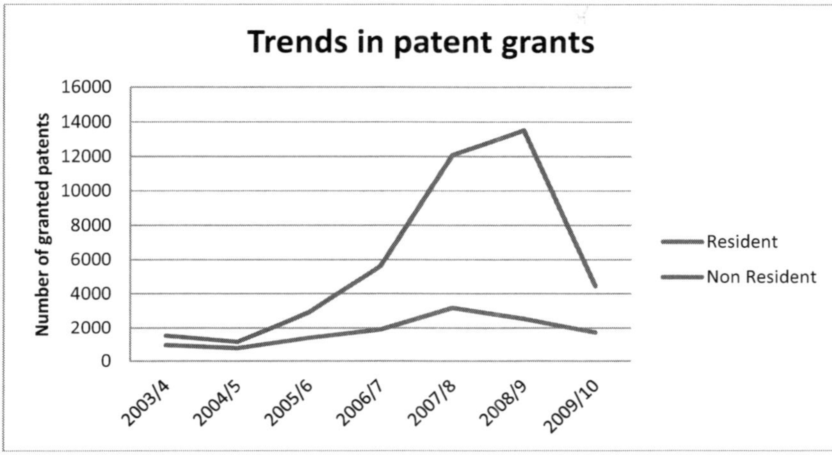

(Source: Based on data from Annual Reports of the Controller General of Patents, Designs, Trademarks and Geographical Indication)

As shown in Figure 5.3, the grant rate of patent applications from 2003 to 2010 remains below 40 percent in India. It is rather disappointing to learn that such a large number of patent applications are rejected at the Indian patent office. Most probably, the majority of them might have failed to reach the strict patentability criteria prescribed in the current Patent Act. From this data it can be reasonably concluded that the high inventive step requirement poses a great barrier for many inventions emanating from the innovation landscape of India. Perhaps most importantly, if the Indian IP legal framework has provided for a UM or petty patent system, a large part of these rejected applications would have been granted an IP right, thereby incentivising such inventive activities in the country. From a policy perspective, most applications that are currently being rejected for not meeting the stringent inventive step requirement would be granted a patent right if there was an STP regime in place.

5.1.2. Protection of Incremental Innovations in India

As interpreted through the lens of the *Ayyanger Report*, the patent system is the most desirable method of encouraging inventors and rewarding them but, at present, Indian inventors take a very small share in the benefits of the system.[671] These observations made in the *Ayyangar Report* also find empirical support from our analysis in the previous section. Nevertheless, there is little reason to conclude that Indians are less innovative. An important reason why there is low domestic participation in patenting is that there is no protection for less technologically advanced inventions in India. A large majority of innovations of SMEs and creative solutions from the rural hinterland are excluded from patent protection. Conversely, it might still be argued that incremental innovation should not be protected at all and deserves to be in the public domain. Obviously, the implementation of stringent patentability criteria makes the patent regime inaccessible for low level simple innovations. Most importantly, Indian IP legal framework does not provide for an STP system such as utility models or petty patents, on one hand. On the other hand, Section 3 and 4 of the Indian Patent Act include a bar on patenting a mere discovery of new forms of known substances, mere arrangement or rearrangement or duplication of known devices, and methods of agriculture or horticulture and inventions which are in effect traditional knowledge.[672] Thus, incremental and minor innovations are specifically excluded from the protection schemes of the current Indian Patent Act.

Critics have pointed out that in particular the patentability criteria under Section 3(d) may even be viewed as an inventive step plus requirement.[673]

671 KS Kardem, 'Patent activities in India: An Overview' (1997) 2 May, Journal of Intellectual Property Rights 113, 113.

672 Department of Industrial Policy and Promotion, Discussion Paper on Utility Model(23 May 2011) para 6, available at: <http://dipp.gov.in/English/Discuss_paper/Utility_Models_13May2011.pdf> (accessed 30 December 2011). See Section 3(d) which states that the mere discovery of a new form of a known substance which does not result in the enhancement of the known efficacy of that substance or the mere discovery of any new property or new use for a known substance or of the mere use of a known process, machine or apparatus cannot be considered as an invention. See also, Section 3 (f) of the Indian Patent Act.

673 A Aggrawal and B Rawat, 'The Indian Patent System Should Grant Utility Model Patents' (2011) Entrepreneurs website, available at: <http://www.entrepreneurswebsite.com/2011/09/08/the-indian-patent-system-should-grant-utility-model-patents/?goback=%2Egde_3297732_member_69774577> (accessed 2 May 2012).

Some commentators including Anil Gupta have lamented over the non-availability of a protection mechanism for incentivising incremental and grassroots innovations in the legal landscape of India. Grassroots innovation are the innovative activities of improving products, techniques and crafts in a random and extensive way by people at the grassroots who have grasped the corresponding techniques and skills. It is a flash in the common people and an embodiment of their wisdom.[674] Obviously, there is no supporting climate for such innovation. Moreover, Mashelkar, a leading Indian IP scholar, has repeatedly emphasized the need of having shorter duration patents for smaller innovations, including specific improvements in traditional knowledge.[675] The system he advocates involves a simple registration-cum-petty patent system where the inventive threshold would be lower, but even a small improvement in material, process, product or use could be protected at much lesser costs and for a shorter duration.[676] Anil Gupta has also followed the same line in arguing that India needs to develop a low transaction cost protection system for small innovators and local communities to make the IP system accessible, based on the Australian innovation patent system.[677] In response to the perceived protection gap and the claim of insufficient incentives for incremental innovations, the Indian government recently took the initial steps in addressing such concerns through the legislative route.

5.1.3. DIPP Discussion Paper

Far too long, Indian scholars have criticized policymakers for not taking into account the special features of Indian intellect, knowledge base and capabilities, nor the ground realities of the pattern of innovations taking

674 L Hua, Y Jiang and Y Lin, 'Grassroots Innovation, Characteristics, Status Quo and Suggestions' (2010) Proceedings of the 7th International Conference on Innovation & Management 2048.

675 RA Mashelkar, 'An Eminent Scientist's New Road-map for India', *GoodNewsIndia* (November 2000) available at : <http://www.goodnewsindia.com/Pages/content/inspirational/mashelkar.html> (accessed 30 January 2011).

676 Ibid.

677 AK Gupta, 'Rewarding Traditional Knowledge and Contemporary Grassroots Creativity: The Role of Intellectual Property Protection' (Centre of International Development, Harvard University 2000) 41-42, available at: <http://www.hks.harvard.edu/sustsci/ists/TWAS_0202/gupta_0500.pdf> (accessed 15 May 2012).

place in the country when drafting IP laws.[678] In view of such critiques, on 13 May 2011, India's Department of Industrial Policy and Promotion (DIPP) released a discussion paper on the possibility of introducing a lower level patent system in India.[679] The discussion paper has admitted that the Indian Patent Act, with its high standard of patentability, may inhibit the protection of creeping and incremental innovation which are no less worth and useful to society.[680] In its DIPP Discussion Paper, the government has observed:

> 'The IP regime in India has undergone significant changes after India's accession to WTO in 1995. After an intense national debate a number of safeguards were incorporated in the amendments made to the Patents Act. These safeguards were designed to prevent evergreening of patents. They included a higher threshold for inventive step and a prohibition from patenting new forms of known substances which do not result in the enhancement of the known efficacy of these substances. Such a stance has been consistent with our obligations under TRIPS and seeks to meet our developmental objectives. While we are firmly committed to resist dilution of patent standards, the need to support the widest possible spectrum of innovative activity in India today, has to be recognized. This Discussion Paper approaches this challenge by examining the viability of introducing utility models into the IPR regime. Utility models are a framework for providing limited protection to those innovations which may not meet the standards of the Patents Act and yet are commercially exploitable and socially relevant'.[681]

Most encouragingly, the Discussion Paper recognized the important role of creeping and incremental innovation has in the innovation landscape of India. Such inventions, though technically less complex than those eligible for a patent, may be exploited by SMEs which in the spirit of *jugaad* technology (a creative or innovative idea producing a quick, alternative way of solving or a fixing a problem), may make minor improvements and adap-

---

678 MD Nair, 'A Case for Grant of 'Petty Patents', *The Hindu* (New Delhi, 10 May 2001) available at: <http://hindu.com/2001/05/10/stories/0610000h.htm> (accessed 15 June 2012).

679 P Ollier, 'Practitioners back Utility Model Patents for India' (July 2011) Managing Intellectual property, available at : <http://www.managingip.com/Article/2848140/Practitioners-back-utility-model-patents-for-India.html> (accessed 15 June 2012).

680 Ibid.

681 Department of Industrial Policy and Promotion of India, 'Utility Models' (2011) Discussion Paper-23 May 2011, para 3-4. available at: <http://dipp.gov.in/nglish/Discuss_paper/Utility_Models_13May2011.pdf> (accessed 30 December 2011).

tations to existing products.[682] These innovations may meet the novelty test, but may not meet the inventive step test and thus are not eligible for protection under the patent law.[683] The Discussion Paper makes out a strong case by bringing in concrete evidence in support of its claim. For example, the National Innovation Foundation (NIF) has documented more than 100,000 grassroots innovations and traditional practices from over 520 districts of the country, out of which even if 40 percent are considered to be eligible to secure a utility model protection, given the more or less acceptable reduced inventive step criteria.[684] Nevertheless, as NIF has pointed out, not all of these innovations are unique, and not all are distinctive enough to satisfy the strict patentability conditions.[685] In other words, if the patentability criteria set out in the Act are applied to these innovations, none of them would be eligible for patent. This brings us to the crucial question of whether the inventions which are new and have practical benefits to the society should be excluded from legal protection for simply being obvious. Seen below are several examples of such innovations cited in the Discussion paper on utility models:

Example 1: Onion Seed Transplanter. "Onion seedlings are usually transplanted manually. This task is time consuming, labour intensive and not standardised. The transplanter is a tractor drawn semi-automatic unit which simultaneously performs three functions viz. transplanting the onion, applying fertilizer and digging the irrigation channels".[686]

Example 2: Clay Refrigerator (Mitticool). "This clay refrigerator, which does not require electricity, keeps food fresh and works on the principle of evaporation. Water from the upper chambers drips down the sides

682 Ibid para7.

683 Ibid.

684 A Aggrawal and B Rawat, 'The Indian Patent System Should Grant Utility Model Patents' (2011) Entrepreneurs website, available at : <http://www.entrepreneurswebsite.com/2011/09/08/the-indian-patent-system-should-grant-utility-model-patents/?goback=%2Egde_3297732_member_69774577> (accessed 2 May 2012).

685 Department of Industrial Policy and Promotion of India, 'Utility Models' (2011) Discussion Paper-23 May 2011, para 8. available at: <http://dipp.gov.in/English/Discuss_paper/Utility_Models_13May2011.pdf> (accessed 30 December 2011).

686 Department of Science and Technology-National Innovation Foundation of India, Official Website, available at: <http://5award.nif.org.in/awardprofile-details.php?page=1&profile_id=1&st_id=4> (accessed 2 July 2012).

and evaporates, leaving the chambers cool. This keeps food, vegetables and milk fresh naturally for more than two days".[687]

Example 3: 'Ribbed Pan (Tawa)'. "With the heating surface made of aluminum with ribs at the bottom. This design increases the surface area available for heating and thus improves the heating capacity of the tawa, minimizing energy use".[688]

Indeed, it is undeniable that in a resource-constrained developing economy like India's, these minor technical inventions which frugally use local resources in a sustainable manner need to be encouraged by providing a legal framework for their protection and commercial exploitation.[689] As it has been argued in the Discussion Paper, such useful, low-cost and relatively simple innovations which create new mechanical devices or contribute to the optimal functioning of existing ones may have commercial value only for a limited time period, before they are replaced by other products or rendered redundant by change of technology.[690] Most importantly, given that such products will primarily be driven by the SME sector, protection would be useful and relevant only if it were provided through a legal framework which is simple, fast and affordable.[691] Presumably, such a legal regime designed to promote small innovation with lesser inventiveness would also remedy the existing inadequacies of the Patent Act. From a practical perspective, UM protection would act as a first level incentive to small innovators and the possession of some kind of legal protection will also facilitate actual commercialization and exploitation of such innovation through licensing and assignment.[692]

"Section X of the Discussion Paper lists eleven 'Issues for Resolution' with an aim to generate more informed discussion on the subject enabling

---

687 Ibid.

688 Ibid.

689 See Department of Industrial Policy and Promotion of India, 'Utility Models' (2011) Discussion Paper-23 May 2011, para 10. available at: <http://dipp.gov.in/English/Discuss_paper/Utility_Models_13May2011.pdf> (accessed 30 December 2011).

690 Ibid.

691 Ibid.

692 See A Aggrawal and B Rawat, 'The Indian Patent System Should Grant Utility Model Patents' (2011) Entrepreneurs website, available at : <http://www.entrepreneurswebsite.com/2011/09/08/the-indian-patent-system-should-grant-utility-modelpatents/?goback=%2Egde_3297732_member_69774577> (accessed 2 May 2012).

the government to take an appropriate policy decision. The issues raised are:

- Does India need a Utility Model Law?
- What should be the scope of protection of such a law, should it be restricted to mechanical devices?
- What parameters should be adopted in the law with respect to inventive threshold, substantive examination, grace period, exhaustion, protection period and registration procedure?
- What novelty criteria should be adopted? Should they be absolute or relative?
- What should be the nature of linkages between this law and the existing Patents Act? How do we ensure that the existing Patents Act, which is a bulwark against the ever greening of patents, remains undiluted?
- What legislative route should be adopted? Should a separate law to protect utility models be enacted? Or should the Patents Act be suitably amended? Or should the Designs Act be amended?
- Should the facility for temporary protection of an invention as a utility model pending grant of a patent be built into the legislation? Should it be specifically mandated that only one form of protection would be available at any time?
- Should applications for patents be transmutable to utility model applications and vice versa whenever the applicant so desires?
- Should any specific provisions be introduced in the proposed utility model law to promote domestic filings as well as applications from SMEs? Can we use this model to protect some part of our traditional knowledge?
- What enforcement procedure should be put in place? What should be the dispute resolution mechanism? Who should be the adjudicating authority?
- To obviate monopolistic dominance, should the adjudicating authority be empowered wherever public interest is involved, to award compensation/royalty in lieu of restraining the infringement?”.[693]

---

693 See Department of Industrial Policy and Promotion of India, ‘Utility Models’ (2011) Discussion Paper-23 May 2011, para 46, available at: <http://dipp.gov.in/English/Discuss_paper/Utility_Models_13May2011.pdf> (accessed 30 December 2011).

The main objective of the Discussion Paper was to develop a suitable framework for granting utility models protection in India, in the event it is felt that this is desirable.[694] The stakeholders have reportedly shown keen interest in the proposals. In terms of responses, the Discussion Paper has received considerable support from domestic industrial sectors. Perhaps most encouragingly, the Federation of Indian Chambers of Commerce and Industry (FICCI) stated that it has received an overwhelming response from micro and small enterprises and Indian innovators who felt that the time is apt and there is a great need for a system which can accord protection to their innovations which are incremental in nature.[695] FICCI has further observed that:

> 'Responses from innovative sectors of India reveal that a lesser inventive threshold in their innovations has been one of the major causes which has not permitted them to get IP protection under the standard patent system. The criteria of higher inventive threshold has led most of them to either withdraw or abandon their patent applications besides discouraging them to even take the route of patent procedures. Further, a lot of instances have been brought to our notice where their innovations have been extensively copied, due to the absence of a regime which can confer upon them the IP rights, which has not only hampered their businesses but also brought to them a lot of dissatisfaction'.[696]

Moreover, according to legal practitioners, it is hoped that a utility model system with a low threshold of inventive step will help India to create a large pool of IP and that can create an innovation driven society.[697] Nevertheless, industrial sectors such as pharmaceutical, biotechnology and IT (software) industries have not supported the move, arguing that a UM regime would be of limited value for them. Leading players in the global software industry have made a strong case against granting UM rights in

694 Ibid para 5.

695 Department of Industrial Policy and Promotion, 'FICCI Suggestions on Discussion Paper on Utility model' (2011) Federation of Indian Chambers of Commerce and Industry, available at: <http://www.ficci.com/SEdocument/20179/UM.pdf> (accessed 2 July 2011).

696 Ibid.

697 P Ollier, 'Practitioners back Utility Model Patents for India' (July 2011) Managing Intellectual property, available at : <http://www.managingip.com/Article/2848140/Practitioners-back-utility-model-patents-for-India.html> (accessed 15 June 2012).

India.[698] They have argued there is no substantial evidence to suggest that a UM regime would really benefit SMEs in India. Moreover, fears have been expressed that a UM regime would lead to unnecessary and excessive litigation. It may also be true that a UM regime would fail to provide advantages to large companies that engage in research intensive industries in high technology sectors. Similarly, more protection does not necessarily mean to increase innovation in India. As pointed out by critics of the Discussion Paper, the real issue lies with the level of awareness of the IP system in India. Thus, policymakers also need to pay more attention to raise the IP awareness through education.

5.1.4. Does India need such a System?

Viewed from a perspective of innovation, in 2012 India ranked 64th in the Global Innovation Index, well behind China (34) and Malaysia (32).[699] Even though India is more scientifically and technologically advanced than other countries in the region, it has not had a very encouraging performance in its innovation landscape, with the exception of the IT and pharmaceutical industries. In that sense, as also pointed out at the outset, India has only scratched its potential. In many industrial sectors, India is still manufacturing low-technology products. Most notably, there is low participation in patenting activities by domestic industries. According to critics, the recent economic boom in India has been propelled by the expansion of its service sector which represented 59 percent of total GDP in 2011 alone. As observed by commentators, although India has now become a hub for international R&D activities of many multinational corporations outsourcing their research activities in India, domestic companies, including the small scale industry sector and individual inventors, are lag-

698 See the Comments from the Global Software Industry (Business Software Alliance) it its letter dated 6 July 2011. See also the Comments from Intel Technology India Pvt. Limited, 'Comments on the Discussion Paper on Utility Models' (30 June 2011) Department of Industrial Policy and Promotion website, available at: <http://dipp.nic.in/English/Discuss_paper/feedback6_Intel_Technology_30June2011.pdf> (accessed 15 June 2012).

699 See S Dutta/INSEAD, *Global Innovation Index 2012* (INSEAD and WIPO 2012) xvii-xix.

ging far behind.[700] India's SME sector, which represents more than 80 percent of all business in India, is still in technological backwaters. The innovations of SMEs are largely from smaller technological improvements and the grassroot innovators from the rural hinterland use marginal or low technology. In fact, laws and policies in India need to meet the needs of the country's industrial structure. However, the existing patent regime appears to be incapable and ineffective in protecting innovative efforts of the majority of domestic industries. All these factors taken together shows a strong case for granting UM rights in India without diluting the patentability standard under Patent Law. Thus, the new Bill proposed by the Indian government should be viewed as a welcome move. The experience from East Asia supports the view that an STP system would be required to create a supporting climate for technology capacity building.

Moreover, as observed in the Discussion Paper, SMEs introduce new products in the market under uncertain conditions.[701] They are unable or unwilling to undertake costly market research prior to the launch of a product and the market value of their invention is unknown and they are forced to take a considerable commercial risk at the time of the product launch.[702] They hesitate to commit significant time and money to protect their inventions by filing for patents.[703] Quick and cheap availability of protection against imitation will help to strengthen their first-mover advantage and consolidate the competitive edge. The utility model system will thus be an attractive option for them.[704] Nevertheless, there are also increasing concerns over potential abuses of the system if a UM system is introduced in India. Critics have warned that a UM regime would, in effect, disincentivise innovation because it would have a blocking effect on

---

700 KS Kardam, 'Utility Model –A Tool for Economic and Technological Development: A Case Study of Japan' (2007) Final Report In Fulfillment of the Long-term Fellowship Sponsored by the World Intellectual Property Office (WIPO) in Collaboration with the Japan Patent Office (from April 2, 2007 to September 28, 2007), 12, available at: <http://www.ipindia.nic.in/research_studies/FinalReport_April2007.pdf> (accessed 15 April 2012).

701 Department of Industrial Policy and Promotion of India, 'Utility Models' (2011) Discussion Paper-23 May 2011, para 41, available at: <http://dipp.gov.in/English/Discuss_paper/Utility_Models_13May2011.pdf> (accessed 30 December 2011).

702 Ibid.

703 Ibid.

704 Ibid.

follow-on innovations. Thus, there is a need to have an enforcement-related check and balance mechanism in the proposed system in order to address the key concerns of the critics. All in all, however, many commentators believe that the introduction of an STP system would encourage more innovations in India if such a regime is appropriately drafted and enforced. Based on the experience of other jurisdictions, it could well be argued that an STP regime encourages more incremental innovation by providing more accessible and affordable means of protection for smaller enterprises and contributes to enhance IP awareness in the country.

5.1.5. What happens Next?

Most enthusiastically, the entire South Asian region is very closely observing the next step that the Indian government will take with regard to the Discussion Paper on Utility Models. It can be safely assumed that a new Act would see the light of day sooner or later. According to the latest information from the office of the Controller General of Patents, Designs, Trademarks and Geographical Indication (CGPDTM) of India, the proposals for introducing a UM system are now before the Sectoral Innovation Councils for consideration.[705] It is apparent that while the work on preparing the draft legislation is proceeding, the Indian government is engaged in further consultations with various sectors involved in innovation. Of course, any new legislation needs to address many of the concerns expressed in response to the Discussion Paper by various stakeholders in India. It is of utmost important to design a more workable and balanced STP regime best suited to the needs of the country.

705 Interview with KS Kardam/Joint Controller of Patents and Designs at Indian Patent Office (New Delhi, 15 March 2013).

5.2. Pakistani Perspectives

> *'If Pakistan is to play its proper role in the world to which its size, manpower and resources entitle it; it must develop industrial potential side by side with its agriculture and give its economy an industrial bias'.*
> *Muhammad Ali Jinnah*[706]

Pakistan is the second-largest economy in South Asia representing about 15 percent of the regional GDP.[707] At the time of the partition in 1947, Pakistan had a negligible industrial base and according to commentators, even after six decades, the Pakistani industrial sector does not play its proper role of contributing to economic development despite having great potential.[708] The industrial development of Pakistan started very early, almost on par with newly industrialized countries such as the Republic of Korea.[709] Despite the fact that the initial industrial policies and plans were focused on import substitution, indigenous technological development remained a missing aspect.[710] One of the factors may be attributed to the type of industry that was mostly primary manufacturing (i.e. textiles and leather) and did not need advanced engineering or technological inputs.[711] According to the World Bank, Pakistan continues to markedly lag behind other nations in South Asia.[712] Presumably, one of the root causes for the country's economic sluggishness is its weak industrial performance. This picture is not very different from its innovation potential. Most notably,

---

706 Cited according to Intellectual Property Organisation of Pakistan, *Annual Report* (2009) Official Website of IP Pakistan. This statement was made by Muhammad Ali Jinnah who is considered to be the founder (father) of Pakistan. Jinnah is officially known as Qualid-e-Azam, available at: <http://www.ipo.gov.pk/UploadedFiles/AnnualReport-2009-81201031025.pdf> (accessed 30 June 2012).

707 World Bank, *Global Economic Prospects Report -January 2013* (World Bank 2013) 139, available at: <http://www.worldbank.org/en/publication/global-economic-prospects> (accessed 30 March 2013).

708 S Jaleel, 'Pakistan Industrial Growth' (2012) The Rawalpindi Chamber of Commerce and Industry 1, available at: <http://www.rcci.org.pk/wp-content/uploads/2012/12/igtip.pdf> (accessed 12 January 2013).

709 HG Ruse-Khan, 'Utility Model Protection in Pakistan-A Feasible Option for Incentivising Incremental Innovation?' (2012), Study conducted for the World Intellectual Property Organisation 70 (copy on file with author).

710 Ibid.

711 Ibid.

712 World Bank, *Global Economic Prospects Report-2012* (World Bank 2012) 139, available at: <http://www.worldbank.org/en/publication/global-economic-prospects> (accessed 30 March 2012).

like India, the Pakistani legal system has failed to provide for a utility model or petty patent system encouraging technological learning to build local technology capacity through minor adaptations or improvements of existing products, imported machinery or equipment by domestic inventors.[713] As commentators have observed:

> 'industrial and economic development of Pakistan has been less than optimal due to the missing 'value addition' part in all economic activities resulting in lack of Intellectual Property usage as a major tool of value addition therein. Therefore Pakistan, thus far, has been an IP importing country. The innovation factor is still not one of the notables for economic activities in Pakistan; in particular the manufacturing and related sectors do not emphasize R&D and its commercialization (in form of IP/patents)'.[714]

5.2.1. The Statistical Story

The statistical evidence from Pakistan's IP office on the number of patent applications and grants provides a reasonable proxy for innovation activities in Pakistan. Comparatively speaking, Pakistan lags far behind its neighbors and other countries in East Asia in terms of patenting activities. As presented in Table 5.3, the number of patent applications in Pakistan not only remains low, but has recorded a slow growth in the recent years. Moreover, the number annual patent grants appears to be very low, given its relatively large size market and population. Commentators have observed that the low number of annual patent applications in Pakistan show a disconnect between domestic economic/industrial activity and the corresponding IP protection.[715] Besides, the industrial sectors in Pakistan are engaged in the production of low technology goods.

---

713 See N Kumar, Intellectual Property Rights, Technology and Economic Development: Experiences of Asian Countries (2003) Commission on Intellectual Property Rights Study Paper 1b, 4-8.

714 HG Ruse-Khan, 'Utility Model Protection in Pakistan-A Feasible Option for Incentivising Incremental Innovation?' (2012), Study conducted for the World Intellectual Property Organisation 70 (copy on file with author).

715 Ibid 72.

Table 5.3: Patent Applications and Grants at IPO Pakistan, 2004-2010

Year	Filed	Granted
2004-05	493	484
2005-06	1406	256
2006-07	1790	299
2007-08	1535	152
2008-09	1365	162
2009-10	1208	252

(Source: Based on data obtained from Annual Reports of IPO Pakistan)

Figure 5.4: Patent Applications by Resident and Non-resident from 2000-2010

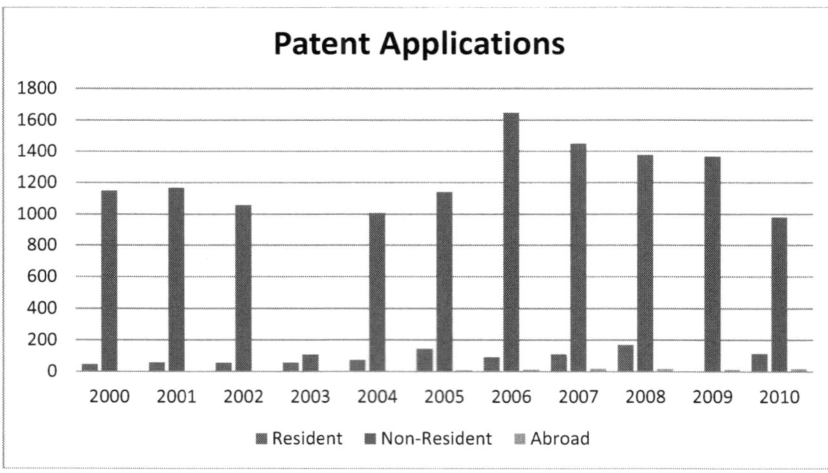

(Source: Based on data obtained from WIPO statistic database)

An analysis of the patent filing trend shows that the majority of patent filers are foreign residents and Pakistani applicants file less than 200 patent applications every year. One possible reason for such low patenting activities may be attributed to the lack of awareness. Nevertheless, it is clear that not many players in the industrial sectors have made good use of the country's patent mechanism. As shown in Figure 5.4, the patent system in Pakistan is overwhelmingly used by foreign filers.

Figure 5.5: A Comparative View of Patent Applications and Grants, 2005-2010

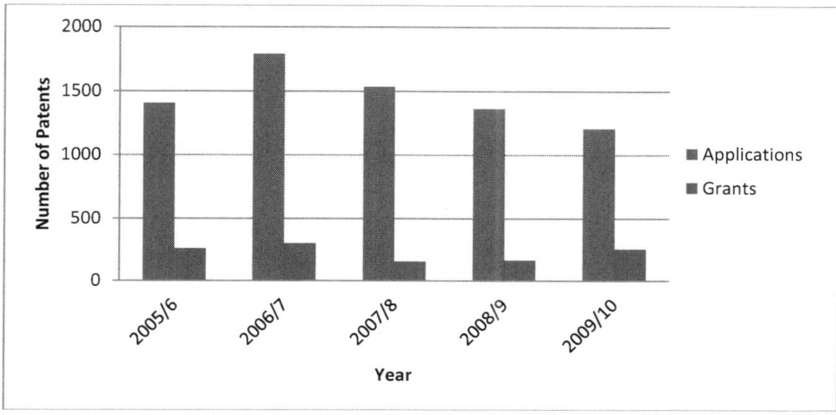

(Source: Based on data obtained from Annual Reports of IPO Pakistan)

Figure 5.5 suggests that the grant rate of patent applications from 2005 to 2010 remained as low as 20 percent and, most strikingly, for the period 2007 to 2008, only 10 percent of total applications have been successful in securing patent rights. The picture painted by these statistics is quite disappointing and a cause for concern. As in the case of India, one of the reasons for this low rate of success may be attributed to stricter novelty and inventive step requirements of existing patent law in Pakistan. Obviously, the patent regime is underutilized and does not seem to cater to the needs of the individual and industrial sectors in the country. From these statistics, it can be concluded that there may be a strong case for adopting a faster, less expensive, uncomplicated and low-threshold protection regime for incentivising domestic innovation in Pakistan.

5.2.2. Protection for Incremental Innovations in Pakistan

The industrial sector is the second largest and an important sector of the Pakistani economy, accounting for 25 percent of the total GDP.[716] Significantly, some of the industries such as light engineering and electrical home appliances have grown significantly in the recent years and expanded their presence in African (fans and electrical motors) and Asian (bicycles) markets.[717] According to the Intellectual Property Organisation (IPO) of Pakistan, incremental innovations are especially evident in the light engineering sector, automotive sector, agricultural machinery, machine tools, and sport and surgical goods industry where SMEs are very active.[718] However, the incremental improvements in technology are not recognized and adequately protected in Pakistan either by the existing patent or design regimes.[719] A recent WIPO study finds that imitation and copying is a very serious issue for the industrial sectors that involve minor and incremental innovations in Pakistan and SMEs are the major victims of absence/weakness of IP protection, creating clear disincentives for their innovative activities.[720] Based on the feedback obtained from Pakistan, the WIPO study further observes that if legal protection for incremental innovation is provided through utility models, then there is a good chance that most of the aforementioned industries[721] would genuinely focus on

716 S Jaleel, 'Pakistan Industrial Growth' (2012) The Rawalpindi Chamber of Commerce and Industry 3, available at: <http://www.rcci.org.pk/wp-content/uploads/2012/12/igtip.pdf> (accessed 12 January 2013).

717 HG Ruse-Khan, 'Utility Model Protection in Pakistan-A Feasible Option for Incentivising Incremental Innovation?' (2012), Study conducted for the World Intellectual Property Organisation 70 (copy on file with author).

718 The Financial Daily, 'IPO to introduce new IP form in Pakistan' (Islamabad, 26 February 2013) reported quoting the Executive Director, IPO Umer Dad Afridi, available at: <http://www.thefinancialdaily.com/NewsDetail/158552.aspx> (accessed 12 March 2013).

719 Interview with M Ismail, Deputy Director IPO (Munich, 28 March 2013).

720 HG Ruse-Khan, 'Utility Model Protection in Pakistan-A Feasible Option for Incentivising Incremental Innovation?' (2012), Study conducted for the World Intellectual Property Organisation, 69 (copy on file with author).

721 Industries mentioned in the study include; surgical goods, electric fans, machinery for pharmaceuticals, bicycles, motorbikes, basic machinery for textiles, automobile parts, steel structures and prefabricated constructions.

achieving such innovation and compete based on innovative products.[722] Thus, the study concludes that in order to promote small-scale, incremental innovative activities by SMEs in particular, introducing a system of utility model protection in Pakistan is a feasible option. Moreover, it has also been argued that if such a protection regime is introduced into the Pakistani IP legal framework, it would provide necessary protection and economic incentives to promote innovation at the domestic level which would eventually facilitate greater awareness and use of the patent system by local inventors.[723]

5.2.3. Recent Initiatives

Based on the WIPO study, the Pakistan government has taken positive steps towards introducing an STP regime in the country. This move may be viewed as one step further than what India has already taken in this regard. In February 2013, the IPO of Pakistan drafted an initial Bill proposing a UM system for Pakistan. The initial draft of IPO is currently before stakeholders for comments. According to the IPO, it is at the stage of assessing whether the proposed UM system would be useful for Pakistan or not, through further consultations.[724] Pursuant to the UM Bill, a utility model shall be granted to any invention which is novel and industrially applicable.[725] Clearly, there is no requirement of an inventive step for a grant of UM right. Notably, like under the German UM system, 'relative novelty' standard has been proposed. In particular, publications in tangible form from anywhere in the world and oral disclosure or use in Pakistan, prior to the filing date of Utility Model application, will be considered as prior art.[726] In other words, neither oral disclosure nor public use abroad can destroy the novelty of a UM application. Thus, it may be argued that the proposed UM regime envisions a lower level of patentability criteria. Like many other countries, animal and plant varieties, chemical compositions,

722 HG Ruse-Khan, 'Utility Model Protection in Pakistan-A Feasible Option for Incentivising Incremental Innovation?' (2012), Study conducted for the World Intellectual Property Organisation, 81 (copy on file with author).

723 Ibid.

724 E-mail from IPO to author (16 March 2013).

725 See Section 5 (1) of the proposed Utility Models Bill of Pakistan 2013.

726 See Section 5 (2) of the proposed Utility Models Bill of Pakistan 2013.

computer programs, processes and methods are specifically excluded from the protectable subject matter.[727] Perhaps even more importantly, it is proposed that the UM right is granted after a preliminary examination and does not involve a substantive examination. Moreover, a mechanism for checks and balances to prevent abuses of the system has been proposed. Specifically, the Bill has provided for an invalidation procedure before the IPO which can be initiated by any person. Moreover, like in Japanese law, any person can request for a 'Utility Model Technical Opinion' as to the registrability of an invention for UM. Last, but not least, the proposed maximum statutory life of the UM will be ten years from the filing date. If passed, the new law would have a significant impact on the entire South Asian region. It is learnt that the legislating process would take, at least, two years for the new Act to see the light of the day.

5.3. Whether and to what extent are these Experiences applicable to Sri Lanka?

Perhaps the most important insight from the above analysis is that the policymakers of both India and Pakistan have signalled their willingness to consider an alternative philosophy for incentivising domestic innovations in their countries. It is even more encouraging to note that, at least by now, countries in South Asia have begun to feel that they lag far behind their East Asian neighbors in terms of innovation. In fact, in the late 1950s, neither of these East Asian economies were much richer than the countries of Sub-Saharan Africa and had virtually no industries.[728] From being predominantly agricultural economies, these nations have transformed their economies into more diversified industrial ones. A snapshot view on selected South and East Asian economies in terms of industrial development indicators is given below:

727 See Section 7 of the proposed Utility Models Bill of Pakistan 2013.

728 D Rodrik, 'Getting Globalization Right: The East Asian Tigers' (2012) OECD Insights, available at: <http://oecdinsights.org/2012/05/03/getting-globalization-right-the-east-asian-tigers/> (accessed 2 June 2012).

Table 5.4: Ranking of Competitive Industrial Performance (CIP) Index 2011

Country	Rank	Country	Rank
India	42	China	5
Pakistan	63	Republic of Korea	7
Bangladesh	69	Thailand	25
Sri Lanka	92	Malaysia	27
Nepal	94	Philippine	33

(Source: Based on data from the UNIDO's Industrial Development Report 2011)

Table 5.5: A Comparative View of Medium and High-Technology Goods Exports

Country	% of all Exports	Country	% of all Exports
India	22.6	Republic of Korea	75.1
Pakistan	8.7	Malaysia	72.1
Bangladesh	3.4	Thailand	61.6
Sri Lanka	7.8	China	57.5
Nepal	9.1	Philippines	81.4

(Source: Based on the data from UNIDO's Industrial Development Report 2009)

Even though IP may only be one factor that affects the technological development of a country, the experience from East Asia indicates that UM regimes have facilitated technological learning through progressive adaptation of foreign technology in their countries. Arguably, all South Asian economies may need to revisit their innovation policies in order to create an eco-system conducive for indigenous innovations. In so doing, individual countries in the South Asian region would have to adopt new legal instruments to incentivise creativity at all levels. Today, both India and Pakistan foresee a UM system in their jurisdictions. Specifically, India has declared 2010-2020 as the 'Decade of Innovation' with the aim of developing an innovation culture in the country to stimulate innovation and to produce solutions for social needs.[729] Sri Lanka, except for its small size market, shares many of the common features such as the agricultural economy and labour intensive industries like those of India and Pakistan. Sri Lanka is a less technological advanced country with a large presence of an underdeveloped SME sector. Thus, the main arguments offered in favour of adopting a UM system in India and Pakistan to encourage incremental and grassroots innovations would be equally applicable for Sri Lanka. Similarly, the designing of a more workable and balanced STP regime to assist SMEs should carry necessary safeguards against possible abuses of the system. To that extent, genuine concerns raised in response to the Indian Discussion Paper and the UM Bill of Pakistan are worth considering by Sri Lankan policymakers in order to minimize unintended negative consequences of the system. Nevertheless, it is important that any system of STP should be tailored to the specific characteristics of the individual country.

5.3.1. Conclusion

It is evident that several countries in the South Asian region are now contemplating adopting an STP regime in order to encourage more indigenous/domestic innovations in their economies. Thus far, the South Asian region has been a notable exception to such a regime. Nevertheless, rigorous patentability criteria prevent most minor and incremental innovations, which are predominantly created by the SME sector in the region, from receiving valuable IP protection. In order to increase the role of SMEs and to build up technological capacity in their countries, both India and Pakistan have taken positive steps towards introducing a UM regime. These moves initially received strong support from domestic industries and it is hoped that new laws would be introduced after further consultations and evaluation of all responses. Nevertheless, there is increasing skepticism of the actual or potential use of the system given the very low level of IP awareness in these countries. Significantly, large players in the market have expressed their dissatisfaction over the possible introduction of such

---

729 See the Press Release of the Department of Science and Technology (Ministry of Science and Technology of India) on 10 March 2010, available at: <http://www.dst.gov.in/whats_new/press-release10/pib_10-3-2010.htm> (accessed 14 June 2012).

a UM system. Most importantly, one of the major concerns that countries need to address is the potential abuses of the system.

6. Designing a Second-Tier Protection Regime for Sri Lanka

> *'Sri Lankans have innovating power and imagination and it is our duty not to stand aside but to give them a hand and push them forward'.*
> *Lalith Athulathmudali* [730]

According to the above observation made by one of the architects of the Sri Lankan Code of IP Act of 1979, Sri Lankans do not lack an innovative spirit. However, Sri Lanka needs to ignite the creative spark of the people by creating the necessary conditions and providing them with incentives to innovate. As evident from the world leading irrigation systems and architectural wonders, during the reign of the ancient kings, Sri Lankans have proven to be a creative and innovative people. However, the country's priorities on technology and innovation seem to have drifted away with the arrival of imperialist powers from across the Indian Ocean in the last couple of centuries.[731] This under-development in the field of science and technology has been one of the reasons why Sri Lanka is economically lagging behind today.[732] Undeniably, innovation is now, if not the driving force, a key determinant of the economic development of a country. By and large, Sri Lanka is a raw material exporter and an agricultural nation. Thus, science, technology and innovation have remained in the backwater of the government's policy-making.

Nevertheless, in recent years, the Sri Lankan government's policies seem to indicate a shift towards more value addition and value creation through innovation as well as advancing the country's science and tech-

---

730 L Athulathmudali-the former Minister of Trade (1977-1993), *Hansard Report-25 May 1979* (The Parliament of Sri Lanka 1979) 503. He made this statement in the second reading of the Code of Intellectual Property Law Bill in Parliament.

731 A Wijesinha, 'Igniting a new fire: Why innovation must be Sri Lanka's new priority' *Daily FT* (Colombo, 12 March 2013, available at: <http://www.ft.lk/2013/03/12/igniting-a-new-fire-why-innovation-must-be-sri-lankas-new-priority/> (accessed 25 March 2013).

732 See Government of Sri Lanka, *Mahinda Chintana-Towards a new Sri Lanka – Policy Document* (Department of National Planning: Ministry of Finance and Planning 2005) 67, available at: <http://www.treasury.gov.lk/publications/mahindaChintanaVision-2010full-eng.pdf> (accessed 25 March 2013).

nology capabilities.[733] Against this background, a consideration of a second-tier protection (STP) regime reinforces the above objectives and the policy goals of the country. As discussed in the initial chapter, due to the almost unfettered policy space left under the multi-national IP treaties, Sri Lanka is free to tailor an STP regime according to the needs of the industrial structure of the country. Since Sri Lanka has no experience with a domestic STP regime, the emerging successful experience from East Asia lends credibility to such a regime. Most encouragingly, the most recent initiatives of the Indian and Pakistani governments in this direction have created enthusiasm to consider the introduction of a UM regime in Sri Lanka. Thus, it is for policymakers to consider an alternative philosophy for incentivising domestic or indigenous innovation in the country. The main arguments offered in favour and against an STP regime can be viewed through administrative, substantive or policy considerations.

6.1. Arguments for introducing an STP in Sri Lanka

One of the main arguments offered in favour of adopting an STP regime in Sri Lanka is the specific characteristics of the innovation landscape of the country. As interpreted through the lens of global innovation indicators, Sri Lanka stands in 94th position out of 141 on the Global Innovation Index 2012.[734] In terms of the Global Competitiveness Index,[735] the Sri Lankan economy was ranked number 68 out of 144 countries. The recent patent statistics provide a telling glimpse of the innovation activities and the technological strength of the nation. As observed in chapter 2, the number of resident patent filings in Sri Lanka is low and the bulk of granted patents are owned by non-residents. Moreover, it is rather disheartening to observe that the rejection rate of patent applications is considerably high, and in 2011 alone, it was more than 60 percent of the total domestic

---

733 National Science and Technology Commission (NASTEC) -Ministry of Science and Technology, *National Science and Technology Policy-2008* (Government of Sri Lanka 2008) 38.

734 S Dutta/INSEAD, *Global Innovation Index 2012* (INSEAD and WIPO 2012) xvii-xix. available at: <http://www.globalinnovationindex.org/gii/main/fullreport/index.html> (accessed 30 August 2012).

735 K Schwab, *The Global Competitiveness Report 2012-2013* (World Economic Forum 2013) 14, available at: <http://reports.weforum.org/global-competitiveness-report-2012-2013/> (accessed 10 November 2012).

patent applications. The low application approval rate indicates that a large area of innovations fall between the no-protection cracks making a strong case for introducing an STP regime in Sri Lanka.[736] From a policy perspective, most applications that are currently being rejected for not meeting the stringent inventive step requirements would be granted protection if there was an STP regime in place. Taken together, all these factors indicate that Sri Lanka's innovation performance is far from satisfactory. Thus, the policymakers need to consider an STP regime to promote innovation at all levels in the country, not only patentable inventions.

Moreover, a UM regime may be used as a tool to advance the technological capabilities of domestic industrial sectors in Sri Lanka. As survey evidence suggests, both large and small industries currently use low and medium technology in their business activities.[737] This might be one of the reasons for a large number of minor and incremental technical advances to have a lower threshold of inventiveness. In fact, Sri Lanka is still on the initial rung of the technological ladder and the SME sector in particular has suffered over the years due to marginal technological capabilities. As commentators have pointed out, Sri Lanka is still making simple products such as tea and garments and very little high-tech complex products.[738] Many firms tend to engage in minimal R&D activities and Sri Lanka's overall expenditure on R&D stands at one of the lowest in the region

---

736 KF Jorda, 'Utility Models: The Panacea for our Broken Patent System' (2007) Germeshausen Center Newsletter 4, available at: <http://www.ipo.org/wp-content/uploads/2013/03/utilitymodels.pdf> (accessed 30 August 2012).

737 The methodology employed to gather information was to conduct face to face interviews and detailed telephone interviews with owners and managers of 25 randomly selected representative SME firms in Sri Lanka, whose contact details were obtained from the government Ministry of Productivity Promotion and other industrial sector organizations. Moreover, interviews with large firms based in Colombo and selected inventors in Sri Lanka based on the contacts provided by the Sri Lanka Inventor's Commission were carried out in 2011 and 2012.

738 S Kelegama, 'SL's lack of innovation, markets limit export growth' *Sunday Times* (Colombo, 13 March 2013), available at: <http://www.sundaytimes.lk/130310/business-times/sls-lack-of-innovation-markets-limit-export-growth-dr-kelegama-35527.html> (accessed 20 March 2013). See also WA Wijewardena, 'Sri Lanka's Future: Convert the Simple Economy into a High-Tech based Complex Economy' *Daily FT* (Colombo, 17 September 2012), available at: <http://www.ft.lk/2012/09/17/sls-future-convert-the-simple-economy-into-a-high-tech-based-complex-economy/> (accessed on 20 March 2013).

which is now 0.11 percent of GDP.[739] Alarmingly, the private sector share of R&D expenditure is just 18 percent.[740] Today, Sri Lanka's high-tech exports have fallen to 1 percent of all manufactured goods. Figure 6.1 below provides a comparative view of high-tech exports of Sri Lanka and selected South and East Asian countries.

Figure 6.1: The Share of High Tech Exports out of the Total Manufactured Exports, 2010

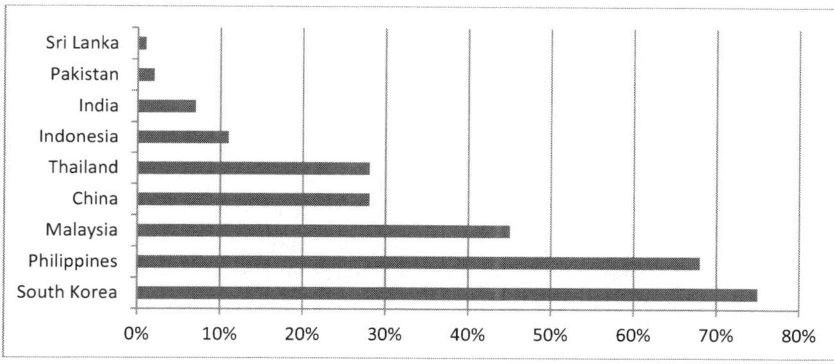

(Source: World Bank Database)[741]

It is apparent that Sri Lanka is a technologically less advanced country. The emerging experience from East Asian countries such as South Korea shows that a UM regime can help those domestic firms who are at the early stages of their industrial development to build their technological capacity.[742] Thus, Sri Lanka should explore an STP system to assist domes-

739 S Kelegama, 'SL's lack of innovation, markets limit export growth' *Sunday Times* (Colombo, 13 March 2013), available at: <http://www.sundaytimes.lk/130310/business-times/sls-lack-of-innovation-markets-limit-export-growth-dr-kelegama-35527.html> (accessed 20 March 2013).

740 Ibid.

741 A Wijesinha, 'Igniting a new fire: Why innovation must be Sri Lanka's new priority' *Daily FT* (Colombo, 12 March 2013, available at: <http://www.ft.lk/2013/03/12/igniting-a-new-fire-why-innovation-must-be-sri-lankas-new-priority/> (accessed 25 March 2013).

742 YK Kim and others, 'Appropriate Intellectual Property Protection and Economic Growth in Countries at Different levels of Development' (2012) 1/4 Research Policy 358, 368, available at: <http://www.sciencedirect.com/science/article/pii/S0048733311001715> (accessed 2 June 2012).

tic industrial sectors to build their technological capabilities. The adoption of a UM system would also help to enhance the technology level of the country's SME sector to the next level. Today, the SME sector in the country is mainly confined to the simple end of technology. Obviously, Sri Lanka has suffered from a low technological capability which has hugely affected the domestic industries predominantly represented by SMEs. Moreover, there is a close nexus between the standard of technology that SMEs use and their productivity and competitiveness, eventually leading to success or failure of the business. Unsurprisingly, most SMEs in Sri Lanka use outdated or substandard technology, and as a result, the quality of products and services produced by them is moderate or is not up to international standards.[743] For instance, the local herbal medicine industry, which has suffered a lot locally and internationally due to substandard products, provides ample examples to prove this claim. Consequently, the SME sector finds it difficult, if not impossible, to compete with relatively high quality cheaper imported products from neighboring markets on one hand, and on the other hand, SMEs are prevented from reaching global or at least the regional markets of South Asia.

Another important argument that speaks in favour of adopting an STP regime is that there are insufficient incentives for minor and incremental innovation in Sri Lanka. The incentive theory holds that economic actors will not tend to engage in economically valuable creativity and innovation without external rewards.[744] The existing patent regime fails to protect technologically less advanced innovations as they do not satisfy the rigorous patentability criteria as applied by the IP office of Sri Lanka. Moreover, the design regime does not accord any protection for the functional aspects of technical innovations. Thus, neither the patent nor the design regime provides a suitable means of protecting sub-patentable innovation. Obviously, such innovations fall through the safety net of IP protection. Moreover, the incentive-based argument can further be supported by recourse to the 'prospect theory or incentive to commercialize thesis'. The prospect theory argues that in the process of technological innovation re-

743 AL Somaratne, 'Access to Finance by SMEs in Sri Lanka' *The Island* (Colombo, 15 August 2012), available at: <http://www.island.lk/index.php?page_cat=article-details&page=article-details&code_title=59282> (accessed 16 August 2012).

744 EE Johnson, 'Intellectual Property and the Incentive Fallacy' (2011) 39 Florida State University Law Review 623, 662.

sources are brought to bear upon an array of prospects.[745] Thus, a UM provides a legal framework that enhances prospects of commercial exploitation of minor but socially desirable innovation. In the Sri Lankan context, the innovation of the SMEs mainly consists in minor adaptations to existing products and they are most vulnerable to copying by competitors. Therefore, it may be argued that a UM or petty patent system would provide adequate incentives for the type of innovations that emanate from the SME sector in Sri Lanka.

Perhaphs even more encouragingly, as interpreted through the lens of the property right theory, a UM regime may provide not only incentives but also much needed legal certainty for minor and incremental innovations. In Sri Lanka, there are no property rights for these types of innovations, leaving the fruits of such investments unprotected. Without some sort of legal protection, such innovations could be freely appropriated by competitors creating disincentives which is tantamount to systematically killing of such innovations. By making a legal right available, the innovative activities of Sri Lankan firms would be encouraged. The property right theory shows the validity of legal protection for private property from an economic point of view.[746] According to commentators, creating exclusive rights and competitive restrictions are necessary so that competition can develop at a particular higher level of activity which is relevant to the economy of consumption, production and innovation.[747] Legal protection of tangible property, as well as of IP, can be viewed as a restraint on consumption, which is required in order to permit competition to arise at the production level; i.e. the owner of an apple orchard would not be interested in the production of apples if anyone could freely snatch away the fruits of his labor.[748] According to von Weizsäcker, if free access to the exisiting stock of goods is excluded by the institution of property, then

745 EW Kitch, 'The Nature and Function of the Patent System' (1977) 20/2 Journal of Law and Economics 265, 266.

746 M Lehmann, 'Property and Intellectual Property-Property Rights as Restrictions on Competition in Furtherance of Competition' (1989) 20/1 International Review of Intellectual Property and Competition Law 1, 2.

747 Ibid 12-13. Also see, C Christan von Weizsäcker, 'Rights and Relations in Modern Economic Theory' (1984) 5 Journal of Economic Behavior and Organization 133, 138.

748 M Lehmann, 'Property and Intellectual Property-Property Rights as Restrictions on Competition in Furtherance of Competition' (1989) 20/1 International Review of Intellectual Property and Competition Law 1, 13.

there emerges a system of incentives.[749] Therefore, a legal mechanism is needed to safegaurd the rights of innovators at the level of consumption. The same is certainly true for restraints in competition by way of property rights at the production level. Arguably, in this scenario, petty patents or utility models also enhance competition at the next higher level, namely the level of innovation (see below).[750]

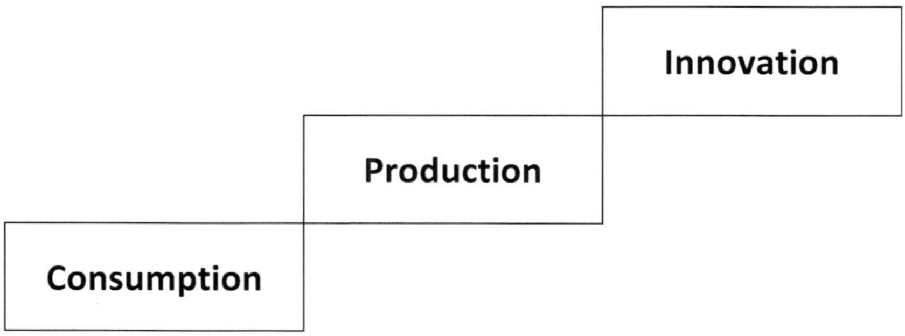

In reality, given the particular vulnerabilty of incremental innovations for copying, as they do not represent sophisticated and complex technologies, free-riders and unfair imitators would lose no time in taking advantages of them. In the absence of a barrier of protection, such incremental innovations become crops in an unfenced field. In crafting the right design of property rights, one of course has to be extremely careful with regard to the scope of the right and its limitations.

Given that the patent system can hardly be used by SMEs, providing a cheaper and accessible source of protection for local SMEs is a vital in unleashing untapped potentials of grassroot innovators. Thus, a legal regime in the nature of utility models can raise the possibility of receiving exclusivity for commercially exploitable and socially-relevant creative solutions

749 C Christan von Weizsäcker, 'Rights and Relations in Modern Economic Theory' (1984) 5 Journal of Economic Behavior and Organization 133, 138.

750 M Lehmann, 'Property and Intellectual Property-Property Rights as Restrictions on Competition in Furtherance of Competition' (1989) 20/1 International Review of Intellectual Property and Competition Law 1, 12. The author has used the argument in analogy for utility model protection.

from the rural hinterland,[751] where nearly 80 percent of Sri Lanka's population lives. These incremental innovations, which use local resources in a suitable manner, would primarily be driven by the SME sector and such protection would only be useful and relevant if it were provided through a legal framework which is simultaneously quick, cheap, undemanding and simple.[752] There is always a criticism that the patent system is similar to a 'luxury hotel' and only very few can afford to get there. Likewise, the patent system is not for all.[753] The cost of obtaining a suitable right and the time it takes to register renders this luxury intellectual property right inappropriate in many cases, especially for small businesses.[754] By way of analogy, one can reasonably argue that the adoption of an STP regime would amount to a 'democratization of the IP system' which has so far been confined to a limited number of foreign and large domestic companies.

From a socio-economic perspective, the introduction of an STP regime would help advance the goal of social justice. It would also respond to the common critique of the patent system that it does not pay enough attention to local needs. In other words, an STP system would contribute to re-balance the IP system by catering to the need of social justice. In the eyes of legal philosophy, John Rawls' theory of justice can also be used to defend this line of argumentation. Rawlsian theory holds that 'justice is the first virtue of social institutions, as truth is the virtue of systems of thought'.[755] In consequence, one can advance an argument that the IP system, as a legal institution which is socially-rooted, needs to create a new institution in

---

751 MS Nair, 'Utility model: DIPP comes out with a discussion paper' (2011) June, China Law & Practice, available at: <http://www.chinalawandpractice.com/> (accessed 12 August 2012).

752 Ibid. Department of Industrial Policy and Promotion, Discussion Paper on Utility Model (23 May 2011) para 10, available at: <http://dipp.gov.in/English/Discuss_paper/Utility_Models_13May2011.pdf> (accessed 30 December 2011).

753 P Torremans, *Holyoak and Torremans Intellectual Property Law* (4th edn, Oxford University Press 2005) 161.

754 Ibid.

755 JA Rawls, *A Theory of Justice* (Clarendon Press 1971) 3-11. Rawls further argues that laws and institutions no matter how efficient and well-arranged must be reformed or abolished if they are unjust. Rawls, in respect of his second principle of justice, argues that 'social and economic inequalities are to be arranged so that (a) they are to be of the greatest benefit to the least-advantaged members of society (the difference principle) and (b) offices and positions must be open to all under conditions of fair equality of opportunity'.

the form of an STP regime that makes the disadvantaged under the conventional patent regime relatively better off. From a social justice perspective, an STP system would be instrumental in affording fair opportunities for accessible protection for all kinds of innovations. Furthermore, no human domain should be immune from the claims of social justice.[756] IP regulates the production and distribution of information and like property law, structures social relations and has profound social effects. Considerations of social justice cannot be peripheral to such a central human institution.[757] As Gupta argues, harnessing intellectual property rights for meeting the ends of social justice is imperative.[758] He makes a strong case for certain specific reforms in the present IP system, including the introduction of a low transaction cost protection mechanism such as the present innovation patent system in Australia, to make IP protection more accessible to small innovators and local communities.[759] Thus, a UM regime would advance social justice by reducing practical difficulties of using the patent system by a broader spectrum of innovators in Sri Lanka.

The other main arguments offered in favour adopting an STP regime in Sri Lanka can be summarized as follows:

– A UM right can be used as collateral to secure financing for the cash-strapped SME sector in Sri Lanka.[760]

756 A Chander and M Sunder, 'Is Nozick Kicking Rawls's Ass? Intellectual Property and Social Justice' (2007) UC Davis Legal Studies Research Paper Series No. 8 563, 578.

757 Ibid.

758 AK Gupta, 'Grassroots to Global: The Knowledge Rights of Creative Communities' (Globalization & Justice: Interdisciplinary Dialogues, School of Law, Seattle University, USA, 21-22 February 2008) 12, available at: <http://www.sristi.org/anilg/papers.php> (accessed 10 June 2011).

759 Ibid. See also AK Gupta, 'Can protecting intellectual property rights be of any consequence for poor people?' (2007) Indian Council for Research on International Economic Relations (ICRIER) 1, 14, available at: <http://www.sristi.org/anilg/papers/> (accessed 10 June 2011).

760 As Jacobs has argued 'collateral is a borrower's promise of specific property if a loan is not repaid. When using intellectual property as a collateral, the borrower is promising the transfer of his intellectual property (i.e. patent, trademark, copyright or a utility model) if he does not repay his loan. Intellectual property was first used as collateral to secure financing by Thomas Edison in the late 1880s. Edison used his patent for the incandescent electric light bulb as collateral to secure financing for his own business.' BW Jacobs, 'Using IP to secure Financing after the Worst Financial Crisis since the Great Depression' (2011) 15 /2 Marquette Intellectual Property Law Review 450, 450.

- It may be a 'title carrier' for business negotiation, especially for licensing agreements and a bargaining tool in litigation.
- An STP right would be an effective vehicle for technology transfer to domestic industries, especially for rural SMEs and TK-based industrial sector in Sri Lanka.
- A utility model system can facilitate adaptive and progressive imitation of foreign technologies by domestic firms, i.e. several East Asian countries relied heavily on utility models in their early development stages, often protecting incremental, non-patentable modifications of imported products.[761]
- An STP regime would provide a realistic opportunity for TK-based innovators to participate in economic development of the country.
- It may be able to provide rapidly enforceable legal rights at a cost that they can afford which can be used as a sword to gain competitive advantage in the market.
- A utility model system can be used as a tool to raise the level of IP awareness among domestic industries.
- An STP system can be a useful supplement and in some cases complement to the existing IP regimes.
- A UM or a petty patent right confers on the right holders a psychological advantage over competitors by creating the (illusory) effect that imitation by competitors will be delayed due to the exclusive rights.[762]

Below is a summary of resposes received from the SME sector on the appropriateness of adopting a UM regime as a legal instrument for protecting small and incremental innovation in Sri Lanka.[763]

761 WIPO, World Intellectual Property Report: The Changing Face of Innovation (2011) WIPO 80.

762 HG Ruse-Khan, 'Utility Model Protection in Pakistan-A Feasible Option for Incentivising Incremental Innovation?' (2012), Study conducted for the World Intellectual Property Organisation 28 (copy on file with author).

763 The methodology employed to gather information was to conduct face to face interviews and detailed telephone interviews with the owners and managers of 25 randomly selected representative SME firms in Sri Lanka, whose contact details were obtained from the government Ministry of Productivity Promotion and other industrial sector organizations.

Figure 6.2: Views of Sri Lankan SMEs on Possible UM System

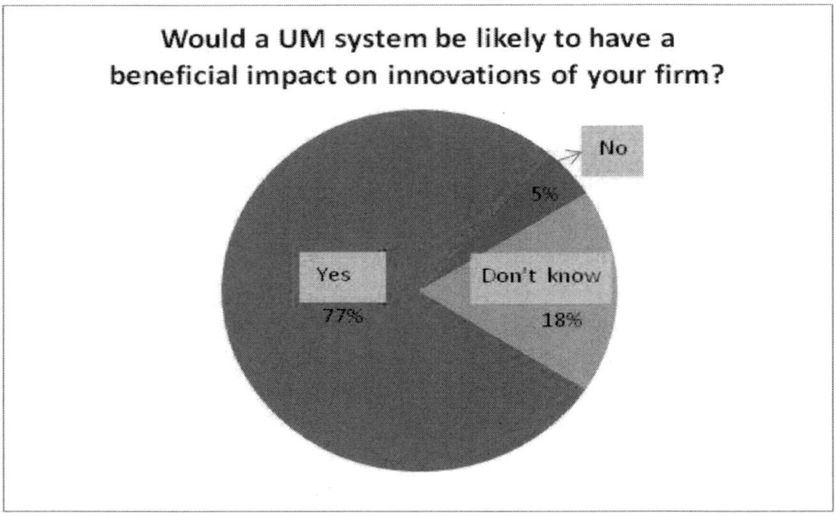

As shown in Figure 6.2, nearly 80 percent of SMEs interviewed have a favourable opinion about the potential benefits of an STP mechanism. Nevertheless, this data should be interpreted with caution, as more than 20 percent of potential users are not clear about the concept of UM or petty patent. Moreover, according to survey evidence, a large majority of IP attorneys and legal academics (over 90 percent) interviewed in Sri Lanka are highly positive about the idea of utility models. Similar responses have been received from the judicary and other innovation-related government institutions (as summarized in Appendix 2). As recent literature has argued, a UM system would benefit the light engineering sector which supplies parts and spares for machinery, equipment and tools.[764] Thus, there are both logical and evidentiary reasons to conclude that an STP regime may be viewed as an appropriate policy choice which can be implemented without diluting patent standards.[765]

---

764 S Kelegama, 'SL's lack of innovation, markets limit export growth' *Sunday Times* (Colombo, 13 March 2013), available at: <http://www.sundaytimes.lk/130310/business-times/sls-lack-of-innovation-markets-limit-export-growth-dr-kelegama-35527.html> (accessed 20 March 2013).

765 Interviews with members of the Sri Lankan judiciary also confirmed the need that high standards patent law should not be diluted.

6.2. Arguments against such an STP Regime

One cannot of course expect a successful system without reasonable critiques. As noted before, many experts are convinced that a UM system may serve as an effective policy instruments in incentivising local innovations. Others, however, strongly argue that the rationale for a utility model system is inherently unsound because the system is open to abuses. From a Sri Lankan perspective, one of the main concerns is that, since IP awareness as well as the use of the IP system is low, the perceived benefits of an STP would not reach the target group, namely the SME sector. Moreover, like in other jurisdictions such as Australia, there is a possibility that the system may be hijacked by large firms and multinational companies for strategic purposes. As noted in chapter 4, abusive filing of innovation patent applications has been a serious issue in Australia. This fear is also reasonable in light of Sri Lanka's legal obligation to provide national treatment and priority rights under the Paris Convention for utility models or petty patents of foreign companies.

As another concern, many critics have argued, copying and freedom of imitation lead to improved and value-added products and the creation of a new IP right would have a detrimental impact on SMEs ability to innovate.[766] An important question here is whether such freedom to imitate has really benefited SMEs in the last six decades in Sri Lanka. There is no significant evidence (at least from the patent data) to conclude that freedom to copy and imitate low-level innovations has brought significant and substantial benefits to the industrial sectors or as a result of such activities the SME sector advanced its technological capabilities in the Sri Lankan industrial landscape. Interestingly, a recent WIPO study has observed that imitation and copying actually discourages innovation due to the fact that all those who are second comers who copy or imitate an original innovator are unlikely or unwilling to engage in innovative activities themselves.[767] Thus, to that extent, this concern should be treated with caution in the Sri Lankan context.

---

766 U Suthersanen, G Dutfield and KB Chow (eds), *Innovation Without Patents* (Edward Elgar 2007) 10.

767 HG Ruse-Khan, 'Utility Model Protection in Pakistan-A Feasible Option for Incentivising Incremental Innovation?' (2012), Study conducted for the World Intellectual Property Organisation 80 (copy on file with author).

Similarly, there is also a risk that big players in the market will apply for a large number of utility models and, in the absence of a proper examination, they will do so even in those cases where the validity is dubious.[768] This could lead to a situation where any competitor, including SMEs, would be threatened with infringement proceedings almost every time it engages in a new development and where the only way out would be by means of expensive litigation.[769] This would result in increased business risk for the SME sector in Sri Lanka. Viewed through the lens of jurisprudence, this would create a scenario that is similar to 'One-shotters (the Have-nots) v Repeat players (the Haves)' which has been introduced by Marc Galanter.[770] There is, of course, a possibility when big players in the market can flex their financial muscle to drive away small businesses, those who already have limited financial capabilities, from using the system. In effect, this would no doubt create disincentives. Paradoxically, the system created to incentivise domestic innovation would in turn create disincentives for SMEs. It is then likely to be a millstone around the neck of local industries.[771]

Furthermore, there may be another concern in Sri Lanka regarding the enforcement mechanism of STP rights. Sri Lanka is a Common Law country with an adversarial system of courts. Even if the granting process for a UM or petty patent right is less expensive and simple, the system would bring limited benefit given the extremely high costs involved in the enforcement of IP rights under an adversarial system. Currently, there are very few IP practitioners and law firms with adequate training in IP law and they generally charge high fees in litigation. Thus, the costs factor in enforcement may discourage SMEs from enforcing their rights. Moreover, the survey evidence from the banking sector in Sri Lanka confirmed that financial institutions are extremely reluctant to accept IP rights as collater-

---

768 P Torremans, Holyoak and Torremans Intellectual Property Law (4th edn OUP 2005) 163.

769 Ibid.

770 M Galanter, 'Why the "Haves" come out Ahead: Speculations on the Limits of Legal Change' (1974) 9/1 Law and Society Review 95, 123. According to Galanter, one-shotters (OS) and repeat players (RP) engage in many similar litigation over time. An OS may not receive quality professional advice because he may simply not be in a position to afford it and there is also doubt whether his case may be properly represented in a fair manner.

771 R Jacob, 'The Stephen Stewart Memorial Lecture: Industrial Property-Industry's Enemy' (1997) 1 Intellectual Property Quarterly 3, 11.

al for granting financial resources to SMEs and innovators.[772] In that case, the UM or the petty patent right would be of limited value for right holders in Sri Lanka. Similarly, since utility models are granted without substantive examination, the potential benefits of licensing and other means of technology transfer would be questionable due to the lack of legal certainty with regard to the scope of the rights. The emerging experience from Malaysia and Kenya also indicates that UM systems sometimes have not attracted much interest from the target group of users. Among other concerns, a UM or petty patent system generates unnecessary litigation, leads to proliferation of trivial patents creating barriers for follow-on innovations, and too many property rights can also lead to 'tragedy of the anticommons'.[773] There are also fears that an STP regime would lead to patent trolls and patent evergreening.[774] There is a reasonable concern among scholars that an introduction of an STP regime may unduly create an erosion of the public domain.[775]

6.3. Design and Structure

A key element of utility model protection is that it is a legal instrument which is outside the sphere of international influence and hence tends to

772 This was revealed during the interviews with the legal managers of five leading banks in Sri Lanka. (details of respondents are available in Appendix 2).

773 The anticommons thesis argues that, when too many people own pieces of one thing, nobody can use it. Too much of ownership leads to wasteful underuse. See MA Heller, 'The Tragedy of the Anticommons: A Concise Introduction and Lexicon' (2013) 76/ 1 The Modern Law Review 6, 8.

774 A patent troll is an entity that neither invents technology nor is interested in developing it; it acquires patents through licensing or purchase and sues another company by claiming that one of its products infringes on the acquired patents. Thus, a patent troll is just a collector of patents with the intention to sue or threaten other business. See R Mittal, 'From Invention to Innovation: Analysing the Tools and Trolls of the Journey' (2012) 54/4 Journal of the Indian Law Institute 489, 490.

775 The phrase 'public domain' is defined by the Oxford English dictionary as the state of belonging or being available to the public as a whole, especially through not being subject to copyright or other legal restrictions. The term 'public domain' can be generally linked to a 'common', in an intellectual rather than a physical sense. For the purpose of this discussion, it is taken to mean information that is not covered by IP rights or held in secret, but it is not itself a recognized legal category in its own right.

be specifically tailored for domestic/regional needs and concerns.[776] Thus, the main rationale of introducing an STP system in Sri Lanka is to incentivise minor and incremental innovation of SMEs in the country. Sri Lanka, as a developing country, may be able to reap the real benefits of adopting an STP system if such a regime is tailored to suit the needs of SMEs and other relevant domestic industries. Thus, the design of the legislation should be structured in such a way to strike the right balance between conflicting interests in the society. While a UM or a petty patent system enables the SME sector to take advantage of the system, it should not, however, discourage follow-on innovation and unduly restrict the public domain. It is certainly true that granting exclusive rights to new but obvious inventions can give rise to abusive behaviors. Therefore, it is of utmost importance to achieve an appropriate balance between private rights of the innovators on the one hand, and the rights of the general public to benefit from free competition on the other. As Roscoe Pound has postulated, the task of law is 'social engineering' and law should balance conflicting social interests in society which would result in legal progress.[777] In this STP scenario, there are three kinds of legally protected interests at stake namely, those of right holders and competitors as well as public interests. In fact, an STP system needs to offer lower barriers to protection in order to incentivize incremental innovation of the SME sector, but at the same time, restrictions and limitations of the right should be embedded in a UM or petty patent legislation, along with necessary safeguards against possible abuses of the system. The most challenging task is the designing of a balanced, effective, inexpensive and more accessible regime for Sri Lanka. As analysed in Chapter 4, the successful experience of other countries which have lived with STP systems for many years provide necessary guidance as 'best practices' to be followed by Sri Lankan policymakers.

---

776 U Suthersanen, 'Utility Models and Innovation in Developing Countries' (2006) UNCTAD-ICTSD Issue Paper No. 13 Project on IPRs and Sustainable Development ix.

777 R Pound, *Social Control Through Law* (Yale University Press, 1942) 64. RWG Friedmann, *Legal Theory* (4th edn, Stevens & Stevens Ltd 1967) 336.

6.4. Core Elements

6.4.1. Protected Subject-Matter/Scope of Protection

The scope of protection should not be restricted to mechanical devices in order to ensure that the STP regime incentivises innovation of a broader spectrum of Sri Lanka's creative class. Hence, the subject matter protected under a UM or a petty patent regime should be narrower than the subject-matter covered under the patent law. It is important that the scope of the new STP right should not contradict the patent provisions in the Sri Lankan IP Act. In this regard, software, pharmaceuticals, biotechnology and high-tech Information Technology (IT) products may be amongst those to be excluded from the utility model protection as the need for substantive examination appears particularly important to prevent abusive and anti-competitive blocking behaviour.[778] Moreover, the experience from Australia shows that the innovation patent system is quite often used by large and multinational companies to protect innovation in the area of software and IT-related technologies for strategic purposes. Like Thailand[779] and some other East Asian countries, a UM legislation in Sri Lanka should specifically exclude the above mentioned technology sectors as an STP regime does not envisage a substantive examination before grant. Interestingly, the option to exclude certain fields of technology from utility model protection appears as an important element of flexibility in designing a system that primarily fits domestic needs and responds to demands for encouraging incremental and minor innovations from SMEs.[780] Accordingly, TK-based innovation may possibly be included for protection as there is considerable interest and need for rapidly granted short-term protection for such innovations. It may also be appropriate for Sri Lanka to initially exclude processes and methods from STP protection which could be reviewed after five years of the implementation of the new regime. Moreover, the discoveries, inventions against public order and morality etc. as

778 HG Ruse-Khan, 'Utility Model Protection in Pakistan-A Feasible Option for Incentivising Incremental Innovation?' (2012), Study conducted for the World Intellectual Property Organisation 70 (copy on file with author).

779 See Section 9 (1) of the Thai Patent Act of 1979 as last amended in 1999.

780 HG Ruse-Khan, 'Utility Model Protection in Pakistan-A Feasible Option for Incentivising Incremental Innovation?' (2012), Study conducted for the World Intellectual Property Organisation 70 (copy on file with author).

excluded from patentability under the IP Act should be left out from the scope of the STP right in order to avoid any inconsistency.

6.4.2. Standard of Novelty

As noted above, the almost unlimited policy space left under the international IP instruments provide necessary freedom for Sri Lankan policymakers to decide whether a UM or petty patent right must satisfy an absolute, relative or local novelty standard. Most importantly, the degree of novelty should be in line with the main rationale of introducing an STP regime in Sri Lanka, namely incentivising minor and incremental innovations of the SME sector. Since the absolute or universal novelty standard[781] may be difficult to achieve by scientifically and technologically less advanced SME sector, Sri Lanka should, taking the German experience into consideration, consider adopting a relative novelty or domestic novelty standard.[782] A more rigid standard of novelty could inhibit adaptive and progressive imitation from receiving protection under the STP regime. Moreover, consideration of prior art abroad would reduce the prospect of securing UM rights for domestic innovators. Nevertheless, a local novelty standard would have several downsides such as protection of technologies that have already been patented abroad. Moreover, an important question is whether domestic novelty is any longer applicable in the era of the Internet where patent databases are accessible online. Furthermore, Sri Lanka should also consider granting a grace period of six months for innovators during which any disclosure by the applicant would not be considered for novelty assessment. This need to be introduced as a

781 Absolute or universal novelty means that invention is new throughout the world and thus all material made available to the public anywhere in the world forms part of the state of the art. In other words, for absolute novelty, the state of the art comprises everything made available to the public by means of a written or oral description, by use, or in any other way, before the date of filing of the application.

782 According to Section 3 of the German UM Act 1986, the state of the art comprises any knowledge made available to the public by means of a *written description* (anywhere in the world) or by *use within the territory of the Republic of Germany*. It is obvious from this wording that neither oral disclosure, nor public use abroad can destroy novelty. Moreover, local novelty is usually restricted to within the country, where only local knowledge and use can destroy such novelty.

safeguard against the lack of IP awareness among in the domestic industrial sector, especially a large majority of SMEs and inventors in Sri Lanka are unaware of their rights and make public disclosure of their inventions via media without knowing the consequences.

6.4.3. Inventive Step Requirement

Like the novelty standard, Sri Lankan policymakers have the flexibility to decide on whether to lessen or eliminate the requirement of inventive step or non-obviousness for the STP regime.[783] It should be in any case a lower or smaller step than is required for the granting of a patent given the different objectives to be achieved under each system. One of the goals of the STP regime is to encourage minor adaptations or improvement of existing products or processes of domestic industries. Moreover, a large part of innovations of the Sri Lankan SME sector involve low or medium level technology resulting in a lower level of inventiveness.[784] Thus, most domestic inventions cannot be patented as they do not satisfy the test of inventive step.[785] A similar observation has been made in the Indian Discussion paper 2011 as discussed in Chapter 5. In fact, a UM right is easy to obtain due to the lower threshold of inventiveness. Since the inventive step requirement is not incorporated into an STP regime in many jurisdictions such as Malaysia, Kenya and Thailand, Sri Lanka should probably do away with this requirement. Nevertheless, if Sri Lanka decides to have an inventive step requirement in its UM legislation, it would be advisable to follow the Australian approach. Otherwise, the system would become less attractive for the target group of users defeating the purpose of adopting such a regime. Australian law requires that an innovation to be not only new, but also that it differs from what was already known in a way that is not merely superficial or peripheral to the invention.[786] The variation

783 Non-obviousness means the invention is different from the prior art in a way that would not be obvious to a person with ordinary skills in the art of the invention at the time of the invention was made.

784 This was revealed in the interviews with Sri Lankan SMEs and inventors. Details of respondents are provided in the Appendix 2. The same finding was confirmed by survey evidence from the NIPO.

785 Based on the survey evidence from the patent examiners at the NIPO.

786 R Gay, 'Editorial: The Innovative Step Conundrum' (2009) April, Managing IP 88, 98-99.

must be of practical significance to the way that the invention works.[787] Unlike for patents, there is, however, no requirement that an innovation must be non-obvious. Moreover, viewed through the experience of other countries, it could be argued that the absence of the inventive step requirement would encourage people in the grassroots level, especially in the agricultural or other rural sectors to register their simple innovations which would in most cases be for practical use in the field.[788] In principle, any innovation that represents a practical or functional advantage over prior art should be protected in order to incentivise minor and incremental innovations of SMEs in Sri Lanka. Such innovations can of course be successive improvements upon existing products and processes which bring out increases in technical efficiency and/or improvements in quality.[789]

6.4.4. Elevated Utility Requirement

As the American inventor and entrepreneur, Thomas Edison, once stated, the value of an idea lies in the using of it'.[790] In many countries where a UM or petty patent protection is available, industrial applicability or utility requirement is one of the main conditions for such protection. The underlying rationale of this concept is that patent protection should not be available for abstract ideas or purely intellectual creations that cannot be put to any use.[791] A patentable invention has to be concrete and should have a technical character.[792] From a policy perspective, an innovation should be useful in order to provide some immediate benefit to the public. In the event that the Sri Lankan policymakers decide to introduce an STP

787 Ibid.

788 See also W Weeraworawit, 'Utility Models in Thailand' in C Heath and A Kamperman-Sanders (eds), *Industrial property in the Bio-Medical Age: Challenges for Asia* (Kluwer Law 2003) 270.

789 RM Galhardi, Small High Technology Firms in Developing Countries: The case of biotechnology (Avebury Press 1994) 49.

790 As cited by Business and Industry Advisory Committee (BIAC) to OECD, Discussion Paper on 'Creativity, Innovation and Economic Growth in the 21st Century: An Affirmative Case for Intellectual property Rights (Paris, December 2003) 3, available at: <http://www.oecd.org/dataoecd/52/45/23375023.pdf> (accessed 10 November 2011).

791 CM Correa, *A Guide to Pharmaceutical Patents* – Volume 1(South Centre 2008) 81.

792 Ibid.

regime, given that there is no requirement for inventive step in such regime, it would be more appropriate to consider an enhanced utility requirement to encourage innovations that are closer to the market. Thus, based on the experience from East Asian countries, Sri Lanka can probably adopt a similar approach. Accordingly, an innovation shall be taken to be capable of industrial application if it can be made or used in any kind of industry, including handicrafts, agriculture and commerce.[793] Specifically, it may be of importance for a developing country like Sri Lanka to encourage innovations that have a utility value that can solve day to day technical problems by providing practical and functional advantages over existing prior art.[794] Moreover, the emerging patent jurisprudence from the US and Japan speaks in favour of a more elevated requirement of utility. In such regimes, there is a need that the claimed invention must show a specific, substantial and credible use.[795] Obviously, the enhanced utility requirement is a regulatory response to prevent certain technology fields such as pharmaceutical and biotechnology, from pushing the boundaries of patent law. This may not be the case for a UM system if such a regime is tailored to protect mechanical innovations. Nevertheless, if Sri Lanka decides to protect traditional medicines under a future UM system then it may be worth considering an elevated utility requirement in order to prevent misuse of the system.

---

793 See the approach of the Thailand's petty patent regime. See Section 8 of the Thailand Patent Act of 1979 as last amended in 1999.

794 For example, as scholars have pointed out, utility models are granted to devices embodying a creative idea applicable to the shape, structure or other technological aspects of a product, such as an improved device capable of reducing the amount of water used to flush a toilet, or a bottle cork remover capable of operating faster than known devices. YK Kim and others, 'Appropriate Intellectual Property Protection and Economic Growth in Countries at Different levels of Development' (2012) 1/4 Research Policy 360, available at: <http://www.sciencedirect.com/science/article/pii/S0048733311001715> (accessed 2 June 2012).

795 See The United States Patent and Trademark Office (USPTO), Guidelines for Examination of Applications for compliance with the Utility Requirement Section 2107.

6.4.5. Granting Procedure

In many jurisdictions, UM rights are granted following a simple registration system. In other words, STP applications are subject to a preliminary examination which covers a formality check and a basic requirement examination. As a result the right is granted within a matter of months. One of the main advantages of the simple registration system is that it gives the right holders an opportunity for early action against any imitator. Therefore, Sri Lanka should consider a granting procedure that does not undergo a substantive examination prior to grant. From a Sri Lankan perspective, one of the main objectives of an STP is to provide for a quick, less expensive and more easily obtainable protection regime for the SME sector. The patent system is often criticized for being too slow, too expensive and too difficult for small innovators.[796] Moreover, critics argue that, in view of the well-known fact that 95 percent of all issued patents never earn any money and are never litigated and, therefore, do not need to undergo a thorough examination.[797] Besides, according to Lemley and Shapiro, most issued patents turn out to have little or no commercial significance, which is one reason why only 1.5 percent of patents are ever litigated, and only 0.1 percent of patents are ever litigated to trial.[798] If this is the case in many major patent jurisdictions, there should not be much concern in a small market like Sri Lanka. Nevertheless, there are concerns that non-substantive examination encourages many UM applications from old technologies to unpatentable technologies including in some cases photocopies of issued patents.[799] The experience from Malaysia shows that the substantive examination of UM applications before grant is one of the reasons for the system to become less attractive and Malaysia is currently considering an Amendment to the existing UI regime. The proposed amendment aims at changing to a non-substantive examination system

796 See LA Hollaar, 'A New Look at Patent Reform' (2004) April, Journal of the Patent and Trademark Office Society 743, 745.

797 KF Jorda, 'Utility Models: The Panacea for our Broken Patent System' (2007) Germeshausen Center Newsletter 5, available at: <http://www.ipo.org/wp-content/uploads/2013/03/utilitymodels.pdf> (accessed 30 August 2012).

798 MA Lemley and C Shapiro, 'Probabilitic Patents' (2005) 19/2 Journal of Economic Perspectives 75.

799 TT Moga, *China's Utility Model Patent System: Innovation Driver or Deterrent* (US Chamber of Commerce 2012) 15.

from the substantive examination before the grant in order to provide cheap and fast grant of right.[800]

6.4.6. Duration of Protection

The statutory life of a UM or a petty patent is one of the key determinants of the commercial exploitation of the exclusive rights granted under such a regime. Thus, there are several considerations to be made for deciding on the length of protection of an STP right. Most importantly, a shorter term of protection than patents is justifiable in view of the lower degree of novelty and inventiveness. Moreover, one of the objectives of a UM system is to provide suitable protection for simple and less technologically advanced innovations with a shorter commercial life because they are copied by competitors as soon as they appear in the market. Nevertheless, the period of exclusive rights should be reasonable to make registration costs and disclosure worth the effort.[801] Sri Lanka can distil experience from other jurisdictions in this regard. International experience shows that countries like Malaysia offer twenty years, while Somalia only provides for a four year term of protection. Thus, it may be argued that Sri Lanka should adopt a term ranging from five to eight years. Such a shorter duration of protection addresses the major concerns of critics such as patent evergreening and potential abuse of the system by the pharmaceutical industry because it needs to undergo compulsory clinical testing before actually getting to the market. Another argument in favour of a shorter term is that it would mitigate the impact of UM rights on follow-on innovation. Therefore, it is recommended that Sri Lanka should decide on an appropriate term of protection by analyzing the needs of the industrial landscape, especially the SME sector, and the underlying goals of such a system.

---

800 See FR Dahalan, 'Utility Models protection in Malaysia-Utility Innovation' (WIPO Regional Conference on the Legislative, Economic and Policy Aspects of utility Models Protection System, Kuala Lumpur, 3-4 September 2012).

801 See PA Cumming, 'From Germany to Australia: Opportunity for a Second Tier Patent System in the United States' (2010) 19 Michigan State Journal of International Law 320.

6.4.7. Exceptions and Limitations

One should not forget that, like all the other rights, IP rights are socially rooted and they are subject to a certain number of limitations imposed by public interests.[802] Therefore, an effective STP regime should contain limits on the exercise of UM rights. In designing exceptions and limitations on the exclusive rights under a UM system, the international IP law framework does not contain provisions comparable to Articles 30, and 31 of the TRIPS Agreement which would have to be adhered to when policymakers in Sri Lanka decide on the issue of exceptions and other limitations (such as compulsory licenses).[803] Thus, Sri Lanka can freely determine which type of uses of the protected utility model do not require any authorisation of the right holder, whether any compensation is owed for such a use and what kind of conditions apply for invoking such an exception.[804] Therefore, Sri Lankan policymakers should consider including research and experimental use provisions and a prior use defence in order to ensure that innovations are not stifled. Moreover, a compulsory license may be used whenever the UM holder is unwilling to license his technology and there is a recognized public interest for its use.[805] The grounds for granting a compulsory license should definitely include non-working and dependent technical advances, government use, failure to supply the domestic market adequately or domestic working requirements as a matter of economic policy choice.[806]

6.5. Prosecution and Enforcement

As lucidly illustrated by Judge Posner in a recent case, patent litigants can be compared with violent beasts, using 'all their teeth and claws' in a

---

802 See generally, C Geiger, 'Fundamental Right, a Safeguard for coherence of Intellectual Property Law?' (2004) 35 International Review of Intellectual Property and Competition Law 268, 270.

803 Hen HG Ruse-Khan, 'Utility Model Protection in Pakistan-A Feasible Option for Incentivising Incremental Innovation?' (2012), Study conducted for the World Intellectual Property Organisation 90 (copy on file with author).

804 Ibid.

805 Ibid.

806 NAO Boztosum, 'Exploring the Utility Models for Fostering Innovation' (2010) 15 Journal of Intellectual Property Rights 429, 435.

'struggle for survival'.[807] A UM right is a negative right to exclude others from using the protected innovation as in the case of patents. The perceived benefits of any UM regime in part depend on the effective enforcement mechanism in the country. Thus, Sri Lanka needs to design enforcement tools for adequate and effective remedies. It should be appropriate to make available legal remedies such as injunctive relief and damages in case of infringement of UM rights. Nevertheless, since STP rights are granted without undergoing a substantive examination, the Court should not grant injunctive relief in infringement lawsuits until the right holder produces an obligatory search/evaluation report obtained from the National IP office.[808] Moreover, there should not be a presumption of validity as an issued UM or petty patent has not been subject to any substantive examination. Nevertheless, a UM right must be presumed valid upon the submission of the search report obtained from the National IP Office of Sri Lanka. As an enforcement related safeguard, there should be provisions for invalidation or cancellation proceedings before the National IP office. Moreover, a search report/evaluation report should also be available to any third party. Since litigation is well beyond the means of the SME sector, Sri Lanka should also consider making available alternative dispute mechanisms for holders of STP rights.

6.6. Interface with other IPR Systems

A UM or a petty patent right may possibly overlap with other IP such as patents and design rights. Since the patent law and the utility model law both set out to protect technical inventions, thus frictions between the two systems cannot be ruled out. Therefore, it is important to design the STP regime in such a way as to ensure a proper balance between the two systems.[809] Significantly, in the Sri Lankan context, any new addition to the existing IP regime has to work within the general IP framework of the country. Under Sri Lankan STP law, there should be a very clear provision

807 Posner J in *Apple Inc. v. Motorola Inc.* No. 1:11-cv-08540, 22 June 2012/District Court for the Northern District of Illinois Eastern Division.

808 In an evaluation report, the IP office should confirm that registered UM or Petty patent right fulfils the conditions of protection.

809 European Commission, 'Green Paper on the Protection of Utility Models in the Single Market Document' COM (95) 370 final.

that allows for no dual protection for the same or identical invention, and it should be made compulsory that UM or petty patent right should be abandoned in the event a patent right is granted. Such a provision is necessary to prevent the potential for double patenting. Nevertheless, it is also important to allow conversion of patent applications to applications for STP, and *vice versa*, especially in view of low level IP awareness in the country. Most innovators and SMEs in Sri Lanka may not have a clear idea of the degree of inventiveness of their innovations. However, it may be also important to keep this right of conversion within limits in order to prevent abusive filing.

6.7. Guarding against Abuse

The unfortunate reputation of utility models of 'easy to get in, hard to get out' is an invitation for free riders and actors.[810] Since STP rights are granted without undergoing any substantive examination, there is always a potential risk of abuse. Therefore, the risk of abuse could be addressed by built-in checks and balance mechanisms which would serve the function of watch dogs or gate keepers. Provisions for invalidation and requiring production of an evaluation report before enforcing the right may be used to discourage such abusive behaviours. As a countermeasure against potential abuse by holders of a UM right, Sri Lanka should possibly introduce an obligatory search/evaluation Report as a precondition for enforcement. Moreover, experience from Australia and China shows that many large companies tend to use the STP regime for strategic purposes. Thus, it is important that Sri Lanka should reduce the scope for such abusive strategies by restricting permissible subject matter, enforcing limitations on conversion and reducing the term of protection. Moreover, the use of compulsory licensing provisions and liability rules can be used to further mitigate potential abuses of the system. Therefore, it is of utmost importance that appropriate safeguards are placed in order to prevent the misuse of the system.

---

810 TT Moga, *China's Utility Model Patent System: Innovation Driver or Deterrent* (Research Paper, US Chamber of Commerce 2012) Forward and Commentary provided by T Pattloch, 4.

6.8. Domestic IP Infrastructure (IP Office, Courts, Professionals)

Not only the legal framework but also the legal infrastructure matters a lot for a developing country that provides for a new IP right. Even though Sri Lanka has a modern legal framework, there are many issues to be resolved. One of the concerns is whether the country's judiciary has the necessary expertise in resolving IP disputes. Even the judiciary in a recent patent litigation observed "at this stage, I should state with humility that I do not possess such knowledge and expertise in the field of engineering to decide on novelty and inventive step of the product and come to a proper conclusion. Therefore I am of the view that this Court may come to an incorrect decision, if the court decides on novelty and inventive step of the product in question, without considering expert opinion".[811] In the event that Sri Lanka introduces a utility model or a petty patent system it has to be implemented through a comprehensive and coordinated approach.[812] Merely legislative and regulatory instruments would not serve the purpose unless the target stakeholders have proper awareness, access and facilitation to use this system coupled with strong enforcement machinery. This system should be used as a trade and industrial policy tool rather than rolling it out merely as another form of IP protection.[813]

One of the major concerns that Sri Lanka has to address is the lack of expertise in the area of IP law. Obviously, there is an acute dearth of experts who can draft patent applications. The same is certainly true for utility models or petty patents. Like most other developing countries, Sri Lanka clearly lags behind in this area and does not have a system of patent attorneys skillful in drafting the claims.[814] Thus, Sri Lanka also needs to consider creating a strong patent attorney profession with the involvement

---

811 See KT Chitrasiri, Decisions on Intellectual property Issues of the Commercial High Court of Sri Lanka (Vishva Lekha 2005) 70. Chitrasiri J in *Michael Laurents Cyrille Cadermanpulle v Mohamed Haniffa Mohamed Ajmal & Another* (2004) Commercial High Court case No:33/2004 (03) (decided on 2 February 2005).

812 HG Ruse-Khan, 'Utility Model Protection in Pakistan-A Feasible Option for Incentivising Incremental Innovation?' (2012) Study conducted for the World Intellectual Property Organisation 95 (copy on file with author).

813 Ibid.

814 W Weeraworawit, 'Utility Models in Thailand' in C Heath and A Kamperman Sanders (eds), *Industrial property in the Bio-Medical Age: Challenges for Asia* (Kluwer Law 2003) 270.

of science and technology graduates passing out from the country's universities. Our survey evidence also supported this proposition that only a handful of law firms are equipped with necessary skills to handle patent cases. If this issue is not sorted out, any new right will suffer the same fate as patents and would not meet the objectives for which it was introduced. Until now, this problem has not caused many concerns for standard patents because most applications are filed from abroad and a good part of local applications are prepared and filed by very few law firms in the capital Colombo. With regard to the patent granting process, the National Intellectual Property Office (NIPO) does not have a sufficient number of qualified patent examiners. It was revealed through our survey evidence that there are currently less than five patent examiners attached to NIPO. Unlike Singapore or Malaysian IP offices, NIPO suffers from a lack of quality human resources. In the light of an expected increase in applications, the need to increase the patent office's ability to handle the increased capacity through training programs for patent examiners is crucially important. Otherwise, even if a UM system is introduced, the industries would not be able to reap its benefits. It may also be important that the Sri Lankan IP office should implement a UM helpdesk concept for users of the STP system which can be used by the SME sector in Sri Lanka.

In order to successfully implement an innovation promotion framework through a UM regime, Sri Lanka needs to raise awareness on and encourage the use of the UM system by establishing 'innovation centres' at the divisional secretariat level[815] through the *'Vidatha'* program which was designed by the government to transfer technology to villages. Officials attached to *Vidatha* resource centres can help to build public awareness of the new system and, in particular to provide counseling to SMEs and individual innovators who are in need of such assistance at the grassroots level. It is worth mentioning here the steps taken by the National Innovation Foundation of India to provide free legal service for the grassroots innovators. Sri Lanka can explore the possibility of devising a system to provide *pro bono* support from the legal community channeled through the Inventors Commission of Sri Lanka whenever so required. It would be unimag-

815 At present, there are 9 Provinces, 25 Districts, and 256 Divisional Secretariats in Sri Lanka. The districts of the Sri Lanka are divided into administrative sub-units known as *divisional secretariats.* See Article 5 and 8th Schedule of the Constitution of Sri Lanka 1978 (as amended).

inable that any system would benefit or reach the rural level unless such a support mechanism is in place. Of course, this system can be implemented by following a bottom-up-approach as opposed to the current top-down-approach taken in relation to the registration of patent rights in the country. As pointed out by many innovators and SMEs during our interviews conducted in Sri Lanka, there should be a 'chain of help' in order to bring budding innovations to reach the NIPO in capital city. In so doing, the government may need to allocate additional resources and should be able to recruit new graduates, after extending specialized training facilities, creating a post of 'innovation promotion officers'. In this way, the government can effectively make use of thousands of graduates from local universities who become mostly unemployed thereafter to contribute to the nation's development.

6.9. TK-based Innovation and Second-Tier Protection

Intellectual creations at all levels should be nurtured so as to develop an innovation culture in a country.[816] TK-based innovations, however, remain on the periphery of the broader discourse on innovation and have only received little attention. At least, in the Sri Lankan context, it is time to increase the role of traditional innovators in its development strategy. TK-based innovations are generally characterized by value addition and incremental steps. The incentive theory informs us that, by affording an appropriate intellectual property protection, a society can encourage and promote such innovation. One of the problems that Sri Lanka's TK-based innovation sector faces is that most companies and family businesses heavily rely on trade secrecy. This has a negative impact on its development in terms of quality. This leads to chilling effects on innovation. For example, a firm might reduce its research and development department to an inefficiently small number of employees, or hire loyal but less-skilled family members in order to protect secrecy.[817] Moreover, TK-based innovation is

816 Federation of Indian Chamber of Commerce and Industry (FICCI), FICCI's Suggestions on Proposed National Intellectual Property Policy (2011) FICCI 3, available at: <http://www.ficci.com/Sedocument/20170/ip-policy.pdf> (accessed 2 June 2012).

817 See RG Bone, 'A New Look at Trade Secret Law: Doctrine in Search of Justification' (1998) 86/2 California Law Review 241, 272-273.

an area that is not primarily served by the patent regime due to stringent patentability criteria. Thus, it is necessary to provide an additional protection option to facilitate TK-inspired innovation in the Sri Lankan context. According to commentators, TK can trigger new product development, especially in sectors of food and beverages, traditional medicines, personal care and cosmetics.[818] In particular, in Sri Lanka, herbal medicine production and cosmetic sectors have indicated great market demand in the recent years. As such, Sri Lankan policymakers should consider including the TK-based innovation sector into the scheme of protection under UM legislation in order to provide necessary incentives for such innovation.

6.9.1. Why is such a Form of Protection Important?

IP is the currency of the knowledge-based economy.[819] Moreover, TK-based innovations have become items of commercial significance in the modern world. Traditional communities are seeking protection for their works similar to that enjoyed by IP owners, endowing works with the ability to earn revenue.[820] Without appropriate IP protection, herbalists and traditional healers would not have incentives to monetize their ideas. The IP system places knowledge and ideas in a market system, acting simultaneously as a legal framework that facilitates disputes over ownership and infringement.[821] Any STP regime is likely to fall short of that expectation if it does not provide protection for TK-based innovations. The current patent regime does not provide a suitable means of protecting minor and incremental innovation of TK-based innovators. The Kenyan experience shows that a UM regime can provide a window of opportunity for TK-

818 See T Cottier and M Panizzon, 'Legal Perspectives on Traditional Knowledge: The case for Intellectual Property Protection' in KE Maskus and JH Reichman (eds), *International Public Goods and Transfer of Technology under a Globalized Intellectual Property Regime* (Cambridge University Press 2005) 564, 567.

819 R Ghafele and B Gibert, 'Promoting Intellectual Property Monetization in Developing Countries: A Review of Issues and Strategies to Support Knowledge-driven Growth' (2012) Policy Research Working Paper 6143-World Bank 14.

820 O Dean, 'From Folklore to Folk Law in South Africa' (2009) May, Managing IP 132.

821 R Ghafele and B Gibert, 'Promoting Intellectual Property Monetization in Developing Countries: A Review of Issues and Strategies to Support Knowledge-driven Growth' (2012) Policy Research Working Paper 6143-World Bank 14.

based innovators, even though the use of the system is very low, mainly due to lack of awareness and other practical hurdles faced by innovators. There is also a strong argument that an STP regime should not extend its protection to TK-based innovation as such a system can be misused by large and multinational firms. But from a practical point of view, one can counter-argue that it is difficult if not impossible to create a system only for the benefit of the SME sector without at the same time creating advantages for large companies. Perhaps even more importantly, to prevent small businesses receiving benefits from the IP system is as bad, if not worse, than letting large companies take advantage of it.[822]

According to commentators, a utility model system is more suited for protecting TK-based innovations.[823] Under a utility model regime, the term of protection should be from eight to ten years and can be more but less than twenty years. Such a system is ideally suited for innovations that build upon existing innovations, without much original contribution and the products have market potential.[824] SMEs and individual entrepreneurs who hold TK and want to develop TK-based innovations can benefit from this scheme. For example an SME that wants to develop and market a TK-based product could come up with an improved process or make the product available in a new form such as a solution or a cream, whereas earlier it was only available as a powder or an extract from dry leaves. The process also increases the efficacy of the product.[825] There should be a more accessible protection mechanism for TK-based innovations that merit protection in order to recognize, respect and reward traditional knowledge innovators.

6.9.2. Herbal and Cosmetic Product Sector

Most of the indigenous knowledge and innovation particularly in the herbal medicine sector may be patentable if they are given modern techno-

822 See the same line of argument by A Gupta in 'Can protecting intellectual property rights be of any consequence for poor people?' (2007) ICRIER Paper 21 <http://www.sristi.org/anilg/papers/> (accessed 10 June 2011).

823 See KR Srinivas, 'Traditional Knowledge and Intellectual Property Rights: A Note on Issues, Some Solutions and Some Suggestions' (2008) 3/1 Asian Journal of WTO & International Health Law and Policy 81, 100..

824 Ibid.

825 Ibid.

logical touches.[826] Unfortunately, for many of the indigenous people this technology is relatively unavailable.[827] Thus, an STP right may be used as a vehicle for technology transfer to TK-based industries in Sri Lanka. Most importantly, the policymaker should design the STP regime so as to include TK-based herbal and cosmetic innovations into the new legislation as these are the main industrial sectors of the domestic SMEs in Sri Lanka that TK-inspired innovations emanate from.[828]

6.9.3. Traditional Medicines: a Potential Candidate for Protection?

All countries in South Asia have a rich heritage of traditional medicine (TM). Traditional systems of medicine are a legacy of several thousands of years of human experience in the selection of plants for preventive and curative healthcare.[829] As is well-known, TM plays a crucial role in health-care and serves the health needs of a large part of the population in developing countries. Access to modern health care services and medicine may be limited in developing countries such Sri Lanka. TM becomes the only affordable treatment available to poor people and the time has come to revisit policies promoting research and development in the area of TM.[830] Viewed from a historical perspective, TM has been practiced in Sri Lanka for 3,000 years. At present, there are four systems of traditional medical systems in Sri Lanka viz. Ayurveda, Siddha, Unani and Deshiya Chikitsa.[831] The most important among them is the Ayurveda, traditional medical system which also forms part of the national health services pro-

826 JM Mbeva, 'Experiences and Lessons Learned regarding the Use of Existing Intellectual Property Rights Instruments for Protection of Traditional Knowledge' (UNCTAD Expert Meeting on Systems and National Experiences for Protecting Traditional Knowledge, Innovations and Practices, Geneva, 2000) 7.

827 Ibid.

828 See CM Correa, Protection and Promotion of Traditional Medicines: Implications for Public Health in Developing Countries (South Center, 2002) 91.

829 K Balasubramaniam, 'Role of Traditional Medicine in Promoting the Well-Being of the People in South Asia' (South Asian Regional Conference of Traditional Medicine, Bangalore, India, July 2006).

830 RA Mashelkar, 'Intellectual Property Rights and The Third World' (2001) 18/8 Current Science 955, available at: <http://www.sristi.org/material/1.2intellectual%20property%20and%20the%20third%20world.pdf> (accessed 15 June 2012).

831 PK Perera, 'Current scenario of herbal medicine in Sri Lanka' (ASSOCHAM, 4th Annual Herbal International Summit, NSIC, New Delhi on 14 -15 April, 2012).

vided by the government of Sri Lanka including a separate ministry for Indigenous Medicine. The word Ayurveda is derived from AYU and VEDA. AYU means life, VEDA means Science or knowledge. That means the science of life. Ayurveda embraces all living things, animate and inanimate. It is divided into three main branches viz. Nara Ayurveda dealing with human life, Satva Ayurveda the science dealing with animal life and its diseases, Vriksha Ayurveda the science dealing with plant life its growth and diseases.[832] At present, Ayurveda serves a large proportion of the population with one Ayurvedic physician per 3,000 people in Sri Lanka. About 60 to 70% of the rural population relies on traditional and natural medicine for their primary health care.[833]

Sri Lanka needs to encourage research and development activities including drug standardization in order to attain a global reach. There is a need to take some positive steps to avoid losing knowledge relating to valuable indigenous medicines. The problem associated with the lack of investment in research and development in Ayurveda research has hampered its development. This may be caused by the lack of protection or security for their rights. The existing knowledge cannot easily be made available to the researcher due to the unwillingness of local healers to reveal such knowledge, especially family recipes of indigenous medicinal treatments including medicines, preparation, dosage and usage. Such knowledge exists either in the form of oral prescriptions jealously guarded as family secrets and sometimes handed down by one generation to the other or it is contained in Ola manuscripts safely locked up in museums, temples or individual homes.[834] As one Sri Lankan commentator has observed:

> 'There is a lot of scope for Sri Lanka to achieve a higher rank in the global market through the export of quality products from medicinal and aromatic plants. But Sri Lanka seems to be lagging behind in using advanced technolo-

---

832 Bandaranaike Memorial Ayurveda Research Institute of Sri Lanka, 'Introduction of Ayurveda and History' (2012) website of BMARISL, available at: <http://www.indigenousmedimini.gov.lk/Research_institute.html> (accessed 10 January 2012).

833 PK Perera, 'Current scenario of herbal medicine in Sri Lanka' (ASSOCHAM, 4th Annual Herbal International Summit, NSIC, New Delhi on 14 -15 April, 2012). .

834 Bandaranaike Memorial Ayurveda Research Institute of Sri Lanka, 'Introduction of Ayurveda and History' (2012) website of BMARISL, available at: <http://www.indigenousmedimini.gov.lk/Research_institute.html> (accessed 10 January 2012).

> gy and standardization procedures in herbal products and is ranked lower in the herbal medicine global market share, while China occupies nearly 30 pecent of the global market with high tech issues. Therefore Sri Lanka needs to be focused on the quality assurance with multidisciplinary researches within the country and collaborative works with other high tech used countries. Further Good Laboratory Practices (GLP) and Good Manufacturing Practices (GMPs) are also needed to apply for produce good quality medicinal products in Sri Lanka. Without overcoming these entire measures the current scenario is not sufficient to increase the global market share of the herbal drug industry and herbal medical practice for Sri Lanka'.[835]

According to our survey evidence, one of the main challenges faced in the development of the TM industry is the lack of funding for R&D efforts.[836] Moreover, the lack of advanced technological capabilities has considerably reduced reaping real benefits from the traditional medicine industry in Sri Lanka. Significantly, there is a huge demand for high quality Ayurvedic medicines and beauticare products. Nevertheless, there is no effective protection mechanism for incremental innovations which occur in this area. Thus, an STP regime would possibly accord a protection option for such innovations which would also facilitate technology transfer through licensing agreements. Most importantly, the STP legislation should specifically allow the protection of non-technical subject inventions, particularly chemical substances.[837]

If Sri Lankan policymakers decide to extend the scope of protection of the STP regime to TK-based innovation and traditional medicines, then there should be specific provisions in the STP law to address the concerns of critics regarding the potential abuses of the system. These safeguards should necessarily include basic principles that have been developed at the international level such as prior informed consent, disclosure of origin and equitable sharing of benefits.[838] Moreover, there are increasing concerns over the erosion of public domain and blocking effect on follow-on inno-

---

835 PK Perera, 'Current scenario of herbal medicine in Sri Lanka' (ASSOCHAM, 4th Annual Herbal International Summit, NSIC, New Delhi on 14 -15 April, 2012).

836 Revealed through personal interviews with the members of the Bandaranaike Memorial Ayurveda Research Institute and the faculty of Indigenous Medicine, University of Colombo, Sri Lanka as well as indigenous medicine practitioners/ (details of respondents are provided in the Appendix 2).

837 See CM Correa, Protection and Promotion of Traditional Medicines: Implications for Public Health in Developing Countries (South Center 2002) 91.

838 See the obligations under Articles 1 and 8 (j) of the Convention on Biological Diversity 1992.

vations if STP rights are granted to TK-inspired innovators. In order to address these fears, Sri Lanka should appropriately use a liability regime embedded into the STP legislation.[839] Under such a Compensatory Liability Regime (CLR), which is built on 'take and pay' principle, the second comers can access and use the protected subject matter for specific purposes without permission, but they must compensate the first comer for the uses in one manner or another.[840] This will also motivate second users to invest in follow-on innovations or incremental innovations.[841] Moreover, one of the other main arguments against granting STP for TK-based innovations is that the protection of such innovations in Sri Lanka would not prevent multinational companies from developed countries from misappropriating them. Nevertheless, the benefits of an STP for TK-based innovation mainly depend on the specific design of the national legislation.

6.10. Conclusion

Sri Lanka is a developing nation with limited technological resources and capabilities. For decades, the country has suffered from a shortage of homegrown creativity due to the low priority of successive governments for science, technology and innovation. The industrial landscape of Sri Lanka is characterized by a large SME sector which is considered to be the backbone of the country's economy. The SME sector is still in the initial stage of the technological ladder and the innovations that emanate from the SME sector mainly consist in minor adaptations to the existing products and are of an informal nature. Moreover, there is a high degree of innovation at the grassroot level involving TK-based less technological advances. It can be argued that current patent and design regimes do not provide suitable means of protecting low-level innovations and thus disincentivise such innovators. Nevertheless, minor and incremental innovations are most vulnerable to unfair copying and imitation, and thus, there exits an apparent need for appropriate legal protection for commercial exploitation of such innovations. Therefore, the findings of this research sup-

839 See JH Reichmann, 'Of Green Tulips and Legal Kudzu: Repacking Rights in Subpatentable Innovation' (2002) 53/6 Vanderbilt Law Review 1743, 1777-1778.

840 See C Correa, 'Designing Patent Policies suited to Developing Countries Needs' (2008) 10/2 Econômica, Rio de Janeiro 82, 89.

841 Ibid.

port the view that an STP system tailored to the specific characteristics of the innovation landscape of Sri Lanka is required to incentivise non-patentable innovations. Nevertheless, further consultation with stakeholders is required in order to make an informed decision. Moreover, the arguments offered in favour of the introduction of a UM regime in India and Pakistan should be taken into account by the policymakers of Sri Lanka. Most importantly, the ideal STP regime should involve much lower requirements for protection than that of patents and should be kept simple, fast and inexpensive in order to encourage the use of the system by the SME sector. However, an STP regime does certainly come with risks. An unexamined right has the inherent quality of uncertainty and such a regime can be manipulated by large players in the market. Thus, appropriate safeguards against potential abuses should be built into the system. The introduction of a new right also involves social costs and if the costs outweigh the benefits then such a system would no doubt become unnecessary and counterproductive. Moreover, the Sri Lankan government needs to take further positive steps to enhance IP awareness in the country and to enhance the capacity of domestic firms to absorb technology. In conclusion, it could well be argued that an appropriately designed STP regime would positively and significantly contribute to technological progress in Sri Lanka.

7. Recommendations and Policy Options for the South Asian Region

'We need to tailor concepts and procedures of our own, suited to our own traditions and needs'.
Judge CG Weeramantry[842]

From a historical perspective, second-tier patent protection is a policy response to perceived deficiencies in patent and design regimes.[843] In many jurisdictions, utility models or petty patents provide protection for minor and incremental innovations such as devices, tools and implementations particularly in the mechanical, optical, and electronic fields.[844] Such a system should, in principle, encourage greater innovation in developing countries as they provide legal protection for simple technological advances that do not qualify for fully-fledged patents because they fail to satisfy rigorous patentability criteria.[845] Perhaps more importantly, the empirical evidence from East Asian countries, especially from South Korea, indicates that a UM regime can help domestic firms in developing countries develop their technological capacity.[846] Despite the fact that South Asian economies rank low on global innovation and technology indicators, no country in the South Asian region has ever had a UM or petty patent regime in its IP law landscape. Interestingly, today there is a rising tide of opinion in the region in favour of the introduction of an STP regime in or-

842 CG Weeramantry, 'Lawyers as Social Engineers' (2004) 5/2 Bar Association Law Journal of Sri Lanka 7, 7.

843 G Dutfield and U Suthersanen, *Global Intellectual Property Law* (Edward Elgar 2008) 13-15.

844 YK Kim and others, 'Appropriate Intellectual Property Protection and Economic Growth in Countries at Different levels of Development' (2012) 1/4 Research Policy 358, 360, available at: <http://www.sciencedirect.com/science/article/pii/S0048733311001715> (accessed 2 June 2012).

845 W Weeraworawit, 'Utility Models in Thailand' in C Heath and A Kamperman-Sanders (eds) *Industrial property in the Bio-Medical Age: Challenges for Asia* (Kluwer Law 2003) 269, 269.

846 YK Kim and others, 'Appropriate Intellectual Property Protection and Economic Growth in Countries at Different levels of Development' (2012) 1/4 Research Policy 358, 368, available at: <http://www.sciencedirect.com/science/article/pii/S0048733311001715> (accessed 2 June 2012).

der to incentivise more incremental innovations among domestic firms, especially SMEs. Apparently, at least, Indian and Pakistani policymakers seem to have understood that certain technological improvements that are new but obvious, can still provide their inventors with a competitive advantage crucial for business and economic success. Even though a UM regime is currently under consideration in both India and Pakistan, designing a balanced, effective and inexpensive regime is a daunting task, and any such system should be adopted only after giving careful consideration to all relevant substantive and practical issues associated with an STP regime.

As noted before, even though India is more scientifically advanced than other South Asian countries, the economies in the South Asian region are generally less technologically advanced when compared with East Asian countries. Countries in the region need to develop indigenous technological capacities in order to achieve and sustain robust economic growth. With the advent of the information revolution, skills and knowledge have become the primary sources of sustainable long-term competitive advantage.[847] Thus, South Asian economies should craft their policies in a manner intended to shift the economy away from reliance on raw material exports and toward value adding and knowledge creating activities. Policies of the governments should be directed towards creating an innovation-friendly climate aimed at reaping the rewards of innovation. Of course, one could reasonably doubt whether the South Asian region suffers from an innovation policy deficit. The decisive question is whether countries in the South Asian region have created the appropriate type of protection mechanisms for the kind of innovation that emanates from their knowledge driven sectors. From a policy perspective, as one critic has elegantly summarized, confining IP rights to rather major and unanticipated solutions could be compared to depriving property rights to holders of small plots of land while granting such rights to big landowners.[848] Arguably, given that the majority of SMEs and grassroot innovators work at low technological levels, depriving such innovators of legal protection is contrary to both the basic rationale of the IP system and the principle of equi-

847 LC Thurow, 'Needed: A New System of Intellectual Property Rights' (1997) September-October, Harvard Business Review 95, 95.

848 NAO Boztosun, 'Exploring the Utility Models for Fostering Innovation' (2010) 15 Journal of Intellectual Property Rights 429, 436.

ty which may also constitute discrimination.[849] Nevertheless, it might still be argued that such innovation does not deserve protection at all. The crucial question is whether leaving less technologically advanced innovations unprotected would benefit the innovation landscape of a developing country in the South Asian region. As noted in previous chapters, the empirical evidence from South Asian countries does not support the view that non-protection of incremental innovation leads to increased innovation and to advances in the technological capacity of the countries, with the exception of certain sectors in India such as IT and pharmaceuticals.

7.1. Policy Options

For more than a century, the world's wealthiest human being was associated with oil, starting with John D Rockefeller in the 19th century and ending with the Sultan of Brunei in the late 20th century. But today, the world's wealthiest person is a knowledge worker.[850] Therefore, it is a priority need for Sri Lanka and other South Asian countries to move away from labour-intensive industrial sectors towards more knowledge-intensive sectors in order to achieve and sustain high economic growth. The policy space retained by individual countries under multinational IP instruments such as the TRIPS Agreement allows individual countries such as Sri Lanka to design an STP regime tailored to the needs of the country's industrial structure. In other words, all options are available for structuring a suitable STP regime for incentivising indigenous innovations. As postulated by Cornish, 'intellectual property may be extended to new subject-matter either by accretion or by emulation. Accretion involves redefining of an existing right so as to encompass the novel material; emulation requires the creation of a new and distinct right'.[851] Accordingly, commentators have pointed out, three main options that policymakers in a developing country can consider:[852]

---

849 Ibid.

850 LC Thurow, 'Needed: A New System of Intellectual Property Rights' (1997) September-October, Harvard Business Review 95, 95.

851 WR Cornish, 'The International Relations of Intellectual Property' (1993) 52/1 Cambridge Law Journal 46, 46-48.

852 U Suthersanen, G Dutfield and KB Chow (eds), *Innovation Without Patents: Harnessing the Creative Spirit in a Diverse World* (Edward Elgar 2007) 69.

- *Status quo approach*; A developing country can accept the existing intellectual property regime, without introducing any new right.
- *Accretion approach*; A developing country can adjust the existing intellectual property regime without introducing a utility model right. This can be done by extending existing intellectual property rights to new subject matter.
- *Emulation approach*; Emulation involves creating new hybrid rights.

In essence, South Asian countries need to decide whether they should

- leave sub-patentable invention unprotected,
- lower the inventive step requirement under the standard patent law in order to accommodate minor and incremental invention, or
- create an alternative protection regime such as that of a UM or a petty patent regime.[853]

Viewed through the lens of innovation activities, almost without exception, all eight countries in the region are IP importing nations. The existing patent regime simply does not provide a suitable means of protecting the type of innovation that emanates from the SME sector in this region. The majority of innovation involves simple technology and lacks a high degree of novelty and inventive step. Thus, there is a need to accord a simple, fast and affordable protection mechanism to incentivise incremental innovation as a stepping stone to further innovation. From a different perspective, there is another reason for not following the 'accretion principle'. If a country were to choose to adopt a lower/diminished inventive step requirement for patent law to accommodate minor technological advances, it could arguably lead to a diluting or polluting effect on the higher quality level of standard patents. A UM or petty patent system does not pose this threat as it provides short term protection for a low-level simple innovation with lower requirements of protection and caters to a different class of users. In the light of the above, South Asian policymakers are likely to decide in favour of the emulation option. Nevertheless, they still need to assess the strengths and limitations of such a regime. As a caveat, it should be born in mind that the emulation option is inherently risky in the sense that new rights are essentially experimental.[854] As Machlup has pointed out, unless compelling evidence suggests that introducing a new system of protection actually does more benefit than harm, one is better off by re-

---

853 Ibid 64.

854 G Dutfield and U Suthersanen, *Global Intellectual Property Law* (Edward Elgar 2008) 13.

taining the status quo.[855] Thus, policymakers in the South Asian region should carefully examine whether the potential social costs of introducing a new UM right exceed the perceived benefit. Most importantly, the lessons emerging from East Asia may provide useful insights for the South Asia region in this regard.

7.1.1. Sri Lanka

Since its independence, Sri Lanka has not been able to make significant strides in terms of innovation and technological progress in the past six decades. According to critics, Sri Lanka's weak performance regarding innovation is a symptom of the low priority given to science and technology and research and development.[856] Policymakers have aptly observed that under-development in the field of science and technology has been one of the reasons for the country's economic backwardness.[857] Today, Sri Lanka embarks on a voyage of economic development after the end of an almost three-decade-long civil war in 2009. It is apparent from the recent policy documents that the Sri Lankan government has acknowledged that it needs to change the direction of its science and technology policies in order to encourage domestic innovation and value creation for economic development.[858] Moreover, the policy agenda of the government clearly spells out

---

855 F Machlup, *An Economic Review of the Patent System* (1958) Study No. 15 of the Subcommittee on Patent, Trademarks and Copyrights of the Senate Committee on the Judiciary 79-80. HG Ruse-Khan, 'Utility Model Protection in Pakistan-A Feasible Option for Incentivising Incremental Innovation?' (2012), Study conducted for the World Intellectual Property Organisation 81 (copy on file with author).

856 A Wijesinha, 'Igniting a new fire: Why innovation must be Sri Lanka's new priority' *Daily FT* (Colombo, 12 March 2013), available at: <http://www.ft.lk/2013/03/12/igniting-a-new-fire-why-innovation-must-be-sri-lankas-new-priority/> (accessed 25 March 2013).

857 Government of Sri Lanka, *Mahinda Chintana-Towards a new Sri Lanka – Policy Document* (Department of National Planning: Ministry of Finance and Planning 2005) 67, available at: <http://www.treasury.gov.lk/publications/mahindaChintanaVision-2010full-eng.pdf> (accessed 25 March 2013).

858 In 2008, the government had observed that previous governments had not considered investment in science and technology as a priority. The investment in R&D has remained around 0.15 percent of GDP for the past several years. See National Science and Technology Commission (NASTEC)-Ministry of Science and Tech-

the government's determination to present the country as a knowledge hub in Asia.[859] Against this background, it is worth considering the introduction of an STP system to incentivise minor and incremental innovations which would reinforce the above policy objectives in Sri Lanka.

Sri Lanka has a good chance of reaping the benefits of innovation if it designs IP policies suited to the specific needs of the country. As noted above, in the event that Sri Lanka decides to introduce an STP regime, it may need to adopt the emulation approach. Since Sri Lankan has followed the practice of codifying all IP categories under the same IP Act, the introduction of a UM or petty patent right can easily be done by amending the current IP Act. Nevertheless, there should be a very clear line of demarcation between patentable inventions and innovation protected by an STP regime in order to avoid any confusions and misunderstandings. According to the Action Plan 2007 to 2016 of the National IP Office of Sri Lanka, the IP office is responsible for proposing policies on IP rights. This includes revising the existing IP regime and introducing improvements.[860] This document provides the necessary platform for the amendment of IP Law in order to introduce a petty patent or utility model system in Sri Lanka. It is argued that the introduction of a separate layer of protection for technologically less advanced innovation would make IP protection more accessible to a broader spectrum of users such as SMEs. As emerging economic literature indicates, Sri Lanka has a great chance to become a 'breakout nation'. A breakout nation is a country that beats expectations or a nation that is able to grow faster than other countries in the same per capita bracket.[861] Nevertheless, critics have warned that Sri Lanka might fall into the Middle-Income Trap if it does not achieve a high economic

---

nology, *National Science and Technology Policy-2008* (Government of Sri Lanka 2008) 5.

859 Department of National Planning-Ministry of Finance and Planning of Sri Lanka, *Mahinda Chintana-Vision for the future* (2010) 68, available at : <http://www.treasury.gov.lk/publications/mahindaChintanaVision-2010full-eng.pdf> (accessed 10 June 2011).

860 National Intellectual Property Office of Sri Lanka (NIPO), *Action Plan 2007-2016* (2007) NIPO 2-4. (file with the authorities).

861 R Sharma, *Breakout Nations: In Pursuit of the Next Economic Miracles* (Allen Lane 2012) 193. Sharma states: "The civil war is over, the process of healing is under way, and there is every chance that Sri Lanka will again become a breakout nation. Despite slowing sharply during the war years, the economy continued to grow at an average pace of nearly 5 percent".

growth rate.[862] In order to avoid the Middle-Income Trap, Sri Lanka needs to promote innovation at all levels and to develop a culture of innovation. For decades, Sri Lanka has suffered from low R&D spending, insufficient incentives to promote innovation, insufficient technology transfer from abroad and lack of clear policy for the promotion of industries in the country, especially for the SME sector. Specifically, Sri Lanka should provide sufficient incentives for all types of innovation to achieve sustained dynamic growth rather than turning to 'low-hanging fruits' such as tourism, exporting raw materials, sending low-skilled labour to the Middle East and far East countries though this may yield short term benefits for the nation.[863] Most importantly, Sri Lanka should have a clear innovation policy in order to guide an innovative nation.

7.1.2. India and Pakistan

The recent initiatives of the Indian and Pakistani policymakers have paved the way for wider discussion of adopting a UM system to promote incremental and creeping innovations in the region. Perhaps even more importantly, the Discussion Paper of the Indian government has generated much attention for a long felt need of providing effective legal protection for minor innovations in the region. Similarly, the Pakistani government has taken steps to draft a Utility Model Bill. Both countries have taken the emula-

---

862 The 'Middle-Income Trap' refers to a situation where countries can get stuck at a level of development in which its populace has been generally lifted out of poverty but has not been elevated to the income levels of more advanced economies. That happens because it is easier to jump from a very poor country to a middle-income nation than it is to advance from that of middle-income status to the ranks of the truly developed. See M Schuman, 'Can China Escape the Middle-Income Trap?' *Times* (New York, 12 March 2013), available at: <http://business.time.com/2013/03/12/can-china-escape-the-middle-income-trap/> (accessed 2 April 2013). WA Wijewardena, 'Will Sri Lanka be snared in a Lower Middle Income Trap before it reaches the Middle Income Trap Proper' *Daily FT* (Colombo, 23 January 2012), available at: <http://www.ft.lk/2012/01/23/will-sri-lanka-be-snared-in-a-lower-middle-income-trap-before-it-reaches-the-middle-income-trap-proper/> (accessed 24 January 2012).

863 A Wijesinha, 'Igniting a new fire: Why innovation must be Sri Lanka's new priority' *Daily FT* (Colombo, 12 March 2013, available at: <http://www.ft.lk/2013/03/12/igniting-a-new-fire-why-innovation-must-be-sri-lankas-new-priority/> (accessed 25 March 2013).

tion approach in order to create a new IP right, without diluting the high standard of the patent regime. Unlike Sri Lanka, these two countries are accustomed to the practice of enacting separate legislation for each type of IP. Therefore, enacting a separate piece of legislation for an STP system seems to be the most likely option for both countries. Given the high degree of innovation at the grassroot level and the type of innovation created by SMEs, the introduction of a new IP regime may provide a low-cost entry point for a broader spectrum of innovators in these countries. From an innovation policy perspective, such a regime may be necessary to assist the industrial sector and in particular the SMEs.

7.1.3. Other South Asian Countries

Other South Asian countries such as Afghanistan, Bangladesh, Nepal, and Bhutan belong to low income economies. Innovation in these countries appears still very low and these countries need to move up the technology and innovation ladder. According to UNIDO Industrial Development Report 2009 (as discussed in Chapter 5) economies in the South Asian region have not performed well on the global Competitive Industrial Performance (CIP) index. Obviously, South Asia has one of the least sophisticated export structures in the world.[864] It is time for these countries to look beyond the low-end operation in fashion cluster (textiles, cloths, shoes, leather, etc.).[865] In view of the experience from India and Pakistan, other developing countries in the region should consider creating a legal mechanism to encourage more domestic innovation in the industrial landscape. Although an IP regime is only one of the factors that contributes to the promotion of innovation in a country, the experience from East Asia shows that an STP regime can significantly contribute as a vehicle for technological learning by domestic industrial sectors. The designing of a balanced, effective, and inexpensive STP regime may be a major challenge for all these countries even though there is unfettered policy space remaining for tailoring a regime suited to the specific needs of an individual country.

---

864 United Nations Industrial Development Organization (UNIDO), *Industrial Development Report -2009* (UNIDO 2009) 120.

865 Ibid.

7.2. General Recommendations and Observations

It may be for historical reasons that an STP regime has not received the consideration it deserves from the South Asian governments. It is therefore desirable to revisit the existing IP laws and policies. At the policy level, the successful experiences of other jurisdictions such as Germany, Australia, China, Malaysia, as well as Kenya may serve as 'best practices' that could be emulated in structuring an appropriate UM or petty patent regime. In the design of any future legislation on STP, the South Asian policymakers should possibly include the following features:[866]

- *Subject matter of protection*: the scope of protection should not be restricted to mechanical devices, but should be narrower than the subject-matter covered under the patent law. There should be a list of excluded subject-matter such as software and pharmaceuticals because such innovation may, in particular, need a substantive examination in order to prevent the abuse of the system. However, TK-based innovation may be included for protection according to the interest and needs of the country.
- *Novelty standard*: novelty should be either relative or domestic in order to advance the interests of domestic innovators and SMEs.
- *Inventiveness threshold*: the level of inventiveness should either be abandoned or be much lower than that of patents. In principle, any innovation that represents a practical or functional advantage over prior art should be protected in order to accommodate adaptive innovations.
- *Substantive examination*: UM or petty patent applications should not undergo any substantive examination prior to grant. A cursory or preliminary examination is recommended.
- *Term of Protection*: the statutory life of the right should not exceed a maximum of eight years as a shorter term can be justified by a lower standard of protection. Moreover, the shorter term would also reduce the possibility of abuses
- *The STP regime should be attractive and user-friendly*: in order to make the new right appeal to domestic industries, it should be a less expensive, quickly granted and a more easily obtainable right.

---

866 U Suthersanen, 'Utility Models and Innovation in Developing Countries' (2006) ICTSD Issue Paper No.13, 38-39, available at: <http://unctad.org/en/docs/iteipc20066en.pdf> (accessed 15 March 2012).

- *Enforcement-related safeguards against abuses*: the risk of abuse could be addressed by in-built check and balance mechanisms. Procedures for invalidation and requiring the production of an evaluation report before enforcing the right may be used to discourage abusive behaviours.
- *Provisions for statutory and compulsory licensing.*
- *Government action to enhance awareness and the use of UM protection*

As noted above, most importantly, the particular features of an STP regime should respond to the objectives and goals of the country concerned. A country needs to examine and evaluate the potential impact of an STP regime on its innovation landscape before introducing such a regime. Without having such a clear understanding of the possible downsides of such a regime, no country can design a system that suits their domestic needs. Moreover, there have been and are concerns regarding possible abuse of the system by large firms. As argued by Fink and Maskus, 'although the existing economic literature on IPRs provides some useful guidance to policymakers in developing countries, there is still a lot we do not know'.[867] Thus countries should carefully assess whether the economic benefit of STP protection outweighs the costs. South Asian nations need to take into account the cost of administering and enforcing the additional layer of protection.[868] Most importantly, the benefit of an STP regime in any country would depend on the specific design of the legislation. In other words, any UM or petty patent system should focus on the needs and interests of the target group, in this case the SMEs.

In addition to introducing an STP regime, South Asian countries should focus their attention on developing the technological capacity of domestic firms to effectively absorb and adapt technologies developed abroad. Most importantly, there is no guarantee that any UM or petty patent would increase minor and incremental innovations unless a country provides the other necessary conditions for innovation to happen viz. appropriate institutions, education and IP awareness. Moreover, the literature on the transfer of technology, based on historical and empirical evidence from East Asia, suggests that a strong IPR protection will hinder rather than facilitate

867 C Fink and KE Maskus (eds), *Intellectual Property and Development: Lessons from Recent Economic Research* (World Bank and Oxford University Press 2005) 13.

868 Ibid.

technology transfer and indigenous learning activities in the early stage of industrialisation.[869] These studies find that it is only after countries have accumulated sufficient domestic capabilities with extensive science and technology infrastructure to undertake creative imitation in the later stage that IPR protection becomes an important element in technology transfer and industrial activities.[870] Even more interestingly, if one takes China as a major success story of the past decade, it has achieved an explosive economic growth in the face of intensive criticism of its IP regime.[871] The Chinese experience suggests that intellectual property protection is not as central a driver of innovation and technological development as is claimed.[872] More often, authors who are too convinced of IP commit the 'mono-causal fallacy'. They argue that in the case of countries that have recently experienced an 'innovation hype' following the introduction of higher standards of IP protection have done so due to their IP policies.[873] This line of argument, however, forgets that IP is just one reason for technological development, and may be not the most decisive one. For in-

---

869 YK Kim and others, 'Appropriate Intellectual Property Protection and Economic Growth in Countries at Different levels of Development' (2012) 1/4 Research Policy 358, 360, available at: <http://www.sciencedirect.com/science/article/pii/S0048733311001715> (accessed 2 June 2012). L Kim, *Technology Transfer and Intellectual property rights: The Korean Experience* (2003) ICTSD-UNCTAD Issue Paper No.2, 5.

870 Ibid.

871 See, F Abbott, 'Towards New Era of Objective Assessment in the Field of TRIPS and Variable Geometry for the Preservation of Multilateralism' (2005) 8/1 Journal of International Economic Law 77, 81. China is a paradigm case. It has pursued a policy of technology appropriation much like those pursued earlier by Japan, Taiwan and Korea, and has enjoyed explosive economic growth and development. Only a revisionist might attempt to correlate China's rapid economic growth to the introduction of strong IP protection. On the contrary, China has been under constant attack by the United States and EU for its IP protection failings.

872 G Dutfield and U Suthersanen, 'Harmonisation or Differentiation in Intellectual Property Protection? Lessons from History' (2005) 23/2 Prometheus 131, 132.

873 Yet, Yang and Maskus argue that stronger IPR would enhance technology transfer through licensing and reduce South firms' marginal production cost, thereby increasing its exports. See L Young and KE Maskus, 'Intellectual Property Rights, Technology Transfer and Exports in Developing Countries' (2008) CESINFO Working Paper No. 2464, Trade Policy. See, Y Chen and T Puttitanun, 'Intellectual Property Rights and Innovation in Developing Counties' (2005) 78 Journal of Development Economics 474, 489.

stance, firms from the US and Europe were willing to transfer a lot of technology to China in recent years although there are serious problems concerning IP enforcement. For them, it was more important to benefit from low wages in China and to be present in the Chinese market. In that sense, technology developments and innovations of the Newly Industrializing Countries (NIC) are largely motivated by cheap labour[874] and market access. All in all, any success of an STP regime may depend on whether a country is sufficiently advanced to generate a significant amount of domestic innovation.

7.3. Conclusion

As noted above, intellectual property protection is one of the central public policy pillars on which knowledge-based industries and global markets of the 21st Century rest.[875] Today, it is hard if not impossible to imagine achieving sustainable economic growth without the protection and the promotion of innovation. In this vein, an STP regime has not been offered its due place in the pantheon of IP law in the South Asian region. The emerging discourse on the feasibility of a UM regime as an appropriate mechanism to incentivise domestic innovation, especially those emanating from SMEs, has triggered Indian and Pakistani policymakers to consider such a regime in their IP laws. Both countries are currently deliberating on the possible adoption of a UM system and are engaging in further consultation with the relevant stakeholders. The Sri Lankan National IP Office is also keen on considering a UM or petty patent option for Sri Lanka soon.[876] Thus, the time is ripe for the other countries in the region to consider ap-

---

874 P Magic, 'International Technology Transfer & Intellectual Property Rights' (2003) University of Texas website, available at: <http://www.cs.utexas.edu/~fussell/courses/econtech/public-final-papers/Peter_Magic_International_IP_Rights.pdf> (accessed 15 May 2011).

875 Business and Industry Advisory Committee (BIAC) to OECD, Discussion Paper on 'Creativity, Innovation and Economic Growth in the 21st Century: An Affirmative Case for Intellectual property Rights (Paris, December 2003), available at : <http://www.oecd.org/dataoecd/52/45/23375023.pdf> (accessed 2 May 2012).

876 Interview with the Director General of NIPO of Sri Lanka (20 December 2012). Based on our personal communication, Sri Lanka is considering an amendment to the IP Act in order to accommodate the utility model or petty patent system.

propriate changes in the legal landscape, although creating a new IP right is only one of the determinants of technological progress. Introducing a new law alone cannot inculcate an innovation culture. It has to go hand in hand with other initiatives, including a strong foundation in technology and science, capacity building and technological learning, incentives for innovation, effective framework and mechanism for transfer of technology, and an effective enforcement of IPRs.[877]

From a policy perspective, most of the main arguments offered in favour of adopting a UM system in India and Pakistan would be equally applicable to Sri Lanka as well as other South Asian economies such as Afghanistan, Bangladesh, Bhutan, Nepal and Maldives. This does not mean that an STP regime would not be without its critics. There is increasing skepticism on the actual or potential use of the system given the very low level of IP awareness in these countries. Significantly, large players in the market have expressed their dissatisfaction over the possible introduction of a UM system. Most importantly, one of the major concerns is that the UM system is prone to be abused as the UM rights are granted without any substantive examinations. Therefore, it is of utmost importance that appropriate safeguards are placed in order to prevent the misuse of the system. Indeed, it is undeniable that an ideal regime of intellectual property rights strikes a balance between private incentives for innovators and the public interest of maximizing access to the fruits of innovation.[878] An STP system is at the beginning of a very long challenging road of producing and maintaining innovation.[879] Arguably, the adoption of an STP regime would be the first step in paving the way for an innovative country and a stepping stone for technological development. In the light of the above, it seems logical to conclude that an STP should be given due consideration in the pantheon of innovation policy in the economies of the

---

877 U Suthersanen, 'Utility Models and Innovation in Developing Countries' (2006) ICTSD Issue Paper No.13, Forward by R Meléndez-Ortiz and S Panitchpakdi ix-x, available at: <http://unctad.org/en/docs/iteipc20066_en.pdf> (accessed 15 March 2012).

878 RA Mashelkar, 'Intellectual Property Rights and the Third World' (2001) October 18/8 Current Science 955, available at: <http://www.sristi.org/material/1.2intellectual%20property%20and%20the%20third%20world.pdf> (accessed 10 January 2012).

879 W Weeraworawit, 'Utility Models in Thailand' in C Heath and A Kamperman-Sanders (eds), *Industrial property in the Bio-Medical Age: Challenges for Asia* (Kluwer Law 2003) 269, 273.

South Asian region. There are compelling reasons for South Asian policymakers to consider a new legal instrument for incentivising less technically advanced innovation in the region. Undoubtedly, choices that policymakers make would have far-reaching repercussion on the innovation landscape of the region. In the final analysis, South Asian nations need forward-looking policies to lay foundations for incentivising indigenous innovation in order to promote domestic creativity.

7.4. Outlook

It is hoped that this study will assist policymakers to think afresh about existing IP laws and policies in Sri Lanka, as well as in other developing countries in the South Asian region. It offers guidance for legislatures in designing an appropriate STP regime to incentivise domestic innovation. Perhaps this would have an impact on the introduction of a new legislation for the protection and promotion of incremental innovation in Sri Lanka. Of course, this research may have not found satisfactory answers to many questions for which future research could offer better solutions. Furthermore research would no doubt be required to draw definite conclusions on the specific issues such as protecting TK-based innovations and products of indigenous and herbal medicines.

8. Summary (in German)

Zusammenfassung der Dissertation

„Die Strukturierung einer zweiten Schutzebene zur Förderung technischer Innovationen bei kleinen und mittleren Unternehmen in Südasien: Ein Modell für Sri Lanka“.

Teil 1: Einleitung und Hintergrund

Ein Patentregime mit einer zweiten Ebene wie etwa einem Gebrauchsmusterschutz oder einem „kleinen Patent“ stellt in einem Immaterialgüterrechtssystem eine Option zu Förderung inkrementeller und kleinerer Innovationen dar. Eine solche zweite Schutzebene ergänzt das Patentsystem und bietet einen einfacher zugänglichen Schutz für einen kürzeren Zeitraum und mit niedrigeren Schutzvoraussetzungen. Eine zweite, mittlere Schutzebene soll ein Immaterialgüterrecht für Innovationen zur Verfügung stellen, die eine technische Verbesserung darstellen, bei denen jedoch der technische Fortschritt zur Erteilung eines regulären Patents nicht ausreicht. Rechtspolitisch kann ein solches Instrument für Entwicklungsländer von Bedeutung sein, deren technologische Kapazität generell geringer ist. Zur Entwicklung einer Innovationskultur in solchen Ländern sollten auf allen Ebenen Innovationsanreize gesetzt werden. Nach der Anreiztheorie würden ohne einen Schutz kleinere und inkrementelle Innovationen mangels Belohnungsperspektive unterbleiben. Ein zweistufiges Schutzregime kann an die Bedürfnisse von lokalen Unternehmen – vor allem von kleinen und mittleren Betrieben – angepasst werden. Es gibt Anhaltspunkte dafür, dass ein Gebrauchsmusterschutzregime für die spezifische Innovationslandschaft in Sri Lanka angemessen wäre. Zudem wäre ein Schutzsystem mit zwei Ebenen besser geeignet für Innovationen, die auf traditionellem Wissen basieren, da Innovationen in diesem Bereich häufig eine geringere Originalität aufweisen. Die multilateralen, internationalrechtlichen Vereinbarungen zum Immaterialgüterrecht belassen einen rechtspolitischen Spielraum für die Einführung eines mehrgliedrigen Schutzsystems, das den spezifischen Bedürfnissen einzelner Länder Rechnung trägt. Die Länder Südasiens sollten die Möglichkeit der Erprobung alternativer rechtlicher Instrumente haben, da eine Vorgehensweise nach dem Prinzip 'one size fits all' die Erwartungen hinsichtlich einer Förderung von Innovationen und Erfindungen nicht vollständig erfüllt hat. Nachdem die Idee eines mehrstufigen Schutzsystems in den Ländern Südasiens bereits seit Jahrzehnten diskutiert worden ist, erhalten die Befürworter in den letzten Jahren an Auftrieb, insbesondere nachdem die indische Regierung dieses Konzept in einem Diskussionspapier über einen Gebrauchsmusterschutz aufgegriffen hat. Daher sollten Sri Lanka und andere Entwicklungsländer Südasiens vorsichtig die Einführung des bislang weit gehend unerforschten Konzeptes eines mehrstufigen Patentsystems zur Förderung lokaler Innovationen diskutieren.

Teil 2: Inkrementelle Innovationen und das bestehende Immaterialgüterschutzsystem in Sri Lanka

Das Immaterialgüterschutzsystem umfasst eine Bandbreite verschiedener Schutzrechte, die traditionell in Urheberrechte und technische Schutzrechte unterteilt werden können. Die Schutzrechtserteilung wird jeweils durch theoretische und philosophische Begründungen legitimiert. In diesem Kapitel, das sich ausschließlich mit Patent- und Designschutz hauptsächlich aus der Perspektive Sri Lankas befasst, wird die Geeignetheit des existierenden Schutzregimes Sri Lankas bei der Förderung inkrementeller und kleinerer Innovationen betrachtet. Innovationspolitisch stellt ein Patent ein Instrument dar, um durch die Erteilung eines Ausschließlichkeitsrechts Investitionen in Forschung und Entwicklung sowie die Kommerzialisierung von Erfindungen zu fördern. Zudem erhofft man sich von einem Patentsystem eine Begünstigung der indigenen technologischen Entwicklung, mehr einheimische Erfindungen, mehr Technologietransfer sowie technologische Lerneffekte. Sri Lanka hat als Land des Commonwealth sein Patentsystem ursprünglich aus dem englischen Rechtskreis übernommen, jedoch schrittweise ein eigenes Schutzregime entwickelt. Obgleich dieses Schutzsystem bereits mehr als einhundertfünfzig Jahre existiert, ist sein Beitrag zur Entwicklung von Wissenschaft und Technologie gering geblieben. Die hohen Anforderungen des gegenwärtigen Patentrechts in Bezug auf das Vorliegen einer globalen Neuheit und eines technologischen Fortschritts stellten ein Hindernis bei dem Schutz von solchen Innovationen dar, die typischerweise von der einheimischen Industrie und vor allem von kleinen und mittleren Unternehmen hervorgebracht werden. Zugleich ist die Rechtsprechung im Bereich des Patentrechts nicht ausreichend fortgeschritten, da nur wenige Fälle in die zweite Instanz gelangen.

Sri Lanka mit einem relativ kleinen Markt und einer technologisch eher gering entwickelten Wirtschaft befindet sich lediglich in einem frühen Stadium der technologischen Entwicklung und bedarf weiterer Fortschritte. Eine empirische Betrachtung zeigt, dass der gegenwärtig verfügbare Patentschutz wenig geeignet ist zum Schutz von denjenigen Innovationen, die von der einheimischen Wirtschaft geleistet werden. Ein Patentschutz scheitert meist an den hohen und komplexen patentrechtlichen Anforderungen vor allem bei dem Kriterium des technischen Fortschritts. Die relativ geringe Anzahl an Patentanträgen und-registrierungen durch einheimische Unternehmen unterstreicht diesen Befund. Es besteht daher die Besorgnis, dass ein Patentsystem nach dem Prinzip 'one size fits all' in Entwicklungsländern nicht das geeignete Instrument zur Förderung einheimischer Innovationen darstellt. Die Regierungspolitik sollte eine intensivere Nutzung des Patentsystems durch Unternehmen anstreben und in Sri Lanka eine Entwicklung von einer arbeitsintensiven Textilindustrie hin zu mehr wissensbasierten Produkten einleiten. Es gibt Anzeichen dafür, dass das Bewusstsein in Bezug auf die Möglichkeit eines Immaterialgüterschutzes bei großen Unternehmen weitaus höher ausgeprägt ist als bei kleinen und mittleren Unternehmen. In einer zusammenfassenden Beurteilung hat das Patentregime in Sri Lanka die gesetzgeberischen Ziele nicht erreicht. Kleine und mittlere Unternehmen arbeiten weit gehend in Außerachtlassung oder in Unkenntnis der Möglichkeit eines Immaterialgüterschutzes. Daher ist-ohne eine Herabsetzung der allgemeinen Patentierungsstandards-die Einführung eines zweistufigen Patentsystems zu bedenken, das bezogen auf den Schutz inkrementeller und kleinerer Innovationen den Bedürfnissen kleiner und mittlerer Unternehmen des Landes besser gerecht wird.

Im Gegensatz zu einem Patentschutz hat ein Designrecht den Schutz des Gesamterscheinungsbildes eines Produktes zum Gegenstand. Mangels eines Konsenses zur internationalen Harmonisierung unterscheiden sich in den verschiedenen Ländern die Voraussetzungen für einen Designschutz. In Sri Lanka muss ein Industriedesign den Standard einer weltweiten Neuigkeit erfüllen. Von noch größerer Bedeutung ist der Ausschluss funktionaler Aspekte des Produktes vom Designschutz. Dadurch ist es schwierig und geradezu ausgeschlossen, einen Designschutz für inkrementelle Innovationen oder für mechanische und technische Innovationen zu erlangen. Anders formuliert, schützt das Designrecht in Sri Lanka keine funktionellen Innovationen. Die Frage, ob ein Designschutz eine Alternative zu einem mehrstufigen Schutzsystem darstellt, ist daher weit gehend zu verneinen. Lediglich in einigen Fällen würde in Sri Lanka ein Designschutz bestehen, wenn die Produkteigenschaften die Erscheinung des Produktes verbessern und nicht primär eine funktionale Rolle spielen. Im Vergleich zum Patentsystem ist die Inanspruchnahme des Designschutzes in den letzten Jahren verhalten geblieben. Empirisch wurde die Mehrzahl der Anträge auf Designschutz durch Einheimische beantragt. Dies bedeutet jedoch nicht, dass bei Beantragung und Registrierung des Designschutzes bedeutende Fortschritte erzielt worden sind. Zusammenfassend sind für Sri Lanka weitere Schritte und ein Paradigmenwechsel erforderlich, um technologische Fortschritte und den Rang einer aufstrebenden Wirtschaftsnation zu erreichen.

Teil 3: Anreizmechanismen für inkrementelle und kleinere Innovationen im Lauterkeitsrecht und im Recht der Geschäftsgeheimnisse in Sri Lanka

Das Lauterkeitsrecht soll ein faires und angemessenes Marktverhalten von Wettbewerbern sichern. Eine Stärke des Lauterkeitsrechts besteht darin, dass ohne unnötige Beeinträchtigung des freien Wettbewerbs ein Schutz über das Immaterialgüterrecht hinaus sowie eine Innovationsförderung erreicht werden können und dass ein Trittbrettfahren verhindert werden kann. Jedoch besteht die Schwäche des Lauterkeitsrechts in der Unbestimmtheit seiner Konzepte. Eine zu starke Ausdehnung des Lauterkeitsrechtsschutzes durch die Gerichte auf zuvor ungeschützte Bereiche kann paradoxerweise eine unerwünschte Beschränkung des freien Wettbewerbs bewirken. Das Gesetz muss daher verantwortungsvolle Unternehmensstrategien fördern, ohne die Balance zwischen fairem Wettbewerb und anderen Bereichen des Immaterialgüterrechts zu stören. Eine weite Auslegung des Lauterkeitsrechts zum Schutz inkrementeller Innovationen wäre dem rechtspolitischen Einwand ausgesetzt, einen Immaterialgüterrechtsschutz durch die Hintertür zu schaffen. Zudem schafft ein Lauterkeitsrechtsschutz-anders als ein Gebrauchsmuster oder ein „kleines Patent“-kein absolutes Recht, das Gegenstand einer Lizenz sein kann.

Bezogen auf Sri Lanka ist es bedauerlich, dass trotz des weiten Schutzes durch das Immaterialgüterrecht, häufig noch auf die lauterkeitsrechtliche passing off action zurückgegriffen wird. Dies ist vermutlich auf ein mangelndes Bewusstsein der Praktiker und ihre Jahrhunderte lange Orientierung auf das Common Law zurückzuführen. Jedoch ist die Entwicklung des Fallrechts der letzten Jahre ermutigend und eine Fortentwicklung des Rechts in Sri Lanka kann unter Rückgriff auf Erfahrungen aus Kontinentaleuropa und insbesondere aus Deutschland erfolgen. Zudem müssen bei der Festlegung der Grenzen des Lauterkeitsrechts die Interessen von Wettbewerbern, Konsumenten sowie der Allgemeinheit zum Ausgleich gebracht werden. Die Gerichte Sri Lankas sollten internationale Entwicklungen und Gesetzgebungen verfolgen, um neuen Konstellationen begegnen zu können. Nur diese Vorgehensweise wird sicherstellen, dass das Lauterkeitsrecht in Sri Lanka dem grundlegenden Ziel einer freien Marktwirtschaft mit fairem Wettbewerb dient. Zusammenfassend können inkrementelle und kleinere Innovationen durch das Lauterkeitsrecht in Sri Lanka geschützt sein. Dies wäre jedoch kein idealer Weg zur Förderung solcher Innovationen

Demgegenüber hat der Schutz von Geschäftsgeheimnissen einen grundlegenden Einfluss auf das Innovationsumfeld in einem Land. Dieser Geheimnisschutz bezieht sich in erster Linie auf den Schutz kommerziell wertvoller Informationen, die der Geheimhaltung unterliegen. Artikel 39 des TRIPS-Abkommens bildet eine Grundlage für die internationale Harmonisierung des Geheimnisschutzes. In Sri Lanka existieren neben dem Schutz durch das Immaterialgüterrecht weitere Schutzmechanismen wie etwa durch das Common Law Rechtsinstitut des Vertrauensbruchs und durch das Vertragsrecht. Bemerkenswerterweise bildet der gesetzliche Schutz von geheimen Informationen einen Teil des Lauterkeitsrechts. In der Zukunft könnte zur Verbesserung des Rechtsschutzes eine spezifische und umfassende Regelung des Geheimnisschutzes erforderlich werden. Geschäftsgeheimnisse sind mehr denn je von Bedeutung bei Unternehmen in Sri Lanka und insbesondere bei Unternehmen im Bereich des traditionellen Wissens. Zu den Gründen für diese Entwicklung zählen die Offenlegungserfordernisse im Patentrecht sowie die Kosten, die mit dem Erwerb, der Erhaltung sowie der Durchsetzung von Immaterialgüterrechten verbunden sind. Aus logischen Überlegungen und tatsächlichen Betrachtungen lässt sich ableiten, dass ein großer Teil der Unternehmen in Sri Lanka auf informelle Mechanismen der Geheimhaltung in ihrer Geschäftstätigkeit zurückgreifen. Obgleich der Geheimnisschutz in einigen Fällen den Schutz durch andere Immaterialgüterrechte ergänzen oder gar vervollständigen kann, bestehen praktische Probleme bei der Durchsetzung des Geheimnisschutzes. So können Verfahren zum Schutz von Geschäftsgeheimnissen zu deren weiterer Verbreitung beitragen. Jedenfalls in Sri Lanka sind diese Fragen nicht ausreichend beantwortet.

Zusammenfassend können sowohl das Lauterkeitsrecht als auch der Schutz von Geschäftsgeheimnissen auf flexible Weise für einige Bereiche Schutz gewähren, die durch die Immaterialgüterrechte nicht erfasst werden. Jedoch besteht die Gefahr, dass die Flexibilität zu Inkohärenz führt. Ein Schutz durch die Hintertür begegnet – wie bereits erwähnt – rechtspolitischen Bedenken und weder das Lauterkeitsrecht noch der Geheimnisschutz bieten einen klar abgegrenzten Schutz und ausreichende Rechtssicherheit. Aus diesen Gründen kann argumentiert werden, dass keines dieser beiden rechtlichen Instrumente eine ausreichende Alternative zu einem zweistufigen Schutzrechtssystem darstellt. Jedoch kann in dem unternehmerischen Umfeld in Sri Lanka der rechtliche Schutz von Geschäftsgeheimnissen durch seinen angemessenen Schutz für einfache und offensichtliche Innovationen, die dem Patentschutz und dem Designschutz nicht unterfallen, und durch das Verbot eines widerrechtlichen Gebrauchs von Geschäftsgeheimnissen einen gewissen Schutz für inkrementelle und kleinere Innovationen leisten.

Teil 4: Mehrstufige Schutzrechtssysteme in anderen Jurisdiktionen: Gesetzgebungsbeispiele aus Ländern von außerhalb Südasiens

Erfahrungen aus entwickelten Ländern

Erfahrungen aus Deutschland

Während die deutsche Erfahrung seit dem Jahre 1891 für viele Länder einen Referenzpunkt darstellt, sollten Sri Lanka und andere Länder Südasiens die unbeabsichtigten Konsequenzen beachten, die sich nachfolgend in dem Schutzsystem ergeben haben. Wie jedes Schutzrechtssystem kann ein zweistufiges Schutzrechtssystem zu negativen Folgen führen, die zunächst nicht bedacht wurden und daher thematisiert werden sollten. Die Gründe zur Etablierung eines Schutzrechtssystems könnten vor allem dann relativiert werden, wenn große Unternehmen das Schutzrechtssystem strategisch ausnutzen. Die Betrachtung der deutschen Mechanismen zur Verhinderung eines Missbrauchs des Systems zeigen auf, wie einem möglichen Fehlgebrauch begegnet werden kann. Es ist festzuhalten, dass der Erfolg eines Schutzrechtssystems mit der gerichtlichen und administrativen Infrastruktur eines Landes zusammenhängt. Das Absehen von einem niedrigeren Standard beim Erfordernis der Erfindungshöhe wird wohl von anderen Ländern nicht übernommen werden. Wenn die erforderliche Erfindungshöhe beim Gebrauchsmusterschutz und beim Patentschutz identisch wäre, so bestünde lediglich ein geringer rechtspolitischer Anlass zur Einführung eines zweistufigen Schutzrechtssystems.

Die erfolgreichen Erfahrungen mit dem deutschen Gebrauchsmusterschutz haben außerhalb Deutschlands die Europäische Kommission dazu veranlasst ab 1995 eine europaweite Harmonisierung des Gebrauchsmusterrechts zu diskutieren. Diese Vorschläge der Europäischen Kommission wären ohne Zweifel als Diskussionsgrundlage dafür geeignet, wie ein Schutzrechtssystem ausgestaltet werden muss, damit es den Bedürfnissen eines Landes am besten gerecht wird. Viele Länder Ostasiens haben von der deutschen Erfahrung mit einem Gebrauchsmusterschutz gelernt und profitiert und eine Betrachtung dieses Systems könnte als erster Referenzpunkt dienen.

Erfahrungen aus Australien

Australien verfügt seit 1979 über ein zweistufiges Schutzrechtssystem („kleines Patent“ und Innovationspatent) und die Erfahrungen können als Modell für Sri Lanka und andere Länder Südasiens dienen. Insbesondere haben mehrere Überprüfungen und Studien bestätigt, dass das zweistufige Schutzrechtssystems den Zielen, die bei seiner Einführung angestrebt wurden, gedient hat und weiterhin dient. Zweifelsohne stellt das australische System einen interessanten Weg dar, um die Interessen einheimischer Innovatoren sowie kleiner und mittlerer Unternehmen durch ein Schutzrecht für inkrementelle und kleinere Innovationen zu fördern, das schnell, billiger und leichter zu erlangen ist. In diesem Sinne können die Überlegungen zu der Erfahrung Australiens für viele Länder einen Anstoß geben, die die Einführung eines zweistufigen Schutzrechtssystems erwägen. Zudem kann von Australien gelernt werden, nach der Einführung eine regelmäßige Überprüfung hinsichtlich des Funktionierens des Schutzrechtsregimes vorzunehmen. Die nachahmenswerten Stärken des Systems bestehen in dem Schutz für nahezu jedes Produkt oder jeden Prozess, soweit diese neuartig und nützlich sind, in der herabgesetzten Erfindungshöhe, in der Schnelligkeit, in den geringen Erteilungskosten und in dem

Erfordernis einer Bestätigung bevor eine Vollstreckung erfolgt. Gleichwohl ist das System nicht frei von Kritik. Obgleich dieser Innovationsschutz einzigartige Vorteile für den einheimischen industriellen Sektor bietet, wird er häufig als strategisches Instrument benutzt. Dabei versuchen große einheimische und ausländische Firmen ein schnell durchsetzbares Recht zu erlangen, indem sie separat beide Schutzrechte beantragen. Dies hat zusammen mit „patent evergreening" und dem Problem der Patentdickichte zu Kritik am australischen Innovationsschutzsystem geführt. Um solchen Missbräuchen zu begegnen, müsste Sri Lanka beim Entwurf eines zweistufigen Schutzrechtssystems wahrscheinlich den Schutzbereich eng ausgestalten, den strategischen Gebrauch beschränken und Computersoftware vom Anwendungsbereich ausnehmen. Zudem würde eine relativ kürzere Schutzdauer die Gefahr eines evergreening bei Schutzrechten im Pharma-Bereich reduzieren. Die geringen Anforderungen an die Erfindungshöhe mögen in einem technologisch fortgeschritteneren Land wie Australien Anlass zu Bedenken geben. Jedoch kann dies nicht auf ein Entwicklungsland wie Sri Lanka übertragen werden, wo die meisten Innovationen durch kleine und mittlere Unternehmen in kleineren Anpassungen und Verbesserungen bei bereits existierenden Produkten bestehen. Zusammenfassend bietet das australische System wertvolle Einsichten für Länder, die die Einführung eines zweistufigen Schutzrechtssystems erwägen.

Erfahrungen aus aufstrebenden Ländern und aus Entwicklungsländern

Erfahrungen aus China

Die beinahe dreißigjährigen chinesischen Erfahrungen können eine gute Fallstudie für Entwicklungsländer wie Sri Lanka darstellen. Abgesehen von der unterschiedlichen Marktgröße kann China viele Lehren für Entwicklungsländer Südasiens zur Verbesserung bei indigenen Innovationen und bei einheimischer Kreativität bieten. Die verfügbaren empirischen Untersuchungen bestätigen, dass das chinesische Gebrauchsmusterschutzregime ein nützliches Schutzrechtsinstrument für kleine und mittlere Unternehmen sowie für individuelle Innovationsträger darstellt. Zweifelsohne können die genannten Beobachtungen des chinesischen Patentamtes auf das heutige Sri Lanka übertragen werden, da der Großteil der Innovationen dem Bereich einfacherer Technologie von kleinen und mittleren

Unternehmen und individuellen Innovationsträgern mit geringen Ausgaben für Forschung und Entwicklung zuzuordnen ist. Folglich kann die chinesische Erfahrung als nützliches Modell für Sri Lanka für die Förderung solcher Innovationen dienen. Zudem hat sich das chinesische Gebrauchsmusterschutzsystem als hilfreich erwiesen, um den einheimischen Industriesektor und insbesondere kleine und mittlere Unternehmen mit dem Patentsystem vertraut zu machen. Wie bereits in Kapitel 2 angemerkt besteht in Sri Lanka ein bedauerlich geringes Bewusstsein von der Existenz des Patentsystems und eine geringe Inanspruchnahme. In diesem Sinne kann Sri Lanka dem chinesischen Beispiel folgend der Industrie und der allgemeinen Öffentlichkeit die Nutzung des Patentsystems als Gewohnheit einschärfen. Zudem ist das Konzept der Evaluierungsberichte nachahmenswert, um mögliche Missbräuche des Systems zu reduzieren. Außerdem sollte dem in vielen Entwicklungsländern fehlenden politischen Willen Chinas zur Förderungen von Innovationen gefolgt werden. Die chinesische Innovationspolitik ist auf eine Innovationsförderung in Wissenschaft und Technologie gerichtet. Mittlerweile hat sich durch einen indigenen Innovationsansatz die Innovationspolitik von einem „made in China" zu einem „innovate in China" gewandelt. Gleichwohl bedeutet dies nicht, dass das chinesische Gebrauchsmusterschutzsystem perfekt ist. Die Qualität der chinesischen Gebrauchsmuster hat in den letzten Jahren Kritik erfahren. Folglich müssen Fälle von Missbrauch und Bedenken bei der Qualität angegangen werden, um das System weiter zu verbessern.

Erfahrungen aus Malaysia

Das gegenwärtige Gebrauchsmusterschutzsystem in Malaysia ähnelt – wie oben angemerkt – stärker dem normalen Patentsystem. Obgleich kein Erfordernis der Erfindungshöhe besteht haben das Erfordernis einer inhaltlichen Prüfung der Gebrauchsmusteranmeldung vor der Erteilung und die Betonung des Standards der absoluten Neuheit möglicherweise für die einheimische Industrie eine Abschreckung dargestellt. Bezogen auf das Ziel eines zweistufigen Schutzrechtssystems sollte das Gebrauchsmusterschutzsystem in Malaysia in der Lage sein, der einheimischen Industrie schnell ein billigeres und einfach zu erlangendes Immaterialgüterrecht zur Verfügung zu stellen. Offensichtlich wird das gegenwärtige System den Bedürfnissen der kleinen und mittleren Unternehmen des Landes jedoch nicht gerecht. Wegen der zeitraubenden inhaltlichen Prüfung kann das

Schutzrechtssystem die Nachfrage nach einem schneller durchsetzbaren Recht für Produkte mit einem relativ kurzen Produktzyklus nicht befriedigen. In praktischer Hinsicht ist das System wegen der Begrenzung der möglichen Ansprüche – nur ein einziger Anspruch ist zulässig- weniger attraktiv. Positiv ist festzuhalten, dass in Malaysia – anders als in vielen Ländern Südostasiens – das System einen weiten Anwendungsbereich vorsieht, der auch Prozesse umfasst. Nach Information der Immaterialgüterrechtsbehörde in Malaysia plant Malaysia gegenwärtig eine Ergänzung des bestehenden Gebrauchsmusterschutzregimes. Diese sieht einen Wechsel weg von dem Erfordernis einer inhaltlichen Prüfung vor Erteilung hin zu einer Erteilung ohne inhaltliche Prüfung. Zudem soll eine schnelle und billige Erteilung erfolgen, es soll ein Antrag auf inhaltliche Prüfung nach Erteilung möglich sein, es sollen mehr Ansprüche gestattet sein und es sollen eine niedrigere Erfindungsschwelle sowie eine angemessene Schutzdauer vorgesehen werden. Insgesamt kann die Erfahrung in Malaysia eine Motivation und wertvolle Einsichten für den Entwurf eines zweistufigen Schutzrechtssystems in Sri Lanka bieten. Jedoch würde eine Übernahme ohne Beachtung der Nachteile zu ungewollten negativen Auswirkungen führen.

Erfahrungen aus Kenia

In Anbetracht der Nachfrage nach einem angemessenen Schutzmechanismus für Innovationen im Bereich traditionellen Wissens in Ländern, die wie Sri Lanka reich an traditionellen Wissen sind, ist es bemerkenswerte, dass Kenia einen Gebrauchsmusterschutz für Kräuter sowie Ernährungsanleitungen mit neuartiger Wirkung vorsieht. Kenia hat den Gebrauchsmusterschutz über den Bereich des traditionellen Wissens hinaus ausgeweitet. Nach den Kommentatoren ist ein Großteil des indigenen Wissens und der indigenen Innovationen durch Gebrauchsmuster schützbar, wenn ihnen ein modernes technologisches Element beigefügt wird. Leider ist diese Technologie für viele indigene Völker nicht verfügbar. In Sri Lanka ist dies vermutlich ähnlich. Zudem wird das Gebrauchsmusterschutzsystem in Kenia erkennbar zu wenig genutzt. Dafür gibt es mehrere Erklärungen. Nach der Erfahrung in Kenia bewirkt eine angemessene rechtliche Regelung alleine keine ausreichende Förderung indigener Innovationen. Vielmehr bedarf es einer Unterstützung für Innovatoren im Bereich des traditionellen Wissens, um ihre innovativen Ideen in Schutzrecht umzusetzen. Die fehlende Vertrautheit der kleinen und mittleren Unternehmen sowie der Öffentlichkeit mit einem Gebrauchsmusterrechtsschutz stellt ein Hindernis für die Wirksamkeit des Systems dar. Ein solches System muss benutzerfreundlich sein und die Zielgruppe ansprechen, also insbesondere individuelle Innovatoren sowie kleine und mittlere Unternehmen. In Kenia ist das Erteilungsverfahren ähnlich und beinahe so zeitintensiv wie bei Patenten. Zudem kann der Standard der absoluten Neuheit eine schwierige Hürde für örtliche Innovatoren darstellen. Offensichtlich stößt auch das Offenlegungserfordernis im Sektor des traditionellen Wissens auf ernste Vorbehalte und wird gleichwohl beibehalten. Möglicherweise stellt aber eine Geheimhaltung nicht den geeigneten Weg zur Förderung von Qualitätsprodukten für eine globale Nachfrage dar. Das Beispiel Kenias zeigt auch, dass Innovatoren im Bereich des traditionellen Wissens Schwierigkeiten bei der Abfassung der Anträge für einen Gebrauchsmusterschutz in der wissenschaftlichen und juristischen Fachsprache begegnen. Ähnliche praktische Probleme können bei möglichen Nutzern des Schutzsystems in Sri Lanka auftreten. Als Erfahrung aus Kenia können einige Aspekte des Gebrauchsmusterschutzes hilfreiche Anregungen darstellen. Jedoch sollten andere Gesichtspunkte, die eine Nutzung des Gebrauchmusterschutzes für einheimische Innovatoren unattraktiv machen, mit Vorsicht gesehen werden.

Teil 5: Die Region Südostasien und zweistufige Schutzsysteme

Die Perspektive Indiens

Bezogen auf Innovationen wurde Indien im Jahr 2012 auf Rang 64 des Global Innovation Index eingeordnet, hinter China (34) und Malaysia (32). Obgleich Indien wissenschaftlich und technologisch fortgeschrittener ist als andere Länder in der Region ist die Innovationsleistung außerhalb des IT- und des Pharma-Sektors nicht sehr ausgeprägt und bleibt hinter den Möglichkeiten zurück. In vielen Bereichen stellt Indien Produkte von geringerer Technologieintensität her und die einheimische Industrie weist wenige Patentanmeldungen auf. Laut Kritikern wurde der jüngere indische Wirtschaftsaufschwung durch eine Ausweitung des Dienstleistungssektors angetrieben, der im Jahr 2011 59 Prozent des Bruttosozialproduktes darstellte. Obgleich sich Indien im Rahmen des Outsourcing internationaler Konzerne zu einem Standort für Forschung und Entwicklung entwickelt hat, wird ein Rückstand bei einheimischen Unternehmen beobachtet. Dies trifft insbesondere auf den Sektor kleiner und mittlerer Unternehmen zu, der mehr als 80 Prozent der Unternehmen in Indien repräsentiert. In diesem Sektor bestehen die Innovationen weitgehend in kleinen technologischen Verbesserungen, und Innovatoren aus dem ländlichen Raum bedienen sich meist einfacher Technologien. Die indische Gesetzgebung sollte den Bedürfnissen der einheimischen Industriestruktur Rechnung tragen. Jedoch scheint das gegenwärtige indische Patentregime den Innovationsaktivitäten eines Großteils der einheimischen Unternehmen nicht gerecht zu werden.

Insgesamt ergeben sich daher gute Gründe für die Einführung eines Gebrauchsmusterschutzes, ohne dass die Patentierbarkeitsvoraussetzungen des Patentrechts dadurch verwässert würden. Der neue indische Gesetzesvorschlag ist daher zu begrüßen. Die Erfahrung aus Südostasien spricht für die Annahme, dass ein zweistufiges Schutzrechtssystem erforderlich ist, um den Aufbau von Technologiekapazität zu fördern. Zudem weist-wie auch das Diskussionspapier beobachtet hat-die Markteinführung neuer Produkte durch kleine und mittlere Unternehmen spezielle Attribute auf: Zu einer kostenintensiven Marktforschung vor der Markteinführung sind diese Unternehmen nicht in der Lage, der Wert ihrer Erfindung ist ihnen nicht bekannt, sie müssen ein erhebliches Geschäftsrisiko eingehen und sie sind zögerlich, den Zeit-und Kostenaufwand eines Patentantrages auf sich zunehmen. Die Verfügbarkeit eines schnellen und billigen Schutzes gegen Imitationen kann ihnen die Ausnutzung ihres Zeitvorsprungs im Wettbewerb erleichtern und stellt daher eine attraktive Option für sie dar. Gleichwohl gibt es zunehmende Bedenken gegenüber einem möglichen Missbrauch des geplanten Gebrauchsmusterschutzsystems. Kritiker befürchten wegen einer möglichen Blockade von Folgeinnovationen einen negativen Effekt auf die Innovationstätigkeit. Diesen Bedenken sollte durch Schutzmechanismen auf der Durchsetzungsseite Rechnung getragen werden. Insgesamt erwarten viele Experten von der Einführung eines Gebrauchsmusterschutzes in Indien einen positiven Einfluss auf die Innovationslandschaft, wenn dieser angemessen ausgestaltet und durchgesetzt wird. Nach der Erfahrung aus anderen Jurisdiktionen kann ein leichter zugängliches zweistufiges Schutzrechtssystem inkrementelle Innovationen kleiner Unternehmen sowie das Bewusstsein für Immaterialgüterrechte fördern.

Das weitere Vorgehen der indischen Regierung nach dem Diskussionspapier zu Gebrauchsmustern wird in der gesamten Region Südostasien aufmerksam verfolgt. Der Erlass eines neuen Gesetzes ist wohl zu erwarten. Nach Auskunft des indischen Office of Controller General of Patents, Designs, Trademarks and Geographical Indication (CGPDTM) liegt der Vorschlag eines Gebrauchsmustergesetzes dem Sectoral Innovation Council zur Beratung vor. Während der Arbeiten an dem Gesetzesvorschlag konsultiert die indische Regierung mit Innovationsträgern aus verschiedenen Sektoren. Natürlich sollte ein neues Gesetz die Bedenken aufnehmen, die als Reaktion auf das Diskussionspapier geäußert wurden. Es ist wichtig, dass ein zweistufiges Schutzrechtssystem funktionsfähig und ausgewogen ist und den Bedürfnissen des Landes Rechnung trägt.

Die Perspektive Pakistans

Auf Grundlage einer WIPO-Studie hat die Regierung Pakistans Schritte zur Einführung eines zweistufigen Schutzrechtsregimes unternommen und ist damit der Entwicklung in Indien voraus. Im Februar 2013 hat die pakistanische Immaterialgüterrechtsbehörde einen Gesetzesentwurf für einen Gebrauchsmusterschutz vorgelegt, der gegenwärtig von Interessengruppen kommentiert wird. Im Rahmen von Konsultationen untersucht die Immaterialgüterrechtsbehörde derzeit, ob das vorgeschlagene Gebrauchsmusterschutzrecht für Pakistan geeignet ist. Nach dem Gesetzesvorschlag kann ein Gebrauchsmuster für jede Erfindung erteilt werden, die neu und industriell verwendbar ist. Das Erfordernis einer bestimmten Erfindungshöhe besteht nicht. Wie im deutschen Gebrauchsmusterschutz wird der Standard einer relativen Neuheit vorgeschlagen. Publikationen weltweit, mündliche Offenlegung oder Gebrauch in Pakistan vor der Antragsstellung werden als Stand der Technik betrachtet. Eine mündliche Offenlegung im Ausland oder ein öffentlicher Gebrauch im Ausland stehen also dem Erfordernis der Neuheit nicht entgegen. Daher kann man argumentieren, dass das vorgeschlagene Gebrauchsmuster einfachere Schutzkriterien vorsieht. Wie in vielen anderen Ländern werden tierische und pflanzliche Variationen, chemische Zusammensetzungen, Computerprogramme, Prozesse und Methoden von der Schutzfähigkeit ausgenommen. Die Erteilung des vorgeschlagenen Gebrauchsmusterrechts erfolgt nach einer vorläufigen Prüfung ohne eine inhaltliche Prüfung. Zudem wird ein Kontrollmechanismus zur Verhinderung von Missbräuchen vorgeschlagen. Insbesondere kann von jeder Person ein Ungültigkeitsverfahren vor der Immaterialgüterrechtsbehörde eingeleitet werden. Zudem kann-wie in Japan- jedermann eine technische Stellungnahme über die Registrierbarkeit eines Gebrauchsmusters beantragen. Die maximale Schutzdauer soll 10 Jahre ab der Beantragung erfassen. Ein Erlass des neuen Gesetzes hätte einen bedeutenden Einfluss auf die gesamte Region Südasien. Erfahrungsgemäß benötigt der Gesetzgebungsprozess bis zum Inkrafttreten des neuen Gesetzes mindestens zwei Jahre.

Die Übertragbarkeit dieser Erfahrungen auf Sri Lanka

Die gesetzgeberischen Pläne in Indien und Pakistan signalisieren die Bereitschaft, den Einsatz alternativer Instrumente zur Förderung einheimischer Innovationen zu diskutieren. Die Länder Südasiens erkennen, dass sie zumindest gegenwärtig im Bereich der Innovation hinter ihren ostasiatischen Nachbarn zurückliegen. In den späten 1950er Jahren war keines dieser ostasiatischen Länder wesentlich wohlhabender als die afrikanischen Länder und verfügten kaum über Industrie. Mittlerweile haben sie eine Transformation von einer vorwiegend agrarwirtschaftlichen Prägung hin zu einer stärker diversifizierten industriellen Prägung erfahren. Wenngleich Immaterialgüterrechte nur einen der Faktoren für die technologische Entwicklung eines Landes repräsentieren, deutet die Erfahrung ostasiatischer Länder darauf hin, dass ein Gebrauchsmusterschutzsystem den technologischen Lernprozess durch schrittweise Anpassung ausländischer Technologien erleichtert hat. Die Innovationspolitik in den Ländern Südasiens bedarf einer Überprüfung, um ein günstigeres Umfeld für indigene Innovationen zu schaffen. Dabei müssten einzelne Länder Südasiens neue rechtliche Instrumente zur Förderung von Kreativität auf allen Ebenen einführen. Sowohl Indien als auch Pakistan planen ein Gebrauchsmusterschutzsystem. Indien hat die Jahre 2010 bis 2020 zum Jahrzehnt der Innovation erklärt und beabsichtigt die Förderung einer Innovationskultur um soziale Bedürfnisse befriedigen zu können.

Sri Lanka weist-abgesehen von der kleineren Marktgröße-in Hinblick auf die Agrarwirtschaft und arbeitsintensive Industrien viele Gemeinsamkeiten mit Indien und Pakistan auf. Zugleich ist Sri Lanka technologisch weniger fortgeschritten mit einem wenig entwickelten Sektor von kleinen und mittleren Unternehmen. Daher sind die Hauptargumente zur Einführung eines Gebrauchsmusterschutzregimes in Indien und Pakistan zur Förderung inkrementeller und kleinerer Innovationen auf Sri Lanka übertragbar. Ebenso sollte der Entwurf eines ausgewogenen und funktionsfähigen zweistufigen Schutzrechtssystems zur Förderung kleiner und mittlerer Unternehmen Vorkehrungen gegen einen Missbrauch des Systems vorsehen. Die berechtigten Bedenken die als Reaktion auf das indische Diskussionspapier und den pakistanischen Gesetzesentwurf geäußert wurden, sollten vom Gesetzgeber in Sri Lanka beachtet werden, um unbeabsichtigten negativen Wirkungen vorzubeugen. Jedenfalls sollte ein zweistufiges Schutzrechtssystem auf die spezifischen Bedürfnisse des jeweiligen Landes zugeschnitten sein. Jedenfalls wird jetzt in einigen südasiatischen Ländern die Einführung eines zweistufigen Schutzrechtssystems zur Förderung indigener und einheimischer Innovationen erörtert. Bislang stellte die südasiatische Region eine Ausnahme bei der Verfügbarkeit eines solchen Systems dar. Zugleich verhindern hier die strengen Patentierungsvoraussetzungen einen wertvollen Schutz für inkrementelle und kleinere Innovationen, die im Wesentlichen von kleinen und mittleren Unternehmen der Region hervorgebracht werden. Pakistan und Indien haben zur Förderung von kleinen und mittleren Unternehmen und zum Aufbau von Technologiekapazität Schritte zur Einführung eines Gebrauchsmusterschutzes unternommen. Dabei haben sie starke Unterstützung durch die einheimischen Industrien erfahren und nach einer Konsultation und Evaluierung der Vorschläge ist eine Einführung der Regelungen zu erhoffen. Dennoch mehren sich angesichts des geringen öffentlichen Bewusstseins für einen Immaterialgüterrechtsschutz Zweifel, ob ein solches System tatsächlich genutzt werden wird. Große Marktteilnehmer haben bereits ihre Skepsis gegenüber der Einführung eines Gebrauchsmusterschutzsystems geäußert. Vor allem ist es wichtig mögliche Missbräuche des Systems, zu diskutieren.

Teil 6: Der Entwurf eines zweistufigen Schutzrechtsregimes für Sri Lanka

Sri Lanka ist ein Entwicklungsland mit begrenzten technologischen Ressourcen und Fähigkeiten. Über Jahrzehnte bestand ein Mangel an einheimischer Kreativitätsförderung, da Regierungen wiederholt Wissenschaft, Technologie und Innovation lediglich eine geringe Priorität zugemessen haben. Ein großer Sektor von kleinen und mittleren Unternehmen stellt den Zentralbereich in der industriellen Struktur Sri Lankas dar. Diese befindet sich erst auf einem frühen Stadium der technologischen Entwicklung und Innovationen bestehen hauptsächlich in kleineren Anpassungen. Eine stärkere Innovationsaktivität lässt sich in frühen Geschäftsstadien sowie eher im Bereich des traditionellen Wissens als der Technologie feststellen. Der gegenwärtige Patent-und Designschutz stellt erkennbar kein geeignetes Mittel zum Schutz kleinerer Innovationen dar. Zugleich können inkrementelle und kleinere Innovationen durch unlautere Imitation stark beeinträchtigt werden. Daher besteht ein sichtbares Bedürfnis nach einen angemessenen rechtlichen Schutz für die kommerzielle Verwertung solcher Innovationen.

Die Ergebnisse dieser Studie zeigen, dass ein zweistufiges Schutzrechtssystem, das an die spezifischen Eigenheiten der Innovationslandschaft Sri Lankas angepasst ist, notwendig zur Förderung von Innovationen ist, die unterhalb des Niveaus der Patentierbarkeit liegen. Dennoch sollten noch eine Konsultation der Betroffenen erfolgen und die Argumente zur Einführung eines Gebrauchsmusterschutzes in Indien und Pakistan beachtet werden. Vor allem sollte ein passendes zweistufiges Schutzrechtsregime weitaus geringere Anforderungen aufstellen als das Patentsystem und es sollte einfach, schnell und preiswert sein, damit es von kleinen und mittleren Unternehmen auch in Anspruch genommen wird. Gleichwohl ist ein zweistufiges Schutzrechtsystem auch Kritik ausgesetzt. Die ungeprüfte Erteilung von Rechten bringt eine inhärente Unsicherheit mit sich und ein solches System kann von größeren Marktteilnehmern ausgenutzt werden. Das System muss daher Absicherungen gegen einen Missbrauch vorsehen. Die Kosten und Nachteile der Einführung eines neuen Rechts dürfen die Vorteile nicht übersteigen. Ferner müssen in Sri Lanka das öffentliche Bewusstsein für einen Immaterialgüterrechtsschutz sowie die Technologieorientierung einheimischer Unternehmen gestärkt werden. Zusammenfassend kann festgestellt werden, dass ein angemessen ausgestaltetes zweistufiges Schutzrechtsystem den technologischen Fortschritt in Sri Lanka maßgeblich stärken würde. Wenn der Gesetzgeber in Sri Lanka den Anwendungsbereich des zweistufigen Schutzrechtssystems auf den Bereich des traditionellen Wissens und der traditionellen Medizin ausweitet, dann sollten spezielle Vorschriften gegen einen Missbrauch des Systems eingeführt werden. Dabei sollten Absicherungen vorgesehen werden, die bereits auf der internationalen Ebene entwickelte wurden, wie etwa vorherige Zustimmung, Offenlegung der Herkunft sowie angemessene Aufteilung der Gewinne. Zudem bestehen verstärkt Einwände gegenüber einer Verkleinerung des schutzfreien Bereichs sowie gegenüber einem Blockadeeffekt in Bezug auf Folgeinnovationen, wenn ein zweistufiger

Schutz im Bereich des traditionellen Wissens gewährt wird. Solchen Bedenken sollte Sri Lanka durch ein angemessenes Entschädigungsregime, ein „Liability Regime", begegnen.

Teil 7: Empfehlungen und rechtspolitische Optionen für die Region Südostasien

Immaterialgüterrechtsschutz spielt eine zentrale Rolle in wissensbasierten Industrien und auf den globalen Märkten des 21. Jahrhunderts. Ohne den Schutz und die Förderung von Innovationen ist ein nachhaltiges Wirtschaftswachstum schwer vorzustellen. In Südasien hat ein zweistufiges Schutzrechtssystem bislang keine angemessene Rolle im System des Immaterialgüterrechts erhalten. Die einsetzende Diskussion über die Umsetzbarkeit eines Gebrauchsmusterrechtsschutzes als angemessenem Instrument zur Förderung einheimischer Innovationen vor allem durch kleine und mittlere Unternehmen hat Indien und Pakistan veranlasst, eine entsprechende Gesetzgebung zu erwägen. Beide Länder führen entsprechende Konsultationen durch. Auch die Immaterialgüterrechtsbehörde in Sri Lanka möchte die baldige Einführung eines Gebrauchsmusterschutzes oder eines „kleinen Patents" erwägen. Daher ist auch für andere Länder der Region die Zeit für rechtliche Änderungen reif, auch wenn die Einführung eines neuen Immaterialgüterrechts nur einen von mehreren Faktoren für technischen Fortschritt darstellt und für sich alleine keine Innovationskultur schaffen kann. Begleitende Initiativen sind erforderlich wie eine Stärkung von Wissenschaft und Technik, technologisches Lernen, Innovationsförderung, Technologietransfer und eine wirksame Durchsetzung von Immaterialgüterrechten.

Die Hauptargumente zur Einführung eines zweistufigen Schutzrechtssystems in Indien und Pakistan sind nicht nur auf Sri Lanka übertragbar, sondern gleichermaßen auf andere südasiatische Länder wie Afghanistan, Bangladesh, Bhutan, Nepal and die Malediven. Dabei wäre eine solche Maßnahme nicht frei von Kritik. Angesichts des lediglich geringen Bewusstseins für Immaterialgüterrechte in diesen Ländern besteht eine gewisse Skepsis, ob ein solches System tatsächlich in Anspruch genommen würde. Große Marktteilnehmer haben ihre Vorbehalte gegenüber der Einführung eines Gebrauchsmusterschutzes bereits geäußert. Eine Hauptsorge besteht in Bezug auf einem möglichen Missbrauch, wenn Gebrauchsmusterschutzrechte ohne inhaltliche Prüfung erteilt werden. Daher sind Mechanismen zur Vermeidung eines Missbrauchs wichtig. Ein optimales System des Immaterialgüterrechtsschutzes muss ein Gleichgewicht finden zwischen der Schaffung von Anreizen und dem öffentlichen Interesse des Zugangs zu den Früchten der Innovation. Ein zweistufiges Schutzrechtssystem steht am Beginn eines schwierigen Weges bei der Schaffung von Innovationen und technischer Entwicklung. Daher sollte einem zweistufigen Schutzrechtssystem eine Rolle im System der Immaterialgüterrechte in Südasien eingeräumt werden. Es gibt überzeugende Gründe für die Gesetzgeber in Südasien ein neues Instrument zur Förderung technisch weniger anspruchsvoller Innovationen zu erwägen. Dies hätte ohne Zweifel weit reichende Folgen für die Innovationslandschaft der Region. Im Ergebnis benötigen die Länder Südasiens eine zukunftsweisende Politik zur Förderung indigener Innovationen und einheimischer Kreativität.

Ausblick

Diese Studie möchte die Gesetzgeber dabei unterstützen, die bestehenden Immaterialgüterrechtssysteme in Sri Lanka und in anderen Entwicklungsländern Südasiens zu überdenken. Sie bietet eine Handreichung für Entwurf eines zweistufigen Schutzrechtssystems zur Förderung einheimischer Innovationen und kann möglicherweise einen Einfluss auf eine neue Gesetzgebung in Sri Lanka zum Schutz inkrementeller Innovationen nehmen. Natürlich können für viele Fragen erst durch zukünftige Forschung genauere Antworten gefunden werden. Insbesondere für die Bereiche traditionelles Wissen und indigene Medizin werden erst künftige Untersuchungen abschließende Schlussfolgerungen finden können.

Bibliography

Abeyesekere IN, 'Copyright Law and Practice in Sri Lanka' (1998) 29/1 International Review of Intellectual Property and Competition Law 27.

Abeyesekere IN, *Sri Lankan Copyright Law and the TRIPS Agreement* (Mahapola Higher Education Scholarship Trust Fund, Sri Lanka 1999).

Abott F, 'Towards New Era of Objective Assessment in the Field of TRIPS and Variable Geometry for the Preservation of Multilateralism' (2005) 8/1 Journal of International Economic Law 77.

Abbot FM, Cottier T and Gurry F, *International Intellectual Property in an Integrated World Economy* (2nd edn, Wolters Kluwer Law, Federick, MD, USA 2011).

Abramowicz M and Duffy J, 'The Inducement Standard of Patentability' (2011) 120 Yale Law Journal 1590.

Adams J, 'History of the Patent System' in Toshiko Takenako (ed), *Patent Law and Theory: Research Handbook of Contemporary Research* (Edward Elgar, Cheltenham, UK, Northampton, MA, USA 2008).

Adelman MJ, Rader RR and Thomas JR, *Cases and Materials on Patent Law* (3rd edn, West Group, USA 2009).

Agreement on Trade-Related Aspects of Intellectual Property Rights (TRIPS), Apr. 15, 1994, Marrakesh Agreement Establishing the World Trade Organization, Annex 1C, The Legal Texts: The Results of the Uruguay Round of Multilateral Trade Negotiations 320 (1999), 1869 UNTS 299, 33 ILM 1197 (1994).

Alavi R, Gee LH and Azmi IM, 'Does IPRs Protection Influence Economic Growth and FDI Inflows in Malaysia' (2008) 9 Journal of World Investment and Trade Law 293.

Alikhan S and Mashelker RA, *Intellectual Property and Competitive Strategies in the 21st century* (Kluwer law, The Netherlands 2004).

Amaradasa RMW and De Silva MAT and Pathirage RP, 'Patent in a Small Developing Economy: A Case Study of Sri Lanka' (2002) 17 Journal of Intellectual Property Rights 395.

Ann C, 'Rushing to the Shadows: How Imitators are Chasing Bavarian SMEs from Patents towards Trade Secret Protection' (13th European Intellectual Property Institutes Network Conference, Munich, 3-5 February 2012).

Arundel A, 'The Relative Effectiveness of Patents and Secrecy for Appropriation' (2001) 30 Research Policy 611.

Australian Government's Advisory Council on Intellectual Property, 'Review of the Innovation Patent System: Issue Paper' (2011) Official Website of Australian Government/Advisory Council on Intellectual Property 8, available at: <http://www.acip.gov.au/reviews/all-reviews/review-innovation-patent-system/> (accessed 12 August 2012).

Azmi IM, Gee LH and Alavi R, *Intellectual Property System and Industrial Development in Malaysia* (IIUM Press, Malaysia 2009).

Bainbridge DI, *Intellectual Property* (8th edn, Person Education, UK 2010).

Balasubramaniam K, 'Intellectual Property Rights & Herbal Medicine' (Conference on Herbal Medicines for the People-Sri Lanka Association for the Advancement of Science Annual Scientific Sessions, Sri Lanka Foundation Institute Colombo, 10 December 2003).

Barton JH, 'Non-Obviousness' (2003) 43 IDEA: The Journal of Law and Technology 475.

Beier KF, 'The Future of Intellectual Property in Europe-Thoughts on the Development of Patent. Utility Model and Industrial Design Law' (1991) 22 International Review of Intellectual Property and Competition Law 157.

Beier FK, 'The Inventive Step in its Historical Development' (1986) 17/3 International Review of Intellectual Property and Competition Law 301.

Bently L and Sherman B, *Intellectual Property Law* (3rd edn, Oxford Universiity Press, Oxford, UK 2008).

Berne Convention for the Protection of Literary and Artistic Works of September 9, 1886, completed at Paris on May 4, 1896, revised at Berlin on November 13, 1908, completed at Berne on March 20, 1914, revised at Rome on June 2, 1928, at Brussels on June 26, 1948, at Stockholm on July 14, 1967, and at Paris on July 24, 1971, and amended on September 28, 1979, Electronic copy available at: <http://www.wipo.int/treaties/en/text.jsp?file_id=283698>(accessed 12 August 2012).

Bittner TL, 'EPO Procedure' (2001) Training Course Materials on Obtaining, Enforcing and Evaluating Intellectual Property Rights in Europe, conducted by Boehmert & Boehmert – Munich, 2-6 July 2001.

Björkwall P, Nyttighetsmodeller: Ett ändamålsenligt innovationskydd? (Utility Models: Adequate Protection for Innovations?) Svenska handelshögskolan, Economics and Society N:o 196 (Helsinhfors, Helsinki, Finland 2009).

Blakeney M and Mengistie G, 'Intellectual Property and Economic Development in Sub-Saharan Africa' (2011) 14/3-4 Journal of World Intellectual Property 353.

Bochnovic J, 'The Inventive Step: Its Evolution in Canada, the United Kingdom, and the United States' (1982) 5 International Review of Intellectual Property and Competition Law 10.

Bodenhausen GHC, *Guide to the Application of the Paris Convention* (BIRPI & WIPO Publication 1968).

Bodkin C, *Patent Law in Australia* (Thomson Lawbook, Sydney, Australia 2008).

Bone RG, 'A New Look at Trade Secret Law: Doctrine in Search of Justification (1998) 86/2 California Law Review 241.

Boztosum NO, 'An Argument in Favour of Adopting Lesser Forms of Patent Protection for Technical Advances' (23 February 2009) Website-IPOSGOODE, available at:<http://www.iposgoode.ca/2009/02/an-argument-in-favour-of-adopting-lesser-forms-of-patent-protection/> (accessed 15 June 2012).

Boztosun NO, 'Exploring the Utility of Utility Models to Foster Innovation' (2010) 15 Journal of Intellectual Property Rights 429.

Cabral H, *The Act No.36 of 2003, The TRIPS Agreement and A Case Digest* (H Cabral, Colombo, Sri Lanka 2004).

Campbell D and Cotter S, *International Intellectual Property Law: New Developments* (Chichester, New York, USA 1995).

Carty H, 'An Analysis of the Modern Action for Breach of Commercial Confidence: When is Protection is merited? (2008) 4 Intellectual Property Quarterly 416.

Carty H, 'Passing Off: Frameworks of Liability Debated' (2012)1 Intellectual Property Quarterly 106.

Central Bank of Sri Lanka, *Annual Report 2011*(2011) Official website- Central Bank of Sri Lanka, available at: <http://www.cbsl.gov.lk/htm/english/10_pub/pub.html> (accessed 17 May 2012).

Chandrasiri S, 'Technological Issues of Small and Medium Scale Enterprises in Sri Lanka' (2003) 4/1 Sri Lanka Economic Journal 59.

Chen Y and Puttitanun T, Intellectual Property Rights and Innovation in Developing Countries' (2005) 78 Journal of Development Economics 474.

Chitrasiri KT, *Decisions on Intellectual Property Issues of the Commercial High Court of Sri Lanka* (Vishva Lekha Publishers, Ratmalana, Sri Lanka 2005).

Christie AF and Moritz SL, *Australia's Second-Tier Patent System: a Preliminary Review* (2004) Intellectual Property Research Institute of Australia (IPRAP) IPRIA Report No. 02/04.

Christie A and Moritz S, 'Harnessing Minor Innovation: National Studies- Austarlia' in Suthersanen U, Dutfield G and Chow KB (eds), *Innovation without Patents: Harnessing the Innovative Spirit in a Diverse World* (Edward Elgar, Cheltenham, UK 2007).

Chaudhry GM and Zafar Iqbal CM, *Chaudhry's Intellectual Property, Intellectual Property Law in Pakistan and International Treaties on Intellectual Property Rights* (Federal Law House, Rawalpindi, Pakistan 2005).

Chaudhry GM, *Guide to Intellectual Property Law* (CPI Publications, Rawalpindi, Pakistan 2008).

Chaudhry GM and Warraich IM, *The Intellectual Property Code* (Federal Law House, Rawalpindi, Pakistan 2005).

Chow KB, Leo KM, Leong S and Hsiao J, 'Harnessing Minor Innovation: National Studies – Chain and Taiwan' in Suthersanen U, Dutfield G and Chow KB (eds), *Innovation without Patents: Harnessing the Innovative Spirit in a Diverse World* (Edward Elgar, Cheltenham, UK 2007).

Cohen W, Nelson R and Walsh J, 'Protecting Their Intellectual Assets: appropriability Conditions and Why US Manufacturing Firms Patent (or Not)', (2000) Working Paper No. 7552, National Bureau of Economic Research, Cambridge, US.

Colston C and Middleton K, *Modern Intellectual Property Law* (2nd edn, Cavendish Publishing, London, UK 2005).

Commission on Intellectual Property Rights, *Integrating Intellectual Property Rights and Development Policy* (London, UK 2002).

Commonwealth Designs Law Review Committee ("Franki Committee"), *Report Relating to Utility Models* (Second Term of Reference), Parl. Paper No. 121 (1973).

Cook T, 'Legal Commentary: Why have Utility Models?' (2005) July/August, Managing Intellectual Property 3.

Cooray A, 'Oriental and Occidental Laws in Harmonious Co-existence: The Case of Trusts in Sri Lanka' (2008) 12/1 Electronic Journal of Comparative Law 1.

Cornish WR, *Intellectual Property: Patents, Copyright, Trademarks and Allied Rights* (7th edn, Sweet and Maxwell, London, UK 2010).

Cornish WR, 'The International Relation of Intellectual Property' (1993) 52/1 Cambridge Law Journal 46.

Correa CM, 'Designing Patent Policies Suited to Developing Countries Needs' (2008) 10/2 Econômica, Rio de Janeiro 82-105.

Correa CM, *Intellectual Property, The World and Developing Countries: The TRIPs Agreement and Policy Options* (Zed Books, London, UK 2000).

CM Correa, *A Guide to Pharmaceutical Patents* (vol I, South Centre Geneva, Switzerland 2008).

Correa CM, 'Protection and Promotion of Traditional Medicine: Implications for Public Health in Developing Countries' (2002 WHO), available at: <http://apps.who.int/medicinedocs/_pdf/s4917e/s4917e.pdf> (accessed 30 December 2011).

Cottier T and Véron P (eds), *Concise International and European Intellectual Property Law: TRIPS, Paris Convention and Transfer of Technology* (Kluwer Law, The Netherlands 2008).

Coulter M, *Property in Ideas: The Patent Question in Mid-Victorian Britain* (The Thomas Jefferson University Press, USA 1991).

Crinson MD 'Is some Novel Protection of Innovation Needed in Canada?' (1997) 12 Intellectual Property Journal 25.

Cummings PA, 'From Germany To Australia: Opportunity For A Second Tier Patent System In The United States' (2010) 19 Michigan State Journal of International Law 297.

Dahalan FR, 'Utility Models protection in Malaysia-Utility Innovation' (2012) WIPO Regional Seminar on the Legislative, Economic and Policy Aspects of utility Models Protection System, Kuala Lumpur, 3-4 September 2012.

Davison MJ, Monotti AL and Wiseman L, *Australian Intellectual Property Law* (2nd edn, Cambridge University Press 2008).

Department of Industrial Policy and Promotion, Discussion Paper on Utility Models (23 May 2011), available at: <http://dipp.gov.in/English/Discuss_paper/Utility_Models_13May2011.pdf> (accessed 30 December 2011).

De Silva MP, *Digest of Reported Cases on the Law of Intellectual Property 1895-2001* (General Printing Services, Colombo, Sri Lanka 2002).

Ding Y, 'Should China Keep the Present Utility Model System? A Look at the Experiences of Germany, Japan, and the United States and Prospect in China' (LLM thesis, MIPLC, Munich, Germany 2011).

Drahos P, *A philosophy of Intellectual Property* (Ashgate Publishing Ltd, Aldershot, UK 2007).

Drexl J, 'Do We Always Favour Dynamic Competition over Static Price Competition When Excluding Imitation' (13th EIPIN Conference, Munich, 3 February 2012).

Dreyfuss R, Zimmerman D and First H (eds), *Expanding the Boundaries of IP: Innovation Policy for the knowledge Society* (Oxford University Press, Oxford, UK 2001).

Dutfield G, 'A Critical Analysis of the Debate on Traditional Knowledge, Drug Discovery and Patent-based Biopiracy' (2011) 33 European Intellectual Property Review 238.

Dutfield G and Suthersanen U, *Global Intellectual Property Law* (Edward Elgar, Cheltenham, UK 2008).

Dutfield G, *Intellectual Property, Biogenetic resources and Traditional Knowledge* (Earthscan, UK, 2004).

Dutfield G and Suthersanen U, 'Harmonisation or Differentiation in Intellectual Property Protection? Lessons from History' (2005) 23/2 Prometheus 131.

Eisenführ G,'Heraus aus dem Demonstrationsschrank!'(2009) 4 Mitteilungen 165.

Encaoua D, Guellec D and Martínez C, 'Patent Systems for Encouraging Innovation: Lessons from Economic Analysis' (2006) 35/9 Research Policy 1423.

European Commission, 'Proposal for a European Directive approximating the legal arrangements for the protection of inventions by utility model Document' COM (97) 691 final.

European Commission, 'The Protection of Utility Models in the Single Market Green Paper' COM (95) 370 final.

Evenson RE and Westphal LE, 'Technological change and technology strategy' in Chenery H and Srinivasan TN (eds), *Handbook of Development Economics* (Springer, Berlin, Germany 1988).

Fagerberg J, Mowery DC and Nelson RR (eds.), *The Oxford Handbook of Innovation* (Oxford University Press, Oxford, UK 2005).

Fink C and Maskus KE (eds), *Intellectual Property and Development: Lessons from Recent Economic Research* (World Bank and Oxford University Press, Oxford, UK 2005).

Fisher T and Henkel J, 'Patent Troll on Markets for Technology-An Empirical Analysis of NPE's Patent Acquisitions' (2012) 41/9 Research Policy 1519.

Fisher W, 'Intellectual Property and Innovation: Theoretical, Empirical, and Historical Perspectives' in *Industrial Property, Innovation and Knowledge-based Economy* (Ashgate, Surrey, UK 2001).

Frankelius P, 'Questioning Two Myths in Innovation Literature' (2009) 20/1 The Journal of High Technology Management Research 40.

Franzosi M, 'Novelty and Non-obviousness-The Relevant Prior Art' (2001) Training Course Materials on Obtaining, Enforcing and Evaluating Intellectual Property Rights in Europe, conducted by Boehmert & Boehmert – Munich, 2-6 July 2001.

Freeman C, *The Economics of Industrial Innovation* (3rd edn, Routledge, Oxfordshire, UK 2000).

Gamage AS, 'Small and Medium Enterprise Development in Sri Lanka: A Review' (2003), available at: <http://202.11.2.113/SEBM/ronso/no3_4/aruna.pdf> (accessed 12 August 2012).

Galhardi R, *Small High Technology Firms in Developing Countries: The Case of Biotechnology* (Avebury, Aldershot, UK, 1994).

Gay R, 'The Inventive Step Conundrum' (2009) April, Managing Intellectual Property 98.

Gee LH, Azmi IM and Alavi R, 'Reforms Towards Intellectual Property-based Economic Development in Malaysia' (2009) 12/4 The Journal of World Intellectual Property 317.

Gee LH, 'The long march-Utility Model Protection for Minor Inventions' (1993) March, Managing Intellectual Property 37.

Gee LH, 'Second Tier Protection for Minor Inventions in Asia: An Appraisal of the Similarities and Differences' (3rd ASLI Conference Shanghai (China), 25-26 May 2006).

Goldstein P and Straus J (eds), Intellectual Property in Asia: Law, Economics, History and Politics (Springer, Berlin, Germany 2009).

Gracey AD, 'Guarantee Mechanisms for Financing Innovative Technology – Survey and Analysis' (2001, European Commission, Luxembourg).

Gupta A, 'Is all TK a prior Art? How to make IPR regime responsive to the needs of small, scattered and disadvantaged innovators and traditional knowledge holders: Honey Bee experience' (2002) WIPO Conference on the Patent System, Geneva, March 25-27.

Gupta A, 'Rewarding Traditional Knowledge and Contemporary Grassroots Creativity: The Role of Intellectual Property Protection' (2002) available at: <http://www.sristi.org/papers> (accessed 12 August 2012).

Hansen SA and VanFleet JW, *Traditional Knowledge and Intellectual Property: A handbook on Issues and Options for traditional Knowledge Holders in protecting their Intellectual Property and Maintaining Biological Diversity* (American Association for the Advancement of Science (AAAS), Washington, DC, USA 2003).

Harankaha M, 'Patent Law Issues: A Third World Perspective with Special Reference to Sri Lanka-Some Substantial Issues and Limitations of Patent Rights' (MPhil thesis, University of Colombo, Sri Lanka 2009) (copy on file with author).

Heath C and Sanders AK (eds), *Industrial Property in the Bio-Medical Age: Challenges for Asia* (Kluwer Law International, The Hague, London, New York 2003).

Heath C (ed), *Intellectual Property Law in Asia* (Kluwer Law International, The Hague, London, New York 2003).

Heath C, 'Utility Models in East and West' in *Current problems of Intellectual Property Law-Writings in honour of Nabao Manya* (1998) (copy on file with author).

Heath C, 'Utility Model Law' in *Encyclopedia of Japanese Law from 1868* (2002) (copy on file with author).

Heller MA and Eisenburg RE, 'Can Patents Deter Innovation? The Anticommons in Biomedical Research Science' (1998) 280-5364 Science, 698.

Henning-Bodewig F, *Unfair Competition Law: European Union and Member States* (Kluwer Law, The Netherlands 2006).

Hollaar LA, 'A New Look at Patent Reform' (2005) 87 Journal of the Patent & Trademark Office Society 743.

Howe M, *Russell-Clarke and Howe on Industrial Designs* (8th edn, Sweet & Maxwell, UK 2010).

Hunt RM, Non-obviousness and the Incentive to Innovate: An Economic Analysis of Intellectual Property Reform (1999) Working Paper No. 99-3, Federal Reserve Bank of Philadelphia.

Indatissa K, *Criminal Prosecutions under the Intellectual Property Act No 36 of 2003* (Centre for Continuing Legal Education, Colombo, Sri Lanka 2005).

International Association for the Protection of Intellectual Property (AIPPI), *Legal and Economic Significance of Protection by Utility Models Q83* (1986) Yearbook- Executive Committee of Rio de Janeiro.

International Association for the Protection of Intellectual Property, *'Introduction of new and harmonization of the existing utility model protection systems Q117'* (1995) AIPPI Yearbook – 36th Montreal Congress.

International Association for the Protection of Intellectual Property, *Report of the Proceedings of the Executive Committee of the AIPPI Copenhagen* 1994.

Jacob R, 'The Stephen Stewart Memorial Lecture: Intellectual Property-Industry's Enemy' (1997) 1 Intellectual Property Quarterly 3.

Janis MD, 'Second Tier Protection System' (1999) 40 Harvard International Law Journal 151.

Japan Intellectual Property Association, 'Opinions on the Proposed Establishment of a Utility Model System in India' (30th June 2011), available at: <http://www.jipa.or.jp/english/opinion/pdf/110704>(accessed 3 May 2012).

Jorda KF, Utility Models: The Panacea for our Broken Patent System – Newsletter (Germeshausen Center 2007) 4, available at : <http://www.ipo.org/wpcontent/uploads/2013/03/utilitymodels.pdf> (accessed 30 March 2013).

Kamperman-Sanders A, *Unfair Competition Law: The Protection of Intellectual and Industrial Creativity* (Oxford University Press, Oxford, UK 1997).

Kardam KS, 'Utility Model –A Tool for Economic and Technological Development: A Case Study of Japan' (2007) Final Report in Fulfillment of the Long-term Fellowship Sponsored by World Intellectual Property Office (WIPO) in Collaboration with the Japan Patent Office (from April 2, 2007 to September 28, 2007), 16-17, available at: <http://www.ipindia.nic.in/research_studies/FinalReport_April2007.pdf> (accessed 15 April 2012).

Karjala DS, 'Misappropriation as a Third Intellectual Property Paradigm' (1994) 94 Colombia law Review 1254.

Karunaratna DM, *A Guide to the Law of Trade Marks and Service Marks in Sri Lanka* (2nd edn, Vishva Lekha Publishers, Ratmalana, Sri Lanka 2007).

Karunaratna DM, *An Introduction to the Law of Copyright and Related Rights in Sri Lanaka* (Vishva Lekha Publishers, Ratmalana, Sri Lanka 2006).

Karunaratna DM, *Elements of the Law of Intellectual Property in Sri Lanka* (Sarasavi Publishers, Nugegoda, Sri Lanka 2010).

Katzarov K, *Katzarov's Manual of Industrial Property* (Katzarov, Geneva 2007).

Kelegama S, 'SL's lack of innovation, markets limit export growth' *Sunday Times* (Colombo, 13 March 2013), available at: <http://www.sundaytimes.lk/130310/business-times/sls-lack-of-innovation-markets-limit-export-growth-dr-kelegama-35527.html>(accessed 20 March 2013).

Kern M, 'Towards a European Utility Model Law' (1994) 25 International Review of Intellectual Property and Competition Law 627.

Kief FS and Nack R, *International, United Sates, and European Intellectual Property: Selected Source Material* (Wolters Kluwer, UK 2011).

Kim L, *Technology Transfer and Intellectual Property Rights: The Experience of Korea* (2003) Issues Paper no. 2 UNCTAD-ICTSD Project on Intellectual Property Rights and Sustainable Development.

Kim YK, Lee K and Park WG, 'Appropriate Intellectual Property Protection and Economic Growth in Countries at Different level of Development (2012) 41/2 Research Policy 358.

Kingston W, *Beyond Intellectual Property: Matching Information Protection to Innovation* (Edward Elgar, Cheltenham, UK 2010).

Kinston W, 'Innovation Patents and Warrants' in Philliphs J (ed) *Patent in Perspectives* (ESC, London, UK 1985).

Kirchmann V, 'The Rise of the Utility Model in Germany' (1995) July/August, Managing Intellectual property 42.

Klicznik A, 'Prior Art from the Internet-A Potential Further reason for Branching off a Utility Model from a Pending Patent Application' in Prinz zu Wal-deck und Pyrmont W, Adelman M, Brauneis R, Drexl J and Nack R (eds), *Patents and Tech-nological Progress in a Globalized World, Liber Amicorum Joseph Straus* (Springer, Berlin, Heidelberg, Germany 2008).

Krasser R, 'Development in Utility Model Law' (1995) 26 International Review of Intellectual Property and Competition Law 950.

Kumar N, Technology and Economic development: Experiences of Asian Countries (2002) Commission of Intellectual Property Rights- Study Paper 1b, available at: <http://www.twnside.org.sg/title2/FTAs/Intellectual_Property/IP_and_Development/IPR_TechnologyandEconomicDevelopment-Nagesh_Kumar.pdf> (accessed 10 January 2011).

Kur A, 'Two Tiered Protection- Designs and Databases as Legislative-Models?' in Ansgar Ohly (ed), *Common Principles of European Intellectual Property Law* (Mohr Siebeck, Germany 2012).

Königer K, 'Registration Without Examination: The Utility Model-A Useful Model?' in Prinz zu Wal-deck und Pyrmont W, Adelman M, Brauneis R, Drexl J and Nack R (eds), *Patents and Tech-nological Progress in a Globalized World, Liber Amicorum Joseph Straus* (Springer, Berlin, Heidelberg 2008).

Lahore J, 'Design and Petty Patents: A Broader Reform Issue' (1996) 7 Australian Intellectual Property Journal 7.

Lees C, 'Do We Need Second Tier Protection?' (1994) Report and Proceedings of the Brocket Hall Symposium – Chartered Institute of Patent Agents.

Lees C, 'Does the United Kingdom Need Second Tier Protection?' (1994) September, Patent World 14.

Lees C, 'Utility Models: A Question of Balance' (1999) May, Patent World 20.

Lee Y and Langley M, 'Invention and Innovation' (2004) August, The CIPA Journal 464.

Lei Y and Maskus KE, 'Intellectual Property Rights, Technology Transfer and Exports in Developing Countries' (2008) CESIFO Working Paper No. 2464, Trade Policy.

Lehmann M, 'Property and Intellectual Property-Property Rights as Restrictions on Competition in Furtherance of Competition' (1989) 20/1 International Review of Intellectual Property and Competition Law 1.

Leith P, *Software and Patents in Europe* (Cambridge University Press, Cambridge, UK 2007).

Leith P, 'Utility Models and SMEs' (2000) 2 The Journal of Information, Law and Technology (JILT), available at: <http://elj.warwick.ac.uk/jilt/00-2/leith.html> (accessed 20 May 2012).

Lemley M and Shapiro C, 'Probabilitic Patents' (2005) 19/2 Journal of Economic Perspectives 75.

Lemley M, 'The Suprising Vertues of Treating Trade Secrets as IP Rights' (2008) 61/2 Stanford Law Review 311.

Letterman G, *Basics of International Intellectual Property* (Transnational Publishers, New York, USA 2001).

Leuven JWMV, 'Patent Statistics as Indicators for Innovation' (1996) November/ December, Patent World 20.

Li Y, *International and Comparative Intellectual property: Law, Policy and Practice* (LexisNexis, Hong Kong 2005).

Li Y, 'Utility Models in China' in Christopher Heath and Anselm kamperman Sanders (eds) *Industrial property in the Bio-Medical Age: Challenges for Asia* (Kluwer Law, The Netherlands 2003).

Liesegang R, 'German Utility Models after the 1990 Reform Act' (1992) 20 American Intellectual Property Law Association (AIPLA) Quarterly Journal 1.

Llewelyn D, *Invisible Gold in Asia: Creating Wealth Through Intellectual Property* (Marshall Cavendish, Singapore 2010).

Llewelyn M, 'Proposals for the Introduction of a Community Utility Model System: A UK Perspective' (1995) 2 Web Journal of Current Legal Issues, available at: <https://www.innovationpolicyplatform.org/content/utility-model-law> (accessed 20 May 2012).

Llewelyn M and Morcom C, 'Second Tier Patent Protection: The European Commission Green Paper on the Protection of Utility Models in the Single Market-A CLIP Seminar Report' (The Intellectual Property Institute, London, UK 1996)

Llewelyn M, 'The Model Myth: The Relevance of the Proposed EC Utility Model System to the United Kingdom' (1996) February, Patent World 36.

Llewelyn M, Utility Model/Second Tier Protection: A Report on the Proposals for the European Commission (The Intellectual Property Institute, London, UK 1996).

Mbeva JM, 'Experience and Lessons learned Regarding the Use of Existing IP Rights Instruments for Protection of Traditional Knowledge: Kenyan Experience' (UNCTAD Expert Meeting on Systems and National Experience for Protection of Traditional Knowledge, Innovation and Practices, Geneva, 30 October-1 November 2000).

Machlup F, *An Economic Review of the Patent System* (1958) Study No. 15 of the Subcommittee on Patent, Trademarks and Copyrights of the Senate Committee on the Judiciary.

Maheshwari V and Bhatnagar P, 'Small Scale Industries and IP Management: Need to Recognize Intellectual Asserts' (2008) 13 Journal of Intellectual Property Rights 139.

Malkawi BH, 'A Critical Look at Trade Secrets Protection in Jordan' (2012) 1 Intellectual Property Quarterly 123.

Mansfield E, 'Patent and Innovation: An Empirical Study' (1986) 32/2 Management Science 173.

Mashelkar RA, 'Intellectual Property Rights and the Third World' (2001) 81/8 Current Science 955.

Maskus KE and Reichman JH(eds.) *International Public Goods and Transfer of Technology under a Globalized Intellectual Property Regime* (Cambridge University Press, Cambridge, UK 2005).

Maskus KE, 'Reforming U.S. Patent Policy: Getting the Incentives Right' (2006) Council on Foreign Relations, CSR No. 19.

Marttz SL and Christie AF, 'Second-Tier Patent System: The Australian Experience' [2006] European Intellectual Property Review 230.

Max Planck Institute, *Proposal for a European Utility Model: Explanatory Report* (1994) 25 International Review of Intellectual Property and Competition Law 700.

Mengistie G, 'The Patent System in Africa: Its Contribution and Potential in Stimulating Innovation, Technology Transfer and Fostering Science and Technology: Part 2' (2010) 16 International Trade Law and Regulation 175.

Mercurio BC, 'Reconceptualising the Debate on Intellectual Property Rights and Economic Development' (2010) 3/1 The Law and Development Review 65, available at: <http://works.bepress.com/bryan_mercurio/2> (accessed 3 July 2012).

Ministry of Traditional Industries and Small Enterprise Development and Department of Development Finance and Planning, *Draft National Policy Framework for Small Medium Enterprise (SME) Development* (Government of Sri lanka, 2014).

Mirando BA, *Critical Analysis of the Provisions Governing Trade Marks under the Code of Intellectual Property Act No. 52 of 1979* (Vijitha Yapa Publications, Colombo, Sri Lanka 1999).

Mott KM, 'The Concept of Small Patent in European Legal Systems and Equivalent Protection under United States Law' (1963) 49/2 Virginia Law Review 232.

Musker D, *Community Design Law: Principles and Practices* (Sweet & Maxwell, London, UK 2002).

Narayana PS, *Intellectual property law in India* (Gogia Law Hyderabad, India 2003).

National Productivity Secretariat (NPS) of the Ministry of Productivity Promotion Sri Lanka, 'Kaizen Entrepreneurs' (2012), available at: <http://nps-kaizen.lk/index.html> (accessed 12 August 2012).

National Science and Technology Commission (NASTEC)-Ministry of Science and Technology, *National Science and Technology Policy-2008* (Government of Sri Lanka 2008).

Nord CA, *The Law of Patents* (2nd edn, Wolters Kluwer, The Netherlands 2010).

Osenga K, 'Entrance Ramps, Tolls, and Express Lanes-Proposals for Decreasing Traffic Congestion in The Patent Office' (2008) 33 Florida State University Law Review 119.

Organisation for Economic Co-operation and development (OECD), Business and Industry Advisory Committee (BIAC) – Discussion Paper on Creativity, Innovation and Economic Growth in the 21st Century: An Affirmative Case for Intellectual property Rights (Paris, December 2003).

Paris Convention for the Protection of Industrial Property of March 20, 1883, as revised at Brussels on December 14, 1900, at Washington on June 2, 1911, at The Hague on November 6, 1925, at London on June 2, 1934, at Lisbon on October 31, 1958, and at Stockholm on July 14, 1967, and as amended on September 28, 1979 Electronic copy available at: <http://www.wipo.int/treaties/en/text.jsp?file_id=288514> (accessed 14 August 2012).

Parkes A, 'Short-Term Patents in Ireland' (1994) 25 International Review of Intellectual Property and Competition Law 204.

Perera PK, 'Current Scenario of Herbal Medicine in Sri Lanka' (ASSOCHAM, 4th Annual Herbal International Summit, NSIC, New Delhi, 14-15 April, 2012).

Philips J, 'A Spanner in the work-or the spanner that work? Patent and Intellectual Property System' in Takenaka T (ed) Patent Law and Theory: A Handbook of Contemporary Research (Edward Elgar, Cheltenham, UK 2008).

Phillips J and Firth A, *Introduction to Intellectual Property Law* (4th edn, Butterworths, London, UK 2001).

Philipp M, 'Novelty and Inventive Step under the European Patent Convention' (2001) Training Course Materials on Obtaining, Enforcing and Evaluating Intellectual Property Rights in Europe, conducted by Boehmert & Boehmert – Munich, 2-6 July 2001.

Porter ME, *The Competitive Advantage of Nations* (Free Press, New York 1990).

Posner RA, 'Do We Have Too Many Intellectual Property Rights?'(2005) 9 Intellectual Property review 173.

Pugatch MP, 'Intellectual Property Policy Making in the 21st Century' (2011) 3/1 World Intellectual Property Journal 71.

Pugatch MP, 'The Process of Intellectual Property Policy-Making in the 21st Century-Shifting from a general Welfare model to a Multi-Dimensional One' (2009) 6 European Intellectual Property Review 307.

Ragavan S, 'Can't We All Get Along? The Case for a Workable Patent Model' (2003) 35 Arizona State Law Journal 117.

Reddy GB, *Intellectual Property Rights and the Law* (3rd edn, Gogia Law Hyderabad, India 2003).

Reichman JH, 'Of Green Tulips and Legal Kundu: Repacking Rights in Subpatentable Innovation' (November 2000) 53/6 Vanderbilt Law Review 1743.

Reichman JH, 'Legal Hybrids between the Patent and Copyright Paradigms' (1994) 94 Colombia Law Review 2432.

Reichman JH and Lewis T, 'Using Liability Rules to Stimulate Local Innovation in Developing Countries: Application to Traditional Knowledge' in Maskus KE and Reichman JH (eds) *International Public Goods and Transfer of Technology under a Globalized Intellectual Property Regime* (Cambridge University Press, Cambridge, UK 2005).

Richards J, 'Utility Model Protection throughout the World' (2010) Internet Publication, available at: <http://www.ipo.org/AM/Template.cfm?Template=/CM/ContentDisplay.cfm&ContentID=25244> (accessed 30 December 2011).

Ruse-Khan HG, 'Utility Model Protection in Pakistan-A Feasible Option for Incentivising Incremental Innovation?' (2012), Study conducted for the World Intellectual Property Organisation 77 (copy on file with author).

Schechter RE, *Intellectual Property* (Thomson West, USA 2006).

Scherer FM, 'The Innovation Lottery' in Dreyfuss RC, Zimmerman DL and First H (eds), *Expanding the Boundaries of Intellectual Property: Innovation Policy for the Knowledge Society* (Oxford University Press, Oxford, UK 2001).

Schricker G, 'Unfair Competition and Consumer Protection in Western Europe' (1970) 1 International Review of Intellectual Property and Competition Law 415.

Schumpeter JA, *The Theory of Economic Development: An Inquiry into Profits, Capital, Credit, Interest, and the Business Cycle* (Transaction Publishers, USA 1982) (Original publication 1934).

Scotchmer S, 'Standing on the Shoulders of the Giants: Cumulative Research and Patent Law' (1991) 5/1 Journal of Economic Perspectives 29.

Segade JAG, 'Editorial: Utility Models-Lost in Translation' (2008) 39/2 International Review of Intellectual Property and Competition Law 135.

Sharma R, *Breakout Nations: In Pursuit of the Next Economic Miracles* (Allen Lane, London, 2012)

Smith A, *An Inquiry into the Nature and Causes of the Wealth of Nations* (Original publication in 1776), available at: <http://www.econlib.org/library/Smith/smWN.html> (accessed 12 March 2012).

Smith GV and Parr RL, *Intellectual Property Valuation, Exploitation, and Infringement Damages* (John Wiley & Sons, New Jersey, USA 2005).

Srinivas KR, 'Traditional Knowledge and Intellectual Property Rights A Note on Issues, Some Solutions and Some Suggestions', available at: <SSRN: http://ssrn.com/abstract=1140623> (accessed 3 March 2012).

Sumanadasa WADJ, 'The Intersection of Contract Law with IP Law in the Protection of Undisclosed Information: A Sri Lankan Perspective' (Annual Research Symposium of the University of Colombo, Sri Lanka (2012).

Suthersanen U and Datfield G, 'The Innovation Dilemma: Intellectual Property and the Historical Legacy of Creativity' (2004) 8 Intellectual Property Quarterly 379.

Suthersanen U and Dutfield G, 'Innovation, Development and Intellectual Property' in Suthersanen U, Dutfield G and Chow KB (eds.) *Innovation without Patents: Harnessing the Innovative Spirit in a Diverse World* (Edward Elgar, Cheltenham, UK 2007).

Suthersanen U and Gee LH, 'Harnessing Minor Innovation: National Studies – The ASEAN States' in Suthersanen U, Dutfield G and Chow KB (eds), *Innovation without Patents: Harnessing the Innovative Spirit in a Diverse World* (Edward Elgar, Cheltenham, UK 2007).

Suthersanen U, 'A Brief Tour of "Utility Model" Law' [1998] European Intellectual Property Review 44.

Suthersanen U, 'Incremental Innovations in Europe: A Legal and Economic Appraisal of Second Tier Patents' (2001) July, Journal of Business Law 319.

Suthersanen U, 'The Economic Efficacy of utility Model Protection' in Christopher Heath and Anselm kamperman Sanders (eds) *Industrial property in the Bio-Medical Age: Challenges for Asia* (Kluwer Law, The Netherlands 2003).

Suthersanen U, *Design Law in Europe* (Sweet & Maxwell, London, UK 2000).

U Suthersanen, 'Utility Models and Innovation in Developing Countries' (2006) ICTSD Issue Paper No.13, available at: <http://unctad.org/en/docs/iteipc20066_en.pdf> (accessed 15 March 2012).

Sykes J, *Intellectual Property in Design* (LexisNexis, UK 2005).

Takeyuki I, 'Modalities of Future Utility Model System' [2004] IIP Bulletin 38, available at: <http://www.iip.or.jp/e/e_summary/pdf/detail2003/e15_06.pdf> (accessed 1 May 2012).

Task Force for Small & Medium Enterprise Sector Development Program, *White Paper on National Strategy for Small and Medium Enterprise Sector Development in Sri Lanka* (Institute of Policy Studies of Sri Lanka, December 2002).

Tensey M and Stembridge B, 'The Challenge of Sustaining the Research and Innovation Process' (2005) 27 World Patent Information 212.

Teece D, 'Profiting from Technological Innovation: Implications for Integration, Collaboration, Licensing and Public Policy' (1986) 15 Research Policy 285.

Thomas JR Richards J, Schwartz HF and Lee SJ, 'Panel I: KSR v. Teleflex: The Nonobviousness Requirement of Patentability' (2007) 17 Fordham Intellectual Property, Media and Entertainment Law Journal 875.

Thurow LC, 'Needed: A New System of Intellectual Property Rights' (1997) September/October, Harvard Business Review 95.

Tootal, 'The European Patent System: Time for Review' (1995) 9 European Intellectual Property Review 415.

Torremans P, *Holyoak and Torremans Intellectual Property Law* (4th edn Oxford University Press, Oxford, UK 2005).

Townend DMR, 'Intellectual Property as Security Interests: Technical Difficulties presented in the Law' (1997) 2 Intellectual Property Quarterly 167.

UK Patent office (UKPO), The Inventive Step Requirement in United Kingdom Patent Law and Practice (2006) UKPO official website, available at: <http://www.ipo.gov.uk/pro-policy/consult/consult-closed/consult-closed-2006/consult-2006-inventive.htm> (accessed 12 April 2012).

UNCTAD and ICTSD, *Resource Book on TRIPS and Development* (Cambridge University Press, Cambridge, UK 2005).

United Nations, 'Systems and National Experiences for Protecting Traditional Knowledge, Innovations and Practices' (United Nations Conference on Trade and Development, Geneva, 22 August 2000, the Background Note by the UNCTAD secretariat, TD/B/COM.1/EM.13/2)

Weeraworawit W, 'Utility Models in Thailand' in Christopher Heath and Anselm kamperman Sanders (eds) *Industrial property in the Bio-Medical Age: Challenges for Asia* (Kluwer Law, The Netherlands 2003).

von Weizäcker CCV, 'Rights and Relations in Modern Economic Theory'(1984) 5 Journal of Economic Behavior and Organization 133.

World Bank, *Changes in Country Classification* (World Bank, 2011), available at: <http://data.worldbank.org/news/2010-GNI-income-classifications> (accessed 30 June 2012).

WIPO-CDIP, 'Patent related Flexibilities in the Multilateral Legal Framework and their Legislative Implementation at the National and Regional Level' (2010) The Document prepared by the Secretariat to the WIPO-CDIP/5/4, 1st March 2010.

WIPO, 'Intellectual Property Rights and Innovation in Small and Medium-Sized Enterprises' (World Intellectual Property Organization, Geneva 2004).

WIPO, 'The Innovation Potential of an SME and the Value of the Intellectual Property Rights' (WIPO/IP/MNL/00/7(b) August 10, 2004) (World Intellectual Property Organization, Geneva 2004).

WIPO, *Intellectual Property Handbook: Policy, Law and Use* (World Intellectual Property Organization, Geneva 2004).

WIPO, *World Intellectual Property Indicators* (World Intellectual Property Organization, Geneva 2011).

WIPO, *Summer School Reading Material* (World Intellectual Property Organization, Geneva 2010).

WIPO, *World Intellectual Property Report: The Changing Face of Innovation* (World Intellectual Property Organization, Geneva 2011).

Wadlow C, 'The Emergent European Law of Unfair Competition and its Consumer Law Origin' (2012) 1 Intellectual Property Quarterly 1.

Wickremasinghe SI, 'The Status of SMEs in Sri Lanka and Promotion of Their Innovation Output Through Networking of S&T Institutions' (2011) July-August, Tech Monitor 11, available at: <http://www.techmonitor.net/tm/images/1/1d/11jul_aug_sf1.pdf>(accessed 30 June 2012).

Wijewardena WA, 'Sri Lanka's Future: Convert the Simple Economy into a High-Tech based Complex Economy' *Daily FT* (Colombo, 17 September 2012), available at: <http://www.ft.lk/2012/09/17/sls-future-convert-the-simple-economy-into-a-high-tech-based-complex-economy/> (accessed 3 March 2013).

Yamamoto S, 'Utility Model Protection in Japan' (1995) July/August, Managing Intellectual property 42.

Yang X, 'Utility Models Have a Vital Role in China' (1995) July/August, Managing Intellectual property 46.

Yonghong L, 'How to Define the Height of Inventiveness of Utility Models?' (2008) 1 China Patents &Trademarks 26.

Vu TA, 'An Insight into the Patent Systems of fast developing ASEAN Countries' (2012) 34 World Patent Information 134.